setting captives free
Pure Freedom

Breaking the Addiction to Pornography
Mike Cleveland

FOCUS PUBLISHING

Setting Captives Free: Pure Freedom
by Mike Cleveland

Copyright © 2002 Focus Publishing

All Rights Reserved under International Copyright Conventions. No part of this book maybe be reproduced in any form or by any means, electronic or mechanical, including photocopying, recording, or by any information storage and retrieval system, without permission from the publisher. Inquiries should be addressed to
Focus Publishing, Rights and Permissions
PO Box 665
Bemidji, Minnesota, 56619

Unless otherwise noted, Scripture is taken from the HOLY BIBLE, NEW INTERNATIONAL VERSION® Copyright © 1973, 1978, 1984 by the International Bible Society. Used by permission of Zondervan Publishing House. All Rights Reserved. The "NIV and "New International Version" trademarks are registered in the United States Patent and Trademark Office by International Bible Society. Use of either trademark requires the permission of International Bible Society.

ISBN: 1-885904-30-4

Printed in the United States of America

Dedication

I lovingly dedicate this book to my wife,

Jody

who, after discovering my involvement with pornography, took it upon herself to become my teammate in fighting against impurity. Without your help, Jody, I would be another statistic of men who ruin their lives.
I love you.

Acknowledgments

This course book is evidence of the transforming power of God in my life, and in the lives of thousands of men and women who experienced the same power and contributed to this work. I would take this opportunity to thank them generally, and thank the following more specifically:

First, my wife Jody has been my suitable helpmeet in overcoming 15 years of bondage to pornography. She worked with me as a teammate when I was hopelessly enslaved, and next to the sovereign grace of God in releasing me from my chains of sin, Jody gets the credit. Then as we sensed God's calling to help others, she provided much godly wisdom and feedback to me through the long hours of writing new course material, all the while rearing and homeschooling our four children, mentoring a full load of female course members and spouses, and being much in demand as a phone counselor to the wives of those in slavery to pornography. Jody, "my rib," this world has been graced with your presence. I love you dearly and am eternally grateful to you.

Next, Dr. Bob Bevington has put much of his time, money and effort into making the **Pure Freedom** course and website a respectable ministry in the eyes of those first coming to visit. His valuable insight into presenting ourselves in a manner that does not detract the reader from the message, and his commitment to the Word of God as being sufficient to release men and women from their prisons of sin, have made this man near and dear to my heart. Bob has a heart for others that is huge, and without him we would still have a black website with small, unreadable, non-standard course material.

Pastor Will Lohnes of Shepherd's Grace Church in Medina, Ohio not only taught me the principles of freedom that come from God's Word, but also walked me out of the darkness with his arm around my shoulder. James 5:20 says, "Whoever turns a sinner from the error of his way will save him from death and cover over a multitude of sins." Pastor Will spent long hours counseling and discipling my wife and me, took many days away from his busy schedule as senior pastor of a growing church to fly across the country as we sought forgiveness from those I had wronged, and has contributed much counsel and provided much support to the ministry of **Setting Captives Free**. Pastor Will, I love you as Onessimus loved Paul, for it was through your love and counsel that God granted me godly sorrow and full repentance unto life.

Finally, to Jan Haley and all our friends at Focus Publishing, we are grateful to God for giving you such a love of His Word, and a desire to publish it to the helping of many. Thank you for the hours of study you have put into the **Pure Freedom** project. May God richly bless your kindness to us. We love you!

Though the names have been changed, the personal testimonies included in this book demonstrate how Satan's wiles lead men and women into the pit of pornography, but also the victory that can be found through Jesus Christ and the Living Water. We are grateful to those who granted us permission to share their testimonies.

Mike Cleveland

Table of Contents

Day		Page
1.	Living Water	2
2.	More Living Water	5
3.	Into the Light	8
4.	The Cross	11
5.	Running Light	14
6.	Turning	17
7.	New Direction	21
8.	Accountability	24
9.	Pure Grace	27
10.	Surprising Grace	30
11.	Ongoing Freedom	34
12.	Radical Amputation	37
13.	Setting Captives Free I	40
14.	Setting Captives Free II	44
15.	Setting Captives Free III	48
16.	Temptation	51
17.	Return to the Lord	54
18.	Exclusive Drinking	57
19.	Purity Precedes Power	60
20.	Idolatry	63
21.	Strength Through Confession	66
22.	Vigilance	69
23.	Enjoying the Light	72
24.	Fleeing Temptation	75
25.	Flee, Abstain, Resist	79
26.	Don't Go Near	82
27.	Growing in Christ	85
28.	Sanctification	88
29.	Our Identity in Christ	92
30.	New Creation in Christ: Salvation Illustrated	95
31.	The Greatness, Majesty, Power And Grace of God	98
32.	Battle Strategies	101
33.	Demolishing Strongholds	104
34.	Demolishing Strongholds II	107
35.	The Love of God and Temptation	110
36.	Break the Chain	114
37.	Seek the Lord	117
38.	Restoration After Loss	120
39.	Specific Steps to Freedom from Sin	124
40.	The Heart, the Mind, and the Actions	127
41.	Battle Strategies	130

Table of Contents

Day		Page
42.	Focus!	133
43.	Dead to Sin, Alive to Christ: Romans 6	136
44.	Dark Night of the Soul: Romans 7	138
45.	No Condemnation: Romans 8	141
46.	Pornography Can't Hold Water	144
47.	Brokenness: Key to Victory	147
48.	But Such Were Some of You	150
49.	Walking in the Spirit	153
50.	Freedom Through Fellowship	156
51.	Live for Pleasure	159
52.	Happy Are the Helpless	162
53.	The Power of the Word	165
54.	Do Everything to Stand	168
55.	Don't Look Back!	171
56.	Normal Sexual Relations	174
57.	Cut Off His Head	177
58.	Final Exam	180
59.	Your Testimony	184
60.	Feedback	185

Introduction

Setting Captives Free: Pure Freedom is a 60-Day study course designed for men and women who seek to be free from pornography and other forms of sexual impurity. Many who have taken this course are walking in freedom today because they implemented the biblical principles found here. As you step out of the darkness and secrecy of pornography, you will find the refreshing cleansing of a relationship with the Lord Jesus Christ which will impact your personal life, and your relationship with others.

The **Pure Freedom** course may be studied individually or in a small group setting.

Small Group Setting:

There should be an appointed leader/teacher to head the group, which will meet weekly. The first meeting of the group should be to get acquainted. The leader will make introductions and explain the method for completing the study. Each group member will work individually through one lesson each day, recording their answers to discuss with the class the next week. At the close of this first meeting the leader will explain from Hebrews 3:13 the importance of daily accountability and he/she will pair up the students as each reports to the other daily of their freedom from sin. The reports may be given on the phone, fax, email, in person, etc., but they should be given daily. At the second meeting the discussion leader will take time to review/expound upon the previous week's material, soliciting the members to share their answers from the material they have studied. The leader will also ask if the members have been providing daily accountability reports to their assigned partner. A Leader's/Mentor's Guide is available.

Individual Study:

When using this course individually, it is highly recommended that you find a trusted Christian friend with whom you may discuss what you are learning from the course material, and who will also be available to you for accountability. This accountability partner should be someone of the same sex who is walking in victory over habitual sin. Possible options include your pastor, an elder in your church, or a fellow Christian. You may also use your spouse for your accountability partner if they are willing. Students need to initiate daily reports to their accountability partner, providing the status of his/her purity.

The genesis of the **Pure Freedom** course began on the internet website, www.settingcaptivesfree.com and continues to operate there successfully. Should you desire to work with an available mentor from the website, you may contact them at feedback@settingcaptivesfree.com
You may contact Mike Cleveland via "snail mail" at the following address:
Setting Captives Free
2325 Medina Road
Medina, OH 44256

To the extent that his schedule allows, Mike is available for conferences and speaking engagements. Please contact him at the above address.

DAY 1—LIVING WATER

Hello, and welcome to **Pure Freedom**. My name is Mike Cleveland, and as the author of this course I will be leading you through the next 60 Days as you seek to be free from pornography, phone sex, sex chatting on the Internet, or any other form of sexual impurity.

First, let me share a bit of my own story with you. I was involved with pornography and many other forms of impurity for 15 years of my life, and my problems only got worse with time. Through my teen years I was involved with pornographic magazines such as Playboy, Hustler, Oui…etc. At 22 years old I was hired as a pilot with Continental Airlines and began laying over in hotels around the world. This is where pornography really got hold of me, for I discovered pornographic movies were available at nearly every hotel. Then came the Internet, and sex chatting became a part of my daily life. All of this led to the breakup of my family, the dissolution of my first marriage, and the death of my dream to have a family that was united in love.

My parents divorced when I was 6 years old and I grieved for a long time the loss of a whole family. So one of my earnest desires was to have a home of love that would last, where there was harmony and mutual support for each member. In my pursuit of this dream, I hastily married for the first time at age 20. But sadly, my first marriage of 14 years did not last; and my involvement with pornography and the consequent dissatisfaction of my heart largely contributed to the divorce.

The rest of my story you will read as you continue on in the course. I've interspersed my story throughout the course material so that you will know that the teaching in the course comes from one who has "been there, done that" and is now free from pornography and all forms of impurity. My desire in sharing my story with you is not to boast in myself. No, I am ashamed of what I had become and the pain I caused so many people. But rather it is to boast in the grace of God who has eradicated the pornography from my life, and to give you hope that He can do the same for you.

Now let me encourage you. **Pure Freedom** is available for you too. You will be completely free from pornography, or whatever your particular struggle is, if you will implement the biblical principles found in the course. I hope this gives you hope that no matter how long you have battled this secret killer called pornography, you can now be successful over it, by applying the truths taught here. Literally thousands of people who have gone through this course ahead of you are now walking in freedom, and you will read some of their testimonies as you continue on in the course.

Now here is Lesson One. I suggest you begin each day by reading the daily introduction, then move to the questions and continuing lesson in the sidebars. Conclude the day's study by reading the Testimony (highlighted in green). These testimonies will give you great encouragement! Finally read the closing Scripture to Consider and answer the accountability questions. The first two lessons have a closing prayer. After that we encourage you to go before God with your own prayer. Enjoy your studies!

Questions

Question 1. List the "water" you've been drinking and describe how it has left you "thirsty."

Question 2. How many relationships did Jesus say that the woman at the well had?
A. 4   B. 5   C. 6

Question 3. To what did Jesus compare these multiple relationships?
A. Eating fruit from a rotten tree
B. Drinking water from a well that does not satisfy

Question 4. What did Jesus mean when He said, "Everyone who drinks this water will be thirsty again"?
A. The water in that well contained a high amount of salt.
B. Ongoing relationships (or pornography) will not ultimately satisfy, and will have to be repeated over and over.

Course member Julie writes:
"Pornography truly is a ball and chain! I have been drinking from the water of lust and relationship..each relationship has failed and I continually thirst for true love; now I know that only Christ can satisfy."

Question 5. What kind of water did Jesus offer the woman at the well?
A. Living Water
B. Well water
C. Tonic water

Question 6. What did Jesus say was the difference between the water she had been drinking of and the living water He offered her?
A. The Living Water was salt-free.
B. The Living Water would satisfy.
C. The Living Water had more nutrients.

Question 7. What did Jesus say the effects of drinking this water would be?
A. More energy and stamina
B. Lower cholesterol
C. Eternal life

Please read through the following Biblical story taken from John 4 and answer the study questions below. (You are about to learn how to be free from sexual enslavement.)

> [7] When a Samaritan woman came to draw water, Jesus said to her, "Will you give me a drink?" [8] (His disciples had gone into the town to buy food.) [9] The Samaritan woman said to him, "You are a Jew and I am a Samaritan woman. How can you ask me for a drink?" (For Jews do not associate with Samaritans.) [10] Jesus answered her, "If you knew the gift of God and who it is that asks you for a drink, you would have asked him and he would have given you living water." [11] "Sir," the woman said, "you have nothing to draw with and the well is deep. Where can you get this living water? [12] Are you greater than our father Jacob, who gave us the well and drank from it himself, as did also his sons and his flocks and herds?" [13] Jesus answered, "Everyone who drinks this water will be thirsty again, [14] but whoever drinks the water I give him will never thirst. Indeed, the water I give him will become in him a spring of water welling up to eternal life." [15] The woman said to him, "Sir, give me this water so that I won't get thirsty and have to keep coming here to draw water." [16] He told her, "Go, call your husband and come back." [17] "I have no husband," she replied. Jesus said to her, "You are right when you say you have no husband. [18] The fact is, you have had five husbands, and the man you now have is not your husband. What you have just said is quite true." [19] "Sir," the woman said, "I can see that you are a prophet. [20] Our fathers worshiped on this mountain, but you Jews claim that the place where we must worship is in Jerusalem." [21] Jesus declared, "Believe me, woman, a time is coming when you will worship the Father neither on this mountain nor in Jerusalem. [22] You Samaritans worship what you do not know; we worship what we do know, for salvation is from the Jews. [23] Yet a time is coming and has now come when the true worshippers will worship the Father in spirit and truth, for they are the kind of worshippers the Father seeks. [24] God is spirit, and his worshippers must worship in spirit and in truth." [25] The woman said, "I know that Messiah" (called Christ) "is coming. When he comes, he will explain everything to us." [26] Then Jesus declared, "I who speak to you am he" [27] Just then his disciples returned and were surprised to find him talking with a woman. But no one asked, "What do you want?" or "Why are you talking with her?" [28] Then, leaving her water jar, the woman went back to the town and said to the people, [29] "Come, see a man who told me everything I ever did. Could this be the Christ?" [30] They came out of the town and made their way toward him (John 4:7-30).

Observe: In the above story, Jesus Christ spoke to a woman about two kinds of water:

1. *"This water,"* which would not satisfy and would not quench thirst. The woman would have to keep coming back again and again to get more of "this water."

2. *"The water I give"* which would quench thirst eternally.

Then Jesus brought up the fact that the woman had had multiple relationships (5 husbands and a current live-in—6 total). Obviously, she was finding no permanent satisfaction in these relationships so she had to keep going back to find a new love, each time hoping that this time would be the last. In bringing up her "unquenchable thirst" for different relationships, Jesus revealed to her that she would never be truly satisfied until she began "drinking" from the water He would give her.

Questions

Note: Jesus offered this woman living water. He said that if she drank it she would not be thirsty anymore; in other words, she would be satisfied and not desire one relationship after another. Here is hope for you and me! Here is the method to **Pure Freedom** from pornography, or any addiction. If you discover how to receive this "living water," and how to drink it, you will not be thirsty anymore; in other words, you will be free from the craving of and slavery to pornography. The remainder of this **Pure Freedom** Course is designed to help you receive and drink.

Question 8. Please describe how this teaching is giving you hope. How is drinking this water going to satisfy you and change the way you live? Be specific.

By admitting that pornography does not permanently satisfy you, that you have to "drink" of it again and again, you are ready to discover what will satisfy. Permanently!

Question 9. Have you attempted to stop viewing pornography in the past but failed?

   A. Yes   B. No

Question 10. According to the teaching that you've learned today, why did you fail last time and what will be different now?

Dear friend, as you contemplate continuing on in this course there is something that must be done, and without doing this there is no real hope for **Pure Freedom.** You must rid yourself of any and all sources of pornography. We have become so accustomed to "drinking" the "water" of pornography that unless we cut it off; we will, out of habit, return to it. Throw away the magazines, cut off the cable, cut off or filter your Internet access, cut off access to pornography newsgroups, and do whatever it takes to rid your house, car, and life of pornography. Enjoy this process; indeed, have fun with it—stomp on it, burn it, drown it in a lake and laugh as it sinks. This is the first step to **Pure Freedom**.

> "And I said to them, 'Each of you, get rid of the vile images you have set your eyes on, and do not defile yourselves with the idols of Egypt. I am the LORD your God'" (Ezekiel 20:7).

Question 11. Will you trash all access to pornography right now? _____

Scripture to Consider:

"Nothing in all creation is hidden from God's sight. Everything is uncovered and laid bare before the eyes of him to whom we must give account" (Hebrews 4:13).

Jesus said: "The Spirit of the Lord is on me, because he has anointed me to preach good news to the poor. He has sent me to proclaim Pure Freedom for the prisoners and recovery of sight for the blind, to release the oppressed, to proclaim the year of the Lords' favor" (Luke 4:18-19).

Prayer for today: "Dear Father, I confess trying to satisfy myself in impure waters. Would you forgive me, and teach me how to truly drink from Jesus Christ? I long to quench my thirst in Him, please satisfy my heart in Jesus. In Jesus' Name, Amen!"

Answer the following accountability questions with each lesson.

Were you free from pornography today?
    Yes   No

Were you free from masturbation today?
    Yes   No

Were you free from sexual immorality today?   Yes   No

Testimony

Every day we will present a testimony for you to read after your course work. **Here is today's testimony from Pastor Ken:**

I grew up in a good Christian home. My father is a pastor, and has been a minister all of my life. I was saved at the age of thirteen at a revival where my Dad was leading the worship; but I never grew in my walk with God until later.

I was hooked by porn at an early age, probably about 11 or 12 years old. I was at my grandparents, where I stayed for a few weeks every summer. One of the neighborhood boys had a magazine he'd stolen from his father. We sneaked into the woods and were mesmerized by the beautiful women we saw there, baring all.

From there, even though I lived in a pastor's home, I would get my hands on some porn from time to time, and eventually I developed a very strong habit of lustful thoughts and masturbation. I carried this addiction into my adult life, even though God called me into full-time ministry at age 17. I had all the "head knowledge", knew the correct Bible answers, had even gone into the ministry at God's calling, but I was not living a pure life sexually.

I was somewhat of a playboy during high school, and sex and girls was kind of "my thing". I attempted at times to be pure, but every time it was on my own strength, and it never lasted. Then, in my second year of college, at age 19, God gave me a wake-up call. My girlfriend (now my wife, by God's hand) became pregnant and we decided to drop out of school and get married. It was rough at first. We had to admit we didn't love each other, and ask God to give us that love. He did; but I still held on to my secret sin; the hook was set deep. My wife did find out, and there was much damage done; my sin put a major strain on our marriage.

But even that wake-up call did not cause me to stop masturbating or viewing porn. It still held me in its terrible grip. I had basically given up hope that I would ever be free of it until this year, at age 31, I stumbled onto the **Pure Freedom** website. I must say honestly that I started the course with little expectation of change. But the course pushed me to a point of being radical in dealing with this sin. God in His grace picked me up, and removed from me the hook of porn. He has given me more of a desire for Him than for my lustful pleasure. He has changed my wicked heart into a heart that seeks Him completely, and I never again want to fill my mind with images or fantasies that will never satisfy. I now have peace, and I now know my identity is fully in Christ.

It's made a difference in the way I approach my family and marriage. God has blessed me with a godly wife and two beautiful daughters—the oldest daughter has surrendered her life to God as a missionary.

And I now have a heart to reach others held in the grasp of porn. God has now opened my eyes to see the many who are trapped in this lie, and I have already had some opportunity in my ministry to encourage others to find **Pure Freedom** from porn. It's been an amazing transformation, and after at least 15 years addicted to porn and masturbation, God has transformed me in 2 months! He is truly a mighty and awesome God, and I now live to serve Him even more. As of July 2001, I've been free for 10 months.

DAY 2— MORE LIVING WATER

"Come, all you who are thirsty, come to the waters; and you who have no money, come, buy and eat! Come, buy wine and milk without money and without cost. ²Why spend money on what is not bread, and your labor on what does not satisfy? Listen, listen to me, and eat what is good, and your soul will delight in the richest of fare. ³Give ear and come to me; hear me that your soul may live. I will make an everlasting covenant with you, my faithful love promised to David (Isaiah 55:1-3).

Pornography, in its essential allurement, promises to quench our thirst. In other words, it promises satisfaction. And honestly, it does satisfy—but only for a time. Pretty soon we discover that we are "thirsty" again, and as the years go by we find that we are really never genuinely satisfied. Right? That is because sin never truly satisfies! It does not fulfill us; it depletes us. I can recall going from soft-core pornography magazines to X Rated videos, to cyber sex…etc. I thought if I could just see that perfect picture, or have that perfect sexual experience, my life would be full and satisfied. This is the nature of sin. It takes us further and further and though it promises to satisfy, it never does satisfy eternally. This is why we keep coming back to it over and over again.

Questions

Question 1. Verse 2 of Isaiah 55 above asks an important question: "Why spend money on what does not satisfy?" Have you done this? How does this relate to our involvement with pornography? Write your answer here:

The verses above in Isaiah 55 are an invitation to the thirsty. Play along with me as we question the author of these verses. He says, "Come, all you who are thirsty."

"Alright, I am thirsty, I will come. But where do I come to quench my thirst?"

"Come to the waters."

"Yes, that makes sense; if I am thirsty I should come to the waters, but where are the waters?"

"Ah, excellent question. 'Listen, listen to me, and eat what is good and your soul will delight in the richest of fare. Give ear and come to me; hear me, that your soul may live.'"

Friend, do you see it now? The water is in the Word of God. Drinking comes by listening. The Bible is our source of true refreshment and quenching of our thirst.

Questions

Question 2. According to verse 2 what is the result of drinking in the Word of God?
- A. Your H2O makeup increases.
- B. You need to use the restroom more often.
- C. Your soul delights in what you are taking in.

Question 3. According to verse 3 what is the result of listening to God's Word?
- A. We become bored and fall asleep.
- B. Our souls are given *life*.

Question 4. Write out your thoughts on this quote: **"None but God can satisfy the longings of an immortal soul; that as the heart was made for Him, so He only can fill it."** (Trench: Notes on the Parables. Prodigal Son)[1]

Yesterday's lesson was about the woman at the well, who had been "drinking" from the wrong water. She was filling herself with one relationship after another (6 total), and she was obviously not satisfied. She was spending herself on what did not satisfy. But Jesus offered her living water, which she could receive as a free gift, which would satisfy her thirst forever. Today, we are admonished to stop spending our time, energy and money on what will never satisfy us, and to drink the water that brings delight, joy and life to our souls. See what we have been missing while involved in pornography?

Question 5. How does this verse relate to what we are studying?

"Death and destruction are never satisfied, and neither are the eyes of man" (Proverbs 27:20).

Friend, I was trapped in pornography for many years as my "eyes were never satisfied." I continued to want excitement, acceptance and all the other things that pornography offers. But at the end of those 15 years I found out that I had been drinking

Questions

from a putrid, impure source of water; and it defiled me and made me unclean. But since January of 1999, I have been drinking the clean, refreshing, satisfying, life-giving, thirst-quenching water of Jesus Christ. The teaching of these past two days is foundational to overcoming pornography. Switch water sources! Pornography never will satisfy us. The porn industry makes its billions of dollars on customer dissatisfaction; and if we stay in it, we will always have a continual lust for more. It is salt water giving more thirst than satisfaction.

Question 6. How does this verse go with today's teaching?

> "Having lost all sensitivity, they have given themselves over to sensuality so as to indulge in every kind of impurity, with a continual lust for more." (Ephesians 4:19).

Question 7. Write your thoughts on this verse:

> "My people have committed two sins: They have forsaken me, the spring of living water, and have dug their own cisterns, broken cisterns that cannot hold water" (Jeremiah. 2:13).

Note: God describes Himself as the "Spring of living water." He alone is the Source of life, refreshment, joy and nourishment for us. He is ever fresh and new, like a spring, and to "drink" of God is to receive life and be satisfied! Turning to pornography is like trying to get water from a jar with holes in it.

Question 8. Please read this quote from the famous preacher, Charles Spurgeon, and record your comments about it: **"Men are in a restless pursuit after satisfaction in earthly things. They will exhaust themselves in the deceitful delights of sin, and, finding them all to be vanity and emptiness, they will become very perplexed and disappointed. But they will continue their fruitless search. Though wearied, they still stagger forward under the influence of spiritual madness, and though there is no result to be reached except that of everlasting disappointment, yet they press forward. They have no forethought for their eternal state; the present hour absorbs them. They turn to another and another of earth's broken cisterns, hoping to find water where not a drop was ever discovered yet."**[2]

Course member Peter writes: "Madness! What a perfect description of my relentless pursuit of the next sexual image that will be the one that will satisfy. As the hours slip away and my eyes grow heavy with sleep I cannot stop. Yet, climax, and moments, even seconds later it starts again. What madness indeed!!!!"

Yesterday we studied the story of the woman at the well. We noticed how she had been "drinking" of the "water" of multiple relationships (6 total); and yet, she was still "thirsty." Jesus offered her "living water" that would quench her thirst eternally. Today, I want to add one final thought about this story, and show how it relates to our involvement with pornography, masturbation, and all forms of sexual impurity. Please read the following verses in John 4—the passage we studied yesterday.

> "Then, leaving her water jar, the woman went back to the town and said to the people, "Come, see a man who told me everything I ever did. Could this be the Christ?" They came out of the town and made their way toward him" (John 4:28-30).

Question 9. After speaking with Jesus, the woman at the well went back into town. What did she do with her water jar?

- A. She took it with her.
- B. She left it with Jesus.
- C. She dropped it.

Question 10. Yesterday we saw that Jesus Christ compared the water in that well to what?

- A. Bad habits that will not truly satisfy.
- B. Ongoing relationships that leave you "thirsty."
- C. Unsatisfied cravings.
- D. All of the above.

Question 11. The fact that the woman at the well left her water jar behind could have meant that…

- A. She forgot it.
- B. She had begun drinking of the water Jesus gave her and no longer needed the other water.

Testimony

The following testimony is from Thomas:

I have attended church all my life. Also from a very early age I have been in bondage to the sin of pornography and masturbation.

We all have had an idol other than the Lord God Almighty, where we have gone to worship in sin. Of course, I tried many times on my own to keep from visiting my idol, but I exhausted myself with my futile efforts. As a matter of fact, before I came to **Pure Freedom**, I was actually at the point of just trying to be comfortable living with this sin in my life.

This is what being comfortable in pornography and masturbation brought to my life: It brought to an end a 16-year marriage, and broken relationships with my children.

I moved on in my life still living in habitual sin. I met a very nice woman after my divorce, and invited her to my church. We even went on a work mission this summer together. But that sin was still in my life.

Finally, the Lord brought me to **Pure Freedom**. I enrolled. Hesitantly. It took me about a week to decide this is what I should do. I knew it wouldn't be easy. Remember I lived most of my life in this sin. And I mentioned the "comfort" that it gave me. Sin is so deceptive.

So I began the course. I was grateful. It started to change my life. I saw that yes, I could live without sin. Truly, I could. I studied sin and salvation. And I studied right along and then we came to the lesson about confession. Boy, this is where the rubber meets the road. The lesson was: You've got to confess this sin to the people it affects.

I was going to have to confess this dirty little secret that I'd kept for years to my Christian girlfriend. I was also faced with con-

Questions

Scripture does not specifically say why the woman left her water jar with Jesus and so we cannot know for certain why she left it. Obviously, she did indeed need to continue to drink physical water even after her encounter with Christ. However, the following truths are seen in the passage: First, Jesus compared the physical thirst of the woman with her attempts to quench the thirst of her soul by having multiple and sinful relationships; and secondly, Jesus offered her "living water" which would quench the thirst of her soul once and for all. Oh, dear friend, here is good news for us! As we learn how to drink living water, that only Jesus can give, we can leave our "water jar" behind.

Question 12. Please read the following quote from Arthur Pink and then write out your thoughts in the space provided.

> **"She left her water pot because she had now found a well of 'living water.' She had come to the well for literal water and that was what her mind was set on. But now that she had obtained salvation, she did not think any more about her water pot. It is always this way. Once our souls truly perceive Christ, once we know Him and receive Him as our personal Savior, we turn away from what we used to think about. Her mind was now fixed on Christ, and she had no thought of well, water, or water pot."**[3]

Granted, even after we come to Christ and learn to drink of His living water, there can be a time when we must learn how to leave the other "water behind" and it is certainly not always an instantaneous exchange of water, as the woman at the well did. We are not saying that it always has to happen in this manner, but what we are saying is that as we drink of Christ's living water we are able to leave behind the sinful water.

Oh, how I remember the day in my pastor's office, when I was challenged to leave behind the filthy waters of pornography, and to begin drinking of the living water. I'll tell you more about this experience as we progress in the course, but for now I will tell you that I never want to go back to drinking that "sewer water" again. My heart's desire now is to see you drinking along with me from the living water—the water that delights the soul and gives it life, and the water that satisfies forever.

Question 13. Please provide your closing thoughts on this day of teaching, and summarize the main thought of the lesson. Have you learned anything new, or been reminded of something you had forgotten? Will anything change in your life as a result of this teaching?

Testimony

fronting the fact that some of the things about our relationship weren't pure. When I heard this I immediately thought of the Gospel where Jesus' disciples started complaining: "This is a hard saying." Confess my sin to my girlfriend, and stop sinning with her. This was a hard saying. I didn't want to do it.

Sin, I discovered is nothing more than telling God I'll do it my way, thank you very much. And that's exactly what I was doing. But God was telling me to stop sinning. Confess. I looked it up in the Bible, in the Gospel of John, 6th chapter. I read it. I choked when Jesus asked the twelve, "Will you go away also?" and Peter said to him, "Lord, to whom shall I go? You have the words of eternal life."

Jesus is the only one who has the words of eternal life. Sin is always a short-term strategy. It will get you through today. If you tell a lie, it will be comfortable for you today, but tomorrow there will be consequences—a broken marriage, a lost job….

So I followed Christ, I confessed my sins and broke off the sinful relationship with my girlfriend. Many things have started to change as a result of my obedience to Christ. I feel like a different person. I've got more energy, more time for important things. It would take a long time to tell all of the blessings that I've begun to receive; but the main thing is that I don't sin in impurity any more. The Lord has begun to bless my new life, and I'm asking that He will continue to bless me with purity from now until eternity.

Friends, you know there will still be struggles. Yes, there is still pain in my heart over the lost relationships in my life; but as my mentor counseled me, it is better to live in pain and righteousness than in sin and deceit.

Scripture to Consider

"You have set our iniquities before you, our secret sins in the light of your presence" (Psalm 90:8).

"Whether you turn to the right or to the left, your ears will hear a voice behind you, saying, 'This is the way; walk in it.' Then you will defile your idols overlaid with silver and your images covered with gold; you will throw them away like a menstrual cloth and say to them, 'Away with you!'" (Isaiah 30:22).

"…being confident of this, that he who began a good work in you will carry it on to completion until the day of Christ Jesus" (Philippians 1:6).

Prayer for today: "Father in heaven, I have wasted much on pornography that has left me empty, parched, and dry. Now I see I need to come to You to be quenched in the Living Water of Jesus Christ. I come to You now, Father, help me to be satisfied with Jesus."

Were you free from pornography since you did the last lesson?

    Yes   No

Were you free from masturbation since you did the last lesson?

    Yes   No

Were you free from sexual immorality since you did the last lesson?

    Yes   No

Question 1. Does this "darkness" scenario fit your situation? Write your answer here:

Here is what eventually happened with me. I met a woman 6 months after my first wife left me, and we began corresponding. My sins were still in secret and over time I convinced this woman, who was a Christian, that I was a fine upstanding Christian man. We married in February of 1998, over a year after we met the first time. But I continued with pornography, masturbation, and sex chatting on the Internet, and my wife soon discovered my sin. She was extremely afraid that if confronted, I would leave our relationship and so she began seeking help from a counselor. Because of her belief in Biblical counseling rather than the psychological approach she searched for a counselor through NANC (National Association Of Nouthetic Counselors), who directed us to Pastor Will Lohnes of Shepherds Grace Church in Medina, Ohio. We began weekly counsel with Pastor Will.

One day during counseling, the subject of pornography came up. I found myself confessing to my pastor about my years in pornography and I asked for his help to stop my habitual sinning in this area. Friend, this was extremely difficult to do! As you can imagine, it was embarrassing and demeaning to my wife, and myself, and it truly broke me to have to admit that I was not on the inside the man that I was claiming to be on the outside. But that very act of humbling myself in front of my pastor was the start of my coming out of the darkness, the sapping of the strength of pornography in my life, and the victory that I am now experiencing on a daily basis since January of 1999. You may not feel able to confess to your spouse or your pastor right now. And this is only the third day in the **Pure Freedom** course, so you no doubt still have "shaky knees" in your newfound walk of freedom. But you have already taken steps to drag this sin into the light, even if they are small ones.

DAY 3— INTO THE LIGHT

So far, we have discussed the necessity of drinking living water from Jesus to quench our thirst. We've seen that God is a "Spring of Living Water" and that turning to anything other than God for satisfaction is spending our life on something that will not satisfy. We have seen that pornography is a "broken cistern" that will not hold water, and will not quench our thirst (Jeremiah 2:13). Today, we will discuss another principle, which if understood and lived out will set us free from pornography.

Have you ever noticed that most fungi grow best in the dark? If you were to turn the light on the fungus it would wither and eventually die. Pornography addiction is the same; it too thrives in the darkness. Typically, pornography is done in secret, where nobody knows, and as long as the sinning remains in the dark it will no doubt continue.

During my years of slavery to pornography, I appeared to be a respectable man. I was an airline captain, had a degree from seminary, taught Sunday school at our church, and appeared to have a good family. But in secret, I was a different man. As a pilot, I would layover in hotels and had much private time. The pornographic channels in the hotel room would draw me

The following testimony is from Jake:

When I was about 7 years old and probably earlier, I assumed masturbation was okay and went ahead and began what would be an ongoing habit. My parents told me I shouldn't do it but never really made a big enough deal of it to really enforce a rule or punish me when I did it (looking back I wish they did). It is easy for me to blame them for not explaining to me and training me enough in that area, but I am ultimately responsible for giving in to these temptations and making this a habit. I chose to remain in it because I thought it was no big deal to God. As I approached my teenage years and even before that I started to hear some voices in the back of my head telling me that I should be ashamed of myself. I felt too trapped into that habit to listen to my conscience. I felt even more trapped as the years went by because I started to view more images and watched TV programs that were not good for my spirit. Though they weren't pornographic, it was just the beginning. Most of my involvement with pornography was progressive and occasional. I let it pull me under those deep waters of deception.

When I was about 15 or so I prayed hard to God that He would tell me whether or not masturbation is wrong. He answered my prayer when I sought out His Word. I concluded that it was indeed wrong but I didn't want to believe it! I wanted God to tell me it was okay—especially since I just thought it was normal all these years. God brought me to Romans 6 and the verse that stuck out the most was 6:21, which says: "What benefit did you reap at that time from the things you are now ashamed of? Those things result in death!"

That same night after midnight, I continued to stumble. I continued to let porn and masturbation be my master for a few more years and in that period discovered that the Spice and Playboy channels on cable existed. I came to those stations and even without paying for the movies all that time was able to hear and see quite a bit of the material, which pulled me further under.

Then one summer, I declared a personal war on this and made a vow to God after one of my stumbles never to masturbate or go to these stations or any of this garbage

powerfully and I would give in repeatedly, year after year after year. I would pray against it, read my Bible, plan not to fall, but as soon as I would get to the privacy of my hotel room, lust would take over and I would plunge into pornography.

I was living two different lives. The person who is living in deceit like this will do everything they can to protect the sinful secret life from being exposed. They become very angry and defensive if questioned about any possible wrong doings. I remember one time preaching very passionately about the evils of pornography and sexual sins, and truly it was a great sermon; but the problem was that I had stayed up most of the night before indulging in pornography. What horrible hypocrisy! And so I know first hand that people involved with pornography have a hidden secret life, and they will do all in their power to keep it from becoming exposed. And yet, this exposure is the very thing necessary to eradicating it from their lives.

What was happening to me during those years that I had no power to overcome? Why did I give in time and time again, especially when I had prayed so much against falling? The answer is that this sinning was all done in the darkness, in secret, where sin thrives. My secret life illustrated the truth of John 3:19-20: "This is the verdict: Light has come into the world, but men loved darkness instead of light because their deeds were evil. Everyone who does evil hates the light, and will not come into the light for fear that his deeds will be exposed."

again. I ended up in the next couple of years stumbling time and time again. I was trying to win the war on my own. It wasn't an every day struggle; however, I would occasionally go back into it and each time the sights and sounds of pornography would make me thirstier. I turned it into a creative game, my own war game, which wasn't necessarily wrong except that I was trying to do it on my own and I wouldn't do it God's way. That was wrong. Determination, motivation and persistence in fighting the battle I did have, but I didn't have one key weapon—humility! I was too prideful and so I fell time and time again. I won some battles but was losing the war badly. There were times years ago where I would actually try to radically amputate pornographic material and I threw away magazines and ripped up stuff, but I didn't amputate everything and didn't have the humility to amputate everything. I thought I could stand face to face with temptation and just say no. It didn't work that way.

Aug. 2, 2000 was my last stumble and it is not hard to believe that it was the deepest that I ever got into pornography. For the first time I viewed hardcore pornography. That night, I got on my knees and cried out to God in desperation for deliverance. I said in tears, "I can't do it! It's all hopeless!" I did cry out to God before about it, especially the weeks leading up to this, but not with those words! God was waiting all this time to bring me to that very point. He then delivered me and I have been free for 11 weeks now! No masturbation, no pornography, complete amputation! I have had my ups and downs with lust, but God is working tremendously in that area cleaning up the leftover garbage. Developing a habit of drinking those living waters of His Word daily does it. It was interesting to me that about a month before He delivered me, He brought me to a verse when I turned at random after praying for deliverance that he would deliver me, and that I would fulfill my vows to Him (Psalm 50).

This is God's grace to me because I not only wanted and accepted it; I cried out for it in humility—I think that is the key word in this whole testimony. It says in the Psalms that The Lord is close to the brokenhearted and He won't despise a broken heart. Please be encouraged; God is good!

Questions

Please read the following passage from 1 John 1:

> [5] This is the message we have heard from him and declare to you: God is light; in him there is no darkness at all. [6] If we claim to have fellowship with him yet walk in the darkness, we lie and do not live by the truth. [7] But if we walk in the light, as he is in the light, we have fellowship with one another, and the blood of Jesus, his Son, purifies us from all sin.
>
> [8] If we claim to be without sin, we deceive ourselves and the truth is not in us. [9] If we confess our sins, he is faithful and just and will forgive us our sins and purify us from all unrighteousness. [10] If we claim we have not sinned, we make him out to be a liar and his word has no place in our lives" (1 John 1:5-10).

Verse 6 above shows that I was deceived while involved with pornography. I was claiming to have fellowship with God, yet I was walking in the darkness, so in reality my life was a lie, and I was not living by the truth. I'm not saying that I wasn't a Christian while involved in pornography, just at the time; I was not walking in truth. This is a very sad scenario, but unfortunately common. I have met so many people who are hiding a vast majority of their lives from their loved ones, co-workers and friends. They present the appearance of being spiritual people who are knowledgeable about the Bible, but appearances are not always reality. We all know that information is not transformation. What these people need to do is to begin to slowly, carefully, and with much discernment as to "who and when" to approach, begin to expose this hidden life to someone else.

Question 2. How about you? Can you relate to the deception of hiding in the dark? Have you been living in secrecy? Write your thoughts here:

Question 3. According to verse 7 there are two results of walking in the light. Please write what each one is:

Did you catch that? Here is truth that packs a punch and can change our lives forever! If we begin walking in the light, not only are we able to fellowship with others who are walking in the light, but also Jesus Himself purifies our lives! *Purity will be the thoroughly enjoyable result of coming into the light, as you have already begun doing!*

> **Course Member Jordan writes:** "Pornography and masturbation are very private activities. Part of the reason we want to be rid of this sin is because of the shame and self-loathing that it creates in our heart. I thought exposing this sin to another would cause me to feel the shame and loathing more intensely. The opposite was really true. What came to me after exposing it was **Pure Freedom** of not having to live the lie. It was not what I expected, but it was a most wonderful gift that God gave to me."

Question 4. Verse 9 tells us the first step to take is to "walk in the light." What is that first step?
  A. Turn all the lights on in the house
  B. Confess our sins
  C. Always carry a flashlight with us

Question 5. Friends, we know that we are to first and foremost confess our sins to God. Find a safe environment for you to write out a prayer of confession to Him. This is the first step toward walking in the light that brings purity. Feel free to drag your sin into the light right here, and write a prayer of confession to God:

Question 6. Can you see how putting this Scripture into practice will result in purity? What ways can you think of to begin walking in the light? Keep in mind that you do not have to do each one of these immediately, but just write out a list of different things that you may eventually need to do, in order to sap sin of its strength. List your thoughts here:

Question 7. Please provide your thoughts on this passage of Scripture; specifically list how you will apply this to your life:

> "For you were once darkness, but now you are light in the Lord. Live as children of light (for the fruit of the light consists in all goodness, righteousness and truth) and find out what pleases the Lord. Have nothing to do with the fruitless deeds of darkness, but rather expose them. For it is shameful even to mention what the disobedient do in secret. But everything exposed by the light becomes visible, for it is light that makes everything visible" (Ephesians 5:8-14).

Write your thoughts here:

Question 8. Finally, write out what things you have learned today, and how you will apply them to your life.

Scripture to Consider

"Here is a trustworthy saying that deserves full acceptance: Christ Jesus came into the world to save sinners—of whom I am the worst" (1 Timothy 1:15).

"How can a young man keep his way pure? By living according to your word" (Psalm 119:9).

"I will repay you for the years the locusts have eaten; the great locust and the young locust, the other locusts and the locust swarm my great army that I sent among you" (Joel 2:25).

Were you free from pornography since you did the last lesson?
    Yes   No

Were you free from masturbation since you did the last lesson?
    Yes   No

Were you free from sexual immorality since you did the last lesson?
    Yes   No

DAY 4—THE CROSS

Today, we want to examine the gospel, and see how it relates to bondage to, and *Pure Freedom* from, pornography. Let's examine the following passages of Scripture:

> "But your iniquities have separated you from your God; your sins have hidden his face from you, so that he will not hear" (Isaiah 59:2).

Friend, when I was doing pornography and masturbation I was separated from God and God did not hear my prayers. In fact, my constant sinning caused Him to hide His face from me because He cannot look on sin. I felt as if my prayers stopped at the ceiling and then fell to the floor. Even though I may have been a Christian I was "darkened in my understanding and separated from the life of God..." (Ephesians 4:18). Indeed, this was a very dark time in my life, as I told you in yesterday's lesson.

Testimony

The following testimony is from Bob:

Well I know God sent this **Pure Freedom** Course to me as one day it just showed up in my email box. But my addiction to porn, as I look back now, started when I was a teenager in the 60's. I found a *Playboy* in my dad's room and I became so excited. But then I went to college and really did not do a lot with porn but maybe a magazine every now and then. But when I got out of college and moved to a big metropolitan city in which there was so much pornography available I found myself starting to get deeper.

I should say that I was addicted for over 20 years to porn. I was mostly involved in topless clubs, movies, magazines and Internet when it came on the scene. As the years went past I even dated topless dancers and was involved in a lot of sexual situations. I wasn't married during this time and I really think God kept me from getting my family involved in this. But as time went on I became so tired of it all.

I took a new job about 5 years ago and moved to a new town. I knew there was something special about this town but I never could figure out what was so special. About a year after I moved here, I had the urge to go to church. I can remember the sermon today as I felt I was the only one in the sanctuary.

Well, as in the past I blew off that feeling or tried to but could not this time. That summer I went back to church and they were having a revival, and I had this strong need to go. So I went Sunday night and then I went the next night. On the third night the Lord had really been working on me, there was an altar call given to come to accept Jesus. Well, my feet would not move but as the evangelist called I accepted Jesus that night.

Now Satan was not a happy camper and tempted me. But this course, which I know was sent by God, has allowed me to finish the job God started over 4 years ago. So to anyone who may have just come to Christ, do not become discouraged when Satan keeps coming back and coming back over and over. I have become so much stronger in my walk with God because of this course. I know I am unworthy of anything he has to offer but through the shedding of the blood of Jesus I am washed clean of the pornography addiction. But I also know Satan is still around and I must always put on the full armor of God and fight Satan each day. I love drinking this wonderful water of Jesus and knowing I am loved. I know now that God will provide me a family one-day and I have this course to thank. Thank you Setting Captives Free for your help, but most of all I thank our Father for never giving up on me.

Questions

Question 1. Can you identify with the feelings of separation from God while involved in pornography? Write your answers here:

Please read the following passage:

> "[21] Once you were alienated from God and were enemies in your minds because of your evil behavior.[22] But now he has reconciled you by Christ's physical body through death to present you holy in his sight, without blemish and free from accusation—[23] if you continue in your faith, established and firm, not moved from the hope held out in the gospel. This is the gospel that you heard and that has been proclaimed to every creature under heaven, and of which I, Paul, have become a servant" (Colossians 1:21-23).

As I came out of pornography the above verses showed my past, my present and my future. I used to be "alienated from God" and was His "enemy" because of my "evil behavior." This was my past as I lived in the darkness of secret sins. Though I claimed to be God's friend, purported myself to be His messenger, and basically told everyone how spiritual I was, the reality is that I was alienated from God, and was His enemy because of my habitual sinning in the area of pornography and masturbation.

But God took action on my behalf. He "reconciled me by Christ's physical body through death." I am no longer His enemy; I am reconciled to God through the death of Jesus Christ. This is the work that He did; it is nothing that I have done.

Now, please understand that not everyone who has been involved in pornography is an enemy of God. You may be a Christian who has fallen into this trap and are eager to be released. For myself, I have concluded that though I used to preach Christ I did not truly know Him in a saving way. I knew about Him, but did not truly know Him through genuine repentance.

These verses in Colossians 1 describe not only how we are saved, but how we come to leave pornography behind, too. So let us look at the above verses from the perspective of how to be free from

Questions

pornography and masturbation. These verses present three things: the problem, the solution, and the results.

First, the problem is that sin, in our case, pornography, separates and alienates us from God. We can become so distanced from God that we feel that our prayers are not heard, and they may not be. Pornography, because it causes us to love the world, eventually leads us to hate God. The following is from an ex-minister of the gospel, after he fell into pornography and sexual impurity. Note how he is now an enemy of God in his mind, because of his evil behavior:

> **Course member James writes:** "Inside of me rages such a depth of anger, so deep it interacts with the depths of hell. It rages and fires against God, all revolving around the loss of the position I cherished so much in ministry. My flesh tells me that God was wrong, unfaithful, incorrect, cruel, and erroneous, and that I should not serve Him who did not keep his word to me. The devil tells me the same. 'He has not met your needs. He has failed you, led you to a position, and then did not rescue you when He could have. Is this the kind of God you want to serve? Does the God who 'screws' you ... leave you defenseless? He has let you go mad. Is this the faithful Deity you want to serve?'"

Friends, I was nearly at this point too. Sin had so hardened my heart, and deceived my very soul, that I was becoming a very hateful and angry person.

Question 2. Have you experienced this hatred for God? Some may say yes, others no. Let me assure you that if you continue in the path of sin you will eventually get to the place where you do indeed hate God. "No man can serve two masters: Either he will love the one and hate the other, or he will be devoted to the one and despise the other" (Matthew 6:24). Write your thoughts here:

Now, let us look at the solution. God has reconciled us by putting Jesus to death. Because pornography causes us to eventually hate God, God took the initiative to reconcile us. He took all our sins off of us and put them onto Jesus, who died to pay for them. On the cross, Jesus was treated as a pornographer, a God-hater, an enemy of God, in order to bring us back to God. On the cross, Jesus removed our sin that prevented us from having a relationship with God. The solution to the problem is Jesus Christ.

Please write out Colossians 1: 22.

Question 3. Where are you with Jesus Christ right now? Can you see that He has dealt with our sin problem?

Dear friend, beware of any teaching, program, or method of finding **Pure Freedom** from pornography that does not have Jesus Christ at the center, for there is no other way to solve the sin problem than Jesus. There is no other way to be reconciled to God, to be changed from His enemy to His friend, to cease the evil behavior, than through Jesus.

I remember how I tried many different avenues to finding freedom from pornography. I went to counseling, read numerous books, sought out the help of a famous evangelist, went to meetings with pastors who had fallen…etc. And now that I have been working with course members, I have found that there are literally hundreds of programs, methods, books, …etc. being offered to help others become free from this addiction. A simple search on the Internet on "Sexual Addiction" will result in literally thousands of websites.

Question 4. Have you tried other methods to be free from pornography? If so, what were they? Please list them here:

So what are the results? The death of Jesus Christ tells us that God has done something about our sin problem. It tells us that He is committed to eradicating sin and has taken radical action to dispose of it, by putting His Son to death in our place.

Notice the results of what Jesus did for us on the cross. (v. 22) "But now he has reconciled you by Christ's physical body through death to present you holy in his sight, without blemish and free from accusation." Oh friends, this is a marvelous truth with practical results. Because of Jesus' death on the cross, we who have been reconciled to God are "holy" "without blemish" and "free from accusation."

Question 5. By way of reflection, please list (1) what you used to be, (2) what God has done, and (3) what you are now, according to today's teaching. Please be thorough.

1.

2.

3.

Question 6. Please provide your comments on the following verses:

> "God made him who had no sin to be sin for us, so that in him we might become the righteousness of God" (2 Corinthians 5:21).

Questions

"For God so loved the world that he gave his one and only Son, that whoever believes in him shall not perish but have eternal life. For God did not send his Son into the world to condemn the world, but to save the world through him" (John 3:16-17).

Yet to all who received him, to those who believed in his name, he gave the right to become children of God, children born not of natural descent, nor of human decision or a husband's will, but born of God" (John 1:12, 13).

Friends, possibly you are still an enemy of God in your mind because of your evil behavior. Maybe it is time to put up the white flag of surrender and ask God to reconcile you to Himself. If you know that you need to be holy, without blemish and free from accusation, then why not ask God right now for help. Here is a place to put your thoughts and prayers to Him in writing:

I remember that after the meeting with my pastor where I confessed to involvement with pornography, I began seeking the Lord earnestly. Up to that point, I thought possibly that I had committed the unpardonable sin, and that God was probably finished with me and I was now useless for the rest of my life. But my pastor pointed me to Deuteronomy chapter 4 verses 25-31. This passage states that the children of God would become corrupt, make themselves idols to worship, assimilate into the practices of the surrounding nations, and do evil against the Lord for many years. But then my eyes fell upon verse 29, which says "But if from there, you seek the LORD your God, you will find Him if you look for Him with all your heart and with all your soul. When you are in distress and all these things have happened to you, then in later days you will return to the LORD your God and obey Him. For the LORD your God is a merciful God; He will not abandon or destroy you or forget the covenant with your forefathers, which he confirmed to them by oath."

Those words penetrated to my soul: "But if from there…." But if from there, you seek the Lord with all your heart, you will find Him. Wherever your "there" is, if you will seek the Lord from "there" you will find Him; and then He will make you holy, without blemish, and free from accusation.

"Ask and it will be given to you; seek and you will find; knock and the door will be opened to you. For everyone who asks receives, he who seeks finds, and to him who knocks, the door will be opened" (Matthew 7:7).

Question 7. Please summarize the teaching of today. I'm specifically looking for your understanding of any changes that will be made in your life because of the Scripture that you have read today.

Scripture to Consider

"Now, brothers, I want to remind you of the gospel I preached to you, which you received and on which you have taken your stand.[2] By this gospel you are saved, if you hold firmly to the word I preached to you. Otherwise, you have believed in vain.[3] For what I received I passed on to you as of first importance: that Christ died for our sins according to the Scriptures,[4] that he was buried, that he was raised on the third day according to the Scriptures" (1 Corinthians 15: 1-4).

Were you free from pornography since you did the last lesson?
    Yes No

Were you free from masturbation since you did the last lesson?
    Yes No

Were you free from sexual immorality since you did the last lesson?
    Yes No

Questions

Question 1. Please describe what things have hindered you from running this race to win:

Question 2. What are we commanded to do with these things that hinder us?

Question 3. So, what things will you throw off so you can run light? Please only list those things that you will get rid of RIGHT NOW.

"But put ye on the Lord Jesus Christ, and make not provision for the flesh, to fulfill the lusts thereof" (Romans 13:14).

Notice the above verse tells us to "make no provision for the flesh?" You see, when I had access to pornography I could pray about not falling all day long, but as soon as I got in to my hotel room, I would go down. Why? Because there was provision made for me to gratify the lusts of my flesh through the TV sitting right in front of me. Pornography was right there beckoning me and for years and years I could not resist its drawing power. But when I removed the TV from my room I was not allowing any provision for my flesh to be gratified.

This is such a key principle to freedom because if we allow ourselves access to that which causes us to sin we will inevitably find ourselves giving in during a weak moment.

DAY 5—RUNNING LIGHT

"Therefore, since we are surrounded by such a great cloud of witnesses, let us throw off everything that hinders and the sin that so easily entangles, and let us run with perseverance the race marked out for us" (Hebrews 12:1).

Friends, this passage of Scripture describes the Christian life as a foot race, and the author tells us that in order to run fast we must run light. We are here instructed to "throw off everything that hinders and the sin that so easily entangles." Here, temptation and sin are described as those things that hinder and entangle, and they must be thrown off.

For me, I had to throw off my TV in the hotel room, give away my notebook computer (as I was using it to do sex-chatting on the Internet), get rid of my TV at home, and avoid certain situations that tempted me.

When I first confessed to my pastor that I had been viewing pornography while on the road in hotels, he told me about this principle of throwing off the sin and everything that entangles. Since that which was entangling me was the TV in my hotel room he suggested I "throw it off" by removing it when I got to my room for the evening. I was desperate to be free of pornography and masturbation, as by now I had pretty much stopped running the race and was entangled in sin. So, I followed my pastor's advice and began physically taking the TV out of my hotel room (which sometimes made for some very interesting discussions the next day).

The following testimony is from Toby:

My earliest recollection of pornography is when I was riding my bike through the town center one Sunday and a pile of magazines under a truck caught my eye. My heart leapt as I discovered them to be pornographic magazines. Although damp, I took them all home and hid them in my wardrobe. I continued to search for other magazines and resorted to buying pictures at school. Now hooked, I continued my fascination, but once in my teens I found TV often provided opportunity to indulge. I would search out the films likely to have some pornographic content. Later I started to attend "X" rated movies at the cinema, although I was under age, I could still get in. The video age assisted this addiction and this developed into watching hard-core movies at home. All this time, although secret about my addiction, I never saw it for what it was.

However, when I was 25, I had an encounter with God, leaving me "born again" and certainly aware of the dangers I was involved in. I cleared out all my sins, literally burning and destroying anything that God showed me. I also married my wife and life seemed to have changed for the better. Although I never told her of my addiction, she had been aware of my "movies". But these were now gone.

For many years, I lived free on the outside, but always within me was a desire of those things. One day, while in a hotel, a movie came on which I should have turned off. I didn't. I just sat and watched it absolutely transfixed. Although I vowed never again to do it, of course I did. I became increasingly hooked and my life in God became increasingly difficult to live.

On the outside, I was a pillar of the church, being the Youth Pastor, a person many came to see for advice. I seemed able to handle all this until one day a man came to see me about pornography. I just couldn't help him, I couldn't even tell him why. He eventually left the Church and has since moved in with another man. I believe I could have helped him had I not been addicted myself.

Now let us review what had transpired up to this point. I was learning to quench myself in Jesus, so I was running to the Bible every time I felt the burning of lust rise within me. I was dragging my sin into the light, and exposing my deeds done in darkness by talking about it with my wife and my pastor. I was asking God to please reconcile me, help me stop the evil deeds that made me an enemy of God in my mind, and now I was beginning to throw off the sin that was entangling me so that I could get back in the race. See all the principles of truth that were being employed? Guess what? Since that meeting with my pastor in January of 1999 where he explained the necessity to throw off anything that hinders and entangles, I have not fallen to pornography one time. My decade long horrible bondage to this terribly destructive sin was over.

Do you see the importance of applying this principle to your own life? As we have been working with people in this *Pure Freedom* course we have discovered that those who apply this teaching to their lives begin to walk in victory over sin. We have also noticed, unfortunately, that those who will not rid their lives of that which is causing them to stumble, just never seem to get free. They confess to falling, get back up and tell us they are sorry and won't be doing that again. We instruct them that they need to remove that which caused them to fall. They make excuses and say that they have learned their lesson, and because temptations are down right after a fall they think that they "have a handle on" it now. We know that it is just a matter of time before they fall again, and sure enough usually within 2 weeks down they go. This will continue unless and until they throw off that which causes them to stumble.

Questions

Question 4. Now, please list any area where you currently still have provision for your flesh to be gratified:

Friend, if you listed any areas above, that is where your next fall to pornography will be. It is just a matter of time. You can be drinking the living water, exposing your sin and asking for help, praying to be reconciled to God, but in a weak moment you WILL fall because there is provision made to fulfill your lusts. So, it is imperative that right now you eradicate that from your life. It has to go. If you keep it around you are trying to run a race with a huge burden on your back, and every time you fall in that area you add weight to the burden. Eventually you will not be able to run the race but will be fallen down, and off to the side of the road in the thorns and weeds.

Question 5. Are you willing to part with that which will make you fall? Will you get rid of it right now?

Testimony

Rather than sober to the seriousness of my plight, I sunk further into watching films. I would sit up late flicking channels to find something on which to feast. My addiction became stronger, and my secrecy more intense.

With the advent of the Internet I delved into pornographic web sites, then chat sites. This was all leading me away from God to the extent I thought of leaving my family, friends and Church to go and live this life elsewhere.

Then one day, I clicked onto a site that advertised "Addicted to Pornography?" I followed the link to "SettingCaptivesFree.com" and enrolled under a false name. I held out little hope, but I knew I was in trouble and would try anything. What I found was the **Pure Freedom** course that addressed my problems, and was filled with testimonies of people just like me, who were now free. I found myself accountable to someone. Although I didn't know this person, I had to give a daily account. The funny thing was that although I became free, I had also become very secret about this course.

Eventually, with God's help, I confessed all this to my wife. She was shocked and confused, but the change in me was apparent and she became very supportive. I have since told my best friend, who likewise has been supportive.

This accountability, and openness to my past addiction, has allowed me to live free. I have been surprised at the acceptance I have received in spite of my shameful behavior. Further, my life has taken on new depths in God, and He is bringing to me people who are addicted to this same sin.

I can only encourage anyone reading this testimony to try this course. Don't worry about all the fears ahead, take a day at a time. God will help you, as he helped me. It's worth it.

Right about now is when we start getting objections. They usually go something like this: "But it is not the Internet that is the problem, it is my heart. Jesus says that out of the heart come the things that defile us, so I don't want to just deal with the symptom, which is viewing pornography, I need to get my relationship right with Jesus so I can be strong enough to say No to pornography no matter where I might be tempted with it."

This is true! We have no quarrel with the above statements. However, what we are talking about in this lesson is the manner in which we get our hearts right with God so that we can say no to pornography when we are tempted by it. And there is only one Scriptural way to do this—the total removal of anything that causes us to stumble. We will talk more about this subject within the next week, but for right now just know that it is a principle of truth that in order to run this race we must remove anything that entangles us. Our hearts will continue to be defiled if we continue to intoxicate ourselves at the devil's bar of pornography and masturbation, and the way to

Questions

be free is to, initially, remove the temptation.

In the beginning, I wanted to be able to look temptation in the face and say "no." I thought that I would know myself to be a strong Christian when I could have the temptation and be able to stand up against it. In reality, I wanted to be strong rather than pure. This is not the way to victory over sin.

Notice this next passage:

> "If your right eye causes you to sin, gouge it out and throw it away. It is better for you to lose one part of your body than for your whole body to be thrown into hell. And if your right hand causes you to sin, cut it off and throw it away. It is better for you to lose one part of your body than for your whole body to go into hell" (Matthew 5:29-30).

Friend, the above verses could be summarized by the words "radical amputation." Now Jesus was not referring to a physical cutting off of our hands or an actual plucking out of the eyeball. Handicapped and blind men still lust. What He was saying was to deal radically with whatever causes us to sin: cut it off, pluck it out, hack it off. Some have stated a desire to be "reasonable" and "balanced" in the approach to overcoming sin. We agree. It is only reasonable to destroy those things in our lives that seek to destroy us. Radically amputating the TV from my hotel room was the most reasonable way to fight this sin. Jesus' method of dealing with sin is radical amputation.

Question 6. Will you, right now, cut off and pluck out anything that is causing you to stumble?

And if the problem is the Internet there are probably three options, if not more to handle this:

1. Get rid of the Internet entirely.
2. Install http://www.afafilter.com/default.htm?27249. This filter prevents all access to pornographic sites and they have unblocked the **Pure Freedom** website. And finally, you can use Integrity Online as your Internet provider. They, too, have unblocked the **Pure Freedom** website and you can find them at http://www.integrityonline.com.

    In the upcoming days you will also learn about a program called "Convenant Eyes" which is like a "computer accountability partner." It will monitor your every keystroke, every URL you visit, and every image you view, and then send an email report to whoever you choose.
3. Only use the Internet while your spouse, friend or another person can be around to monitor the activity.

Dear friends, run the race to win! Remove that which hinders you, and anything that entangles you. It's worth it to be running light! I am no longer encumbered with the heavy and growing burden of habitual sin. I can actually run the race marked out for me and know that I am running to win, because God has enabled me to throw off the sin that so easily besets me.

Please, take this teaching of Scripture seriously. We have seen some students who delay in removing that which trips them up, and some who only remove it part way, and in every instance of a half-done job there is a fall that is soon to come. Don't hesitate to be radical in dealing with this. After all, God was radical in dealing with sin. He gave His one and only Son to suffer and die on the cross. That's radical! Be willing to part with that which you have loved in the past. Be willing to sacrifice it to be free from it.

Question 7. How are things going for you today?

Scripture to Consider

"I made a covenant with my eyes not to look lustfully at a girl" (Job 31:1).

"Therefore, if anyone is in Christ, he is a new creation; the old has gone, the new has come!" (2 Corinthians 5:17).

"For what I received I passed on to you as of first importance: that Christ died for our sins according to the Scriptures, that he was buried, that he was raised on the third day according to the Scriptures" (1 Corinthians 15:3-4).

"The thief comes only to steal and kill and destroy; I have come that they may have life, and have it to the full" (John 10:10).

Were you free from pornography since you did the last lesson?

    Yes No

Were you free from masturbation since you did the last lesson?

    Yes No

Were you free from sexual immorality since you did the last lesson?

    Yes No

DAY 6—TURNING

Today we are going to discuss the subject of repentance, and see from Scripture exactly what repentance is.

> "⁴ For we know, brothers loved by God, that he has chosen you, ⁵ because our gospel came to you not simply with words, but also with power, with the Holy Spirit and with deep conviction. You know how we lived among you for your sake. ⁶ You became imitators of us and of the Lord; in spite of severe suffering, you welcomed the message with the joy given by the Holy Spirit. ⁷ And so you became a model to all the believers in Macedonia and Achaia. ⁸ The Lord's message rang out from you not only in Macedonia and Achaia—your faith in God has become known everywhere. Therefore we do not need to say anything about it, ⁹ for they themselves report what kind of reception you gave us. They tell how you turned to God from idols to serve the living and true God, ¹⁰ and to wait for his Son from heaven, whom he raised from the dead—Jesus, who rescues us from the coming wrath" (1 Thessalonians 1:4-10).

Please answer the following questions as we think through this most important issue of repentance together.

Questions

Question 1. According to verse 5, in what manner did the gospel come to the Thessalonians?

Question 2. According to verses 8 and 9, what things were being reported about these Thessalonian believers?

Friend, here is true repentance summarized: "They tell how you turned to God from idols to serve the living and true God" (v. 9).

Repentance has often been described as "doing a 180" meaning we turn away from sin and turn to God. This is the very reason that psychology and humanistic programs fall short of truly assisting people who are trapped in sin. They attempt to get the person to turn away from sin, but cannot instruct them to turn to God, so they are in essence instructing us to do a 90-degree turn. This half-turning is never sufficient to truly eradicate sin from our lives. True repentance is not only turning *from sin,* it is turning *to God* and serving Him.

Question 3. Write the words from verse 9 that define true repentance:

I was involved in pornography for many years, and I went through many periods of repentance followed by sin, followed by repentance again. But when God granted me genuine repentance I turned away completely and have not ever returned. I'm not saying that my repentance before wasn't genuine, but at the very least I did not learn how to walk away from the sin that I turned away from.

> "For, He that would love life, and see good days, let him refrain his tongue from evil, and his lips that they speak no guile: And let him turn away from evil, and do good; Let him seek peace, and pursue it" (1 Peter 3:10-11ᴷᴶⱽ).

Question 4. How does the above verse define repentance? What are the "negative" aspects of true repentance, and what are the "positive?"

We can see from Scripture that genuine repentance is a complete turnaround from our previous course. For me, that meant totally turning away from the sins of pornography and masturbation, and turning to God. The turn must be complete! We must put our backs to the sin and walk away from it, never to return again. And we must face Christ and walk towards Him. No half-hearted turning will free us from the power of sin; no partial turning will enable us to escape the trap of the devil in pornography and masturbation.

Oh, the pain in my heart during those long years where I would sin and confess, sin and confess, while not truly turning away from the sin. I was like Lot's wife, who did indeed leave the burning city, but longed for it in her heart and turned back just to have a look. Her turning away from the sin of that city was not complete, and she perished in her sin, turning to a pillar of salt. We should **remember Lot's wife**, for she is a monument to all who will not fully turn away from sin. God has now granted me the repentance that makes me hate my previous way of life and therefore turn completely away from it.

This is my hope and prayer for you, too. That God would enable you to truly turn away from sin for good, and to begin to walk away from it as fast as you can, and to get as far away from it as possible.

Now, here is another excellent passage that describes the attitude of genuine repentance:

> "Come near to God and he will come near to you. Wash your hands, you sinners, and purify your hearts, you double-minded. Grieve, mourn and wail. Change your laughter to mourning and your joy to gloom. Humble yourselves before the Lord, and he will lift you up" (James 4:7-10^{KJV}).

Here is how we can tell when God is granting somebody repentance. They not only make a 180-degree turn around, but they also lose their silliness, their hollow laughter, their joking, and their pride. They become earnest in being rid of their sin. They feel sorrow over their sins and even become somewhat gloomy, as the above verses mention. This does not mean that they live like this the rest of their lives, because joy comes into the life that is committed to purity. But there is a time where all the levity is gone, and there comes a need to be done with sin for good.

I remember as I first came out of pornography I was a very gloomy and mournful man, because God had made me earnest in repenting. I listened carefully to what others who were walking in purity told me, and I begged God for real repentance. In January of 1999, I made a full turn away from pornography, and began running as fast as I could away from it. My heart ached because of the offenses I had committed against God and others, and I was very sad. As I write this, that was nearly 2 years ago, but I can remember the sorrow that I felt and the gloom that I experienced, and recall it as good and healthy for the soul.

Question 5. Please read the following quote and give your comments below:

"Conviction of sin is one of the rarest things that ever strikes a man. It is the threshold of an understanding of God. Jesus Christ said that when the Holy Spirit came He would convict of sin, and when the Holy Spirit rouses a man's conscience and brings him into the presence of God, it is not his relationship with men that bothers him, but his relationship with God—'against Thee, Thee only, have I sinned, and done this evil in Thy sight'. Conviction of sin, the marvel of forgiveness, and holiness are so interwoven that it is only the forgiven man who is the holy man, he proves he is forgiven by being the opposite to what

The following testimony is from Daryl:

I thank the Lord Jesus Christ for His perfect, pure, and holy sacrifice that has redeemed me from my life of sin and destruction. All the glory and honor goes to the one, true, holy, righteous, omnipresent, omnipotent Lord of all of the universe and creator of ALL things. Amen.

My sins against the Lord growing up were many, and affected many different areas of my life. But for the purposes of this ministry, I will only explain how the Lord pulled me out of the pit of pornography and masturbation that I may have a new life in the name of my Lord Jesus Christ.

I started masturbating at an early age (around 9). It seemed like harmless experimentation at the time but as I became older it led to more and greater sins in this area of my life. This spirit of lust that had a hold of me led to strip bars, pornography sites on the Internet and prostitution as well.

In biblical terms, I was an adulterer and fornicator at least 4 times a week for 29 years. This became a major part of my life and because of my desires to fulfill my lust it corrupted my heart and mind as well. This was my "secret" sin as well, in that none of my friends or family knew about this.

I heard a preacher on the AM Radio early one morning 4 years ago while driving home from work. To put things simply he told it how it was. When he spoke of the judgment of God it sent shock waves into my life. I would imagine it was initially because of the scary thought of experiencing hell for the rest of my life. I listened to him that night, and then I listened again the next, and then the next. One thing he always said was "look, don't take my word for it. Go out and get yourself a King James Bible and read it for yourself". Now, I have to say that I was brought up with many false Christian religious beliefs, and I was not a Christian by any sense, but if someone would have asked me if I was I would have told them yes, certainly.

As I read the Bible, the Holy Spirit spoke to me Scripture by Scripture. I repented of my wickedness before the Lord and asked him to lead and guide my life because I KNEW that I had made a rotten mess of it. As each day went on I learned something new. Point by point, my life was starting to be addressed. At first it was the false religion that I was born, raised and baptized into, then it was the language I was using, then as I stopped using it, it was the language that my football buddies were using (football was MY god on Sunday). Each word was like a dagger in my heart, and at this point I knew that something was happening in my life. Then it was the drunkenness that was addressed, then this and then that. But there was one thing that I was never able to overcome like I did the others, and that was pornography and masturbation.

As I grew in the Lord, I started to be filled with words of salvation to give to coworkers. I started handing out tracts and I was led by the Lord to a Bible believing church. But there continued to be one problem in my life and that was this lust that would overcome me. If you have ever been in the situation where you were professing godliness but falling continually to pornography and masturbation you will certainly know the sheer torment that I was under in my mind and my heart. This torment showed me the clear picture of Satan and who he really is and what I was really up against. Through my OWN WILL, I decided to attack this and I just didn't want to do this sin anymore! I would have success for 1, 2, 3, sometimes 14 days in a row. The problem is that when the floodwaters started rising, I would find myself falling to this dragon and feeling tormented, guilty, miserable, and even completely lost at times. I would hear, "Ha, you really did it this time! There's no saving you now." This continued for about 3 3/4 years since my conversion, it is only through the grace of God that I found relief from this hellish torment.

One day in August 2000, a Christian friend sent me an e-card from www.Crossdaily.com. At the top of the card was this flashing ban-

Testimony

ner that spoke of freedom from porno-graphy. I immediately went into the site, while ensuring that my co-workers weren't seeing what I was doing. You see, once again this was my "secret sin". The more I read about the program the more I liked it. I certainly knew that this was a sin in my life that encompassed my heart and was going to lead me to death and destruction. So I signed up for the course at home that night (August 24th, 2000).

I remember the first day of the ministry as if it was yesterday. I had heard of the story of the Lord meeting up with the Samaritan women at the well, but not until this day did I understand the significance of it. This truth from day one (Pornography does not truly satisfy) set the groundwork for the rest of my life. The more I read, the more I understood. I started applying the principals of freedom through Jesus Christ into my life.

Remember; before I started this course I was wrestling this demon myself and I was trying to will it away with no success. It is only through the grace, mercy and longsuffering of the Lord God that I am where I am today. As I went through these lessons I learned more about the grace of God, the forgiveness of God, the longsuffering of God, the desire of the Lord for us to be free from the bondage of this world. There are so many important truths that were brought forth in this ministry to have complete freedom from pornography and masturbation THROUGH OUR LORD JESUS CHRIST. So as each truth was brought forth I applied it to my life. Then I had truth upon truth upon truth, etc.

It is through the grace of God that I have been led to the understanding of the importance of abiding in the Lord always. I can tell you as fact that as I abide in the Lord there is peace and joy, but as I take my focus off of the throne of grace and put it on myself, the floodwaters begin to rise. There is no middle ground that I once thought there was. As is clearly stated in the Bible "you are either for me, or against me". So knowing this, the choice was mine. Do I continue in sin so that grace may abound? GOD FORBID! To me, the choice is obvious. For years I have suffered much mental, physical, and spiritual anguish under the harsh slavery of Satan. Now, what I have in front of me is no longer a curse but a blessing. No longer is it torment, it is now peace. It is no longer death, it is now life. So here I am, a son of God who has been saved by the grace of God and called to be holy and blameless before the Lord. Do I accomplish this on my own power? God forbid! I have tried to do this in the past and have failed miserably and so will anyone else who tries to take this on themselves without divine intervention. This is a simple truth. It is only through the power of God that we will be able to walk through the fire without burning. Thank you, Father, for giving us your Son so that we may live eternally giving you all praise, honor, glory and thanksgiving. You alone are worthy of all praise, all of the time. Amen.

Questions

he was, by Gods grace. Repentance always brings a man to this point: I have sinned. The surest sign that God is at work is when a man says that and means it. Anything less than this is remorse for having made blunders, the reflex action of disgust at himself.

"The entrance into the Kingdom is through the panging pains of repentance crashing into a man's respectable goodness; then the Holy Ghost, Who produces these agonies, begins the formation of the Son of God in the life. The new life will manifest itself in conscious repentance and unconscious holiness, never the other way about. The bedrock of Christianity is repentance. Strictly speaking, a man cannot repent when he chooses; repentance is a gift of God. The old Puritans used to pray for the gift of tears. If ever you cease to know the virtue of repentance, you are in darkness. Examine yourself and see if you have forgotten how to be sorry" (Oswald Chambers, My Utmost For His Highest, December 7th Devotional).[4]

Comments:

Questions

Did you catch that "repentance is a gift from God?" This comes from 2 Timothy 2: 25: *"Those who oppose him (the servant of God) he must gently instruct, in the hope that God will grant them repentance leading them to a knowledge of the truth, and that they will come to their senses and escape from the trap of the devil, who has taken them captive to do his will."* Notice that repentance is the only way to escape from the devil's trap.

Question 6. Are you escaping the trap? If so, can you see how God has granted you repentance? Explain a little about this repentance. Do you have it? If so, are you enjoying it? If not, will you seek God for it?

Course Member Tim writes: "Yes, I am escaping the trap of Satan with God's help and this course. God for sure has granted me repentance and I know that this is a precious gift of God. After realizing that God was watching me through the eyes of Jesus and seeing all the filth I put in front of His eyes and to do the things he saw me do in masturbation. Yes, I know that God has forgiven me and granted me the gift of repentance."

Next, let us examine one final passage of Scripture and note the elements of repentance contained in it:

> ⁶ Seek the LORD while he may be found; call on him while he is near. ⁷ Let the wicked forsake his way and the evil man his thoughts. Let him turn to the LORD, and he will have mercy on him, and to our God, for he will freely pardon" (Isaiah 55:7).

Question 7. Please list the 4 defining elements of repentance as stated in Isaiah 55:7 above. The first one is "Seek the Lord"

1:_____

2:_____

3:_____

4:_____

Question 8. Please make an honest assessment of your life right now. Are you seeking the Lord, calling on Him, forsaking your sin, and turning to the Lord?

Dear friend, there is much good news to be found in repentance. It is not as if we were merely turning away from sin only to be left empty and with no excitement in life. You see, as you turn from pornography and turn to God there is a blessed life of satisfaction and joy to be found in Jesus Christ. In reality, we are leaving the lesser and temporary pleasures for the greater and eternal ones. Yes, we are giving up the pleasures of sin, but we are gaining the pleasures of Christ, and Psalm 16:11 describes the pleasures of Christ as "eternal."

Course Member Jack writes: "My sorrow was in that I was offending God and was not getting close to Him at all. When I confessed in this area, I fell with a broken heart to my knees wanting to be delivered and desiring a closer relationship with God. Repentance is a by-product of God's grace. He is the one who breaks hearts. I believe a broken heart before God over any sin, and a turning from it, is repentance."

Scripture to Consider

"Or do you show contempt for the riches of his kindness, tolerance and patience, not realizing that God's kindness leads you toward repentance?" (Romans 2:4).

"Come now, let us reason together," says the LORD. "Though your sins are like scarlet, they shall be as white as snow; though they are red as crimson, they shall be like wool" (Isaiah 1:18).

Were you free from pornography since you did the last lesson?

    Yes No

Were you free from masturbation since you did the last lesson?

    Yes No

Were you free from sexual immorality since you did the last lesson?

    Yes No

DAY 7—NEW DIRECTION

⁸ "Even if I caused you sorrow by my letter, I do not regret it. Though I did regret it I see that my letter hurt you, but only for a little while ⁹ yet now I am happy, not because you were made sorry, but because your sorrow led you to repentance. For you became sorrowful as God intended and so were not harmed in any way by us. ¹⁰ Godly sorrow brings repentance that leads to salvation and leaves no regret, but worldly sorrow brings death. ¹¹ See what this godly sorrow has produced in you: what earnestness, what eagerness to clear yourselves, what indignation, what alarm, what longing, what concern, what readiness to see justice done. At every point you have proved yourselves to be innocent in this matter. ¹² So even though I wrote to you, it was not on account of the one who did the wrong or of the injured party, but rather that before God you could see for yourselves how devoted to us you are. ¹³ By all this we are encouraged" (2 Corinthians 7:8-13).

Questions

Question 1. From verse 11, write out the seven ways that godly sorrow showed itself in the life of the Corinthians.

1.

2.

3.

4.

5.

6.

7.

Question 2. Go through this portion of Scripture and count the number of times Paul uses the words "sorry," "sorrow" or "sorrowful." How many times?

Question 3. According to verses 9 and 10, what does godly sorrow over sin bring about?

Note this well: True sorrowing over sin brings about real repentance. So, this being true, we need to pray for sorrow in our hearts that it might lead us to repentance.

The first time my sins had been exposed to my pastor, and I was driving away from his office, I began weeping and sobbing uncontrollably. My heart was breaking at the shame I had cast on the name of Christ. I was also hurting about what I had made of my life, and all the pain I had caused others. My sorrow was so great that I felt the need to pull the car over and park so I could sit and weep over my sin. This sorrow began working within me a resolve to never return to pornography again, and to this day I have not. Godly sorrow brings about repentance, and so this sorrow is our friend. Pray for it and seek after it.

Testimony

The following testimony is from Gill:

I have been involved in masturbation as far back as I can remember and sometimes it reached over to pornography. Usually, I was in college and seminary and didn't have cable in the house, but when I would head home for the holidays or weekends I would watch late night cable television, and this would fuel my addiction. I always knew that masturbation was a sin, but I just couldn't seem to give it up.

Then, in 1999 I moved overseas to teach English and it was the first time that pornography became readily available in my life. For some amazing reason I had never been tempted with internet...I had never chatted and I can count on one hand the numbers of time I visited a website the four years previous to 1999. Being in a new culture and not having any friends or a place to worship, I slowly deteriorated.

For many years I would go through times in my life where I would wonder when I would test God's grace enough and he would let me be swallowed up in my sin. I truly did love Him, but it seemed like I loved the sin more because I kept clinging to it.

While overseas I found places where I could rent movies cheap. First it started out with little skin shown, but grew and grew and when I had to come home for an emergency I found some porn at a friend's house (which I had previously used and became more and more involved in it). Then at the same time one night I was on the Internet site and started looking at pornography, and for two months I hit a deep depression and just stayed in M and P constantly. One night I was chatting on the Internet and I could tell that the lady I was chatting with was trying to turn the conversation. I didn't do it, but just the fact I almost did scared me, and I knew if I didn't do something quick I would slowly slip away past the point of no return. I was fixing to go back overseas and I knew that it would get worse and worse and eventually lead to acting out with others. I cried out (I had cried out before but nothing ever really happened and I would give up), but this time I decided I would cry out until God saved me or I had passed the point of no return.

I didn't know if God would show up, but I was going to go down fighting. Well...He did show up mainly through this **Pure Freedom** course. Since starting the course I got

Continued on page 22

Questions

Question 4. What does worldly sorrow bring about?

Question 5. Godly sorrow is the mourning one goes through when he has grieved the Holy Spirit of God with sin. When you are only sorry about your sin because you got caught or because of its consequences, what kind of sorrow would you call it?

Question 6. According to verse 10, what is the ultimate end of only having this kind of sorrow?

Note: We can see from this study on repentance that godly sorrow leads to and is a part of repentance that leads to life, whereas worldly sorrow leads to death.

Question 7. Honestly assess your heart right now. Ask the Holy Spirit to illuminate your understanding to know whether you have been granted godly sorrow and genuine repentance unto life, or if you only have worldly sorrow. What are your thoughts?

Now we have seen that part of repentance is experiencing a godly sorrow over sins committed against God. How do the following verses define repentance?

> ¹⁴ And it will be said: "Build up, build up, prepare the road! Remove the obstacles out of the way of my people." ¹⁵For this is what the high and lofty One says—he who lives forever, whose name is holy: "I live in a high and holy place, but also with him who is contrite and lowly in spirit, to revive the spirit of the lowly and to revive the heart of the contrite" (Isaiah 57: 14-15).

Your thoughts:

Friends, the habitual viewing of pornography hardened my heart and puffed me up with pride. Sin, pride and hardness of heart always go together (Hebrews 3:13). Genuine repentance brings with it lowliness and contriteness. I remember when I first came out of pornography, though I was a theology major and had been to years of Bible school and seminary, I kept quiet and asked my pastor for help. I asked him questions, asked for his input, asked for accountability. I realized all my head knowledge was worthless.

We can recognize this humility in people as they begin to ask questions, and ask for help, instead of presenting all their biblical knowledge and their viewpoints on everything. They become humble and teachable, lowly and contrite.

This repentance is the key to lasting victory over sin. Anything short of true repentance will leave one wanting to return to the sin. This is why real repentance is a must, and only God can grant repentance. So, please seek the Lord and ask Him for the gift of repentance, and then repent with horror and disgust at past sins.

Course member Maggie writes: "My sorrow was in that I was offending God and was not getting close to Him at all. When I confessed in this area, I fell with a broken heart to my knees wanting to be delivered and desiring a closer relationship with God. Repentance is a by-product of God's grace. He is the one who breaks hearts. I believe a broken heart before God over any sin is equivalent to repentance."

Testimony

Gill's testimony continues ...

free from pornography. Over the last 74 days I have only had 9 days that have involved masturbation and 3 days that involved pornography. I'm not happy with this because I want complete freedom, but this is truly a work of God because before this I never went more than 2 or 3 days without pornography since I was about 14 (I'm now 31).

In conclusion, I know it is only through the grace of God that I am saved. I know that if I ever quit seeking Him I would be back there. Today, I feel like I am completely free of pornography, I've radically amputated my life from it, I can pass the movie store without the desire to go in, etc. etc. In masturbation I feel like I'm going towards freedom, but maybe not quite there...that urge still hits a couple of times a week, but I've learned I don't have to satisfy it and I don't really "white knuckle" like I did for the first several days of this course. The temptation is still stronger, but God gives me the grace each night to deal with the temptation and to pass on it and the daydreaming that led to that sin has stopped. How? I don't know. Because I tried for many years to stop and I gave it over to God on more than one occasion, but I think this is the first time I truly have taken the offensive against this sin. I may or may not have another relapse with masturbation, if I do I know I'm forgiven, but I also know now that I have the power of Christ in me and I'm growing more and more in love with him each and every day and as his grace increases in my life this sin slowly fades away. I will close with a short chorus that has become my prayer not only in this fight, but also for my whole life.

Jesus, draw me close
Closer Lord to you
Let the world around me fade away

Jesus, draw me close to you
Closer Lord to you
For I desire to worship and obey.

Questions

Friends, the teaching of both yesterday and today define what true repentance is. It is a turning completely away from sin, doing an about face, and then pursuing God with a reckless abandon. And it is also sorrowing over sin to such an extent that the heart begins to hate the sin and turns from it in disgust. This is repentance, and if either of these elements are missing the "freedom" from sin will not be lasting. If one merely feels sorrow over the sin but does not turn from it then he is not free. Or if one merely turns from the sin but does not develop a heart-sorrow over it he is not free either. Both must be there.

Question 8. Are both of these qualities of repentance becoming evident in your life? Are you turning away from sin toward God, and are you sorrowing in your heart over sin?

Next, notice how repentance works itself out in worship. These next few verses show what true worship looks like, and admonishes us to conform:

> "Guard your steps when you go to the house of God. Go near to listen, rather than to offer the sacrifice of fools, who do not know that they do wrong. Do not be quick with your mouth; do not be hasty in your heart to utter anything before God. God is in heaven, and you are on earth, so let your words be few. Much dreaming, and many words are meaningless. Therefore stand in awe of God!" (Ecclesiastes 1-2,7)

This passage of Scripture shows that worship of God from a repentant soul brings quietness and an awe of God. I think back on my years in pornography and they were loud years, with much talking and teaching and making myself out to be somebody. All my many words were evidence that I was not in awe of God, but was instead taken with myself. But when God brought me low, and caused my heart to fear Him, I immediately shut up, and began being in awe of God. He was in heaven and I was on earth. I finally saw Him for Who He was, and myself for the loud-mouthed, irreverent man I was.

Now I don't believe Scripture here is saying that just because we are in awe of God that we cannot talk. Some people are naturally more talkative than others, and may not be sinning in doing so. But what these verses are referring to is the loud and obnoxious man who feels that what he has to say is so important, and who does not reverence the Lord.

True repentance evidences itself in the worship of God. It shows us the Majestic Deity of God, and His holiness and power, grace and love, and His awesome character. We begin to develop awe for Him and we listen more than talk.

Question 9. What is your life currently like in relationship to this truth? Are you discovering awe of God and becoming quiet before Him?

Finally, please notice the definition of repentance from this verse: "Therefore say to the house of Israel, 'This is what the Sovereign Lord says: Repent! Turn from your idols and renounce all your detestable practices" (Ezekiel 14:6). This can apply to those of us who have been involved with pornography and masturbation. Pornography has become an "idol" and we are to turn away from it, and masturbation has become a "detestable practice" and we are to renounce it.

Scripture to Consider

"If at any time I announce that a nation or kingdom is to be uprooted, torn down and destroyed, and if that nation I warned repents of its evil, then I will relent and not inflict on it the disaster I had planned" (Jeremiah 18:7-8).

"I tell you that in the same way there will be more rejoicing in heaven over one sinner who repents than over ninety-nine righteous persons who do not need to repent" (Luke 15:7).

"[46] "When they sin against you—for there is no one who does not sin—and you become angry with them and give them over to the enemy, who takes them captive to his own land, far away or near; [47] and if they have a change of heart in the land where they are held captive, and repent and plead with you in the land of their conquerors and say, 'We have sinned, we have done wrong, we have acted wickedly'; [48] and if they turn back to you with all their heart and soul in the land of their enemies who took them captive, and pray to you toward the land you gave their fathers, toward the city you have chosen and the temple I have built for your Name; [49] then from heaven, your dwelling place, hear their prayer and their plea, and uphold their cause. [50] And forgive your people, who have sinned against you; forgive all the offenses they have committed against you, and cause their conquerors to show them mercy; [51] for they are your people and your inheritance, whom you brought out of Egypt, out of that iron-smelting furnace" (1 Kings 8:46-51).

Were you free from pornography since you did the last lesson?
    Yes No

Were you free from masturbation since you did the last lesson?
    Yes No

Were you free from sexual immorality since you did the last lesson?
    Yes No

DAY 8—ACCOUNTABILITY

There is an aspect to overcoming pornography, or any sin really, that is extremely important: One alone may be overcome; two can be victorious.

Read and observe the following passage from Ecclesiastes 4:

> Vs. 9—Two are better than one, because they have a good return for their work: Vs.10—If one falls down, his friend can help him up. But pity the man who falls and has no one to help him up! Vs.11—Also, if two lie down together, they will keep warm. But how can one keep warm alone? Vs. 12—Though one may be overpowered, two can defend themselves. A cord of three strands is not quickly broken (Ecclesiastes 4:9-12).

Today, we will see the value and necessity of finding and maintaining an accountability partner.

Questions

Question 1. According to verse 9, why are two better than one?

A study was done with horses to determine the true value of team effort. The study revealed that one horse pulling alone was able to pull 2,500 pounds. The test was then repeated with two horses pulling together; the two horses were able to pull 12,500 pounds! The two horses together were able to pull 5 times the amount of weight that the one horse alone could pull!

Ecclesiastes 4:9 is about spiritual fruit. Teamwork is critical in overcoming pornography and sexual sin. As I have told you, I was in bondage to pornography for 15 years, the last 10 of which were as a Christian. I kept my sins a secret because I was too proud to tell anyone else. But God brought me very low and then began teaching me the necessity of having an accountability partner. My wife and my pastor became my accountability partners. I've been totally free from all forms of pornography for three years now (as of January 2002). Two are better than one. My freedom and victory are intimately related to the accountability that has come into my life.

"Two are better than one, and more happy jointly than either of them could be separately, more pleased in one another than they could be in themselves only, mutually serviceable to each other's welfare, and by a united strength more likely to do good to others." (Matthew Henry)[5]

Have you ever read Pilgrim's Progress? It is a wonderful allegory of the Christian life. In the 9th scene a man by the name of "Hope" finds himself desiring to take a nap in the land of Enchantment. But Christian reminds him of 1 Thessalonians 5:6 that says, "let us not sleep, as do others; but let us watch and be sober." Hope, being reminded of the truth of Scripture, becomes very thankful for Christian. He says these words: "I acknowledge that I was wrong; and if I would have been here alone, by myself sleeping I would have been in danger of death. I see it is true what that wise man said, 'Two are better than one.' Therefore you being here has been a mercy to me; and you will have a good reward for your labor."

My friend, an accountability partner should, by love of the Scriptures and care for your soul, be able to detect when you are about to "sleep" in the "land of enchantment," which, in our case, is pornography. "Hope" is restored when another "Christian" helps to wake us up. That accountability partner is indispensable.

Read Ecclesiastes 4:10 *"If one falls down, his friend can help him up. But pity the man who falls and has no one to help him up!"* (Ecclesiastes 4:10)

Testimony

The following testimony is from Lucas:

Like the drunk in the AA meeting, I only had a little problem with porn, not like the rest of the world. There is no such thing as a little problem with porn!

Maybe I didn't buy as many tapes or books as others, didn't go to strip bars, etc. It doesn't matter. There is no such thing as a little problem. Like gangrene, there is no little problem. The poison soon kills you while destroying your entire body, unless you cut it off!

Thanks to Christ working through this course I have been able to cut it off. The poison is out of my body and I am clean. Oh, that doesn't mean that my flesh has so soon forgotten the poison it relished. R rated movies (which would have been X-rated only a few years ago) are still capable of waking the monster within—thus the need for continued vigilance.

So I prescribe these words to anyone (mostly myself) in dealing with porn:

Cut it off, run away, feed on the Word daily, attack the enemy using God's weapons and Never give up, Never give up, Never, Never, Never give up (Winston Churchill).

Questions

Question 2. Can you recall a time when you've "fallen" into pornography and then had no strength to "get up?" What were the results? What happened? What did you do?

Read Galations 6:1: "Brothers, if someone is caught in a sin, you who are spiritual should restore him gently. But watch yourself, or you also may be tempted."

Question 3. We all need an accountability partner. From Galatians 6:1 above, what qualifications does your future partner need to possess in order to help you?

Question 4. Have you ever had anyone to come along side and "help you pull more?" Someone to "help you up" when you fell into pornography or sexual impurity?

Read Hebrews 3:13: "But encourage one another, as long as it is called Today, so that none of you may be hardened by sin's deceitfulness."

Question 5. Notice how "daily encouragement" is an antidote to sin. According to this verse, how often should you and your accountability partner communicate?

If we are serious about overcoming we must utilize an accountability partner. Here's how:

Church is important. If you are involved in church speak with your pastor or another elder. Simply ask his help in overcoming pornography, and ask if he can be an accountability partner with you.

Your spouse, if you are married, should eventually become your number one accountability partner. Have you shared your struggles with him or her and asked for their help? If not, possibly this may be the time to do so.

Finally, if you are doing this course within a group, the men in the group can be your accountability partners at your request.

Here are some guidelines to follow when you initiate accountability with your partner:

1. You agree to openness and honesty. Bondage to pornography brings deception with it; some of us have been deceptive for years. If we want to lose the slavery to sin it starts with honesty, even if it is humbling. If your accountability partner asks how you are doing, and you have just fallen into masturbation or pornography, you must honestly admit this.
2. You agree to prepare and share with your accountability partner your "break the chain" plan as described on Day 9. Expect your accountability partner to help you by making suggestions to your plan and holding you accountable to it.
3. You agree to give your partner freedom to ask the hard questions, without taking offense. For instance, "have you seen any pornography today?"
4. You agree to initiate communication daily for the first 30 days, as far as is possible.

"It is good for two to travel together, for if one happens to fall, he may be lost for want of a little help. If a man falls into sin, his friend will help to restore him with the spirit of meekness; if he falls into trouble, his friend will help to comfort him and assuage his grief" (Matthew Henry).[6]

Course Member Jesse writes: "Have you had anyone to help you up? Since I had hidden it so well (even from myself to a point) no, I did not have someone to pull me up until recently. Oh, I would pick my head up from the muck every once in a while by myself - usually after a good sermon - or some devotional reading struck too close to home, but I never stayed above water too long. That is until I once again was picked up by God, shook off and placed in front of a mirror to see the filth I was in (that was about 18 days ago now), then He lead me to your site, which has given me inner strength to fight the demon of lust in my life and the courage to go to my accountability partner (who I never truly let in to this secret - though I had hinted of a potential problem) and confessed my need for his help here as well."

Read Ecclesiastes 4:11 "Also, if two lie down together, they will keep warm. But how can one keep warm alone?"

Question 6. How does the verse above apply to our topic of study?

Note: In Revelation 3 Jesus tells the church of Laodicea that it had grown "lukewarm." They needed to repent of their sin and open the door to Jesus Christ and restore fellowship.

Question 7. How is your spiritual zeal?

"If two lie together, they have heat. So virtuous and gracious affections are excited by good society, and Christians warm one another by provoking one another to love and to good works" (Matthew Henry).[7]

And now, we will examine the final verse in this important "accountability" section. Ecclesiastes 4:12 says, "one may be overpowered, two can defend themselves."

Questions

We have discovered that two working together can produce spiritual fruit (vs. 9), that it can provide spiritual restoration (vs. 10), prompt spiritual zeal (vs. 11), and now we will see that two working together can provide spiritual protection.

Question 8. What does verse 12 teach that "two together" can provide?

Question 9. Has this spiritual protection been missing in your life in the past? Yes   No

Question 10. Have you contacted someone yet to be an accountability partner with you? Yes   No

To be honest, if you are unwilling to maintain an accountability relationship, most likely you will not win the battle against pornography for any length of time. Remember, "one can be overpowered." (I proved the truth of this fact in my life for 15 years. I did not have accountability and I was overpowered again and again.) However, if you will contact your pastor, spouse, or others, then "two can defend themselves" and you can experience victory too! (Wow, is it ever good to be done with pornography and masturbation!) We are in a battle, dear friend. We can either be "overpowered" or we can "defend ourselves," depending on our willingness to find a partner.

"**United strength. If an enemy find a man alone, he is likely to prevail against him; with his own single strength he cannot win, but, if he have a second, he may do well enough: two shall withstand him**" (Matthew Henry).[8]

Notice this Biblical story, which reinforces the truth we have been studying:

> "Joab saw that there were battle lines in front of him and behind him; so he selected some of the best troops in Israel and deployed them against the Arameans. [10] He put the rest of the men under the command of Abishai his brother and deployed them against the Ammonites. [11] Joab said, 'If the Arameans are too strong for me, then you are to come to my rescue; but if the Ammonites are too strong for you, then I will come to rescue you.' [12] Be strong and let us fight bravely for our people and the cities of our God. The LORD will do what is good in his sight" (2 Samuel 10:9-12).

The end result of this battle was victory for the Israelites. Joab in essence said, "You help me with my enemy, and I'll help you with yours." And so together they were victorious whereas separately they would have been conquered. This is an important aspect of an accountability relationship. We should provide one another with spiritual protection from our mutual enemy. The way we do this is to pray for each other, share "battle tips" that helped us, take each other to the Word of God, and help each other amputate the causes of sin. This is a winnable war. But it takes two!

"We Christians need each other. There is strength in numbers. When isolated and separated from our brothers, we are easy pickings for the Enemy of our souls" (Robert Daniels, *The War Within*).[9]

Please provide your comments on the following passages of Scripture:

> "Let us hold unswervingly to the hope we profess, for he who promised is faithful. [24] And let us consider how we may spur one another on toward love and good deeds. [25] Let us not give up meeting together, as some are in the habit of doing, but let us encourage one another—and all the more as you see the Day approaching" (Hebrews 10:23-25).

Scripture to Consider

"As iron sharpens iron, so one man sharpens another" (Proverbs 27:17).

Were you free from pornography since you did the last lesson? Yes   No

Were you free from masturbation since you did the last lesson? Yes   No

Were you free from sexual immorality since you did the last lesson? Yes   No

DAY 9—PURE GRACE

For the next several days, we are going to examine a pivotal teaching of the Scriptures. The necessity of understanding this cannot be overstated. Simply put, grace is what saves us, sanctifies us and will ultimately glorify us. The grace of God is responsible for rescuing us from pornography and keeping us out of it until the end.

The value of this truth is that grace can do what the law cannot. In other words, if I am caught in the trap of pornography I cannot escape through obeying the law. The law condemns my behavior as sinful but provides no power to help me stop. On the other hand, the grace of God actually releases us from the trap of the devil, redeems us from slavery to the devil, and rescues us from the kingdom of the devil.

"To run and work the law commands, but gives us neither feet nor hands. But better news the gospel brings, it bids us fly and gives us wings." (unknown author)

I wonder if you are familiar with the strangle-knot. It is an excellent knot to be used as a running knot for a snare because the more force that is applied from inside the loop the more firmly the running knot prevents opening of the loop. In short, the harder you pull against the knot the tighter the knot becomes! The only way to break free of this snare is by cutting the rope with a knife.

Pornography is a strangle-knot for us. All of our own efforts to break free from sin only serve to increase its death-grip on us. The truth is that it is the grace of God alone that can break our bondage and free us from certain death. God's grace is like the knife that can free us from the strangle-knot.

Please read the following biblical story of "Pure Grace", and answer the questions.

"But Jesus went to the Mount of Olives. ² At dawn he appeared again in the temple courts; where all the people gathered around him, and he sat down to teach them. ³ The teachers of the law and the Pharisees brought in a woman caught in adultery. They made her stand before the group ⁴ and said to Jesus, 'Teacher, this woman was caught in the act of adultery. ⁵ In the Law Moses commanded us to stone such women. Now what do you say?' ⁶ They were using this question as a trap, in order to have a basis for accusing him. But Jesus bent down and started to write on the ground with his finger. ⁷ When they kept on questioning him, he straightened up and said to them, 'If any one of you is without sin, let him be the first to throw a stone at her.' ⁸ Again he stooped down and wrote on the ground. ⁹ At this, those who heard began to go away one at a time, the older ones first, until only Jesus was left, with the woman still standing there. ¹⁰ Jesus straightened up and asked her, 'Woman, where are they? Has no one condemned you?' ¹¹ 'No one, sir,' she said. 'Then neither do I condemn you, Jesus declared. Go now and leave your life of sin'" (John 8:1-11).

Nothing is more humiliating than being caught in an act of disobedience! Whether it's a child with his hand in the cookie jar or an adult driving over the speed limit, we all know the sinking feeling of being caught. In John 8, a woman is caught in the act of adultery. Let us study her story and learn. (Some of the following questions are taken from Lesson Builder by Logos).¹⁰

Questions

Question 1. From the early verses of this passage, what do we know about the character and motive of those who bring this woman to Jesus?

Question 2. How do you think the woman feels when the men make her "stand before the group" and publicly expose her sin?

Question 3. While it is obvious that this woman is guilty, what elements of injustice can you find in this situation?

Note: The Pharisees and scribes continued to press their point. They were not after the poor woman as much as they were after Jesus. They were saying this "testing" Jesus (v. 6). They wanted grounds for "accusing" Jesus. He is the one they are really after here.

This self-righteous, self-appointed group of Pharisees were acting as judge and jury and wanting to stone this woman; but don't mistake it, their ultimate goal was the death of Jesus. They were filled with self-righteous hatred toward Jesus. They kept stressing their point. "They persisted in asking Him" (v. 7a). They kept the pressure on Jesus. "Come on, tell us teacher, what do You say? Will you kill the woman or kill the Law?"

Scripture makes no definitive statement as to what Jesus wrote in the dirt. Here is a thought: There are only 2 other times in Scripture where God is shown to write something with His hand or finger, and both times what was written condemned those to whom He wrote. The first time was when God wrote the Law on tablets of stone, the second time was when He wrote on the wall of King Belshazzar. One opinion is that he wrote the sins of the accusers. Note Job 13:26— "For you write down bitter things against me and make me inherit the sins of my youth."

Question 4. The Pharisees and teachers were often very self-righteous. Why did they go away instead of stoning the woman?

Question 5. Was Jesus condoning the woman's sin by not condemning her? Please explain.

Thoughts: As these religious leaders persisted in questioning him, Jesus stood up and invited any one among them who was sinless to throw the first stone. By this statement they could not possibly say Jesus rejected the law. Jesus specifically told them to throw the first stone. Go ahead, you are right, the Law says stone her. She is guilty. Now, you, which one of you, is sinless?

Question 6. Why are we tempted to condemn other people's sins rather than our own?

Course Member Dave writes:
"Amazingly, when I was so deep in sexual sin, I would condemn a man for ...sexual sin, yet I would have no problem looking at girls in a sexualizing way at the swimming pool. Apparently it was easier for me to throw stones at others for my own sins than myself."

Question 7. How would you describe Jesus' attitude towards the woman? (Notice Jesus was the only one who talked to her; the others only talked about her).

Please notice the last statement of Jesus: "Neither do I condemn you..." This is pure grace. The law required punishment and death of the woman caught in the act of adultery, Jesus forgave her and gave her life. The woman did not make any excuses (v. 11). She was guilty. She knew it. She stood condemned. She didn't have to be convinced of that fact. She needed grace. She did not deserve it. "The wages of sin is death." "The soul that sins will surely die." She couldn't earn it. She was a spiritual pauper in need of the riches of God's marvelous grace.

Jesus said to her, "Neither do I condemn you; go your way; from now on sin no more" (v. 11). Let those words soak in. "Neither do I . . . " "Neither do I condemn you."

How could Jesus offer such a sinner no condemnation? He did it the same way He does to us. He knew that He was going to the cross to die for her sins. "For while we were still helpless" sinners. That is the way all sinners are. Helpless. A helpless sinner doesn't merit forgiveness. A helpless sinner doesn't earn forgiveness. "For while we were still helpless [sinners], at the right time Christ died for the ungodly" (Romans 5:6^{NAS}).

Moreover, "God demonstrates His own love toward us, in that while we were yet sinners, Christ died for us" (v. 8).

To every guilt-ridden sinner who puts their trust in Jesus Christ as their savior the LORD God comes today and whispers in your ear "neither do I condemn you." "There is now no condemnation for those who are in Christ Jesus" (Romans 8:1).

But Jesus' statement of grace is immediately followed by an admonition to "go and sin no more." Theologians have made terms that describe what Jesus did here: Justification and Sanctification. Justification is: "Neither do I condemn you." Sanctification is: "Go and sin no more." And it is critical to see the order of Jesus' statements, for He did not say, "Go and sin no more, neither do I condemn you." "Clean up your act and then I will forgive you." Jesus Christ here uses grace as the motive for pure living.

The following testimony is from Sean:

The first memory I have of sexual activity is at the age of approximately age 4 when an older female molested me. From then on, I was drawn to girls. I was 'married' to a classmate at the age of 7 behind the bushes at school, and can remember feelings of love and desire from that age on. There wasn't any sexual attraction at that time; I was just a child, of course, but there was a continuous history of `worship' that escalated as I aged. I tore pictures out of National Geographic, looked in Bible storybooks around the home of loosely clothed women and feasted on the Sears catalogs in the lingerie section. At the age of probably 11, a friend masturbated in front of me to show me this 'cool' thing he learned. From that point on, I was hooked. I of course was drawn to pornography like a bee to honey, and when there's a will, there's ALWAYS a way. From the age of 12 until I was married at 19, I engaged in pornography and masturbation at least once a day.

I repented or as the phrase is coined elsewhere 'Let Jesus in my heart', and joined the church I was raised in. Everything was ok for a while; (I thought). I started to fall again; whether it was masturbation in the middle of the night, or getting a magazine, viewing it and subsequently destroying it, or a movie every great once in a while. Then the great Internet was born. When I told the elder of our church that I still masturbated occasionally, he looked at me like I was weird, and he couldn't believe it. He said `But you're married; why are you doing this?' I knew it was wrong; but I needed advice from someone who knew what it took to break free. I was starting to get lazy and scarred by my sins. When I fell, I was just guilty and sorry, not repentant anymore. I hadn't really tried to stop doing this for years! I was content to sin, and then put on the complacent face of sorrow, at least until the next time I was tempted.

I can say with certainty I was destined for hell. I was living the life of a Christian, but my private and personal life was a lie and an abomination to Him. I was so scared that

Question 8. If you were the woman, how would you feel as you left Jesus' presence?

Course Member Lilly writes: "I have been like that woman, and have experienced Him saying to me, Neither do I condemn you, go and sin no more...It is such a wonderful experience to simply admit my sin, accept His love and forgiveness, and walk away knowing that He loves me and is helping me to stop sin."

Friends, let us bring this teaching home. Doing pornography is adultery. Jesus said, "anyone who looks at a woman lustfully has already committed adultery with her in his heart" (Matthew 5:28). Let us call it what it is—it is not just "stumbling" or "slipping up" it is spiritual adultery of the heart. We are adulterers—guilty before God, condemned before men, caught in the act—adulterers. If we are married and doing pornography, we are committing the sin of heart adultery against our spouse as well.

And yet, there is a place where adulterers can go to find pardon and forgiveness. It is in Jesus, who "justifies the wicked" (Romans 4:5). It is in Jesus, who was "pierced for our transgressions, and crushed for our iniquities." And it is also in Jesus where we find grace to live differently. For it is the grace of God (not the law of God) that teaches us to say "no" to ungodliness (Titus 2:12). Pure grace. We need it. He has it.

In summary, a snare was set for this woman; she was in a strangle-knot with no way to break free. But Jesus cut the knot, by the knife of pure grace. He can do the same for us!

I'd find a site that was full of deceit and dead men's bones, for what good would it do for me to get freed from one thing, yet equally deceived in another? I went through the first day's course with much wariness, but when I clicked on the devotions and heard that beautiful, 4 part old-fashioned piano music, I knew this was my home. I broke down weeping in relief for the first time in years; I knew I was on the road to freedom.

I went through the course one day at a time, and I finished it a freed man. The lessons were perfectly practical and no punches pulled; I got the admonition I needed if I started getting lazy!! As the victories started to come, I got stronger and stronger. Seeing the posts of fellow soldiers on the discussion group and giving them encouragement was such a blessing to me, and it makes me want to practice what I preach. I have to walk the walk, not just talk it. I believe that I have the knowledge and the grace of God I need for continuing, eternal victory. May I stay humble and reliant on Him so this grace may continue.

I am now a full-time mentor with Setting Captives Free, and also a discussion group moderator. I have a passionate hatred for the bonds that had a hold on me at one time, and I want to help others learn and have the belief that they can break free from this sin's trap, too. I served the devil well for years; it is my prayer I can serve the Lord ten times better in my few moments on this soil before the glories of Heaven. It is such a blessing to be able to see God's grace traveling the face of the earth; calling lost, hurting souls back home while the door of grace is yet open. Freedom awaits the humble repentant sinner!!!

Scripture to Consider

"I, even I, am he who blots out your transgressions, for my own sake, and remembers your sins no more" (Isaiah 43:25).

"John testifies concerning him. He cries out, saying, "This was he of whom I said, 'He who comes after me has surpassed me because he was before me.'" [16] From the fullness of his grace we have all received one blessing after another. [17] For the law was given through Moses; grace and truth came through Jesus Christ" (John 1:15-17).

"If we confess our sins, he is faithful and just and will forgive us our sins and purify us from all unrighteousness" (1 John 1:9).

Were you free from pornography since you did the last lesson?
    Yes No

Were you free from masturbation since you did the last lesson?
    Yes No

Were you free from sexual immorality since you did the last lesson?
    Yes No

DAY 10— SURPRISING GRACE

There was once a great and noble King whose land was terrorized by a crafty dragon. Like a massive bird of prey, the scaly beast delighted in ravaging villages with his fiery breath. Hapless victims ran from their burning homes, only to be snatched into the dragon's jaws or talons. Those devoured instantly were deemed more fortunate than those carried back to the dragon's lair to be devoured at his leisure. The King led his sons and knights in many valiant battles against the dragon.

Riding alone in the forest, one of the King's sons heard his name purred low and soft. In the shadows of the ferns and trees, curled among the boulders, lay the dragon. The creature's heavy-lidded eyes fastened on the prince, and the reptilian mouth stretched into a friendly smile.

"Don't be alarmed," said the dragon, as gray wisps of smoke rose lazily from his nostrils. "I am not what your father thinks."

"What are you, then?" asked the prince, warily drawing his sword as he pulled in the reins to keep his fearful horse from bolting.

"I am pleasure," said the dragon. "Ride on my back and you will experience more than you ever imagined. Come now. I have no harmful intentions. I seek a friend, someone to share flights with me. Have you never dreamed of flying? Never longed to soar in the clouds?"

Visions of soaring high above the forested hills drew the prince hesitantly from his horse. The dragon unfurled one great webbed wing to serve as a ramp to his ridged back. Between the spiny projections, the prince found a secure seat. Then the creature snapped his powerful wings twice and launched them into the sky. The prince's apprehension melted into awe and exhilaration.

From then on, he met the dragon often, but secretly, for how could he tell his father, brothers or the knights that he had befriended the enemy? The prince felt separate from them all. Their concerns were no longer his concerns. Even when he wasn't with the dragon, he spent less time with those he loved and more time alone.

The skin on the prince's legs became calloused from gripping the ridged back of the dragon, and his hands grew rough and hardened. He began wearing gloves to hide the malady. After many nights of riding, he discovered scales growing on the backs of his hands as well. With dread he realized his fate were he to continue, and so he resolved to return no more to the dragon.

But, after a fortnight, he again sought out the dragon, having been tormented with desire. And so it transpired many times over. No matter what his determination, the prince eventually found himself pulled back, as if by the cords of an invisible web. Silently, patiently, the dragon always waited.

One cold, moonless night their excursion became a foray against a sleeping village. Torching the thatched roofs with fiery blasts from his nostrils, the dragon roared with delight when terrified victims fled from their burning homes. Swooping down, the serpent belched again and flames engulfed a cluster of screaming villagers. The prince closed his eyes tightly in an attempt to shut out the carnage.

Questions

Question 1. What are your thoughts on this story? Do you see parallels with your own life? What are your comments?

Have you been so disgusted and shame-filled over your pornography slavery that you resolved to never do it again only to find yourself pulled back as if by the cords of an invisible web? I have. I resolved over and over to stop, to never do that again, and yet all my resolve melted in the heat of the temptation. I was receiving God's grace in vain.

Friends, it is possible to "receive the grace of God in vain" (2 Corinthians 6:1); that is, with no associated heart and life change. So let us examine Scripture and see that the grace and love of God is the cure for any bondage. Sin is a spiritual problem and requires spiritual solutions. God's grace given us at the cross is the solution.

> "For if, by the trespass of the one man, death reigned through that one man, how much more will those who receive God's abundant provision of grace and of the gift of righteousness reign in life through the one man, Jesus Christ" (Romans 5:17).

Question 2. According to this passage, what will those who receive grace do?

> "For I am the least of the apostles and do not even deserve to be called an apostle, because I persecuted the church of God. But by the grace of God I am what I am, and his grace to me was not without effect. No, I worked harder than all of them — yet not I, but the grace of God that was with me..." (1 Corinthians 15:9-10).

Question 3. Paul says that the grace God gave to Paul was not without effect. What was the effect of God's grace to Paul?

In the pre-dawn hours, when the prince crept back from his dragon trysts, the road outside his father's castle usually remained empty. But not tonight. Terrified refugees streamed into the protective walls of the castle. The prince attempted to slip through the crowd to close himself in his chambers, but some of the survivors stared and pointed toward him.

"He was there," one woman cried out, "I saw him on the back of the dragon." Others nodded their heads in angry agreement. Horrified, the prince saw that his father, the King, was in the courtyard holding a bleeding child in his arms. The King's face mirrored the agony of his people as his eyes found the prince's. The son fled, hoping to escape into the night, but the guards apprehended him as if he were a common thief. They brought him to the great hall where his father sat solemnly on the throne. The people on every side railed against the prince.

"Banish him!" he heard one of his own brothers angrily cry out.

"Burn him alive!" other voices shouted.

As the king rose from his throne, bloodstains from the wounded shone darkly on his royal robes. The crowd fell silent in expectation of his decree. The prince, who could not bear to look into his father's face, stared at the flagstones of the floor.

"Take off your gloves and your tunic," the King commanded. The prince obeyed slowly, dreading to have his metamorphosis uncovered before the kingdom. Was his shame not already enough? He had hoped for a quick death without further humiliation. Sounds of revulsion rippled through the crowd at the sight of the prince's thick, scaled skin and the ridge growing along his spine.

The king strode toward his son, and the prince steeled himself, fully expecting a back-handed blow even though he had never been struck so by his father. Instead, his father embraced him and wept as he held him tightly. In shocked disbelief, the prince buried his face against his father's shoulder.

"Do you wish to be freed from the dragon, my son?"

The prince answered in despair, "I have wished it many times, but there is no hope for me."

"Not alone," said the King. "You cannot win against the serpent alone."

"Father, I am no longer your son. I am half beast," sobbed the prince.

But his father replied, "My blood runs in your veins. My nobility has always been stamped deep within your soul."

With his face still hidden tearfully in his father's embrace, the prince heard the King instruct the crowd, "The dragon is crafty. Some fall victim to his wiles and some to his violence. There will be mercy for all who wish to be freed. Who else among you has ridden the dragon?"

The prince lifted his head to see someone emerge from the crowd. To his amazement, he recognized an older brother, one who had been lauded throughout the kingdom for his onslaughts against the dragon in battle and for his many good deeds. Others came, some weeping, others hanging their heads in shame.

The King embraced them all.

"This is our most powerful weapon against the dragon," he announced. "Truth. No more hidden flights. Alone you cannot resist him."[11]

Questions

"Now this is our boast: Our conscience testifies that we have conducted ourselves in the world, and especially in our relations with you, in the holiness and sincerity that are from God. We have done so not according to worldly wisdom but according to Gods grace" (2 Corinthians 1:12).

Question 4. How did Paul conduct himself while among the Corinthians?

Question 5. What was the source of Paul's ability to conduct himself in "holiness and sincerity?"

Question 6. They acted in holiness according to what?

"And God is able to make all grace abound to you, so that in all things at all times, having all that you need, you will abound in every good work" (2 Cor. 9:8).

Question 7. What does it take in order to "abound in every good work?"

"For the grace of God that brings salvation has appeared to all men. It teaches us to say No to ungodliness and worldly passions, and to live self-controlled, upright and godly lives in this present age" (Titus 2:11-12).

Question 8. If we are ever to learn to say "no" to ungodliness, if we are ever to deny worldly passions, if we are ever to live a self-controlled life, what will it take?

Questions

Friend, hopefully these verses have taught us one very basic but essential truth: the grace of God alone will enable us to conquer any sin habit. But, since we acknowledge that grace is a sovereign gift of God, how may we acquire it?

Answer: We must humble ourselves, rid our lives of idols, seek after it, and don't miss it. This is a very serious matter, because if we miss the grace of God we miss eternal life. Let us look at how we may acquire this grace and life.

- **Humble ourselves:** "God opposes the proud but gives grace to the humble. ⁷ Submit yourselves, then, to God. Resist the devil, and he will flee from you. ⁸ Come near to God and he will come near to you. Wash your hands, you sinners, and purify your hearts, you double-minded. ⁹ Grieve, mourn and wail. Change your laughter to mourning and your joy to gloom. ¹⁰ Humble yourselves before the Lord, and he will lift you up" (James 4:6-10).
- **Rid our lives of idols:** Those who cling to worthless idols forfeit the grace that could be theirs. Whatever is between God and us must be given up in order to get grace. Either forfeit the idols or forfeit grace.
- **Seek after it:** "Ask and it will be given to you; seek and you will find; knock and the door will be opened to you. For everyone who asks receives; he who seeks finds; and to him who knocks, the door will be opened" (Mat. 7:7-8).
- **Don't miss it:** "See to it that no one misses the grace of God and that no bitter root grows up to cause trouble and defile many" (Hebrews 12:15). See to it. Make it your primary objective. Do not miss the grace of God. Humble yourself, rid your life of any idol, seek after it, and don't miss it. The result? God gives grace, grace makes us more than conquerors through Him who loves us, we reign in life, and we overcome pornography.

Often recall the proverb: "The eye is not satisfied with seeing nor the ear filled with hearing." Try, moreover, to turn your heart from the love of things visible and bring yourself to things invisible. For they who follow their own evil passions stain their consciences and lose the grace of God.

Testimony

The following testimony is from Herman:

Glory to God.

If you wonder why the first three words of my testimony were these, it is because I have learned in sixty days that these should be the first and last sentences, or some of the same meaning, of our days now and forever. I remember the day I first experienced pornographic magazines. It was winter and I was thirteen years old, the age for young boys when the body suddenly erupts chemically and the beginning of a chaotic ride begins. I haven't done any studying and cannot spew statistics to you about how long this ride typically lasts, but my chaos lasted fifteen years.

Louisiana winters are nothing extreme, normally requiring nothing heavier than flannel shirts, but that winter I wore extra clothes. I chose that day to wear insulated coveralls and as I ventured out of the house, had no idea what a horrid turn my life was about to take. I stood beneath a large, beautiful live oak tree - the kind that most people see only in the movies - with limbs as thick as my teenage torso that curved gently to the ground. The canopy was so large that once under the tree, I felt as if I was safe inside a building. An old chest of drawers stood near the tree, discarded.

This was not my home, but I lived there temporarily and was left alone for the day. The place was nearly twenty miles from the nearest town, so there was not much trouble I could get into. I didn't wonder about the chest until that day and decided to look inside the drawers in case there was something interesting there to rummage through. I opened the top drawer and it was empty, then the second. As the image registered in my brain, I recoiled as if a snake lay curled inside. This was no snake, but a drawer full of pornographic magazines like Hustler, Jugs, Playboy and even Playgirl. I looked around, paranoid that someone could see me. I knew I was alone, but my senses came alive and in my immaturity didn't know how to handle it. I stuffed magazines inside my coveralls and fled to the nearby woodlands to view them among the hungry blips and tweets of red-breasted robins.

My parents divorced before I was a teen and both were alcoholics, lost within themselves and didn't have the capacity to raise us. We lived with them alternately, but they didn't really raise us, so I plunged deep within the dark recesses of masturbation and sexual deviation with myself.

Several times I was asked about mysterious bruises and there were other times that I injured my back to the point that it hampered my physical activities at school. This behavior went on until only recently when I found **Pure Freedom**. It came and went between the beginning and end of the fifteen years, but Satan had me bound the entire fifteen or so years. Keep in mind I NEVER had a partner, was not sexually active until I got married. Before I fell in love with my future wife, I had no desire to be with other women, because I was in love with myself and I knew no woman could accept the types of activities I involved myself in on a regular basis. I have been married for ten years and my wife had no idea of any of this for the first nine years.

I have always been a writer, but only in the past several months have I committed myself to it full time. When I went full time, I got involved with a publishing house that publishes pornographic novels. Keep in mind that I did not start out writing pornography—I was a suspense writer—but the enemy knew my heart at the time and convinced me to change to filth the one last part of my life that I thought was truly my own. Looking back now it makes perfect sense—like the prince riding the dragon I was being consumed. Upon my salvation, I knew instantly that I could no longer write what I had been writing and walk with the Lord and was terrified. I remember thinking, "Lord if I can't write, what will I do?" I am a writer to the core of my soul and the Lord revealed to me: You WILL write, but for ME.

At the time of my salvation this past Easter, I was experiencing a time of temporary success abstaining from viewing porn that we all went through several times before finding Jesus, so pornography was out of my mind at the time and it was something I didn't leave at the foot of the cross and the devil used it against me when I wasn't expecting it to come back.

My addiction was secretly birthed in the woods and died in my living room fifteen long years later. It took Jesus Christ to put it to death, because I could not do it on my own.

Glory to God.

Question 9. Are you truly committed to receiving God's grace? Will you employ the four principles? Please list those four principles and tell how you will practically do them:

Principle #1—

Principle #2—

Principle #3—

Principle #4—

Question 10. Write out anything you have learned in this lesson, or any new thoughts or ideas you have had today.

Scripture to Consider

"For it is by grace you have been saved, through faith—and this not from yourselves, it is the gift of God— not by works, so that no one can boast" (Ephesians 2:8-9).

Were you free from pornography since you did the last lesson?
    Yes   No

Were you free from masturbation since you did the last lesson?
    Yes   No

Were you free from sexual immorality since you did the last lesson?
    Yes   No

DAY 11— ONGOING FREEDOM

"Therefore, I urge you, brothers, in view of God's mercy, to offer your bodies as living sacrifices, holy and pleasing to God—this is your spiritual act of worship. Do not conform any longer to the pattern of this world, but be transformed by the renewing of your mind. Then you will be able to test and approve what God's will is—his good, pleasing and perfect will" (Romans 12:1-2).

In the above passage, the apostle Paul teaches us that the receiving of God's compassion should prompt us to offer our bodies up to the Lord as a living sacrifice. He shows us that God's mercy motivates us to offer ourselves to the Lord, which is why we placed this lesson after the two days of teaching on grace. Grace leads us to holiness, to pleasing the Lord with our bodies, and to true worship.

The language of Paul in these verses reminds us of animal sacrifices that God's people in the Old Testament were taught to offer unto the Lord. As atonement for sin, they were required to bring a lamb and present it to the priest as an offering. The priest would sacrifice the animal, which pointed for-

Questions

Question 1. You may want to take a moment and write out a prayer to God and present Him with your body. If so, here is a place for you to do this:

Here some clarity is brought to what it means to worship God. Is worshiping God going to church and singing songs? Is it hearing a sermon and receiving the Word planted in our hearts? Is it singing in the choir, or participating in prayer? It sure can be. But the above verses tell us that presenting our bodies as living sacrifices to God is our "spiritual act of worship." If you want to experience worship in the most powerful way, just offer up your body to God for Him to live in, work through and draw others to Himself.

Question 2. At this time, it will be wise for you to develop a daily habit of presenting your body to the Lord as soon as you awake. First thing each morning, present your body to the Lord as a living sacrifice. This takes the grace of God to accomplish, as we have already discussed; so, will you seek God for grace to offer yourself to Him daily?

The verses in this lesson describe precisely how we can overcome the habitual habit of viewing pornography, and of masturbation. Notice verse 2: *"Do not conform any longer to the pattern of this world, but be transformed by the renewing of your mind."* We are not to be conformed but transformed. And this is accomplished by renewing our minds. What does this look like in the life of one who has been enslaved to pornography?

Well, viewing pornography is like a pouring of gas on the fire of lust. It makes us walk around all day long with lust in our hearts because of the pornographic images that are in our minds, and those images can drag us in to masturbation. This is a very frustrating thing for people who wish to be free from this habitual sin because the images torment our minds. It is as if the devil is mocking us, or worse yet it is as if he is raping our souls.

I remember that a pornographic image would get lodged in my brain from something I had viewed even several years back, or maybe it was from a magazine I had seen at the airport that morning, and I could not stop thinking about that pornographic picture no matter what. And finally, by the time my flying day was over and I was in my hotel room I was so stirred up with lust that masturbation was inevitable. So how do we combat this?

Testimony

The following testimony is from Tyler:

"Wow, what a great God we have; the very fact that I am alive and sharing this testimony is evidence of His power!

Mine is a very ordinary story in a way, I am just an ordinary Christian. But to me it is a story of extraordinary life.

I grew up as an introvert in a typically modern dysfunctional family. Having a shyness with real girls, I gravitated to 'girly magazines' to satisfy my curiosity in that area during my early teens. It became a habit very quickly. Soon I had a stash of magazines carefully hidden from prying eyes, and it was my substitute for the 'real thing,' the girls that my brothers bragged about. I can recall, somehow, feeling self-righteously indignant at their moral infractions, feeling that my aberrant behavior somehow wasn't as bad as theirs, though deep down I well knew it was wrong. What did frighten me was the power that my lust for these 2 dimensional pictures had over me. I tried not to think about that too much though. I was at the same time grappling with trying to understand the great Why of life and beginning to come into a primitive relationship with the Lord.

At the age of 19, I met Carrie, fell in love, and we married 10 months later. All thoughts of and desires for pornography evaporated. I guess that's not too unusual an experience, the 'real thing' displaces the fake substitute. At least for a time!

Over the next 20 years the battles with pornography were few and far between. For the most part I was busy taking care of my wife and children, and seeking a relationship with the Lord. However, my faith was extremely legalistic, and that would eventually prove to be near fatal.

I say the battles with pornography were few and far between. In fact, often only fleeting. Like when I would accidentally find a Playboy magazine in a circumstance of privacy, and not be able to resist the temptation to peruse it. It worried me, that I could never resist the temptation, but the times were infrequent and I found it better to try to forget, and do better in future.

About 8 years ago, during a time of great personal stress for both my wife and myself,

ward to the death of Jesus Christ to pay for our sins, and the person presenting the sacrifice would be released from guilt, and in presenting this sacrifice he was worshiping God.

In the same manner we are to present to God, not an animal sacrifice, but the sacrifice of our own body. And just as the member of God's family in the Old Testament would present the entire animal as a sacrifice, holding no part back, so we are to offer God our entire being: heart, mind, hands, feet, sexual organs, indeed all of ourselves are to be presented to God.

In light of God's grace and mercy, it is time for us to begin offering up our bodies as living sacrifices to God. He gave His all for us, now we are to give our all for Him. I remember learning this truth just a few years back, and I was so eager to give all of myself to God that I burst out into prayer. I remember I prayed something like this: "Oh God, how I have abused this body You gave me. I have used it for wickedness and pleasing my flesh. I have given my eyes over to viewing pornography, my mind over to sex chatting, my heart to lusting after impurity of all sorts. Oh God, I now present me, all of me to You, and ask You to receive me as a living sacrifice. May my body now be dead to those things that dishonor You so much, and may Your Holy Spirit live in me. I worship You as I present this offering to You."

Questions

First, we "radically amputate" (more on this tomorrow) by "cutting off" and "plucking out" the source of those images; and second, we "radically transform" our minds by renewing them. Here is how:

The first thing I do in the morning is present my body to the Lord as a living sacrifice. Then I sit down with my Bible and I read it. As I meditate over the truths I undergo a change in my thinking. I begin dwelling on Jesus Christ and His perfect sacrifice on the cross, and how I am to die to my flesh. I then begin planning out the day from a spiritual perspective. What will I do to avoid temptation completely? What will I do if I have a "surprise attack?" How will I handle this situation, and that situation…etc?

This "renewing my mind" is really just "thinking differently" and thinking differently leads to acting differently.

Question 3. What will be some ways that you will begin to "renew your mind" by the grace of God? Please be specific.

---

we succumbed to the temptation together, rationalizing that 'a little bit of voyeurism spiced up the sex life.' For Carrie there was no great moral problem because she was still not a Christian, and her interest soon waned anyway. The turmoil for me though was horrendous. On one side the utter condemnation of a vengeful and wrathful God (my legalistic church life!) and on the other the exhilaration and new heights of sexual pleasure after our relations having become stale with neglect over the years (I had not realized this neglect at the time though, or indeed the fullness of joy God intended in sexual union between a husband and wife).

After several attempts to rid my bedroom and my mind of this material that was holding me in bondage, I soon became desperate. Each time I simply found the desire for this filth too much. I can remember the last year of this trial falling to such depths that on a trip to a church convention I took a detour of several hours specifically to pick up some more videos, and spent half the time at the convention praising God and the other half shaming Him and His beloved Son. The condemnation I felt both at my weakness and my hypocrisy, going to church, preaching even (in a very minor capacity), and yet falling back into sin again at night (No, I should be honest and say, diving headlong back into sin.) was becoming too much. I had been taught that obedience was the key by my church, but it simply didn't work, and, oh how miserable a creature I was.

The last 6 months was a bitter period of my life. Every night as I tried to find sleep, the same image came clearly into my mind, the image of a gun at my temple, and the final blast, and silence. Oh how I wanted to die. Thankfully guns of any kind are rare in Australia, let alone hand guns. But thoughts of suicide as the only way out consumed my mind, when it wasn't consumed by the pornography. I was even creating my own filthy images and 'stories' in my mind, so obsessed was I. I realize now how deep the scars are that we carve into our minds with sin, as it becomes an addiction. Soon thoughts of actually ending it all were taking clear shape.

Thankfully our little church was at the same time going through a mighty change, from Old Covenant legalism into the New Covenant of Grace. I think that this was what saved me, as in the few rational moments left I was studying these issues with our Bible study group and gradually absorbing some of this new knowledge.

Continued on page 36

---

[2] "Do not conform any longer to the pattern of this world, but be transformed by the renewing of your mind."

Notice here that renewing our minds leads to a transformation. The Greek word for this is "metamorphoo" which is where we get our word "metamorphosis." This metamorphosis, which comes by renewing our minds, makes a total change in our nature, and is what enables us to have freedom on a daily basis. Therefore, it is critical to renew our minds. We do this by reading the Bible, and earnestly seeking the Lord in prayer. This gives us "the mind of Christ" (1 Corinthians 2:16) and enables us to think differently, which produces a real change in our character. Metamorphosis is the same word we use to describe what happens to a caterpillar that changes into a butterfly. What used to inch along the ground, in the mud and dirt, can now soar heavenward in **Pure Freedom** of flight.

Friends, I was crawling in the dirt and mud of pornography and masturbation for 15 long years, inching my way along the road that goes nowhere. But in January of 1999, 3 years ago as of this writing, a metamorphosis began to take place in my heart and life, by the grace of God. I began actually applying biblical principles to my life, instead of just reading about them and preaching them. God made me serious about eradicating pornography, sex chatting, and all sexual impurity from my life. As I began offering my body as a living sacrifice every morning, and renewing my mind in His Word, I have been experiencing changes in my thoughts, my desires, my goals in life—everything! Everything is changing, and I feel as though I have been given wings of grace to soar to the presence of God.

Practically speaking, this means that I no longer have pornographic images lodged in my brain all day (or any part of the day for that matter). So, here you are coming up on your second week in this course, and you may be struggling because some images may not have been washed away from your mind yet. Let me assure you that they will indeed go away, if you have cut off the source of pornography and if you are renewing your mind. Those two things will ensure your continued success.

I love this metamorphosis, and don't ever want to go back to crawling in the mud. How about you? This is day 11 for you, and most people begin to see ongoing victory just up ahead. But also about this time period the devil begins stomping his feet and throwing a temper tantrum over his captives leaving. Some people begin having pornographic dreams, others find that suddenly temptation is all around them, and still others find that pornography becomes available where it never was before. Hang in there, friend. The hardest part for most people is from the 14-day period up to and including the 30th day. I'm telling you this as a warning that things may get harder before they get easier, and to be forewarned is to be forearmed.

Question 4. So, are you sensing a "metamorphosis" in your life? What are some of the changes taking place in the following areas: heart, life, marriage (if married), work environment, home, etc.

To review, we learned or reviewed two key principles to overcoming pornography and masturbation today.

1—Offer up our bodies as living sacrifices

2—Renew our minds, and be metamorphosed as a result

And we can only do these things "in view of God's mercy." In other words, Jesus Christ offered up His body as a sacrifice to the Father, to satisfy God's hatred toward sin, and to forgive us our sins. He held nothing back, but presented all of Who He is to God. His back was whipped, His beard was pulled off, His hands and feet were nailed to the cross, His head was crowned with thorns. His side was pierced by the soldier's sword, His heart imploded and poured out blood and water, and then He died. Jesus' death on the cross was the demonstration of God's mercy, and in light of that mercy we too should offer our own bodies as living sacrifices, and renew our minds to be transformed.

Question 5. What are your final thoughts on this teaching today? Did you learn anything new, or were you reminded of any truths that may have been neglected before?

Scripture to Consider

[8] "For you were once darkness, but now you are light in the Lord. Live as children of light [9] (for the fruit of the light consists in all goodness, righteousness and truth) [10] and find out what pleases the Lord" (Ephesians 5:8-10).

[18] "The LORD is near to all who call on him, to all who call on him in truth" (Psalm 145:18).

Were you free from pornography since you did the last lesson?	Yes	No
Were you free from masturbation since you did the last lesson?	Yes	No
Were you free from sexual immorality since you did the last lesson?	Yes	No

Tyler's testimony continues ...

But my misery was deepening. I had just a few weeks earlier been through the cycle of ridding my home of the porn, and then a few days later restocking, and I was feeling incredibly shattered at my total inability to control myself. One evening I told my wife I was going back to work for a few hours to catch up. But I had a rope on the floor behind the drivers seat, and I knew just where to tie it up out in the detailing shed at work, on a beam next to a high workbench. I know that I had not quite reached the bitter end that night, as I did not take the rope out of the car as I went in to work. But I went out to the back paddock, and just stood there and cried. After a bit I looked up into the crystal clear sky and cried out, "Lord, I can't do it!" in desperation. And then it was that I heard, so gentle, so still and so small, His voice, "Yes, Tyler, but I can."

That was a revelation. It was like a divine awareness flooded through me. Of course I couldn't overcome. That was impossible, me trying to overcome, even with His help. It was all back to front. I looked up and said, "OK, Lord, you do it." The most powerful thing was the realization that He really loved me, even right there in the midst of my putrid sin. He loved me, tenderly, affectionately. Those five words were full of love.

Wow that was incredible, I had been struggling as much because I had always thought God hates me, detests me, and this locked me into the cycle of sin. Sin, self-condemnation, sin, self-condemnation..........

I went home and rid myself of the disgusting material I had just bought a few weeks earlier. I had done this several times before, but always before with a feeling of regret at losing the objects of my lust. I had done it out of obedience to God, not desire for Him. This time it was out of desire and thirst for more of this divine awareness and JOY! For Him alone.

As soon as this all happened, I began to focus on Him, His glory, His Holiness, His purity. What a joy. I rejoiced in my freedom, freedom from evil desire, because He had given me desire for Him. The chains are broken, I flee to Him, to thoughts of my Savior, who saved my physical life that starry night, and who has saved me for eternity. And in Him I am now growing in grace and knowledge and strength. Praise our tender and merciful God.

May He be your Salvation and freedom too. This is my prayer for all who struggle as I once did.

DAY 12—RADICAL AMPUTATION

"If your hand causes you to sin, cut it off. It is better for you to enter life maimed than with two hands to go into hell, where the fire never goes out. And if your foot causes you to sin, cut it off. It is better for you to enter life crippled than to have two feet and be thrown into hell. And if your eye causes you to sin, pluck it out. It is better for you to enter the kingdom of God with one eye than to have two eyes and be thrown into hell..." (Mark 9:43-47).

Dear friend, we need to separate ourselves completely from whatever has caused our pornographic addiction. This may not seem reasonable but in dealing with sin being radical is only reasonable.

After 15 years of pornographic addiction, I desperately needed and wanted to be free. With the assistance of my pastor and my wife, I began to cut off every source of pornography and sexual impurity that was in my life.

For instance, when I would go to hotels I could resolve all day long not to watch pornography, and then find myself suddenly turning on the TV to late-night porn and giving in to lust. (You've been hit with this sudden "surprise attack" right?) My pastor helped me understand the need to amputate porn from my life. He suggested I begin unplugging and unhooking the TV and carrying it into one of my co-workers rooms and to leave it with him overnight. That way I had no access to pornography. Also, because I was doing "romantic chatting" on the Internet, I gave my notebook computer away. Everything was cut off. What may seem "radical" to others who do not struggle with this problem is reasonable and the right thing to do for us.

Jesus said that we should "cut off" and "pluck out" whatever causes us to sin, and He warned us that if we don't radically amputate the cause of our sin we could end up in hell. Friend, do not take this lightly. We are talking life and death here; heaven and hell. If you thought you were "just playing" with pornography please know this: pornography will take you farther than you want to go, keep you longer than you want to stay, and cost you more than you want to pay.

Jesus is not referring to a physical cutting off of your foot or a plucking out of your eyeball. Blind men still lust. He's referring to the complete removal of the causes of your sin. He's saying that if we want to be free from this, some things in our lives have to go, and we must do whatever it takes. For me, this meant getting rid of the TV in my hotel room and my home and giving away my notebook computer.

This teaching may seem less than reasonable, indeed it may come across as quite radical. Some people, rather than cut off the causes of sin, want to stare it in the face and say "no." (We will read about this on Day 19.) That would be true victory for them. However, this desire to be strong rather than pure will not result in victory.

Questions

Question 1. Please list what "complete removal" means to you.

Question 2. Please list here the things that have caused you to sin in the area of sexual impurity.

Question 3. We looked at Mark 9:43-47: What did Jesus say to do with things that cause us to sin?

Question 4. Truth time: Have you totally "amputated" everything that has caused you to sin?

Questions

Notice the "radical amputation" principle in the following story:
Timothy Salzman writes:

> "When I was 14 years old I was riding my bicycle across an open field on my way home from school and found a copy of a pornographic magazine. That discovery introduced me to masturbation and eventually fornication. The addiction has followed me, even into my marriage. In fact, marriage has amplified the problem many-fold. I am beginning to get the problem under control by using very extreme measures. For example, I voluntarily gave up my access to our bank account. I have no way to withdraw or spend money at all. That is extremely drastic, but it has worked: no money, no ability to participate in the 'action.' Surprisingly, when I know I can't go to the girly bars, or other places because of a lack of money, the desire is slowly diminishing."[12]

Okay friend, today is the day to clean house! Are you hiding anything anywhere that can cause you to sin? If so, go throw it away. Get rid of it. Have a "burn party" (Acts 19:19) where you throw all pornography away—for good. View it as the fire of God's love consuming your old life.

Question 5. Please comment on Hebrews 12:1 as it relates to our study today: "Therefore, since we are surrounded by such a great cloud of witnesses, let us throw off everything that hinders and the sin that so easily entangles, and let us run with perseverance the race marked out for us."

The following is Matthew Henry's commentary on Mark 9:43-47:

1. The case supposed, that our own hand, or eye, or foot, offend us; that the impure corruption we indulge is as dear to us as an eye or a hand, or that which is to us as an eye or a hand, is become an invisible temptation to sin, or occasion of it. Suppose the beloved is become a sin, or the sin a beloved. Suppose we cannot keep that which is dear to us, but it will be a snare and a stumbling block; suppose we must part with it, or part with Christ and a good conscience.

2. The duty prescribed in that case; Pluck out the eye, cut off the hand and foot, mortify the darling lust, kill it, crucify it, starve it, make no provision for it. Let the idols that have been delectable things, be cast away as detestable things; keep at a distance from that which is a temptation, though ever so pleasing. It is necessary that the part, which is gangrened, should be taken off for the preservation of the whole. The part that is incurably wounded must be cut off, lest the parts that are sound be corrupted. We must put ourselves to pain, that we may not bring ourselves to ruin; self must be denied, that it may not be destroyed.

3. The necessity of doing this. The flesh must be mortified, that we may enter into life (v. 43, 45), into the kingdom of God, v. 47. Though, by abandoning sin, we may, for the present, feel ourselves as if we were halt and maimed (it may seem to be a force put upon ourselves, and may create us some uneasiness), yet it is for life; and all that men have, they will give for their lives: it is for a kingdom, the kingdom of God, which we cannot otherwise obtain; these halts and maims will be the marks of the Lord Jesus, will be in that kingdom scars of honor.

Testimony

The following testimony is from Ellis.

I am an overcomer in Christ Jesus. Born with cerebral palsy, a crippling muscle disease, I had to work hard to get what came naturally for everyone else – from walking to talking to driving a car.

From an early age, I knew that I was different from other children. I grew up in a loving Christian home, and my parents taught me that God had made me this way for a reason. I believed at an early age that God had a purpose for life. I gave my life to the Lord when I was 12 years old. Growing up was not easy for me. Doctors, therapists and specialists in my native Texas doubted that I would ever live or work on my own. My parents doubted it, too. Even I sometimes wondered what kind of life I could make for myself. Knowing that I could do nothing on my own, I turned my eyes to God and trusted in Him.

God blessed my life richly, allowing me to attend regular schools and even to excel. Because of my disability, I did not have much social interaction with other young people. It was during this time as a lonely teen-ager that I felt myself beginning to drift away from God and from the godly principles that had been so firmly instilled in me. I continued to go to church and tried to serve the Lord, but I was starting down a path that would take me far away from the presence of God.

I was about 15 years old when I began experimenting with masturbation. I knew that it was wrong. I knew it was wrong the first time I did it. Yet, it offered me something that I had never had before. With my disability, I doubted that I would ever be with a woman romantically. I turned to masturbation as a way of finding "a satisfaction" that I thought I would never get from a woman.

At first, I wasn't too worried about it. I knew that a lot of young boys tried it, and I assured myself that it was just a phase and that I would soon "grow out of it." Instead, it became an addiction that would affect my life and my relationship with God for nearly 15 years. I tried to stop many times. I prayed for deliverance on many occasions but never was able to go more than a week at time without relapsing.

For many years, masturbation was as far as I went. In all other areas of my life, I seemed to be a Christian. I was involved in my church, I prayed and read the Bible. Still, something wasn't right. The sin in my life was keeping me from growing in the Lord. I knew that God still had His hand on my life even when I wasn't living for Him. The Lord blessed me with the ability to write. I became a writer for my high school newspaper, and despite those who said I would never live on my own, I went on to college where I received a degree in journalism.

Finding a job after college was difficult. After numerous rejections from one newspaper after another, I finally saw my dream of achieving independence become a reality. I was hired as a copy editor at an area newspaper and moved into my own

Testimony

apartment. My life seemed to be on track. However, I had continued to struggle with masturbation all these years. It would get even worse before I would find my freedom. Once I was on my own, I was free to do as I wanted. No one ever knew about the secret life that I lived.

I invested in a computer for my work, which would lead me even farther down the path of destruction. While before it was only masturbation, now I became involved in pornography. I got online and began spending hours on pornographic sites.

I still believed God had a purpose for my life. I always believed that He would use me through my writing. I even began writing a book about faith and how I had used my faith to overcome the obstacles of living with a disability. The Lord granted me favor, and the book, *Through Eyes of Faith*, was published in 1998.

For two more years, however, I continued to explore pornography on the Internet. I became more and more addicted to it. My relationship with God became non-existent. I knew that God would never be able to fully use me for His service until I turned back to Him and away from masturbation and pornography. I thought I could find a way out of the sin and pornography on my own. It was only when I realized that I couldn't do it on my own that I began to see God move in my life.

Out of desperation, I prayed that God would show me a way out. I asked God to forgive me and gave "my burden" over to Him. One night while I surfing the Internet, God led me to the Setting Captives Free web site, an online study course on breaking the addiction of pornography. I immediately knew that this was my "way out." God set me completely free. Since starting the course nearly two months ago, I have seen God move in my life in a new way. The growth that had been halted by the sin in my life was now beginning again. I have truly experienced new life in Christ.

When I look back on my life, and the bad choices I made early on, I regret all the time I wasted. However, I believe it must be in God's timing and that He will somehow use this experience to encourage others. That is my prayer. I thank God for His wonderful grace.

Course Member Toby writes: Comments on Hebrews 12:1: "I knew when I started this course that if I kept any hidden books or magazines that I would simply fail to get free. So I got rid of everything. And now I am running the race set for me, unhindered by any hidden source of temptation."

Questions

4. The danger of not doing this. The matter is brought to this issue that either sin must die, or we must die. If we will lay this Delilah in our bosom, it will betray us; if we be ruled by sin, we shall inevitably be ruined by it; if we must keep our two hands, and two eyes, and two feet, we must with them be cast into hell. Our Savior often pressed our duty upon us, from the consideration of the torments of hell, which we run ourselves into if we continue in sin. With what an emphasis of terror are those words repeated three times here, Where their worm dieth not, and the fire is not quenched! The words are quoted from Isaiah 66:24. The reflections and reproaches of the sinners own conscience are the worm that dieth not; which will cleave to the damned soul as the worms do to the dead body, and prey upon it, and never leave it till it is quite devoured. Matthew Henry.[13]

Question 6. How do you respond to this reading?

Scripture to Consider

"Therefore do not be foolish, but understand what the Lord's will is. Do not get drunk on wine, which leads to debauchery. Instead, be filled with the Spirit. Speak to one another with psalms, hymns and spiritual songs. Sing and make music in your heart to the Lord, always giving thanks to God the Father for everything, in the name of our Lord Jesus Christ" (Ephesians 5:17-20).

"The thief comes only to steal and kill and destroy; I have come that they may have life, and have it to the full" (John 10:10).

"May the groans of the prisoners come before you; by the strength of your arm preserve those condemned to die" (Psalm 79:11).

Were you free from pornography since you did the last lesson?
    Yes   No

Were you free from masturbation since you did the last lesson?
    Yes   No

Were you free from sexual immorality since you did the last lesson?
    Yes   No

DAY 13— SETTING CAPTIVES FREE 1

> ³¹ To the Jews who had believed him, Jesus said, "If you hold to my teaching, you are really my disciples. ³² Then you will know the truth, and the truth will set you free." ³³ They answered him, "We are Abraham's descendants and have never been slaves of anyone. How can you say that we shall be set free?"
> ³⁴ Jesus replied, "I tell you the truth, everyone who sins is a slave to sin.
> ³⁵ Now a slave has no permanent place in the family, but a son belongs to it forever. ³⁶ So if the Son sets you free, you will be free indeed." (John 8:31-36)

This passage contains amazing truth for us who have been involved with pornography and masturbation. Let's examine it by answering some questions.

Questions

Question 1. According to verse 31 and 32, what will be the result of holding to Jesus' teachings?

Here we see a very important reason for Bible study. How can we know the truth if we do not study the teachings of Jesus? And if we do not know the truth, we will not be set free. But it is not only Bible study that is important. I studied the Bible all throughout the years that I was a captive to pornography and masturbation. Many people come to this **Pure Freedom** course knowing much Scripture because of having studied much. No, it is not just studying the Bible that frees us from sin's captivity. Jesus said, "If you *hold to* my teaching…" indicating that it is not merely studying the Scriptures but embracing them that brings freedom. Holding Jesus' teachings has to do with keeping them ever before me so that when I am tempted I recognize the lie in the temptation, and flee from it so as to not indulge in it. This is the holding on to Jesus' teaching and is the truth that sets us free.

Question 2. What did Jesus say would happen when we know the truth?

According to verses 34-36 Jesus stated that the truth sets us free from sin's slavery. Slaves are not free people, but rather they have a master and must do his bidding. I remember how a pornographic image would lodge in my brain, and I could try to pray it away, and read the Bible, but it kept after me until I would eventually give in and obey the demands to masturbate. Then I would feel bad and ask for God's forgiveness,

Testimony

The following testimony is from Kirk:

I was 11 or 12 years old when I came into my brother's room and saw a Playboy magazine laid out across his bed. I had looked at it before with friends at the grocery store, but now I had time to gaze at the pages of this magazine and many more editions to come after that day.

It started as extreme curiosity and became a thrilling encounter. My heart would beat so hard when I opened my brother's bottom drawer and saw a new one. Masturbation and pornography was so prominent in my life as long as I had access to those magazines all through high school.

My parents never knew about the magazines during those years. They had brought me up in a good 'do what's right' home, and I always had to go to my Methodist Sunday school and church when I was young and learned all about Jesus and God. I even prayed for Christ to come into my life when I was about 15 and re-prayed the sinner's prayer many times to make sure I was saved. As a young Christian, I mostly knew what was right and wrong, and felt guilty and convicted when I sinned, but why was I so into pornography? The reason is because it was too good. I couldn't believe the excitement I felt when I looked at a magazine. Oh, I was always feeling guilty about it and would pray to God to forgive me and I would keep away from it. I would feel some peace and believed I was right with God, but my brother's room was only next-door, and I would eventually give in for a quick look, which led to indulging in it.

I was a pretty shy guy in high school too, since I had always been. I did go on 3 or 4 dates, only when I could get up the nerve to ask someone out. If people only knew how I would undress every female, especially the ones who were filled out like the girls in the magazines.

I was able to express myself in sports pretty well and my baseball abilities led me to a scholarship to a division 1 college. Actually, in the first year of college, I had gone to many Bible studies with other athletes/jocks and some were serious Christians and I learned more truth about a personal relationship with Jesus and that's the way I believed. The ex-ball player who led the studies was looked upon to be too extreme, but I never denied that he knew the happiness and joy of a relationship with Christ. He encouraged me by giving me some hip Christian music and I actually began to get some peace from the Lord and was getting up early and reading a devotional and a quick prayer.

But the other guys I hung around were weak like me and we were kind of the silent Christian sinners, but at least we were Christians, right? This was college and there were women out there to be sought and I couldn't see meeting a woman as quick as I could with these guys. I made the Spring trip that year and got to go to Florida for two weeks on a charter bus. All we did from town to town was read the many porn magazines that had to be purchased by the 'rookies' as kind of an initiation. We had at least 10 different magazines going around to all the players and coaches just fueled my pornography addiction.

The next few years I "grew up" and was dating and having sex. When I would go home, I would go to my brother's room, who had moved out, but left his magazines in the same drawer. My mom knew about them by then and would just say that my brother needed to get rid of them and they shouldn't be in the house. She knew I wouldn't have any interest for them, but I did. All the time. I eventually got out of college and moved to the big city on my own as a pharmaceutical sales rep. I had one night stands from time to time and dated a couple of women for a good while, but it was all for the sex. That is all I wanted.

I had a portable VCR that I took to the doctor's offices to show nurses product videos. I remember the first time I got the nerve to go and buy an X-rated video. I felt so cheap and dirty, until I got in my car and headed home. I couldn't wait and was so excited and would go home and indulge in it. The next day I would feel like a cheap nothing, just like I always did when I read my brother's magazines.

I would turn to God and make commitment after commitment. I would get involved in a youth group at a Baptist church and had fellowship, but the need for women and the nightlife always won the battle. I could never accept the porn life style; because I knew oh so well in my heart that it was wrong, so all I did throughout my life was hate myself over it, over and over. I hated myself whenever I would do pornography and always wondered why I didn't have the strength.

I thought everything would die down during marriage, but it didn't. It didn't matter if sex was great at times or if I was in the doghouse with my wife. I needed the porn life. Going to adult video store or buying a magazine was nothing to me. It would always give me something to look forward to and then let me down by feeling so guilty and just wanting more the next day. Then, one day I joined a company that gave me a laptop computer and I was introduced to Internet porn. I couldn't believe the convenience and privacy I could have with no one knowing what I was doing. I am a salesman and can stay in my office or be on the road at my own discretion, so I had flexible time to access the Internet. Naturally, I got into porn thicker and thicker, wondering what it would be like to go to a strip club by myself or get a prostitute.

Here I was with 2 little boys and getting them up early to go to church every Sunday, and I was so involved in porn and after so many years. What was I coming to and what more could I do to get out of this? I would try porn blocker, just to uninstall them the next day. I would order satellite TV porn, just to cancel the subscription after I viewed a movie and said I would stop. I would buy a video and watch it once, then throw it away. Another $30 dollars down the drain.

Continued on page 42

but soon after I would be masturbating over a different image, over and over. This is slavery to sin. Even the therapeutic world, which is minus the gospel, recognizes this loss of free will when involved in pornography. From one report: "I found that once addicted, whether to just the pornography or the later pattern of sexual acting out, they really lost their "free agency." It was like a drug addiction. And in this case their drug was sex. They could not stop the pattern of their behavior, no matter how high-risk for them it was."

Question 3. Have you had this type of "slavery" experience?

But notice it is the truth that sets us free. You see, if we are slaves to sin we are deceived. We believe a lie. The lie may be that pornography will satisfy us, or that masturbation will relieve the stress (when we all know the stress will be back later, and to give in only makes it easier to give in the next time), or that giving in to lust will make us happier. For instance, when I was being tempted in the hotel rooms to view pornographic movies, the main lie I believed is that I would not be lonely. Here, in these movies I had people who wanted to be with me, who would love and accept me, who would make my evening go better. But was that the truth? I think we all know the answer to that.

Question 4. What are some lies you have believed in pornography, masturbation, or sexual impurity?

Now we know that part of our leaving pornography behind is to embrace truth. Examine every temptation and ask, "Is this true?" Will indulging in this sin bring the satisfaction it promises? Will it satisfy me eternally, or will it leave me with guilt and regret?

Question 5. Compare verse 32 and 36 in the lesson. What do they have in common?

Friends, Jesus Christ is the Truth that sets us free. When we embrace HIM, we know the truth, which sets us free. Jesus says in John 14:8, "I am the Way, the Truth, and the Life. No man comes

Questions

to the Father but through Me." And in Proverbs 8 Jesus Christ is portrayed as "wisdom" and is shown to be the "way" (verse 2), the "truth" (verse 7) and the "life" (verse 35).

Question 6. How does John 14:8 ("I am the Way, the Truth, and the Life. No man comes to the Father but through Me.") compare with verses 32 and 36 in today's lesson?

The above makes it clear that Jesus Christ is the Truth that sets us free! He declares: "So if the Son sets you free, you will be free indeed."

Friend, let's be clear about this. There is no program, or system, or counseling technique that can set us free from the slavery to sin. This course will not set you free apart from Christ. Only Jesus, the Truth, can release us from sin. "Salvation is found in no one else, for there is no other name under heaven given to men by which we must be saved" (Acts 4:12). And the way He sets us free is by enabling us to embrace the Truth, rather than deception and lies.

Involving ourselves in pornography is the same as believing lies, and living in a world of deception. Pornography does not satisfy, as it promises to do. It is like drinking from a stream of polluted water, which leaves one "thirstier" than before. In order to overcome this sin we must drink the living water, which quenches our thirst eternally, and we must begin to embrace the truth as it is in Jesus.

Begin to speak the truth, to forsake lies, to refuse to live in any form of deception. Drag your sin into the light, and begin to be honest in all your dealings with others. You see, it is because of our sins that we are taken captive and are made slaves. Notice the following verses from the New Living Translation: "The Lord asks, 'Did I sell you as slaves to my creditors? Is that why you are not here? Is your mother gone because I divorced her and sent her away? No, you went away as captives because of your sins. And your mother, too, was taken because of your sins'" (Jeremiah 50:1^{NLT}).

It is the main mission of the Messiah to release men and women from their chains of captivity. Jesus declares what His mission was in Luke 4:18-19: "The Spirit of the Lord is on me, because he has anointed me to preach good news to the poor. He has sent me to proclaim freedom for the prisoners and recovery of sight for the blind, to release the oppressed, to proclaim the year of the Lord's favor." He came to release us from captivity to our sins, and to bring freedom from bondage and slavery. His freedom is real. He breaks the power of sin, and releases us from the prison of sin. I testify that I have been free from pornography and masturbation for over three years, not to brag about my own strength to overcome for I have none, but rather to glorify Jesus who came to earth for this very purpose.

Testimony

Kirk's testimony continues...

Finally, I went to a search engine and instead of typing some porn star's name, I typed in "pornography addiction". There I saw the SettingCaptivesFree.com site and went there. Here was a course I could take for 60 days to be free from pornography. I wanted to try it and it was a Christian site. I desired so much to get out of this crap.

After the first couple of days, I felt like maybe there was a chance that I would make it, but once I fell I didn't know it was worth continuing the course, but my email accountable friend encouraged me and showed me truth from God's Word that I had never really applied to my life. So many references are in the Bible relating to sexual immorality or sexual sin. God knows how luring it can be. I learned that asking for forgiveness is only one part of repentance. The other part is turning away from my sin and this is the part I struggled with.

I had been around this stuff so much in my life and I wanted to dabble in it, but I could not experience any freedom and God's power until I truly ran from it and literally threw it completely out of my life. I struggled and fell a few times until I finally got all sources out of my life at about day 40. It was then that I began feeling freed from it and knew that Jesus does love me and wants me to experience victory over sin.

The thing I really learned through all of this is how much God wants our attention and wants us to please him. Everything will be all right if we just put our attention on him. I am experiencing the peace and contentment that overcomes the desire for pornography. Don't get me wrong. I still get tempted and am still a sexual being, but this is now only for my wife. Also, I have, and need the encouragement from a Christian friend to make it through, which I didn't have before. I've exposed the darkness of this terrible sin to my wife and she has helped me eliminate all sources and made me accountable.

God is real in my life now and he has given me more assurance each day as I grow with him. I now believe I am truly on the right track, and through daily prayer, devotion, and humble communion with Jesus, I know my God will prevail over sin. May all glory be to God. Amen.

Questions

Question 7. Please provide your thoughts on the following verses.

Jeremiah 29:12-14: "Then you will call upon me and come and pray to me, and I will listen to you. ¹³ You will seek me and find me when you seek me with all your heart. ¹⁴ I will be found by you," declares the LORD, "and will bring you back from captivity."

Isaiah 48:20: "Yet even now, be free from your captivity! Leave Babylon and the Babylonians, singing as you go! Shout to the ends of the earth that the Lord has redeemed his servants, the people of Israel."(NLT)

Ezekiel 39:25: "So now the Sovereign Lord says: I will end the captivity of my people; I will have mercy on Israel, for I am jealous for my holy reputation!" (NLT)

So, to summarize: Pornography, indeed all sin, makes us slaves. It deceives us so that as we partake of it we believe a lie. But Jesus came to break the power of sin, to release us from slavery to sin, to set the captives free! This is why Jesus came to earth.

Question 8. Finally, it is reflection time. Where are you with the above teaching? Is Jesus releasing you from sin's captivity? Do you see how you've believed lies while in pornography, and are you seeking to embrace truth now?

Friends, I can recall my captivity very clearly even today, three years later. If my "master" Lust told me to go and view pornography, I would have to obey. If he told me to get involved with sin on the Internet, then I followed his orders. I was a slave to my lusts, and captive to evil desires. But now Jesus Christ has freed me, by causing me to embrace the truth. And freedom is very precious to me, and I never want to return to my slavery again. Jesus made me His prisoner now: "But thanks be to God, who made us his captives and leads us along in Christ's triumphal procession. Now wherever we go he uses us to tell others about the Lord and to spread the Good News like a sweet perfume. Our lives are a fragrance presented by Christ to God" (2 Corinthians 2:14ᴺᴸᵀ). And when God makes us captives of Christ we also become prisoners of hope: "Come back to the place of safety, all you prisoners of hope, for there is yet hope!" (Zecharaiah 9:12ᴺᴸᵀ) So let us be clear, that with Jesus Christ freedom is not only possible, it is inevitable. We must beg Christ to do His work in our hearts, for when He does we will be free. No more slavery to sin, no more giving in just because the impulse comes to do so, no more masturbating five and ten times a day and reliving the guilt and stress each time. Freedom from habitual sin is real. My prayer is that you will experience and enjoy it!

Scripture to Consider

"¹ When the LORD brought back the captives to Zion, we were like men who dreamed. ² Our mouths were filled with laughter, our tongues with songs of joy. Then it was said among the nations, "The LORD has done great things for them." ³ The LORD has done great things for us, and we are filled with joy" (Psalm 126:1-3).

"The Spirit of the Sovereign Lord is upon me, because the Lord has appointed me to bring good news to the poor. He has sent me to comfort the brokenhearted and to announce that captives will be released and prisoners will be freed" (Isaiah. 61:1ᴺᴸᵀ).

"God, the Lord, created the heavens and stretched them out. He created the earth and everything in it. He gives breath and life to everyone in all the world. And it is he who says, ⁶ 'I, the Lord, have called you to demonstrate my righteousness. I will guard and support you, for I have given you to my people as the personal confirmation of my covenant with them. And you will be a light to guide all nations to me. ⁷ You will open the eyes of the blind and free the captives from prison. You will release those who sit in dark dungeons'" (Isaiah. 42:5-7ᴺᴸᵀ).

Were you free from pornography since you did the last lesson?
    Yes No

Were you free from masturbation since you did the last lesson?
    Yes No

Were you free from sexual immorality since you did the last lesson?
    Yes No

DAY 14—
SETTING CAPTIVES FREE 2

Precisely how does salvation work? Who is it for? What does it look like in the every day life of someone who was once in bondage to pornography?

These are the questions we will seek to answer today. And there will be much encouragement from the Scriptures as we dig into God's Word.

We are about to embark on a fascinating study! You will discover that God had a purpose in your addiction. Read through the following verses and answer the questions below.

> "vs. 10—Some sat in darkness and the deepest gloom, prisoners suffering in iron chains, vs. 11—for they had rebelled against the words of God and despised the counsel of the Most High. vs. 12—So He subjected them to bitter labor; they stumbled, and there was no one to help. vs. 13—Then they cried to the Lord in their trouble, and He saved them from their distress. vs. 14—He brought them out of darkness and the deepest gloom and broke away their chains. vs. 15—Let them give thanks to the Lord for his unfailing love and his wonderful deeds for men, vs. 16—for he breaks down gates of bronze and cuts through bars of iron" (Psalm 107: 10-16).

Today, let us do a verse-by-verse study, and notice together the spiritual condition of the above people, and also let us note the reason why things were so bad for them.

> "vs. 10—Some sat in darkness and the deepest gloom, prisoners suffering in iron chains,"

Question 1. As you read through the previous description of someone enslaved to sin, which number(s) described your past porn prison the most?

And now, let us notice the reason why these people were in such bad shape:

> vs. 11—for they had rebelled against the words of God and despised the counsel of the Most High.

And look what God did next:

> vs. 12—So He subjected them to bitter labor; they stumbled, and there was no one to help.

Notice the three things that happened to these people because of their rebellion:

1. God subjected them to bitter labor. Were your pornography habits ever "bitter labor" to you? Mine sure were. The words "bitter labor" are the same words used in Exodus 1 referring to the slavery of the Israelites. Pornography can reduce us to "slave labor."
2. They stumbled. Friends, please do not miss this: pornography will be your downfall if you do not totally forsake it. They stumbled and fell. So did I.
3. There was no one to help them up. You probably know this already, but it is possible to go so far into pornography that nobody can help you.

Question 2. Are you identifying with all this? Have you ever felt that you were in this very predicament? Explain please:

Testimony

The following testimony is from Julie:

I had the wonderful privilege of being born into a home where God was loved, served, and obeyed. I can say with Timothy that from a child I was taught the Holy Scriptures, which were able to make me wise unto salvation. I was always the good little girl that did the expected thing. I was never outwardly rebellious and conformed to what I was taught. I made a profession of faith at the age of 16. At 18, I married a young seminary student. In time, God blessed us with 8 children.

To the onlooker, I had the model life. It was not perfect, but it was good. I was a devoted wife and mother and was looked up to as a godly woman in the church. I was very religious in my thinking and as I said before, very well taught in the Scriptures. Now that I look back on it, there were always struggles with my thought life. I would go through periods of time that my thought life was very ungodly, but outwardly my life appeared the same; faithful day in and day out. I am amazed now that I didn't realize that there was a serious problem and that I should have seen it coming.

This verse states 5 things about these people. They were:

1. in darkness
2. in deepest gloom
3. prisoners
4. suffering
5. in iron chains

There may not be a better description of the spiritual condition of a pornography addict in all of Scripture. Note:

#1—They are in darkness. It is spiritually pitch black in the life of a porn addict. His (or her) lusts are continually stirred up by visual images that have been burned into his mind; his mind is dark because of the sin that dominates him; he lacks genuine spiritual light, which is wisdom and understanding. Life is dark for the porn addict.

#2—They are in deepest gloom. Oh, not at the beginning, or the middle when the excitement of a new image floods their hearts and minds, but as the addiction continues the gloom increases. And this is not just "ordinary" gloom, this is "deepest gloom,"—spiritual gloom, dread, fear, pessimism, hopelessness.

#3—They are prisoners. They are captivated to the "rush" of pornography, imprisoned by the next impulse to look at porn, which they are unable to fight off. They are not free to simply choose to stop, or "just say no" anymore than a prisoner is free to leave his prison any time he wants.

#4—They are suffering. Pornography causes suffering. Examine the end of anyone who has been addicted to pornography, and you will see suffering in their lives. I personally suffer for my years of involvement with pornography.

#5—They are in iron chains. This is a reference to the strength of the sinful habit patterns. Pornography is an "iron chain" addiction—too strong for man to break.

Questions

Course Member Patrick writes: "This Psalm's description is right on target. I rebelled against God, and my reward was bitter addiction to the next image, the next sensuous picture or imagination; it would pull me in when I didn't want it to... I would ignore my family for my lust; I would go even out in cold bitter rain to satisfy my wicked desires. Then I would suffer horrible guilt and shame and feel so trapped, so alone."

Concentrate for just a moment on the words from verse 12, "And there was no one to help them up." This is the condition to which God takes all whom he will eventually save. He brings them to the point that they must cast themselves totally on His mercy. They cannot help themselves. Nobody else can help them. They are helpless and hopeless. And yet, what is impossible with man is possible with God!

"If the Son sets you free, you will be free indeed!" (John 8:36)

vs. 13—"Then they cried to the Lord in their trouble, and He saved them from their distress. vs. 14—He brought them out of darkness and the deepest gloom and broke away their chains. vs. 15—Let them give thanks to the Lord for His unfailing love and His wonderful deeds for men, vs. 16—for He breaks down the gates of bronze and cuts through bars of iron" (Psalm 107:13-16).

Oh, dear friend, here is a prescription for freedom from pornography. Cry to the Lord. But you say, "I HAVE called to Him and I'm still falling." Keep crying out to Him! Have you ever noticed that when the Israelites first began calling to the Lord for help that their slavery increased?

God eventually delivered the Israelites by the blood of the lamb, and He can deliver you, too. It is the godless that won't cry to God, and keep crying until He answers: "The godless in heart harbor resentment; even when he fetters them, they do not cry for help" (Job 36:13).

Be like Jacob and wrestle with God in prayer until He blesses you with salvation from pornographic sin. God purposely takes us to the place where we cannot help ourselves, and there is no one else to help us. In fact, in this same chapter that we are studying (Psalm 107) it says that certain people were "at their wits' end (vs. 27)." They were at the end of their rope. But they cried to the Lord. And He saved them! Friends, when you are at the end of your rope, you are at

Testimony

Sometime in the year of 1998 the computer entered our home. I didn't even want one. At first I was scared to use it, but then decided it would be fun to communicate with family via email. My children had to show me how to do it. Then a family member told us about ICQ. I started chatting with family members and then soon discovered that I could chat with people from around the world. That appealed to my curious side, and I was very interested in learning about and getting acquainted with other people. I realize now that I had a great curiosity about the world out there from which I had always been so sheltered. I started chatting with men.

Looking back now I see how naïve I really was. But before long, I was being drawn into another world, and I was enjoying it. I ended up having several online "friendships" with men. I "met" a man from Europe. We developed an intense relationship that involved daily chats and emails. We soon professed our "love" for one another and were making plans to be together. My sin was taking a great toll on me physically, spiritually, and mentally. I chose to believe so many lies and was so hardened in my sin,

Continued on page 46

the beginning of hope. Real hope. Call, call, call, and keep calling. He will answer, in His time.

Question 3. From verses 13-16 above, notice the 5 things that God does in response to people crying out to Him. Please write all five here.

The above verses tell us that when God saves someone He destroys the work of the devil in their lives. He frees from the grip of the devil, removes oppression (though not temptation), rescues from slavery to sin and sets us free. We must ever pray for ongoing help and be on guard against backsliding, but the work of salvation is a thorough and ongoing deliverance from sin.

So, to answer the questions we asked at the beginning of Day 14:

#1—How does salvation work? People rebel against God, God hands them over to slavery, they come to the end of their rope and nobody helps them, they cry to the Lord, He saves them.

#2—Who is it for? Salvation is for those who have rebelled, those who have gone against the teaching of God's Word, those who have been in prison to sin.

#3—What does it look like in the every day life of someone who was once addicted to pornography? We come to know that we are powerless to stop using pornography. We see very clearly that we are enslaved and imprisoned by it. We hear that salvation is available through the cross and we begin to cry out. Oftentimes, God waits until we are truly repentant. He alone knows when we are ready for deliverance. We cry more, and louder. God hears, rescues, redeems, and saves. We are no longer in bondage to pornography. The Son of God has set us free, and we are free indeed.

Question 4. Honesty time. Where are you in the above scenario? Enslaved? In prison? Calling? Or free indeed?

Course Member Teresa writes: "I could/can relate to every verse in this Psalm! I was bound with iron, sitting in a pit that I had dug with my own 2 hands. I couldn't eat (their soul abhors all manner of meat). I've been told that I had a "dead" look in my eyes during that time (they draw near unto the gates of death). It all came because I rebelled against the words of God. The way of the transgressor is hard. I fell down and there was no one to help. I didn't even want help! He has shown me once again that He alone satisfies the longing soul. Anything else is only temporary satisfaction with a heavy price to pay in the end. The cup of sin tastes sweet, but at the end are bitter dregs. But, praise God, he sends deliverance to the captives and saves those that call out to Him in their distress. That makes me want to fall on my face before Him in humble adoration! What a merciful, great, and awesome God He is!"

Julie's testimony continues ...

that I actually had myself convinced that I had never really belonged in the world that I had grown up in and was purely a product of my environment. My husband ended up finding us out; I fled the home at that point, because I knew that if I stayed, I would be forced to give up my sinful activity.

I didn't go far and ended up going back home within a few days. We received some biblical counseling and made great efforts to put our lives back together. God was certainly merciful to me even then.

In June of 1999 my husband was called to pastor another church, and we moved our family 1000 miles away from where I had lived most of my life. A whole new life-just what I needed!

After home schooling for 12 years, the church we were now in had a school, so I was no longer home educating our children. Due to a busier church life, my husband's time was more taken up with his work. I had longer periods of time home alone with just my two youngest children. Little did I know that I was about to go through the deepest waters of my life. I decided that it would be okay to chat with just "Christian" men. I met a man that even held to the same doctrines that I had grown up with and there was an immediate connection. I won't get into details, but that was really the beginning of the end for me.

It went from bad to worse, and I ended up delving into sin that I would never have dreamed that I would have become involved in. I sank to the depths. All the while I was trying to maintain my status as a well-respected pastor's wife. I remember leading the ladies of our church through a study on "The Excellent Wife" (Martha Peace, Focus Publishing) while indulging myself in sin. I was having major inner turmoil and struggle. Obviously so! I would go through periods of time that I would try to reform. I would gain a new resolve to stop, but soon would fall again. I would confess parts of my sin to my husband, but not nearly all of it. I always would make a provision so that I could go back to my sin. You see, way down at the root, I was still in love with it and had never really broken with it in my heart.

In June of 2000 after so many struggles, I heard a couple of sermons about bearing fruit that struck me. I realized that I had been trying to tape another man's fruit on my dead tree and that is why I had never had any real victory! It was like an eye-opener to me! At first I felt such peace! That explained everything! I wasn't saved at all. I shared my discovery with my husband. I confessed to our church that I wasn't saved and was removed from the membership.

Upon that profession of my lost state, my life took a nosedive. I started to indulge myself in my sin with no restraint, except my husband, friends, and family getting in my way. My marriage was disintegrating. I did everything that I could to destroy it. I couldn't stand to be in the same room with the man that had been my faithful husband for 20 years.

I was very unfaithful to my husband and left him once again. I had met a man on the Internet. We were planning out a life together. I had myself convinced that I had been in a very oppressive, cultic-type religious environment, in which I didn't belong. I believed that I owed it to my children to give them another option rather than the one that they were having "forced" upon them. As I write this now, I am amazed at the deceitful and hardening nature of sin. I was completely sucked in and my life was in the self-destruct mode. Little did I know that God was about to stop me in my tracks and draw me to Himself!

I will just say that when I got to my destination, the thought hit me that I was in a horrible pit, and that if I did not get out right then and there, that I would die. I ended up walking the streets of a strange city at night all alone with nowhere to go. Me, the respected pastor's wife! I remember walking alone on those sidewalks and it was as if God spoke to my heart and He said, "I still have not left you alone!" That hit me like a ton of bricks. I managed to walk to a motel room. I made contact with my husband, and after talking with me, he started to make arrangements to bring me home.

But I still had all night alone in that motel room. I had hit the absolute bottom of the pit. I cried out to God to grant me true repentance and faith. I told Him that I knew that He would be completely just if He were to cast me into hell, and if He chose to do that, so be it, but I would go there clinging to Him, because I had nowhere else to go.

As I returned home, I still was unsure of what God was going to do with me. I told my husband that even if he chose to divorce me and I lost him and the children and everything that I had, that I must have Christ. I had to have Christ! It was at that point that I came to the end of myself and saw Christ as my only hope that He broke the chains of sin and death and set me free. I am no longer the same. The sin that so long had enslaved me no longer has its death grip on me. I am free! I believe now that I had never died to myself and experienced new life in Christ. I had never experienced the power of sin being broken in my life. Praise God, I now know and have experienced what that really means!

The remembrances and consequences of my sin continue to bring much pain at times. When I look at what I have done, it is cause for despair. But then I am led to joy and rejoicing when I reflect on how God has redeemed my life from destruction, turned my mourning into dancing, and put a new song in my mouth.

There are two practical essentials that I have learned are a necessity to put into practice when dealing with these habitual sexual sins:
1) Radical amputation. Before I always made some provision for my sin, and I always went back to it. I have learned that we must be ruthless in cutting away the sources of our sin, burning our bridges behind us.
2) Accountability. I have realized the necessity of telling all to my husband and having him hold me accountable.

By the grace of God, my family has been restored. I am now able to walk in true spiritual union with my husband and able to serve God with him here. That is bringing me much joy. I am able to be the kind of mother that God intends for me to be. But more than that, I am enjoying new life in Christ, and all of those truths that I was taught from a child have sprung forth in my heart, taken root and budded. God is able to restore all that sin has stolen. He is able to break the power of sin and free us from its grip forever. Only Christ can fill the deepest longings of the soul. He can and He does!

Course Member Dick writes: "Where are you in Psalm 107? Enslaved? In prison? Calling? Or free indeed?" Regarding pornography- calling and free. I really believe God has given me insight and freedom in this. I think it is of the utmost importance to build an accountability relationship with someone- I know I can't do this on my own. Regarding the sin attitudes of my heart- pride, not being completely doors wide open consistently with God- a struggle. Calling from prison, I know of His deliverance. I believe He has shown me mercy. In a way I could care less about the pornography issue- but what a special thing to just know Him, and to receive from Him—to be filled, and remain in Him, to have Him in all His fullness in all areas of my heart. Mostly the ones of hurt or emptiness or discouragement, to truly know and experience and receive His forgiveness and completeness in full measure- to remain there."

Question 5. How are you doing today?

Course Member Philip writes: "I always knew that there was help, if I only could drop my pride and be accountable to a brother. So, I continued suffering from the remorse of masturbation until I found this website that finally gave me a good kick in the rear to confess to someone. That was all that I needed, and I always knew that God would help me, but only under the condition of letting go my pride in this area."

Scripture to Consider

"For there is no distinction between Jew and Greek, for the same Lord over all is rich to all who call upon Him. For "whoever calls on the name of the LORD shall be saved." (Romans 10:12-13 NKJV)

Were you free from pornography since you did the last lesson?
    Yes No
Were you free from masturbation since you did the last lesson?
    Yes No
Were you free from sexual immorality since you did the last lesson?
    Yes No

Question 1. How is being addicted to pornography like being a slave? Write your answer here:

Course member Daryl writes:
"Addiction to pornography takes away all your personal rights and freedoms. You feel like someone else owns you. In this state you come to understand that they will use you whenever they want, and they do not care if you are tired, hurt, injured, or just can't go on. Each day after being beat up by those who own you-you go back to your slave hut and try to lick your wounds like an animal would lick a cut on it's paw. Each and every step is painful, and the worst is that you know you will not have time to heal, before being dragged out and forced to dig in and re-injure yourself again and again. It breaks your spirit; it makes you bitter, it makes you angry, it makes you want to lash out at those around you-even those who are trying to help you with your wounds. You do not want anyone to come near you. In fact, there is a certain satisfaction of being more comfortable in your misery than you are of venturing into the new world of freedom."

Course member Riley writes: "Once subdued, it pushes you more and more to isolate yourself from anything that might free you or conflict with it's power over you. It lets you live only enough to barely survive and have the strength to serve it eventually, at the same time putting you through whatever it takes to numb your brain to it's cruel control."

Question 2. Have you, yourself, gotten to the "slavery" part of pornography yet?

Question 3. When the Israelites were slaves, what did they do to get help?

DAY 15— SETTING CAPTIVES FREE 3

In the Book of Exodus in the Bible, God's people were in slavery to the Egyptians. They had been in slavery for 400 years, and theirs was a very hard and bitter slavery. The Egyptians were "ruthless," and "harsh" taskmasters. Notice the wording in Exodus 1:11-14:

> "So they put slave masters over them to oppress them with forced labor...and worked them ruthlessly. They made their lives bitter with hard labor in brick, and mortar and with all kinds of work in the fields; in all their hard labor the Egyptians used them ruthlessly."

Friend, this is a picture of our condition in the grips of pornography and sexual impurity. We become "slaves" to that all-exciting image on the TV or the computer. Romans 6:20 illustrates this truth: "When you were slaves to sin, you were free from the control of righteousness." Pornography made me a slave. If I had a thought that told me to watch a pornographic movie when I got to the hotel I would obey it and watch. If my heart told me to do some "romantic" chatting on the Internet, or my body craved visual stimulation from pornography, I obeyed. My impulses controlled my actions for years. I was a slave. My master was pornography. And it was a harsh master. Can you relate?

But the Israelites began to cry out to God in their slavery. Oh friend, God will not turn a deaf ear to "Help me, Oh God. Please. I beg you." And so He said to His people, "I have indeed seen the misery of my people in Egypt. I have heard them crying out because of their slave drivers, and I am concerned about their suffering. So I have come down to rescue them from the hand of the Egyptians and to bring them up out of that land into a good and spacious land..." (Exodus 3:7-8)

God "came down" to "bring them up." Dear friend, God never changes. The cross of Jesus Christ, where He died, was God "coming down" to "bring us up." He is now coming down to you...in the midst of your slavery. He has seen your misery, He's heard your cries for help, and He's concerned about your suffering. His purpose in coming to you is to "rescue" you and "bring you up." Do you see that? In a little while we will see how He does that, and that will be an exciting discovery. But for now, please answer the following questions.

Question 4. Did God hear their cry for help?

Question 5. Read the above verses. What words does the Bible use to describe how God felt about His people while they were in slavery?

Question 6. How has pornography enslaved you in the past?

Testimony

The following testimony is from Kris:

As humans, it is our propensity to compare ourselves to others. I was never that bad, or I could never be that good. Thankfully God does not use a sliding scale to determine our worth. Over many years, I have struggled with the fight over pornography.

My first exposure was in a mall with my brother and his best friend. In one of the bookstores, the friend pulled down a Playboy and showed me the centerfold. I was not even a teen-ager yet. While I was not sexually excited by what I saw, I was very curious and interested, but I knew it was wrong and so acted like I didn't want to see it. A few years later, I was house sitting for a neighbor while they were out of town. In the process of bringing in the mail, I was again exposed to the same magazine, but this time, I could peruse it without anyone seeing me. I would not be exposed to porn again until I was in my 4th year of college.

Meanwhile, as a sophomore in college, I heard a friend talk about how he was getting victory over masturbation, and since I had honestly never done it to that point, I was curious how he could be entrapped and so tried it myself. (Looking back, that sounds stupid, and it was.) Soon I was masturbating several times a week. I didn't think it was all that wrong, after all I wasn't viewing porn, I was only responding physically to the thoughts that "God had placed in my mind". It was not God that placed them there.

When a couple of years later I was re-exposed to porn, I still acted like I disdained what my co-workers were doing, but then would secretly view the porn when they were not around, but now there was the additional addictive component of masturbation. During this whole time, I thought myself better than others because I had not lost my virginity (I still count this as a gift from God, but no longer a source of pride.) What I didn't realize is that I was going further into the trap of porn. I never once bought a movie, and only once bought a magazine, because others too easily saw those. I was instead getting it from the Internet where I could get it free and anonymously. I was no longer just viewing women, but I was now viewing couples (hetero and lesbian) and being titillated by the interaction I was seeing. I am sure that if God had allowed me to continue, I would have turned to physical expression with others to try some of what I was seeing.

Many times I tried to quit and not view porn again. Although my going cold turkey was the only approach, it only works when you have the right support from God and others. It was only when I began (through the **Pure Freedom** course) to study scripture with the intent of finding escape that I was set free from the chains that the enemy kept using to pull me back to porn.

It has now been over 60 days that I have been porn free. Some of those times have had stronger temptations than others, but I am glad to say that God has rescued me from temptation. I am learning more every day about how to fight by running away. I know that God has rescued me from a pit that I could never climb out of by myself, and am grateful for that. I know that He is willing to rescue you as well. In fact the rope is there for you to climb out, but until you grasp hold of it, you will continue to slip further into the trap you have chosen for yourself. If you are in porn, it is an addiction, but it is also SIN. You (like I) chose to allow yourself into it; you must now choose to let God help you out. Please make this change today!

Questions

Now for the life-changing part of this Biblical story! The Israelites cried out to God and He came down to rescue the slaves. First He sent a bunch of plagues (frogs, hail, locusts...etc.) on the Egyptians to display His power. Finally, because Pharaoh's heart was hard and he would not let God's people go, God sent word that He would destroy the firstborn son of every Egyptian household. But, in order to protect His own people, He instructed them to kill a lamb and put it's blood on the doorposts, and when the destroying Angel "saw the blood" he would "pass over" that house and not destroy the firstborn.

Dear friend, the Bible says that Jesus Christ is our "Passover Lamb" (1 Corinthians 5:7). He was sacrificed on the cross, 2000 years ago, and His blood protects us from death. Oh friend, ask that God would place the blood of His Son Jesus on the doorposts of your heart. LOVE the blood of Jesus, as your only protecting agent to save you from death. He died so we can live!

But now watch this! Not only were the Israelites told to put the blood of the lamb on their doorposts, they were also instructed to eat the lamb. And here are some of the most instructive words in Scripture: "This is how you are to eat it: with your cloak tucked into your belt, your sandals on your feet and your staff in your hand. Eat it in haste; it is the Lord's Passover" (Exodus 12:11).

Question 7. Consider this for a moment, and please record your thoughts on why they were to eat the Passover Lamb with their cloaks tucked into their belts, their sandals on their feet, and their staffs in their hands. Write your thoughts here:

The Israelites were to eat the lamb with their cloak tucked in, their sandals on, and their staff in their hands. In other words they were to be ready to go. God was saying to them: "Be ready to go, because as soon as you eat the lamb you will leave Egypt." Please don't miss this teaching for here is real and lasting help for us: The Israelites literally ate their way out of slavery! And so can we! This is the message that is taught to us today: When we feed on the Passover Lamb we will leave slavery.

Questions

So, how do I "eat my way out of slavery?" Answer: Feed on the Word of God! Let's talk about that, and then we will have some questions for you.

The way that you and I, today, "eat the Lamb," is to take Scripture and chew on it. We take a small passage and eat it up, so to speak. Eating involves taking some food in to nourish us, and that is what Jesus Christ is: Food for the soul! Jesus Christ came not only to die for our sins, and give us eternal life by His death, but He also came to be eaten, and to provide nourishment for our hungry souls. Now, let's get to some questions.

Question 8. How is meditating through a passage of Scripture like "eating the Lamb?"

A. Both are nourishing
B. Both provide freedom
C. Both give life
D. All of the above

There is a way out of slavery to pornography! It is through feeding on Jesus Christ. As we become full of Him, through meditating on the Bible, we will discover our freedom. Freedom follows fullness.

Now, to be very practical with this teaching, we're going to ask you to "feed" on the following Scriptures. Write down your thoughts that you get from thinking through these Scriptures. And as you "feed" and get "full" you will leave the Egypt of pornography and sexual impurity behind. Always remember that sexual purity and freedom from pornography is a by-product of "feeding" on Jesus Christ through thinking on, meditating in, and acting on Scripture. We can't "try" our hardest not to do pornography and be successful; we will always fail. But we can "eat" our way out of slavery. Now, come do what Paul told Timothy to do: "Reflect on these things, and the Lord will give you insight" (2 Timothy 2:7).

Psalm 1:2, 3: "His delight is in the law of the Lord, and on His law He meditates day and night. He is like a tree planted by streams of water, which yields its fruit in season and whose leaf does not wither."

Deuteronomy 8:3: "Man does not live by bread alone, but by every word that comes from the mouth of God."

John 6:48-51: "I am the bread of life. Your forefathers ate the manna in the desert, yet they died. But here is the bread that comes down from heaven, which a man may eat and not die. I am the living bread that came down from heaven. If anyone eats of this bread, he will live forever. This bread is my flesh, which I will give for the life of the world."

Jeremiah 15:16: "When your words came, I ate them. They were my joy and my heart's delight."

John 17:17: "Sanctify them (set them apart from sin) by the truth: your Word is truth!"

Joshua 1:8: "Do not let this book of the Law depart from your mouth. Meditate on it day and night, so that you may be careful to do everything written in it. Then you will be prosperous and successful."

Question 9. Have you learned something today? Does this teaching give you hope? How will you implement the teaching in your own life?

Course Member Michel writes: "I have never seen how this passage applies to me before, and I have never understood why the Israelites had to eat the lamb all prepared to go. Now it makes perfect sense. The light dawned on me today, while reading this lesson, and I believe I will be free from pornography from now on, as before I had tried to leave slavery without being full of Christ. Now I get it! Now I see! Eat and leave, eat and leave."

Scripture to Consider

"Captives also enjoy their ease; they no longer hear the slave driver's shout. The small and the great are there, and the slave is freed from his master" (Job 3:18-19).

"When the LORD brought back the captives to Zion, we were like men who dreamed. Our mouths were filled with laughter, our tongues with songs of joy. Then it was said among the nations, 'The LORD has done great things for them.' The LORD has done great things for us, and we are filled with joy" (Psalm 126:1-3).

Were you free from pornography since you did the last lesson?
    Yes   No

Were you free from masturbation since you did the last lesson?
    Yes   No

Were you free from sexual immorality since you did the last lesson?
    Yes   No

DAY 16—TEMPTATION

Today we will study the subject of temptation. We want to discover the nature of temptation as well as how to combat it. Please read the following passage.

> "Jesus, full of the Holy Spirit, returned from the Jordan and was led by the Spirit in the desert, ² where for forty days he was tempted by the devil. He ate nothing during those days, and at the end of them he was hungry. ³ The devil said to him, "If you are the Son of God, tell this stone to become bread." ⁴ Jesus answered, "It is written: 'Man does not live on bread alone.'" ⁵ The devil led him up to a high place and showed him in an instant all the kingdoms of the world. ⁶ And he said to him, "I will give you all their authority and splendor, for it has been given to me, and I can give it to anyone I want to. ⁷ So if you worship me, it will all be yours." ⁸ Jesus answered, "It is written: 'Worship the Lord your God and serve him only.'" ⁹ The devil led him to Jerusalem and had him stand on the highest point of the temple. "If you are the Son of God," he said, "throw yourself down from here. ¹⁰ For it is written: "'He will command his angels concerning you to guard you carefully; ¹¹ they will lift you up in their hands, so that you will not strike your foot against a stone.'" ¹² Jesus answered, "It says: 'Do not put the Lord your God to the test.'" ¹³ When the devil had finished all this tempting, he left him until an opportune time" (Luke 4:1-13).

The parallel passage in Matthew 4 records that this temptation of Jesus happened directly after he was baptized in the Jordan, where Heaven was opened to Him and the Holy Spirit descended upon Him. He received the approval of His Father in heaven who said, "This is my beloved Son in Whom I am well pleased." So the first thing we can learn about temptation is that it often happens directly after a high spiritual experience.

I have a friend who preaches weekly and he says that Sunday afternoon is usually a difficult time for him. Remember Paul who, after He experienced wonderful revelations from God, was given a "thorn in the flesh," a messenger of Satan for his humbling?

Questions

Question 1. If you are a Christian, have you been tempted after a special time of closeness with God, or after a high spiritual experience at a retreat, conference, church meeting…etc.?

Next, let us notice that this temptation took place during a time of physical weakness. It says Jesus did not eat during those 40 days and there must have been a huge physical strain on Jesus' body. Temptations often transpire during a time of physical sickness, or when the body is in a weak state or when hungry or tired.

Question 2. Have you had an experience where you were hit with temptations during a time of physical weakness?

Then let us note Jesus was alone when tempted. He was not hit with these fierce onslaughts while in company with His disciples, but only as He was alone in the desert.

Question 3. Have you ever noticed that you can be with people all day long and be fine, but when you get alone you are beset by intense temptation?

Scripture warns us to expect it, and helps to remove our isolation when we are admonished: "Be self-controlled and alert. Your enemy the devil prowls around like a roaring lion looking for someone to devour. ⁹ Resist him, standing firm in the faith, because you know that your brothers throughout the world are undergoing the same kind of sufferings" (1 Peter 5:8-9).

Question 4. What "alone time" is a temptation for you? Explain it here:

Testimony

The following testimony is from Wood:

When I was a kid, 11 or 12 perhaps, I first remember being stimulated by a scantily clad woman in the local TV guide. I had the same reaction to TV shows. Over the next couple of years, some friends always had Playboy magazines. Of course, I had the same reaction to the pictures, but I didn't have a wild desire to go out and buy some magazines.

I don't know how much later it was that I tried masturbation. It could have been a couple of years. Honestly, I remember almost nothing about how it got started. Before long, I was doing masturbation on a regular basis. I sometimes used pictures in magazines (not porn), or ordinary catalog lingerie pictures to be stimulated. Often times, I could be stimulated just by memories of the pictures or real girls that I had seen. (I suppose that I have a pretty active imagination, and that got me even more addicted later on).

I guess that even in my unsaved condition, I knew that it (porn/masturbation) wasn't right, but had no idea how to deal with it or stop. There were times that I wanted to die because of this problem, but had no idea how to express it. In the end, I simply chose not to think about it.

Continued on page 52

Next, let us notice the design of the temptations. The design of the temptations was to get Jesus to sin against God, and to disqualify Him for being the ultimate Sacrifice for the sins of others. All through this temptation Satan attempts to get Jesus to bypass the cross, by which He would save all believing mankind. Satan knew that if He could get Jesus to short-circuit the cross that all mankind would be lost, and must suffer in eternal hell to pay the price for their sins.

Questions

Let us learn this lesson well, for every temptation for us is designed by the enemy of our souls to cause us to disobey God, and to bypass our own cross. Satan's design is for us to give in and disobey rather than to resist and offer our bodies a living sacrifice; to indulge our flesh, rather than crucify it.

Next, let us note another design by Satan in tempting us. He wants us to doubt our relationship with God, and to become independent of Him in meeting our own needs.

Notice the first temptation: ³The devil said to him, "If you are the Son of God, tell this stone to become bread." ⁴ Jesus answered, "It is written: 'Man does not live on bread alone.'" The devil said, "IF You are the Son of God." See how he attempts to cast doubt upon Jesus' identity and relationship with His Father? Notice again, that the devil said, "Tell these stones to become bread." He did not say, "Pray to your Father in heaven and ask for bread," but rather "take matters into your own hands and provide for your own needs." The devil hates anything requiring humility and dependence upon God, and loves to tell us of our own self-sufficiency. The great thing that Satan aims at in tempting a Christian is to overthrow their relation to God as a Father, so as to cut off their dependence on Him.

To apply this teaching, you and I have needs of intimacy, and God promises to supply our every need. Will you believe Him and wait for Him to meet your need? Or will you believe the lies of the devil who says that viewing pornography will meet your need for intimacy?

Question 5. If you are a Christian, do you see how the devil can use pornography to get you to break your relationship from God and to declare your independence from God? Please explain here:

Next, notice how the temptation was resisted and overcome:
1. Christ refused to comply with it. In this one aspect, the teaching of the world to "just say no" is correct, but it falls short because it does not teach the next point, which is:
2. He was ready to reply to it. He quoted from Scripture, saying, "It is written." Isn't it amazing that Christ answered and baffled all the temptations of Satan with "It is written." Not only was He the Living Word of God, but also God's Word lived in Him and He was strong and overcame the evil one by the Word of God.

Question 6. How does the following verse compare with our subject of study today?

"I write to you, young men, because you are strong, and the word of God lives in you, and you have overcome the evil one" (1 John 2:14).

Friend, it is not so much our knowing Scripture that gives us the victory, it is the Word of God living in us that enables us to "overcome the evil one." We see many people come to this course who have much knowledge of Scripture, yet are habitually defeated by pornography. Scripture takes up residence in the heart only through obedience (Psalm 111:10).

Next, notice the second temptation: "⁵The devil led him up to a high place and showed him in an instant all the kingdoms of the world. ⁶And he said to him, "I will give you all their authority and splendor, for it has been given to me, and I can give it to anyone I want to. ⁷ So if you worship me, it will all be yours."

In this temptation the devil showed Jesus all the splendor of the world. All the beauty, the glory, the power, the magnificence, the grandeur and the luxury of the world was shown to him. Friends, we don't have to be involved with pornography long to see this same offer displayed on our computer screens or TV monitors. The models shimmer with beauty and magnificence, and they are luxurious and glamorous. They "offer us the world" of excitement and pleasure and heart-pounding fun!

The problem is that pornography is demonic (1 Corinthians 10:20), and that there is worship involved with it. Just as Jesus had to "worship" the devil if he was to enjoy the splendor and power of the world, so the devil is after our worship and offers us pornography as the enticement.

Even though I was a professing Christian for 10 of the 15 years I was involved with pornography, I was unknowingly worshiping at a demonic altar. The truth is clear from this passage that the devil is after our worship, just as He was with Jesus.

Testimony

Wood's testimony continues ...

Things went pretty well, or so I thought. I was "in control" enough so that my porn problem wasn't affecting me outwardly.

About this time I had developed an interest in spiritual things. I was raised up in the Catholic Church, so I had no idea about what it really meant to be a Christian. I started to watch Christian TV, because I didn't want to go to church. Finally I got the nerve to go and eventually was saved by the Grace of God. Although the problem with porn lessened a bit, it was still there and I knew it. I struggled for the last 5 1/2 years, going to different ministers for help. As helpful as they tried to be the message that I got was (mostly) try harder. Read more scripture, pray more, listen to preaching tapes more, take a vow to stop etc. Yes, they shared with me about God's grace, but they either did not have the time or experience to disciple me until I could turn to the Lord for victory over this sin. That is the wonderful thing about Setting Captives Free. Although an Internet connection can never replace a real person, you were there every day with a Bible study and counsel that seemed to be just what I needed. Although I know that I am still tempted, the temptation is lessening over time. This may sound a little crazy, but it is almost like I just "forgot" about my addiction to porn. Crazy, but true! As long as I keep my eyes on the Lord, he will be faithful to keep me from falling.

Questions

Question 7. Please provide your thoughts on this commentary by Matthew Henry:

*"'All this will I give thee'. And what was all that? It was but a map, a picture, a mere phantasm, that had nothing in it real or solid, and this he would give him; a goodly prize! Yet such are Satan's proffers. Note, Multitudes lose the sight of that which is, by setting their eyes on that which is not. The devil's baits are all a sham; they are shows and shadows with which he deceives them, or rather they deceive themselves.'"[14]

Question 8. What did you learn today, and how are you doing now?

Notice how Jesus warded off this assault and conquered the enemy:

1. With abhorrence and detestation. A parallel passage says, "Get away from me Satan" (Matthew 4:10). If we are ever going to win this battle against pornography we must ask God to give us a holy detestation of it, as if we cannot bear the thought of it.
2. With Scripture. "It is written: 'Worship the Lord your God and serve him only.'" When dealing with fierce and intense temptations, answer from Scripture, and answer in brief.

Finally, the third temptation: [9] The devil led him to Jerusalem and had him stand on the highest point of the temple. "If you are the Son of God," he said, "throw yourself down from here. [10] For it is written: '"He will command his angels concerning you to guard you carefully; [11] they will lift you up in their hands, so that you will not strike your foot against a stone."' [12] Jesus answered, "It says: 'Do not put the Lord your God to the test.'"

Here, the devil tempts Jesus to presume upon the promises of God. We presume upon the promises of God when we purposely sin, while clinging to a promise of God. If Jesus had purposely sinned by throwing Himself down from the temple, He would have been testing God to try to rely on God's promise to not let Him fall.

This has direct application to us who have been involved in pornography. If I purposely view pornography while claiming God's promise to forgive sin, I am testing God. It's the same as praying, "God please forgive me for this sin I am about to commit", which presumes upon God's grace.

Please get this principle. The devil will throw all kinds of Scripture our way to get us to sin against God in viewing pornography. "I will forgive your sins, and remember your wickedness no more," "All manner of sin and blasphemy will be forgiven among men," "Nothing can separate us from the love of God," "The evil I do not want to do, this I keep on doing," "If we confess our sins, He is faithful and just to forgive us our sins…" and so on. How do we know it is the devil using Scripture and not our own minds? If that Scripture is being used to lure us into sin it is coming from the evil one.

Scripture to Consider

"[13] No temptation has seized you except what is common to man. And God is faithful; he will not let you be tempted beyond what you can bear. But when you are tempted, he will also provide a way out so that you can stand up under it" (1 Corinthians 10:13).

Were you free from pornography since you did the last lesson?
    Yes   No

Were you free from masturbation since you did the last lesson?
    Yes   No

Were you free from sexual immorality since you did the last lesson?
    Yes   No

DAY 17— RETURN TO THE LORD

Scripture records that Solomon's Temple was radiant in its splendor, and brilliant with the Shekinah glory of the Lord. "...the cloud filled the temple of the LORD. 11 And the priests could not perform their service because of the cloud, for the glory of the LORD filled his temple" (1 Kings 8:10). This Temple was the house of God, "I have indeed built a magnificent temple for You, a place for you to dwell forever" (1 Kings 8:12) and was meant to be a "light for all nations." It was "imposing" (1 Kings 9:8) and magnificent, a holy and glorious dwelling place for God.

It served several purposes: It was a place of worship, a place to find forgiveness of sins, a place where the presence of God was seen, a place where unbelievers could find God and learn how to worship Him. God's presence made it glorious, pure, holy, radiant with splendor and majestic in beauty.

But the book of Ezekiel in the Old Testament records the slow departure of the glory of the Lord from the nation of Israel. The Shekina glory cloud (which symbolized the presence of God) left the Most Holy Place of the Temple, then left the Temple itself, then the entire land of Israel. The departing of God and His glory brought about monumental changes to the nation of Israel. They no longer had the presence of the Lord, their enemies ransacked their nation, taking captive men, women and children, and they were left without a witness to the nations. They became "Ichabod" which means, "The glory of the Lord has departed." Why did God depart and leave Israel as Ichabod?

Questions

Question 1. Take a tour of the book of Ezekiel and I believe we can discover what it was that drove the presence of God from the Temple and the nation. Please note what these verses say about why He withdrew from the Temple, and record your thoughts below each verse:

"As surely as I live, declares the Sovereign LORD, because you have defiled my sanctuary with all your vile images and detestable practices, I myself will withdraw my favor; I will not look on you with pity or spare you" (Ezekiel 5:11).

"But as for those whose hearts are devoted to their vile images and detestable idols, I will bring down on their own heads what they have done, declares the Sovereign LORD" (Ezekiel 20:11).

"I said to them, each of you, get rid of the vile images you have set your eyes on, and do not defile yourselves with the idols of Egypt. I am the LORD your God. But they rebelled against me and would not listen to me; they did not get rid of the vile images they had set their eyes on, nor did they forsake the idols of Egypt" (Ezekiel 20: 7).

"This is what the Sovereign LORD says: Will you defile yourselves the way your fathers did and lust after their vile images?" (Ezekiel 20:30).

Testimony

The following testimony is from Dillon:

I first saw a Playboy magazine when I was seven years old. My stepfather was surprised that it intrigued me. After that I would sneak looks at his magazines and when I got older masturbate. Over the years I got more deeply involved in my sexual sin. The magazines got raunchier; there were strip clubs, sex with men, sex with women, going to prostitutes. Sex took over my life for many years. Even after I was married I struggled with my sin of pornography and masturbation. Even after I received Christ into my life I struggled.

After becoming a Christian sometimes I went up to a year without viewing pornography, but I would toy with temptation with magazines at the supermarket. If my wife went away on a trip I would fall big time with videos. Recently as my marriage has struggled I fell badly into visiting adult bookstores and masturbating in the peep show booths. I would pray before and after but I couldn't stop myself. I felt extremely guilty. Here I was helping with a Bible study at the prison and teaching children in Sunday school and I was enslaved to this filth. I could never think of whom I might talk with about my problem. I was afraid of gossip in my church.

Then God rescued me. He put the idea into my mind to look for a website that would help. I found Setting Captives Free and timidly at first I started the Pure Freedom course. That was 60 days ago and the whole time I have been free of pornography and masturbation. God has been gracious to me. I have freedom. I am in love with Jesus. My life is restored.

Questions

It becomes obvious from reading these verses that the people of God were "setting their eyes on vile images" and "defiling themselves with vile images" and "detestable practices." They were idolatrous and this is why God withdrew His presence. Sin that is tolerated in the nation, or the home, or the individual always drives the Holy Spirit of God away.

Course Member Jeremy writes: "Oh sure, before I knew what I believed, or at least what I professed to believe. I attended church and paid my tithe and tried to show outward signs of Christianity, but it was all tainted by my repugnant sin towards God and myself. I was damaging His temple, the dwelling place of God. He couldn't live with that unrighteousness so I was pushing Him out. I cried out and He heard me through that nightmare and answered me and drew me out of that pit. I am on my way and ever growing in His light and love."

So what does this teaching on the Temple have to do with pornography and us?

"The body is not meant for sexual immorality, but for the Lord, and the Lord for the body" (1 Corinthians 6:13).

Question 2. According to verse 13 above, what is your body meant for?
  A. To be gratified through lust
  B. Sexual Immorality
  C. God

Question 3. In your own words, please tell what you think the statement that our bodies are meant for the Lord actually means.

"By his power God raised the Lord from the dead, and he will raise us also" (verse 14).

Question 4. Verse 13 states that our bodies are not meant for sexual immorality, but they are meant for the Lord. The very next verse speaks about the resurrection of Jesus Christ and states that we will be raised as well. What connection do you see between these two verses?

Question 5. What are your thoughts on verses 15-17?

"Flee from sexual immorality. All other sins a man commits are outside his body, but he who sins sexually sins against his own body" (verse 18).

Question 6. Dear friend, it is clear from the above verse that we are to flee from sexual immorality. Like Joseph, who ran from Potiphar's wife, we are to flee. Please think through times when you are specifically hit with heavy temptations, and write how you will "flee." Write your thoughts here:

Question 7. Verse 18 contains an admonishment regarding sexual immorality. What are we to do to overcome it?
  A. Stare it in the face and say "No."
  B. Be strong and fight it.
  C. Flee from it! Get out of there! Run away!

"Do you not know that your body is a temple of the Holy Spirit, who is in you, whom you have received from God? You are not your own;" (vs. 19)

Question 8. Verse 19 describes the body as what?

"…you were bought at a price. Therefore honor God with your body…" (1 Corinthians 6: 20)

Question 9. According to the same verse, who owns the Temple of my body?
  A. I do. It is my body and I own it.
  B. God owns my body; it is His home.

Question 10. Verse 20 tells us "we were bought at a price." What was the purchase price?

[15] Do you not know that your bodies are members of Christ himself? Shall I then take the members of Christ and unite them with a prostitute? Never! [16] Do you not know that he who unites himself with a prostitute is one with her in body? For it is said, The two will become one flesh. [17] But he who unites himself with the Lord is one with him in spirit.

Friends, these verses tell us that our bodies are temples belonging to the Lord. The Temple of the Old Testament became "Ichabod" because the people of God were "lusting after idolatrous images" in their hearts and committing "detestable practices." God slowly left them, and they were dispersed into foreign lands where they became "captives."

We, too, have spent time lusting after idolatrous images (pornography) and have been involved in detestable practices (masturbation). And depending on how long we were involved we may have lost the presence and power of God. Our lives may have become "Ichabod." It may have happened slowly, over time, but now we are destitute of power, spiritual weaklings trying to fight "principalities and powers of darkness" without Christ. We have been handed over to the enemy and are now "captives" in exile. But there is hope.

Question 11. Please read and comment on our final portion of Scripture today:

> "Therefore say: This is what the Sovereign LORD says: I will gather you from the nations and bring you back from the countries where you have been scattered, and I will give you back the land of Israel again. They will return to it and remove all its vile images and detestable idols. I will give them an undivided heart and put a new spirit in them; I will remove from them their heart of stone and give them a heart of flesh. Then they will follow my decrees and be careful to keep my laws. They will be my people, and I will be their God. But as for those whose hearts are devoted to their vile images and detestable idols, I will bring down on their own heads what they have done, declares the Sovereign LORD. Then the cherubim, with the wheels beside them, spread their wings, and the glory of the God of Israel was above them" (Ezekiel 11:17-22).

Notice the "removal of the detestable images" brought the captives back to the land and the glory of God returned to the people. Ichabod no more! The glory returned. Friend, are you wondering if, since you have devoted yourself to detestable pornographic images, you will ever enjoy the presence of God again? Remove those vile images and the detestable practices, and the presence and power and purity of God will return. Your body is a Temple.

One of the objections we hear from course members quite often is that they feel that God will not return to them; that they will not experience his presence again. This passage of Scripture should confirm to the questioning soul that God returns to those who repent and return to Him.

Question 12. What are your thoughts and insights on today's teaching? Specifically, how will you apply what you are learning?

Dear friend, I lost the presence and power of God through my involvement in pornography and masturbation, and I didn't even know it. Samson lost the presence of God through his lust, but was not aware of it: "Then she called, 'Samson, the Philistines are upon you!' He awoke from his sleep and thought, 'I'll go out as before and shake myself free.' *But he did not know that the LORD had left him*" (Judges 16:20). But since God has granted me repentance and I've been away from pornography and all forms of impurity for over 2 years, I can attest to the presence of God returning to me. I sense closeness with Him, unity with Him, and love from and to Him. But this has been a slow process.

Scripture to Consider

"Ever since the time of your forefathers you have turned away from my decrees and have not kept them. Return to me, and I will return to you," says the LORD Almighty" (Malachi 3:7).

"Arise, shine, for your light has come, and the glory of the LORD rises upon you. ² See, darkness covers the earth and thick darkness is over the peoples, but the LORD rises upon you and his glory appears over you. ³ Nations will come to your light, and kings to the brightness of your dawn" (Isaiah 60:1-3).

"This is what the LORD Almighty says: 'Return to me,' declares the LORD Almighty, 'and I will return to you,' says the LORD Almighty. ⁴ Do not be like your forefathers, to whom the earlier prophets proclaimed: This is what the LORD Almighty says: 'Turn from your evil ways and your evil practices.' But they would not listen or pay attention to me, declares the LORD" (Zechariah 1:3-4).

"Come to me, all you who are weary and burdened, and I will give you rest. ²⁹ Take my yoke upon you and learn from me, for I am gentle and humble in heart, and you will find rest for your souls. ³⁰ For my yoke is easy and my burden is light" (Matthew 11:28-30).

Were you free from pornography since you did the last lesson?
    Yes   No

Were you free from masturbation since you did the last lesson?
    Yes   No

Were you free from sexual immorality since you did the last lesson?
    Yes   No

DAY 18— EXCLUSIVE DRINKING

Dear friend,

The first few days of this course were about satisfying ourselves in the Living Water of Jesus Christ. Today we want to be very practical in providing help in overcoming pornography and sexual impurity. What does it mean to "drink the living water"? What does it look like in daily living to be satisfied in Christ? And how does drinking living water actually enable us to leave our water pots of sin behind? These are the questions we will seek to answer today.

Let us begin with the first question: what does it mean to drink the living water? At the risk of sounding simplistic, it is as basic as reading the Bible. However, it is possible to read the Bible and not drink of the living water. So what is the difference?

Drinking implies taking something into your system, and receiving nourishment and sustenance from it. I can read that Jesus is living water all day long and not drink of Him. Drinking is directly related to the application of Scripture in my life, and it is much more than mere reading. When you read the Scripture, ask God to apply it to your heart and to change your life by the reading of it. This is what it means to drink the living water.

The next question is what does it look like in daily living to be satisfied in Christ? It means rejoicing in the love, forgiveness and grace of God on a daily basis. It is discovering Christ fresh every day and being irresistibly drawn to him by what we discover. When we become happy in Him we need not look for happiness in pornography, food, or other sins. So then, as one of the Puritans of long ago said, "our first duty as Christians is to get ourselves happy in God." This is the only sure means of avoiding pornography. This is what Jesus taught the Samaritan woman in John chapter 4 that we studied in our first lesson.

And how does this drinking actually enable us to leave pornography behind? Simply put, if we are full and satisfied in Jesus Christ we don't need anything else. Our heart has found its rejoicing place and needs no other.

The problem is that today's society offers so many other "water fountains" to drink from; each one promising joyful satisfaction and delight. Pornography, in its basic intent, promises to satisfy. It is an invitation to drink of happiness. These same promises are subtly conveyed through the allurement of alcohol, smoking, TV, card playing, money chasing, relationships, gambling, drugs, etc. Even seemingly innocent fun can be an attempt to satisfy the heart; things such as family, religion, sports, theme parks, the Internet, vacations, newspaper reading, work, etc. How do we live in today's society that offers so many fountains to drink from? The answer is to be "exclusive drinkers." What do we mean by that? Notice the following verse:

"As they make music they will say, 'All my fountains are in you.'" (Psalm 87:7). The context of this passage is that God is gracious to outsiders. He brings pagan gentiles into his family and calls them his own. And it is those heathen outsiders, who, by the grace of God have been brought into God's family, who sing of their enjoyment of God: "all my fountains are in you."
Continued on page 58

Questions

Question 1. Where were these people during this event?
- A. At the Taj Mahal
- B. In Egypt
- C. In the desert

Question 2. Why were they complaining?
- A. They missed the Coke machines of Egypt
- B. They were thirsty
- C. They did not like living in tents

Question 3. What did God tell them to do about their thirst?

Compare the following passage: "They all ate the same spiritual food and drank the same spiritual drink; for they drank from the spiritual rock that accompanied them, and that rock was Christ" (1 Corinthians 10:3-4).

Question 4. According to the above verses, whom did the rock represent?
- A. Moses
- B. Jesus Christ
- C. Muhammad

Question 5. What did Moses have to do to the rock before the people could drink from it?
- A. Speak to it in
- B. Drill a hole in it
- C. Strike it

Notice the teaching from this passage of Scripture. The rock that was struck poured forth water for the people to drink. This rock represents Jesus Christ. Oh friend, here is lasting satisfaction; Jesus Christ, on the cross, was "struck," and he poured out his life that we may drink and live. But that rock that was struck in the wilderness was God's only provision at this time to quench their thirst. They had to drink from that rock.

Are you still thirsting? Looking in pornography to be quenched? You never will be. But come to the cross of Jesus Christ. He was pierced by a Roman soldier and his life gushed out. It is the cross of Jesus Christ where the "Rock" was struck.

But friend, we must drink only from the Rock. We must say "all my fountains are in You." We must be exclusive drinkers.

Question 6. Are there other "fountains" in your life from which you have been drinking? If so, what are they? List them here:

Question 7. Will you now make a conscious effort to rid your life of all other "drinking" sources? Will you, by the grace of God, say from now on "All my fountains are in You?"
- A. Yes, by God's grace I will now be an exclusive drinker
- B. No, I am not ready to give up all other sources of satisfaction yet

Please comment on this quote from Matthew Henry:

"Nothing will supply the needs, and satisfy the desires of a soul, but water out of this rock Jesus Christ, this fountain opened. The pleasures of sense are puddle-water; spiritual delights are rock water, so pure, so clear, and so refreshing — rivers of pleasure".[15]

Question 8. According to Matthew Henry's quote above, what would you say is a major difference between "drinking" from pornography and drinking from Jesus? Write your answer here:

Course member Devon writes: "It is amazing that something which you know causes such anguish is at the same time so alluring. It's like being addicted to an electric fence."

Day 18 continued:

This is an affirmation of the truth that we have been studying from the beginning of the course; **Jesus alone can satisfy.** And it is a commitment to have no other source of life, refreshment or satisfaction than can be found in Jesus. It is a statement of fact, that they would be "exclusive drinkers."

Now we will examine some very practical ways to ensure that all our fountains are only in Jesus Christ. Please read the following passage and answer the questions below.

> The whole Israelite community set out from the Desert of Sin, traveling from place to place as the LORD commanded. They camped at Rephidim, but there was no water for the people to drink. ² So they quarreled with Moses and said, "Give us water to drink." Moses replied, "Why do you quarrel with me? Why do you put the LORD to the test?" ³ But the people were thirsty for water there, and they grumbled against Moses. They said, "Why did you bring us up out of Egypt to make us and our children and livestock die of thirst?" ⁴ Then Moses cried out to the LORD, "What am I to do with these people? They are almost ready to stone me." ⁵ The LORD answered Moses, "Walk on ahead of the people. Take with you some of the elders of Israel and take in your hand the staff with which you struck the Nile, and go. ⁶ I will stand there before you by the rock at Horeb. Strike the rock, and water will come out of it for the people to drink." So Moses did this in the sight of the elders of Israel (Exodus 17:1-6).

The following testimony is from Jules:

I was raised in a broken home, and my father rarely came to visit. My older brother sexually abused me when I was 10 and then I discovered pornography in my early teens. This began a 22-year addiction, which I tried literally hundreds of times to break. Though I appeared to be a professional, respectable, businessman, and was well liked by my peers, yet inside me there was this horrible secret bondage to pornography. Looking back on it now, I can see that I was an idolater. I drank from numerous fountains such as work, religion, sports, and entertainment.

As I mentioned earlier, I had tried numerous things to cease the addiction to pornography. I attended sexual addiction meetings, went to support groups, read books, and talked with psychiatrists. None of these helped. And in June of 2000, I did a search on the Internet and found the Setting Captives Free course and enrolled in **Pure Freedom.** In that course, I discovered that I had been looking for Jesus Christ, and soon thereafter began earnestly seeking for him. I radically amputated all access to pornography, took up my Bible and began seeking God with a passion. I found him. And now, with God's help, I will never return to the sewer water of pornography again. My heart and my life are now satisfied in Jesus Christ. I am so thankful for those who put together this course and that it has pointed me to Christ and taught me how to drink the living water, and to quench my thirst in Jesus. Thank you!

Course Member Micah writes: "Porn is like the puddle. The water is shallow, stagnant and full of impurities. It might satisfy for a moment, but it cannot last and it contains elements that do me lasting harm. Drinking from Jesus however, is like drinking from the rock. The water is cool, clear and flowing. It contains no impurities and does me lasting good. And the supply is renewing and lasting, unlike the puddle, which disappears and goes away, forcing me to seek after another puddle. In porn, that relates to the constant quest for new pictures and thrills. It is also like seeking new experiences in entertainment. Only in drinking the water of Christ can I be satisfied and find true contentment. When that contentment is found, however, it has a profound effect on my life."

Course Member Lawrence writes: "Selfish, indulgent, sinful water is like puddle water. It is contaminated with the poison of pornography, muddied by chaos, stagnant of spirit, and small in volume, and quick to dry up, leaving a cracked and broken crust of a soul. The living water from Jesus is like the streams of fresh mountain water, which melts from the pure white snow and runs quickly down the mountain over clean rocks — refreshing and satisfying. In another way, one can think of the living water, being pure and clean, washes away all of the contamination, replacing it with pure, fresh life giving water which satisfies the thirst."

"Then the angel showed me the river of the water of life, as clear as crystal, flowing from the throne of God and of the Lamb [2] down the middle of the great street of the city. On each side of the river stood the tree of life, bearing twelve crops of fruit, yielding its fruit every month. And the leaves of the tree are for the healing of the nations. [3] No longer will there be any curse" (Revelation 22:1-3).

Question 9. How do the above verses in Revelation coincide with the teaching in today's lesson?

Question 10. Please write out a paragraph that summarizes the teaching of today:

Question 11. How is your life going right now? Are you beginning to walk in victory by God's grace?

Scripture to Consider

"[37] On the last and greatest day of the Feast, Jesus stood and said in a loud voice, 'If anyone is thirsty, let him come to me and drink. [38] Whoever believes in me, as the Scripture has said, streams of living water will flow from within him.' [39] By this he meant the Spirit, whom those who believed in him were later to receive" (John 7:37-39).

"They are before the throne of God and serve him day and night in his temple; and he who sits on the throne will spread his tent over them. [16] Never again will they hunger; never again will they thirst. The sun will not beat upon them, nor any scorching heat. [17] For the Lamb at the center of the throne will be their shepherd; he will lead them to springs of living water. And God will wipe away every tear from their eyes" (Revelation 7:15-17).

Were you free from pornography since you did the last lesson?
    Yes   No

Were you free from masturbation since you did the last lesson?
    Yes   No

Were you free from sexual immorality since you did the last lesson?
    Yes   No

DAY 19—PURITY PRECEDES POWER

Question 1. What is the title of Day 19?

Read the following Scriptural account and notice how serious these people were about radical amputation.

> "Many of those who believed now came and openly confessed their evil deeds. A number who had practiced sorcery brought their scrolls together and burned them publicly. When they calculated the value of the scrolls, the total came to fifty thousand drachmas. In this way the word of the Lord spread widely and grew in power" (Acts 19:18-20).

There! Did you notice it? Immediately after Scripture records the people "radically amputating" their books of sorcery, it records the power that came with it. Read it again: "In this way the word of the Lord spread widely and grew in power!" Purity precedes power.

But now, let us examine one of the ways that the devil keeps people enslaved to pornography. He tries to turn things upside down and make us think that power precedes purity. Look at an email we received several months ago from an anonymous writer: "I have not continued on in the course because I have been doing pornography. In response to your advice that I 'cut off and throw away the CDROM' that has the porn on it I respond that it is not the CDROM that causes me to sin, it is my own heart. It would not be reasonable to cut off the CDROM and throw it away, as I would just find something else to view. My idea of victory is to be able to have the CDROM nearby and say no to it. I will continue looking for another method of freedom."

This man will not find power to say "no" until he radically amputates his sin.

Here is another response we received to "radical amputation": "The TV and computer haven't 'caused' me to sin, it has been my own sinful desires. As the Bible tells us, we are drawn by our own sinful desires. I can see this can apply if I were going to a strip bar or porn shop. But, to get rid of TV and a computer all together because I can't trust myself around them doesn't really get rid of the problem. Yes, I may be great when not being faced with the temptation but do I really have victory? Is an alcoholic reformed and walking in victory because he is never around alcohol and doesn't drink? I say, he is wise to stay out of the bars but if he is around alcohol in daily life and still doesn't drink, he is truly reformed. To me, this parallels porn addiction or food addiction or whatever addictions one may have. I am not going into clubs [like an alcoholic to bars] but I do have TV and computers in my daily life. I think it too radical to say I will get rid of both because I can't trust

Now let us see a powerful demonstration of this truth taught in story form. Here is the background: The Israelites had just won a great victory over the very fortified city of Jericho and were preparing for battle against the small town of Ai They were not too concerned about the outcome of this battle, due to how small Ai was. But, they lost! And were humiliated. Notice why they lost:

> "Israel has sinned; they have violated my covenant, which I commanded them to keep. They have taken some of the devoted things; they have stolen, they have lied, they have put them with their own possessions. That is why the Israelites cannot stand against their enemies...You can not stand against your enemies until you remove it!" (Joshua 7:11-13)

As it turns out, a man by the name of Achan took a "beautiful robe, two hundred shekels of silver and a wedge of gold" (verse 21) from the victory at Jericho, and was cherishing and hiding them. But notice the words that God used to show why the Israelites lost the battle: "You can not stand against your enemies until you remove it."

This is highly instructive for us today. Until we remove that which has caused us to sin we cannot expect power over the enemy. Purity precedes power. Notice what happens next:

> "Then Joshua, together with all Israel, took Achan son of Zerah, the silver, the robe, the gold wedge, his sons and daughters, his cattle, donkeys and sheep, his tent and all that he had, to the Valley of Achor. Then all Israel stoned him, and after they had stoned the rest, they burned them."

Now that is radical amputation. It is removing that which has caused sin. Notice what happened next:

> "Twelve thousand men and women fell that day—all the people of Ai. So Joshua burned Ai and made it a permanent heap of ruins, a desolate place to this day" (Joshua 8:25-28).

Friend, if we want to make pornography "a permanent heap of ruins—a desolate place" in our lives then we must cut off that which causes us to sin. Purity precedes power.

Question 2. Why did Israel lose the battle with Ai?

   A. They were outnumbered
   B. They were unskilled in battle
   C. Achan was hiding items devoted to destruction.

Question 3. What words did God use to tell the Israelites why Ai had defeated them?

myself. Just as a dieter has to expect to be around sweets in their daily life, even if they rid their whole home of them, and still not eat them, then that is victory. I find more strength in having tons of junk food around and STILL not eating it. I agree we have to remove temptations or stay away from them as much as is reasonable but that is the key, reasonable and I don't feel getting rid of TV and computers [which both have also been a source of Bible teaching as well as porno] is the answer."

Notice the references to being "reasonable," and the negative use of the word "radical." Incidentally, to our knowledge this lady has not become free of pornography (nor overeating).

> *Jodi, one of our mentors, writes:* "I've been meditating on this whole issue and thinking about how some of those on Day 19 testified that their strength against sin wasn't really being put to the test unless they stood when being faced with it. That is so unbiblical. God NEVER tells us to do that. He says, 'Flee'—Get out of there! Don't stick around! I believe that that is yet another tactic of Satan to cause us to fall flat. I believe that it is only tempting/testing the goodness of God in His grace of past deliverance to be dumb enough to put myself back in the path of sin."

Now, read the battle plan that one man devised and see how he was willing to be radical to halt the sin. He did the following things:

1. Locked up the TV and VCR and gave his wife the key.
2. He carried no money or credit cards. He knew that to rent impure videos takes money.
3. He told several men and his wife about his struggles and asked them to hold him accountable. These accountability partners would regularly ask him questions about whether he was following his plan or not. They were also available to him for confession if he stumbled and prayer support if he was tempted." [16]

Warning: those who trifle with the Word of God's clear teaching that we are to deal radically with sin will not achieve lasting purity, will not perceive spiritual matters correctly and will not receive God's power in their lives.

"There must be a divorce! Within the egg of sin there sleeps the seed of damnation! Man, there must be a divorce between you and your sins. Not a mere separation for a season, but a clear divorce. Cut off the right arm; pluck out the right eye, and cast them from you, or else you cannot enter into eternal life" (Charles Spurgeon, The Chief of Sinners). [17]

"Why ask for trouble and cause your own downfall...?" (2 Chronicles 25:19)

Question 4. What did the Israelites do to the man who was cherishing and hiding items of destruction?
   A. They learned how to fight while he was still with them.
   B. They ignored him and kept fighting battles.
   C. They amputated him.

Note: They did not only eradicate Achan, but his entire family, cattle, donkey, sheep and "all that he had." They stoned him, stoned the rest, and then burned them all. Here is truth for us. To become pure and powerful in battle we need to thoroughly destroy everything remotely connected to our previous bondage to pornography.

Questions

Stone it, burn it, and bury all of its "relatives." Then watch how powerful God makes us.

Question 5. What did it take for the Israelites to have power in battle?
   A. It took learning battle strategy
   B. Purity

Friends, there is a spiritual principle taught in the above passage that has everything to do with our fight against the sin of pornography. If we will radically amputate anything that can trip us up, God will fight for us. We will have power that results from purity. We cannot expect victory over porn while keeping an "Achan" in the camp. Get rid of it. Cut it off, and experience true power over temptation. Remember, **"you can not stand against your enemy until you remove it!"**

Question 6. Where are you right now with your level of understanding and commitment?

> "Throw out your calf-idol, O Samaria! My anger burns against them. How long will they be incapable of purity?" (Hosea 8:5)

Question 7. Did you learn anything new in this lesson today, and what will you put into practice?

Questions

Course Member Chris writes: "Radical amputation seems obvious, I got rid of everything when I started this course. Obviously I still know what the wrong way back would be, so this lesson reminds me to take care and not to approach any source of sin. It is tempting to test yourself and see how strong you are against sin. It is tempting because it is a trick of the devil. I am not strong; I am weak. I am glad I have been 19 days free but I am not proud of it. I am just doing what I always should have done."

Course Member Maggie writes: "I am committed to being pure. No matter how hard this battle gets, I am not going back or giving up. I'm drinking of the living water and eating the living bread from heaven. NO more porn, no more masturbation, I'm done with it, I want it gone out of my life. I'm tired of the bondage, tired of hiding it, fearing to be found out. I hate the way it fills my mind with filth so that I can't be pure. I may be standing before the Red Sea with an army behind me, but God will get me through this. My eyes are on Him."

Course Member Mac writes: "Yes! This was a great lesson. I am committed to purity. Purity is so wonderful, so clean, so pure, so healthy, so invigorating. It gives us strength to fight off death and the devil: uncleanliness, pornography, smut, dirt, and nakedness. Jesus said to clothe the naked, not unclothe the clothed, right??? So lets give thanks for purity. Purity of mind, purity of heart, purity of body, purity of emotions, sexual purity."

Course Member Ed writes: "I truly believe that all forms of ungodliness in our lives must be amputated. If it takes turning off the computer, getting rid of the VCR or Cable then so be it! I only desire purity in life, for only the PURE in heart will see the kingdom of God! I cannot imagine keeping the CDROM or what have you as a temptation. It is clear in God's example what happens when there are even images that are within the abode. Can God put up with that? God forbid!"

Testimony

The following testimony is from Tim:

My first exposure to pornography was when I was very young. My friends showed me a porn magazine at a friend's house. My years from that early time until I went to college were filled with purchasing and viewing pornography. The desires for more excitement continued to grow.

I joined the military a short time later and found that pornography was in abundance. Pornography wasn't the only temptation back then. I traveled to Germany and visited the "red light district." This area in Frankfurt was a small community filled with every imaginable sin of the flesh. Any kind of sexual sin you desired could be obtained. There were blocks in many directions that contained strip clubs, prostitute houses and video stores. There was no limit to what a person could get into there if you had the money.

Many years passed, and I married my wonderful wife from Kentucky. We started to attend church and became Christians. My bad habits didn't stop. I found ways to hide them, and continue on doing what I wanted even while going to church. I eventually became a deacon, treasurer, Sunday school teacher and witness for Christ. During this time I fought my desires as much as possible. I was able to keep that outward appearance but inside I was dead. I knew what I was, but for my kids and wife. I had to continue to show those around me that I was a respectable and upstanding Christian.

I finally hit bottom and went through a period determined to stop doing pornography. The Internet made it too easy, and the temptations were too great. I tried for years to stop. I was ashamed, embarrassed and hated myself for what I did. If I could make it two days without viewing pornography, I felt pretty good about myself. But I always came back for more. I finally had enough of this roller coaster ride that Satan had me on, and I was determined to get out. I searched for help and God brought me to Setting Captives Free.

I was so ashamed of my behavior I lied to Mike about my name. Just in case they wanted to find out who I really was. My embarrassment was at an all time high. When I started the course I found an immediate release from pornography. I really felt like I was going to make it. I found others going though the same thing as I and our stories paralleled. I replaced pornography in my life with Christ. That is the only way I can explain it. Get porn out and put God in its place. God brought me out of this nightmare I have been in for many years. I owe all to the Lord for allowing me to find this web site that has been a valuable tool in over coming pornography addiction. While the web site was the tool, there is no doubt that God was and is my strength and power to continue to resist temptation and use the tools this web site has given me to continue to be free from pornography. I thank God daily for His guidance to this web site and for His strength. Only God could overcome something with such a grasp on me as porn has had.

Scripture to Consider

"[8] For it is by grace you have been saved, through faith—and this not from yourselves, it is the gift of God— [9] not by works, so that no one can boast" (Ephesians 2:8-9).

Were you free from pornography since you did the last lesson?   Yes   No

Were you free from masturbation since you did the last lesson?   Yes   No

Were you free from sexual immorality since you did the last lesson?   Yes   No

DAY 20—IDOLATRY

Friends, doing pornography and masturbating is deceitful, self-pleasing, rebellious idolatry and heart-adultery. At times in the history of the nation of Israel, they were given over to sins of the same nature. Read the following passage, and then answer the questions below:

> ⁹ These are rebellious people, deceitful children, children unwilling to listen to the Lord's instruction. ¹⁰ They say to the seers, "See no more visions!" and to the prophets, "Give us no more visions of what is right! Tell us pleasant things, prophesy illusions. ¹¹Leave this way, get off this path, and stop confronting us with the Holy One of Israel!" (Isaiah 30:9-11).

The above Scripture describes the life of one who habitually views pornography. It mentions 4 specific things about them:

A. They are rebellious people.
B. They are deceitful.
C. They are unwilling to listen to godly instruction.
D. They do not wish to be confronted about their sin.

I remember how rebellious my heart was during my 15 years of enslavement to pornography. I would read Scripture that taught me not to look lustfully at a woman, for to do so was committing adultery in my heart (Matt. 5:27-28) and yet I loved my sin, and willfully chose to rebel. I was deceitful, as I would pretend to others that I was some great Bible student, and zealous for Christ, when in reality I was hopelessly trapped in sin. I lied about being involved in pornography, deceived those who wanted to help me, and lived a life that was a total lie. Toward the end of my 15 years, many Christians tried to reach me but I would not listen. I stopped going to church because I did not want to hear "the Lord's instruction" and avoided godly men and women. One time a group of five Christians confronted me with my sin, and I was nothing but angry over their confrontation. See how my life was evidencing the truth of the above Scripture?

Questions

Question 1. How has your life in the past resembled these four truths? Which one described you best? Rebellious, deceitful, unwilling to listen, or not wanting to be confronted? Write out an explanation of your life here:

> ¹² Therefore, this is what the Holy One of Israel says: "Because you have rejected this message, relied on oppression and depended on deceit, ¹³ this sin will become for you like a high wall, cracked and bulging, that collapses suddenly, in an instant. ¹⁴ It will break in pieces like pottery, shattered so mercilessly that among its pieces not a fragment will be found for taking coals from a hearth or scooping water out of a cistern" (Isaiah 30:12-14).

All who continue in pornography, masturbation and sexual impurity will find that their lives will come crashing down to the ground and be smashed to pieces. After my first wife left me and moved across the country, I ended up in a tiny hotel room, without family and without friends, nearly losing my job over emotional distress and turmoil. Soon after I found myself in this situation I had to have surgery, and as I was lying on the hospital table waiting to be put to sleep, I secretly wished I would not awake. I was as hopeless as any man has ever been. I was "broken to pieces like pottery, and shattered mercilessly" (verse 14).

And now that this **Pure Freedom** course has been around for one year (as of January, 2001) we have seen numerous stories of great devastation. Families split apart, jobs lost, pastors asked to resign, criminals taken in to custody…etc. Possibly your life has come crashing down around you because of your sin. Or you are not at that stage yet, maybe you're just "having fun" with pornography and have not experienced this "crash." Maybe you have gone for 10, 20 or even 30 years with seemingly no, or minimal adverse side effects. But like the giant tree that finally topples after years of internal decay, if you continue on in impurity your life will fall to pieces, because God cannot be mocked.

Testimony

The following testimony is from Millie:

The CHAIN
My inspiration during this course has been the picture on the main web page of the hands with the broken chain, and the cross. I noticed it immediately, and said that's what I want. My goal wasn't so much finishing the course, but more a goal of the chain breaking.

My Past—the chain is fastened
My involvement with porn started in my teenage years. I didn't think much about it, as I felt it was a normal part of growing up. It was an infrequent habit, as I didn't really have much access to porn. It was a few movies here and there, or books that just happened to have sex scenes in them. At age 16, I became a born-again Christian. That day the war started in my life. I continued to view porn when available. With the dawning of cable TV, it was a bit more often. Right away I knew God didn't approve. I would go to God almost every time, and confess it. The next time the temptation came along I gave in. Life continued that way for years, even through a short 6-year marriage that was full of turmoil. With the introduction of the Internet, I first started reading newsgroups, and story after story. Then people started

Continued on page 64

Questions

Question 2. Please explain where you are with this teaching. Have you crashed yet?

[15] This is what the Sovereign LORD, the Holy One of Israel, says: "In repentance and rest is your salvation, in quietness and trust is your strength, but you would have none of it. [16] You said, 'No, we will flee on horses.' Therefore you will flee! You said, 'We will ride off on swift horses.' Therefore your pursuers will be swift! [17] A thousand will flee at the threat of one; at the threat of five you will all flee away, till you are left like a flagstaff on a mountaintop, like a banner on a hill" (Isaiah 30:15-17).

Some things caused by habitual sin are: Escapism and Paranoia.

Escapism is where a person knows he is guilty and he has a bad conscience, and seeks to escape his trouble by running away. This escapism is described above as "fleeing away on swift horses" and shows the desire of these people to get away from it all.

Paranoia is where a person exhibits irrational fear of people, places or things, and any of these can literally terrify them. When a person is in habitual sin there is a fear of getting caught, and they always wonder if they've covered their tracks sufficiently. They can become paranoid that someone will find out, or that God will strike them dead.

Sue writes the following, as she describes what life was like while she was in open sin: "I became extremely paranoid during this period of time. I became a faithful seat belt wearer, because I was convinced that the Lord was going to take my life; that He wouldn't let me get by with this." This paranoia is described above, as "a thousand will flee at the threat of one; at the threat of five you will all flee away."

Question 3. Have you ever experienced this type of escapism or paranoia?

Testimony

Millie's testimony continues...

posting connections to web sites. Most of them were geared toward men, so they didn't interest me. Recently though, there is a new trend toward web sites designed for women. Now it wasn't only the written word, the pictures were also interesting. After awhile, that got boring, too. I saw the ads for the video clips. All I had to do was enter my credit card number. So, one sad day, I entered my number, and said to myself, I have just sold my soul to the devil. All these years, Satan had slowly been fastening the chain. This was the final link. I was trapped, and I knew it. I cried out to God, and said I want out now! And God led me that night to the Setting Captives Free web site.

The course—well, yeah, I want the chain to break—maybe
I had no idea what effort it would take to break the chain. By day two, I was stating that I was only here because God considers porn sin. I saw God as a mean ruler over my life. I was being forced by God to be here. I didn't like it here. For example, my mentor wanted to know what caused me to view porn that day. Sorry, I'm a Christian young lady; I don't talk about those things! But I continued on...with the Bible studies, and with my porn. One minute I was on my knees crying to God that I wanted the chain broke, and the next minute back at the computer with my porn. I was determined to finish the course, but all these stupid suggestions—first, Lord, I don't need a mentor, I can do this on my own. Second, no I will not block access to porn; no, I will not be accountable to another person.

Repentance—the chain broke
One night, I finally realized this cycle of one minute God, one-minute porn, could go on forever. I was 20 some days into the course. I loved the Bible studies, I loved my porn, I loved God, and I loved my sin. Finally, I'd had enough. I knew something was wrong. I was confessing my sins, but nothing was changing. Finally, God put the word "repentance" on my heart. At this point, I realized that I had been a Christian for 26 years, and had no clue what the word really meant. So, I humbled myself and asked. In tears, I read notes about what repentance was, and God turned me around, and the chain broke.

Results of a broken chain
I stopped fighting with God. I am less stubborn toward others. Satan and I are at odds which is fine. I haven't viewed porn on the computer since that day. I have blocking software plus a Christian internet service provider. I have come to value my mentor (who also served as an accountability partner) for her prayers and advice. I will not listen to or read current fiction books, because of the sex involved. On the positive side, my Bible reading, which has never been a problem for me, now has so much more meaning. I have a prayer life now, and know the meaning of "pray without ceasing." I have also told a Christian friend about the porn and she can keep me accountable on more of a long-term basis.

The Future—Satan carries a chain
My life knows a joy that has never been there. I love my God. I enjoy talking to Him. I want that to continue. Another lesson resulted after a short fall from the victory I was experiencing. I found Satan is still alive and well, and I must be careful. I view myself as walking down a road cleansed from this horrible sin, with my hand in Jesus' hand. On the side of the road stands Satan. He holds one hand out with things he knows would interest me. In the other hand behind his back.... is a chain. I don't want that chain clamped on again. I know I have to continue to live a life of caution. I can't escape totally from this world's garbage. I can't escape from my body that gets a little crazy once in awhile. But I can escape and run to my all-powerful God.

My Special Reminder
Isaiah 1:18—"though your sins be as scarlet, they shall be as white as snow." This verse has a special meaning for me. Years from now, people in my city will look back on December 2000, and remember the record-breaking snow, and cold. I will remember back to the December when my Lord felt I needed large blocks of time to spend with Him, and to work on this area of my life. The weather changed many plans that month, but at least for me there was a reason for it.

Yes, I am sincerely thankful for the course, and to the people who developed and maintain the web site. Yes, I will be forever thankful that God rescued me from pornography.

Questions

> Yet the LORD longs to be gracious to you; he rises to show you compassion. For the LORD is a God of justice. Blessed are all who wait for him! (Isaiah 30:18).

Friends, if you find yourself described in the above scenario there is one thing that will fix it all: the grace of God! The solution to sin is the grace of God. And it is not as though God doesn't want to be gracious, for He "longs to be gracious to you." Another version of the above verse reads that God "waits to be gracious to you." The answer to a life reduced to rubble by the power of sin, is the grace of God. It is not to turn to the psychologists and psychiatrists, for that does not go to the root of the problem. It is not to learn behavior modification, for that does not reach the heart of the problem. Only God's grace changes the heart and goes to the root.

> [19] O people of Zion, who live in Jerusalem, you will weep no more. How gracious he will be when you cry for help! As soon as he hears, he will answer you. [20] Although the Lord gives you the bread of adversity and the water of affliction, your teachers will be hidden no more; with your own eyes you will see them. [21] Whether you turn to the right or to the left, your ears will hear a voice behind you, saying, "This is the way; walk in it." [22] Then you will defile your idols overlaid with silver and your images covered with gold; you will throw them away like a menstrual cloth and say to them, "Away with you!" (Isaiah 30:19-22).

The answer to a pornography addiction is to cry out to God for help. When He hears, He will be gracious to you and answer you. He will send you "teachers" to help you learn and grow, and His Holy Spirit will help you to walk in purity, and provide you direction in life.

And the result of God showing you His grace will be that you begin to detest pornography and all forms of sexual impurity, and you will rid your life of them: "Then (after God gives His grace) you will defile your idols.... and images...you will throw them away like a menstrual cloth and say to them, 'Away with you!'" We can always tell when God is granting grace to someone, because they willingly rid their lives of their former idols, and it is not uncommon to hear them use strong language of hatred for their former idols such as "menstrual cloth."

Sexual impurity is idolatry: "[5] Put to death, therefore, whatever belongs to your earthly nature: sexual immorality, impurity, lust, evil desires and greed, which is idolatry" (Colossians 3:5). When God grants us grace we can't get rid of the idol fast enough!

Question 4. Where are you in the above passage of Scripture? Are you yet rebellious, deceitful, and unwilling to listen and trying to avoid confrontation? Or are you crying out to God for grace? Or are you ridding your life of idols and calling them names?

> "[23] He will also send you rain for the seed you sow in the ground, and the food that comes from the land will be rich and plentiful. In that day your cattle will graze in broad meadows. [24] The oxen and donkeys that work the soil will eat fodder and mash, spread out with fork and shovel. [25] In the day of great slaughter, when the towers fall, streams of water will flow on every high mountain and every lofty hill. [26] The moon will shine like the sun, and the sunlight will be seven times brighter, like the light of seven full days, when the LORD binds up the bruises of his people and heals the wounds he inflicted" (Isaiah 30:23-26).

When God gives His grace of forgiveness, He also restores fully. Sometimes sin causes such ruin that some relationships cannot be restored (divorce), nor victims brought back (murder) but even so, God gives grace to endure these difficulties. God's restoration can even make things "better" than before. Notice the above passage "the moon will shine like the sun," the sunlight will be seven times brighter...when the Lord binds up the bruises of His people and heals the wounds he inflicted.

As of this writing (January, 2002) it has been nearly 6 years since my sin was found out, and my wife left me, taking our two children with her. I eventually remarried. My wife Jody is a loving and God-fearing woman and is a great help to me. Together we have one son and twin daughters, a wonderful church with good friends, and are active in ministry. Our ministry together is more effective than anything I have done before, and God is blessing our hearts and lives together with much grace. No, it is not the ideal situation to be divorced and remarried; yet God's grace is plentiful and has made our lives so much better than before. It has been almost 36 months since I have viewed pornography, and I can honestly say that I am content with Christ and my wife and our home of love. Quite a contrast from the man I was when I did not want to wake up from the operating table just a few years ago. Thank you God, for the grace of forgiveness and restoration.

Testimony

I also thank Him for those who walked along beside me, and guided me. But more than that, during the course, out of necessity, I developed a prayer life. Since the day I became a Christian, my prayers have consisted of one-sentence prayers, with the exception of a few crisis times in my life. I have gone from seeing God as a mean ruler who didn't like what I was doing, to a God that cares about me, and that I want to get to know better. He is no longer just a God that could work miracles in other people's lives; He worked one in mine. This renewed relationship with my Lord means more than words can ever express.

Scripture to Consider

"How great is the love the Father has lavished on us, that we should be called children of God! And that is what we are! The reason the world does not know us is that it did not know him. Dear friends, now we are children of God, and what we will be has not yet been made known. But we know that when he appears, we shall be like him, for we shall see him as he is. Everyone who has this hope in him purifies himself, just as he is pure" (1 John 3:1-3).

Were you free from pornography since you did the last lesson?
    Yes No

Were you free from masturbation since you did the last lesson?
    Yes No

Were you free from sexual immorality since you did the last lesson?
    Yes No

DAY 21—STRENGTH THROUGH CONFESSION

This aspect to fighting pornography is very important: confession of sins. We'll examine this today and you will discover that spiritual strength to overcome sin is directly tied in to confession of sins. Read the following verses and answer the questions about this passage that follows.

> "³ When I kept silent, my bones wasted away through my groaning all day long. ⁴ For day and night your hand was heavy upon me; my strength was sapped as in the heat of summer" (Psalm 32:3-4).

Questions

Question 1. The verses in this lesson describe someone in a lethargic condition. His bones were "wasting away," and his strength was "sapped" as in the heat of summer, and God's hand was against him. What was the reason for his affliction?

Question 2. The context of this passage makes it clear that David was keeping silent about a sin he had committed. So what happens when people hide their sin? And do you now, or have you ever felt like that person?

1. Forgiveness (vs. 5). God "forgave the guilt of my sin." Before David "confessed his sin" God did not forgive him; indeed God's hand was "heavy upon him."
2. Discovering God (vs. 6). "Let everyone who is godly pray to you while you may be found." This verse teaches that the only way to "find God" is through forgiveness of sins. And forgiveness of sins only comes through acknowledgment and confession of sin.
3. Spiritual Strength (vs. 6). "...surely when the mighty waters rise, they will not reach him." You know what this is like, right: At times, sin comes rushing in like a flood. It overwhelms us and we sink. But notice that confession of sin is immediately followed by this promise of victory. In owning up to our sins we will find that God will protect us from being overcome by the floods of sin.
4. Spiritual Protection (vs. 7). "You are my hiding place; you will protect me from trouble and surround me with songs of deliverance."

Note: Sin is debilitating, exhausting, paralyzing. This "sapping of strength" keeps us powerless to fight the Enemy, and ineffective in serving God. It is the opposite of "I can do all things through Christ who strengthens me," and it leaves us spent, tired, and emotionally drained. But, there is a way out!

> "Then I acknowledged my sin to you and did not cover up my iniquity. I said, 'I will confess my transgressions to the Lord—and you forgave the guilt of my sin.' ⁶Therefore let everyone who is godly pray to you while you may be found; surely when the mighty waters rise, they will not reach him. You are my hiding place; you will protect me from trouble and surround me with songs of deliverance" (Psalm 32:3-7).

Notice that when David "kept silent" his bones wasted away and his strength was "sapped" as in the heat of summer. But, we will see that there were four specific benefits to David when he "acknowledged" his sin and "did not cover up" his iniquity but "confessed" his transgressions to the Lord. They are:

Testimony

The following testimony is from Terri:

My testimony is that I was once caught up in the sin of pornography and masturbation. I was seeking to meet my relational needs through those avenues.

In actuality masturbation was more of a "problem" than was pornography. The role of pornography was to give me mental pictures to feed my fantasy life and so I didn't frequent porn sites unless I felt like I needed to get a refill so to speak, so it was usually a few months between viewings of pornography. But when it came to masturbation, I felt totally helpless and powerless to overcome and as a result usually just gave in when the desire came up instead of fighting it even though I always felt so much shame and guilt afterwards. When I did fight, I always lost, usually because I was only pretend fighting.

Then one day I found out about Setting Captives Free through the men's forum on Crosswalk.com and decided to check it out. Right away I knew I was supposed to go through the course, because way down deep I truly wanted to be free from slavery to the sin of pornography and masturbation. Through taking the **Pure Freedom** course I learned to stop drinking from dry broken cisterns and to begin drinking from the living water of Jesus Christ and his word. I finally realized that pornography never satisfies and neither will masturbation fulfill whatever un-met needs I might have.

I learned that it is only by the grace and mercy of God that I can be free from pornography and masturbation. I cannot be free by any other means except by the grace of God. As I cry out to God for deliverance, in his grace he comes and delivers me. So, that is what I do now to stay free, cry out to God and he delivers me. I also drink living water each day by reading the Bible purposefully, by doing a combined study/reading so I make sure I get something out of it. I have been free a month now and I know it is not over yet, but as I grow I will experience more and more freedom in Christ and the life he gives.

Questions

So, to summarize: hiding our sins (we actually can not hide them from God, He knows) and refusing to confess them brings about spiritual sickness, loss of strength against further sin attacks, and the anger of God. Confession of sin brings forgiveness, knowing God, spiritual strength and protection. "He who conceals his sins does not prosper, but whoever confesses and renounces them finds mercy" (Proverbs 28:13).

Dear friend,

Even though this may be difficult, it is important that you make a full confession and disclosure of your sins. This must first be to God, as all sins are against God. But it also must be to the person, or people whom you have sinned against. If you are married and have been doing pornography, you have been sinning against your spouse. This needs to be confessed before you can expect real and lasting victory. However, while confessing it to God must be total, complete and immediate, confessing it to others requires wisdom and discernment as to timing and detail. If you are now contemplating making a confession to someone, you might be apprehensive. Most times confession is not an easy thing to do. I understand. If you have felt the consequences of hiding sin, and now see the value of fully confessing, but are just a bit scared and need someone to talk to, please contact your mentor and ask for help. We want your victory in the Lord, and we pray for it.

Confession is a necessary part of that victory. Don't put it off. Next, we will look at how confession brings strength and victory.

> "² It was a long time, twenty years in all, that the ark remained at Kiriath Jearim, and all the people of Israel mourned and sought after the LORD. ³ And Samuel said to the whole house of Israel, 'If you are returning to the LORD with all your hearts, then rid yourselves of the foreign gods and the Ashtoreths and commit yourselves to the LORD and serve him only, and he will deliver you out of the hand of the Philistines.' ⁴ So the Israelites put away their Baals and Ashtoreths, and served the LORD only. ⁵ Then Samuel said, 'Assemble all Israel at Mizpah and I will intercede with the LORD for you.' ⁶ When they had assembled at Mizpah, they drew water and poured it out before the LORD. On that day they fasted and there they confessed, 'We have sinned against the LORD.' And Samuel was leader of Israel at Mizpah.
>
> ⁷ When the Philistines heard that Israel had assembled at Mizpah, the rulers of the Philistines came up to attack them. And when the Israelites heard of it, they were afraid because of the Philistines. ⁸ They said to Samuel, 'Do not stop crying out to the LORD our God for us, that he may rescue us from the hand of the Philistines.' ⁹ Then Samuel took a suckling lamb and offered it up as a whole burnt offering to the LORD. He cried out to the LORD on Israel's behalf, and the LORD answered him. ¹⁰ While Samuel was sacrificing the burnt offering, the Philistines drew near to engage Israel in battle. But that day the LORD thundered with loud thunder against the Philistines and threw them into such a panic that they were routed before the Israelites. ¹¹ The men of Israel rushed out of Mizpah and pursued the Philistines, slaughtering them along the way to a point below Beth Car" (1 Samuel 7:2-11).

Question 3. We want to discover how the Israelites were victorious over their enemies from this passage. The Israelites employed several of the teachings that we have been studying through this course in the past few days. Can you find and name them? Write your findings in the space below.

Question 4. Write out what the Israelites said in verse 6:

Note: Notice how "radical amputation" in verses 3 and 4 is followed by "confession" in verses 5 and 6, and "victory" in verse 11. Now, let us note the steps to victory. Write them next to each verse. We will do the first one for you.

1 Samuel 7:2— First step: **Seeking the Lord**

1 Samuel 7:3,4—Second step: _____

1 Samuel 7:5—Third step: _____

1 Samuel 7:6—Fourth step:_____

Question 5. Where are you in this scenario? Have you radically amputated? Or are you rationalizing and excusing? Have you made all necessary confessions (or are you, at least, planning to as the Lord opens doors for you)? If you have done these things, please share the victories the Lord is giving you.

Finally, note this very well worded and impassioned commitment to confession from ***Course Member Carl:***

> "I have been reflecting on God's wonderful grace and the sin from which He has so lovingly delivered me. I had tried so many times to stop myself from my sin, that I had thought that I had failed too many times and that God had given me up to my lusts.

Questions

"If we confess our sins, he is faithful and just to forgive us our sins, and to cleanse us from all unrighteousness." I thought and hoped, desperately hoped, that I would never have to confess this sin, except to God Himself. But that is pride. I was not broken enough, not contrite enough, not desirous of Him enough to confess my sin to others. And it defeated me. My unwillingness to do everything, to completely submit, undid me.

"I now want God and His Forgiveness, His Love, His Grace and His Mercy more than anything else. I know now that I can't hide. I need Him. I am willing to do anything and everything to secure my portion of Him. I will risk all and forsake all that I previously held too dear to endanger by my confession.

"God gave Himself for me. I am nothing, but I willingly give myself to Him. Not in return for what He did, because that would be futile and ridiculous. I can't ever repay or compensate Him. Just because He Loves me and paid the Price for me, I am His without reservation or condition."

Friends, words are not enough, for "the kingdom of God is not a matter of talk but of power" (for action)—1 Corinthians 4:20. Unfortunately, the man who wrote that beautifully articulated letter above, failed to confess his sin to his wife as he knew he should, and has now returned to the slavery of pornography "as a dog returns to it's vomit" (2 Peter 2:22). Please pray that God would genuinely recover him and grant him true repentance.

Course Member Joey writes: "Hiding sin eats you alive. I have felt like this, yes. I do not now because I am confessing sin to others. But I remember all too well the bearing sin in silence, not so much because I wasn't confessing it before God, which is the context here, but because I was afraid to confess it to others. The Christian circles I grew up in didn't lend themselves to admitting sin to each other. We know we're sinners, God knows we're sinners, but we have a hard time admitting to one another that we're sinners."

Course Member Jerry writes: "This guy (in Psalm 32) had not confessed his sins, and God's hand was against him. That is a horrible place to be. Sometimes, in the past, after giving in to lust, I was a wreck the next day. I would feel weak, tired, sick, probably more spiritually than physically. Which is worse? I would rather be sick physically than spiritually. I am familiar with confession, all too well. Today I experienced the refreshment that comes after confession. Although I wish I didn't have to."

"Beside that, dear friends, although we have confessed to ignorance, in many sins we did not know a great deal. Come; let me quicken your memories. There were times when you knew that such an action was wrong, when you started back from it. You looked at the gain it would bring you, and you sold your soul for that price and deliberately did what you were well aware was wrong. Are there not some here, saved by Christ, who must confess that, at times, they did violence to their conscience? They despised the Spirit of God, quenched the light of heaven, drove the Spirit away from them, distinctly knowing what they were doing. Let us bow before God in the silence of our hearts and own to all of this. We hear the Master say, Father, forgive them; for they know not what they do. Let us add our own tears as we say, and forgive us, also, because in some things we did know;" (Charles Spurgeon: *Jesus, The Pleading Savior*).[18]

Comments:

Scripture to Consider

"When anyone is guilty in any of these ways, he must confess in what way he has sinned..." (Leviticus 5:5).

Were you free from pornography since you did the last lesson?
    Yes   No

Were you free from masturbation since you did the last lesson?
    Yes   No

Were you free from sexual immorality since you did the last lesson?
    Yes   No

DAY 22—VIGILANCE

"I have come back to this course. I stopped taking the course because I believed the lie that I was completely delivered and totally healed from the sin. After completing 21 days of this course I stopped because I thought I was free, but I should have learned to stay vigilant because I plummeted right back into pornography, worse than ever, for approximately 2 weeks. So I make a fresh commitment to the Lord and to this course."

Such is one of numerous emails we receive. Today we want to teach on a subject that Scripture speaks much about: the necessity to be vigilant against sin creeping back in to our lives after a period of victory. Let's notice several passages:

> "⁷ Do not be idolaters, as some of them were; as it is written: 'The people sat down to eat and drink and got up to indulge in pagan revelry.' ⁸ We should not commit sexual immorality, as some of them did—and in one day twenty-three thousand of them died. ⁹ We should not test the Lord, as some of them did—and were killed by snakes. ¹⁰ And do not grumble, as some of them did—and were killed by the destroying angel. ¹¹These things happened to them as examples and were written down as warnings for us, on whom the fulfillment of the ages has come. ¹² So, if you think you are standing firm, be careful that you don't fall!" (1 Cor. 10:7-12)

This passage traces the history of the nation of Israel after they had been released from their slavery in Egypt. They had come to the desert where they were involved in the idolatry of sexual immorality, and God's wrath broke out against them and He killed 23,000 of them by snakes. The Apostle Paul tells us that the experiences of the nation of Israel were given as examples and warnings for us. What are we to learn from the experience recorded above? To be vigilant! "So, if you think you are standing firm, be careful that you don't fall."

Testimony

The following testimony is from Cameron:

When I was very young I began to be involved in exhibitionism and masturbation. I can't remember very much of my childhood and don't know how I got started. It was more the thrill of being naked. Over the years the bondage increased and I begin masturbating also. I can't remember any place where I have ever lived or been where I did not do it. One day my father gave me "the talk." He basically told me to masturbate instead of having sex. Boy that helped a lot, I went headlong into masturbation that I had already being playing around with.

Even after receiving Christ in my early teens, I remained involved in this sin. I entered ministry early and stayed involved in this sin. I talked to youth about not having sex, while I was having sex with myself. The shame and inner conflict grew and grew. Eventually I just resigned myself to the fact that I would always be like this. After I got married it still didn't stop. In fact it got worse. Sex seemed to release the dragon I had managed to control to some degree for all these years. I was in bondage for more than 25 years, parking my car in the early morning hours and walking naked for blocks and blocks. Sometimes I could not remember where I parked and had to find my way back

Continued on page 70

Questions

Question 1. Can you think of a time when you thought you had mastered sin, and were "standing" only to fall?

We have seen course members begin walking in victory over their past sins, and truly be overcomers for many days in a row, and then we notice some pride creeping in and their answers and postings to the discussion group become quite instructive as if they were the authority. It isn't long before they fall, and oftentimes we never see these people again. Their fall came because of pride, and pride keeps them in their fallen condition. There is much caution needed, especially when we begin to experience victory.

> "⁴⁰ Then he returned to his disciples and found them sleeping. 'Could you men not keep watch with me for one hour?' he asked Peter. ⁴¹ 'Watch and pray so that you will not fall into temptation. The spirit is willing, but the body is weak.' (Matthew 26:40-41).

The above verses describe the scenario leading up to Judas' betrayal of Jesus. Jesus knew He would be betrayed and knew He needed strength from above to endure the coming events, so He was seeking His Father in prayer. And it is right here that Jesus instructs His disciples, and us, on how not to fall: "Watch and pray so that you will not fall into temptation." Be vigilant. Watch against a developing chain of events that lead to a fall into sin, and remove a link in the chain. Watch for familiar areas in which you are tempted, watch for the uprising of the flesh, watch out for when you are tired; watch out for when you have just had a high spiritual experience, WATCH. But don't watch only. Watch and pray. Pray that God will keep you from falling. Pray that He would give you grace to endure temptation without giving in. Pray for power from above to extinguish the fiery darts of the devil.

Question 2. What are some specific areas of temptation that you need to be watchful of and pray about?

Questions

Friends, no matter how many victories we have had, nor how long we have been walking in them we always have a need to be vigilant. The reason for this is because "the flesh is weak." The flesh is always weak, no matter how long we've been pure or how strong we are in faith. There is no saint alive who does not have weak flesh, hence the need to watch and pray against falling. Many a Christian has fallen to the lies of the devil in the last hour of his life, and we must pray to guard against this.

> "[8] Be self-controlled and alert. Your enemy the devil prowls around like a roaring lion looking for someone to devour. [9] Resist him, standing firm in the faith, because you know that your brothers throughout the world are undergoing the same kind of sufferings" (1 Peter 5:8-9).

The above passage instructs us to "be self-controlled and alert" which is translated in the KJV as "be vigilant." We not only must be vigilant because our flesh is weak, but because our enemy is strong—like a lion. He prowls around looking to devour us. Should he find us not watching and not praying, he finds easy prey to devour.

Question 3. Are you aware of the strength of your enemy? What experiences have you with the enemy where you've felt his strength?

In the book *Pilgrim's Progress*, Christian is often assaulted by numerous enemies and, in time, comes to watch for them and pray against them. He writes this poem based upon his experiences of surprise attacks from his enemies:

> "The trials that those men do meet withal,
> That are obedient to the heavenly call,
> Are manifold, and suited to the flesh,
> And come, and come, and come again afresh;
> That now, or some time else, we by them may
> Be taken, overcome, and cast away.
> O let the pilgrims, let the pilgrims then,
> Be vigilant, and quit themselves like men." [19]

Notice that the purposes of the trials and temptations, and assaults of the enemy, are that we might be "taken, overcome, and cast away." That is what our prowling enemy seeks to do to us, is cast us away from the faith. We must be watchful unto prayer, being ever vigilant.

> "[5] You are all sons of the light and sons of the day. We do not belong to the night or to the darkness. [6] So then, let us not be like others, who are asleep, but let us be alert and self-controlled. [7] For those who sleep, sleep at night, and those who get drunk, get drunk at night. [8] But since we belong to the day, let us be self-controlled, putting on faith and love as a breastplate, and the hope of salvation as a helmet" (1 Thessalonians 5:5-8).

In the above passage we are admonished not to "sleep," which obviously does not refer to refusing the nightly rest that the body needs, but rather to being vigilant against temptation. The disciples in the garden were sleeping when they should have been watching and praying. Likewise, we sleep when we go about our day ignorant of the power of our enemy, and ignorant of the weakness of our flesh, which work together to cast us down and destroy our faith and make us reprobates.

Question 4. Please state what circumstances, in the future, might cause you to "sleep" when you should be watching and praying.

Course Member Cole writes: "I tend to 'sleep' spiritually when I am sleepy physically. I'm just not alert enough to watch and pray and often fall into sin when I'm tired. This lesson helped me as now I know I need to go to bed at a decent hour that will allow me enough sleep so as to not 'sleep' spiritually and be overtaken by sin. Thank you!"

Finally, notice a parable of Jesus that illustrates this need to not sleep and be vigilant:

> "[24]Jesus told them another parable: "The kingdom of heaven is like a man who sowed good seed in his field. [25] But while everyone was sleeping, his enemy came and sowed weeds among the wheat, and went away. [26] When the wheat sprouted and formed heads, then the weeds also appeared. [27] The owner's servants came to him and said, 'Sir, didn't you sow good seed in your field? Where then did the weeds come from?' [28] 'An enemy did this,' he replied. The servants asked him, 'Do you want us to go and pull them up?' [29]'No,' he answered, 'because while you are pulling the weeds, you may root up the wheat with them. [30] Let both grow together until the harvest. At that time I will tell the harvesters: First collect the weeds and tie them in bundles to be burned; then gather the wheat and bring it into my barn.' " (Matthew 13:24-30)

Testimony

Cameron's testimony continues ...

in the nude. I don't want to describe all the horrible dirty things I have done over these past decades.

The turning point came a few months ago when I was standing outside naked in the front yard at mid-day behind a tree with neighbors within eyeshot from all directions. Now I was letting people see me. I was searching for porn on the web at work and masturbating in the nude in my office. I was going deeper and deeper and could not stop. I was loosing control. A preacher friend of mine, sent this website to all his friends. I thought, this guy is crazy, people are going to think he's into this stuff. But I clicked on it anyway. For the first time in my life I saw light at the end of the tunnel. I might actually get free. I confessed to my wife and began to find freedom through the Word. It was the secrecy that gave power to the chains. For several months now I have been free from porn, masturbation and exhibitionism. I am finally enjoying the grace I have preached about. I am enjoying my family and my wife. It feels great to be free and pure.

There is so much more I want and may need to say, but I'm running out of space. I am free and loving life for the first time. I've finally left my water pot. Thank God and Thank you.

Question 5. How does this parable illustrate the truth in today's lesson? Write your thoughts here.

Friends, Jesus Christ declared that He whom the Son sets free would be free indeed (John 8:36). And part of His work of making us free is to help us be vigilant. May we not be like those who walk many years in victory, only to fall through lack of vigilance. Watch and pray. Here are some specific ways you can do this:

1. Make sure to attend a Bible-believing church (Hebrews 10:25). The importance of this cannot be overemphasized.
2. Have daily accountability (Ecclesiastes 4:9-12; Hebrews 3:13).
3. Seek the Lord daily (Proverbs 2:1-5; Hebrews 11:6)
4. Drag every known sin, and even temptation into the light. If you struggle with something, humble yourself and talk to someone about it (John 3:19-21).

Question 6. What are some other things you can do to be vigilant against sin? Write them here:

Scripture to Consider

"I will set before my eyes no vile thing" (Psalm 101:3).

"Therefore, prepare your minds for action; be self-controlled; set your hope fully on the grace to be given you when Jesus Christ is revealed" (1 Peter 1:13).

"You will be like one sleeping on the high seas, lying on top of the rigging. 'They hit me,' you will say, 'but I'm not hurt! They beat me, but I don't feel it! When will I wake up so I can find another drink?'" (Proverbs 23: 34-35).

"But you, brothers, are not in darkness so that this day should surprise you like a thief. You are all sons of the light and sons of the day. We do not belong to the night or to the darkness. So then, let us not be like others, who are asleep, but let us be alert and self-controlled. For those who sleep, sleep at night, and those who get drunk, get drunk at night. But since we belong to the day, let us be self-controlled, putting on faith and love as a breastplate, and the hope of salvation as a helmet. For God did not appoint us to suffer wrath but to receive salvation through our Lord Jesus Christ" (1 Thessalonians 5:4-9).

Were you free from pornography since you did the last lesson?
    Yes   No

Were you free from masturbation since you did the last lesson?
    Yes   No

Were you free from sexual immorality since you did the last lesson?
    Yes   No

DAY 23—
ENJOYING THE LIGHT

Dear friend,

Earlier in this course we touched on a subject, in brief, that we would like to dwell on more thoroughly at this point. When I was enslaved to pornography I had a secret and hidden sin. There was an area of my life that nobody knew about, that was off-limits even to my wife, and that was protected carefully so as not to be exposed. This hidden area is precisely what sin thrives on as the darkness conceals the deeds done.

> ***Course Member Jeff writes:*** "I can remember closing all the doors, pulling down the shades on the windows, drawing the curtains, turning off all lights in the house, and then, only after everything was dark, did I sit down at the computer for my time of sinning in pornography and masturbation. Like some mutant, cancerous rat, sin loves to hide in the darkness."

So part of gaining the victory over sin is to drag this secret life into the light, and expose it. This is always a scary prospect, but in this lesson I hope to give you helps to exposing the sin in the least painful way, and to assure you that God is always with the one who will begin this task. Please examine the following Scripture and answer the questions…

> "The night is nearly over; the day is almost here. So let us put aside the deeds of darkness and put on the armor of light. ¹³ Let us behave decently, as in the daytime, not in orgies and drunkenness, not in sexual immorality and debauchery, not in dissension and jealousy. ¹⁴ Rather, clothe yourselves with the Lord Jesus Christ, and do not think about how to gratify the desires of the sinful nature" (Romans 13:12-14).

Questions

Question 1. What are the "deeds of darkness" listed in verse 13? Write them here:

Question 2. What are the "deeds of darkness" that you have been doing in the past?

Question 3. What are we instructed to do with these deeds of darkness?

Question 4. Getting specific now, in what exact way can you "lay aside" those deeds of darkness?

Question 5. What is light compared with?
 A. A purifying element
 B. Heat
 C. Armor

Friends, the verses tell us that the light is armor, and armor protects a soldier from the attacks of the enemy. This is an important understanding to have: Light, in the spiritual realm, is armor. The enemy always shoots at us in the darkness, and if we expose our sin to the light we have protection from his assaults. So, I can tell you based on the authority of Scripture, if you will expose your sin to the light you will have protection from ongoing attacks of the devil.

After we "lay aside" the deeds of darkness, we are to clothe ourselves with the Lord Jesus Christ. We are to put Him on, to wear Him as our protection against the enemy, and to find our life in Him. I remember that after I came to my pastor and exposed my sin to the Light, not only did I have the protection that the light offers, but I also began to find my life in Christ. I loved studying God's Word,

Testimony

This testimony is from Conner

I was involved in pornography and masturbation for 15 years of my life. It all started when I began viewing porn movies on my next-door neighbors television set at age 10. I came from an abusive home life where it seemed no matter what I did my mom was always angry with me. I tried to win her love but I couldn't so I turned to other sources for it. I began having imaginary love affairs with TV characters and would masturbate every night.

I was a young girl who felt unloved and unwanted by everyone and I would get love no matter what kind anyway I could. On top of my rich sinful fantasy life, I would read romantic teen novels. When I was twelve, I went to live with an aunt and uncle in Arizona and it stopped for a while and the imaginary romances were no more.

I masturbated occasionally except now it was real people I was attracted to that were my fantasy lovers. I knew about God and had been raised in church, but I kept on doing my own thing. I accepted Christ into my life at fifteen in a Teen Challenge center for troubled girls.

My life was full but I kept God at a distance. Sure he could change my life if he wanted to, but I knew he could never love me if he knew what I had done.

Questions

singing songs to Jesus in private, praying often and long, going to church to receive God's Word and to fellowship with other believers...etc. Though I didn't know it at the time, I was learning to do what the above verses speak of: lay aside the deeds of darkness, and clothe yourself with Jesus Christ.

Question 6. How will you specifically begin clothing yourself with Jesus Christ?

The above verse tells us to lay aside things done in darkness, and to clothe ourselves with the Light of Jesus Christ. Part of our clothing ourselves in Jesus is coming into the light, and exposing our sins.

We can't emphasize enough, that though it can be frightening to come into the light, the results will be immediate purity. A fungus that is exposed to the light is sapped of its strength and eventually withers away and dies. Sin that is exposed to the light loses all its power and eventually is no more. Despite the initial difficulty of doing this, it is well worth the trouble to do it. It will indeed provide **Pure Freedom**!

Let's read additional verses on this subject.

> "When this became known to the Jews and Greeks living in Ephesus, they were all seized with fear, and the name of the Lord Jesus was held in high honor. ¹⁸Many of those who believed now came and openly confessed their evil deeds. ¹⁹A number who had practiced sorcery brought their scrolls together and burned them publicly. When they calculated the value of the scrolls, the total came to fifty thousand drachmas. ²⁰ In this way the word of the Lord spread widely and grew in power" (Acts 19:17-20).

The verses that precede this passage show the healing power of Jesus as He cast out unclean spirits. It is when this power of God was displayed that people were seized with fear and were in awe of Jesus' Name.

Question 7. Verses 18 and 19 show that those who were reverencing the Name of Christ did two specific things. What two things did they do?

First, notice that they **"openly confessed their evil deeds."** They dragged their sin into the light, exposed and confessed it. Friends, let us be clear about this: there will be no true victory over pornography without an "open confession." I know that's scary; I've been there, remember? I had a good reputation and standing in the community, a lovely family and a good job. I had much to lose. But I became so scared that my sins were dragging me into hell that I finally had to confess. First I confessed to my wife, then to my pastor, then a general apology to my children, then to my accountability at church, and finally this website. I'm in the light now, aren't I?

Now here is something that will help you. I want you to write down a proposed plan of how you can openly confess your evil deeds. Now understand that you do not have to do all that is on your plan right now, this can be done over time, but please develop a plan that includes who you will openly confess to, and in what order. Again, developing this plan does not mean you will do this right away, it is only a "seed plan" to begin working towards. So, please write here who and what you will confess to. Don't leave anything or anyone out.

Testimony

Life went on as usual and God did some amazing changes in my life but I always felt unworthy, unwanted, and distant from God for many years. In the fall of 1994 I went to Bible College. I had been reading Christian romance novels but now I had access to a library with hard-core romance novels and I was caught hook line and sinker. Soon it went from once a week to two and more. I swayed from promising myself only to read good Christian romance but always went back to the hard-core stuff.

Then I discovered online chatting at my boyfriend's house. Man was I in deep! I always felt guilty afterwards, but began justifying why I had to continue doing it. Then I discovered porn sites and all kinds of trash to feed my need for intimacy. It wasn't until I had been married for about six months that my eyes were opened to what I was doing to myself.

This came about through inner healing seminars we were having at church and also the Holy Spirit who used all that to help me see I was in deep trouble. He then led me to search for a site where I could get help, then had me confess to Pat, my husband, and then confess to my church at a Sunday night prayer meeting on October 22, 2000. It's been a long hard road and I am sure its not over yet but I praise God for every new day I have an opportunity to live free from pornography and lust in my life.

Second, notice that these people did not stop at public confession they also "**radically amputated**" those things which had caused them to sin. They burned their scrolls publicly. Let me share with you that only confessing your sin will not be enough to keep you from sinning in the future. There must be a cutting off, a plucking out, a burning, or a total destruction of that which trips us up. This needs to be done with a vengeance, or "with attitude" as we are destroying that which would have destroyed us.

Question 8. Have you "burned" (or somehow destroyed) every trace of every ounce of sinful material that has caused you to sin in the past? If not, now is the time, and today is the day. Please write down here if you have radically amputated anything that causes you to sin.

Now let us get some additional "light" on this subject:

> "This is the verdict: Light has come into the world, but men loved darkness instead of light because their deeds were evil. Everyone who does evil hates the light, and will not come into the light for fear that his deeds will be exposed. But whoever lives by the truth comes into the light, so that it may be seen plainly that what he has done has been done through God" (John 3:19-21).

Friend, are you aware of the extreme importance of the teaching we are considering? The above verses tell us that all who do evil hate the light, and will not come into the light for fear that their deeds will be exposed, while those who live by the truth will come into the light. Which are you?

And finally, notice something else that exposing sin does: "The visions of your prophets were false and worthless; they did not expose your sin to ward off your captivity. The oracles they gave you were false and misleading" (Lamentations 2:14).

Question 9. What does the above verse state would have happened if these false prophets would have exposed the sin of the people?

That's right! Exposing the sin would have warded off captivity. Let us be real clear on this: leaving sin covered by refusing to expose it leads to captivity. We become captives to the power of sin while it is hidden and kept secret. But, if we expose it we ward off captivity, and live as free men and women!

I can't tell you the relief I feel now that I am no longer sneaking around, trying to hide my sin, always looking over my shoulder to see if I would be caught. Confession and amputation (with accountability) will produce complete and total freedom from pornography, forever.

> "For whatever is hidden is meant to be disclosed, and whatever is concealed is meant to be brought out into the open" (Mark 4:22).

Friend, do you need help doing what you need to do? Talk to your mentor, and pray about your situation, and he will offer suggestions and counsel as to how to proceed. But please do not lose the value of the teaching in the Scriptures today, by continuing to hide and sin in the dark. Begin coming into the light. Confess openly, and amputate radically, and by God's grace you will be free!

Course Member John writes: "I just wanted to tell you of some radical amputation. The other night I sat down with my wife and confessed my sin to her. She was incredibly gracious and she has promised to help me overcome my struggle with pornography. I have agreed with her that I will not look at the Internet unless she is around and she is going to hold me accountable to that and to me continuing with the **Pure Freedom** course. I have tried all these things before, but the difference is that I always tried to do them while hiding them from my wife. My sin was still in the darkness, at least in my own home where the rubber meets the road. Thank you for all your prayers and for encouraging me to bring my sin into the light."

Course Member Tom writes: "I am all done with hiding! I have pulled my sin out from the cellar of my life and am turning high-intensity aircraft lights on it. Yes, I can see that my addiction has lost it's strength now, and that purity and freedom are now mine. Praise God!"

Scripture to Consider

"Therefore, since we have this ministry, as we have received mercy, we do not lose heart. But we have renounced the hidden things of shame, not walking in craftiness nor handling the word of God deceitfully, but by manifestation of the truth commending ourselves to every man's conscience in the sight of God." (2 Corinthians 4:1-2 NKJV)

"So there is hope for your future," declares the LORD. "Your children will return to their own land" (Jeremiah 31:17).

"The visions of your prophets were false and worthless; they did not expose your sin to ward off your captivity. The oracles they gave you were false and misleading" (Lamentations 2:14).

Were you free from pornography since you did the last lesson?
    Yes   No

Were you free from masturbation since you did the last lesson?
    Yes   No

Were you free from sexual immorality since you did the last lesson?
    Yes   No

DAY 24— FLEEING TEMPTATION

Today, we will see a biblical story of victory! We will examine this story closely to see how the victory was won and how we can apply these truths to our own lives. Are you starting to enjoy victory over this deadly spiritual disease called Pornography? Me too! Please read the following story and answer the questions at the bottom.

"⁶Now Joseph was well-built and handsome, ⁷and after awhile His master's wife took notice of Joseph and said, 'Come to bed with me!' ⁸But he refused. 'With me in charge,' he told her, 'my master does not concern himself with anything in the house; everything he owns he has entrusted to my care. ⁹No one is greater in this house than I am. My master has withheld nothing from me except you, because you are his wife. How then could I do such a wicked thing and sin against God?' ¹⁰And though she spoke to Joseph day after day, he refused to go to bed with her or even be with her. ¹¹One day he went into the house to attend to his duties, and none of the household servants was inside. ¹²She caught him by his cloak and said, 'Come to bed with me!' But he left his cloak in her hand and ran out of the house" (Genesis 39: 6-12).

Questions

Question 1. What did Joseph say to his master's wife when she wanted to sleep with him?
- A. "Well, nobody will see, so I guess so."
- B. "No way!"
- C. "I'll think about it."

Question 2. Read vs.9 and answer who Joseph was thinking about when he said "no."
- A. Her husband catching them
- B. Himself
- C. God

Question 3. Please write your thoughts about this story. Why did Joseph "win?" How did he win? How will you apply this to your own situation?

Testimony

A testimony from Sally:

Well, my journey into pornography started at the age of 12. I found pornographic magazines and novels in my Dad's den. I was just naturally curious as any kid at that age. However, at that time, I realize now, Satan got his hook in me. Little did I know this would lead to 31 years of bondage and almost total destruction of my life. I got most of my sex education from those books and quickly learned about masturbation. I soon developed a fear of men, as I thought all they wanted was sex. Because of this and the shame and guilt I was feeling, I somehow turned to food for comfort and soon had a serious weight problem, which in hindsight, has kept men away from me most of my life. During my teen-age years and through my twenties I spent many lonely years looking for happiness. When I got a VCR I started renting x-rated videos, which further fueled my addiction and unhappiness. I believed what I was doing was wrong, but couldn't stop no matter how I tried.

At the age of 30, I gave my heart and life to Jesus Christ. I was very happy and God led me to a great church and a singles group where I met people and felt accepted for the first time in my life. I was totally free from porn for about a year, but then fell back. The guilt and shame were harder to handle now. I was doing something that was against everything I believed in. Even before I became a Christian, I always believed that sex was only for marriage, and I vowed that I would wait until marriage for this intimacy. I am thankful that the Lord has helped me to keep this vow, despite all the impurity. It confuses me though, that I could be so strong in this area, and then on the other hand, give in to the other activities so easily. I knew God was not happy with my sin, and I would confess it to him and pray for deliverance, however I continued to struggle. I could not read the Word with any consistency because I was too convicted of my sin. I finally told a few close Christian friends, and 2 pastors whom I respected about my

Continued on page 76

Being tempted in this way is very difficult to handle (as you no doubt know)! But Joseph was focused. Did you see who he was focused on from verse 9? It was God. To Joseph, God was very real and he was "aware" of God always being with him. Keep in close contact with Him, and you will find strength against temptation, and saying "no" will be a lot easier. Next time you are tempted, act like Jesus is right there with you. He really is! Focus on Him. Enjoy His presence and you will run from sin!

Now let us notice something important from the previous story: Sin keeps coming after us. Notice that Joseph's master's wife kept after him. She kept pressing him, kept tempting him. She "spoke to Joseph day after day." Possibly you've experienced the same thing with pornography. The images come at you once, and maybe you are able to pass them off once or twice. But they keep coming back, don't they? You may send them away again but soon, like Potiphar's wife, they are begging and pleading with you and tempting you again.

Questions

To illustrate the truth that sin keeps pressing you, please read this account of Samson, found in Judges 16: 4-18.

> [4] Some time later, he fell in love with a woman in the Valley of Sorek whose name was Delilah. [5] The rulers of the Philistines went to her and said, "See if you can lure him into showing you the secret of his great strength and how we can overpower him so we may tie him up and subdue him. Each one of us will give you eleven hundred shekels of silver." [6] So Delilah said to Samson, "Tell me the secret of your great strength and how you can be tied up and subdued." [7] Samson answered her, "If anyone ties me with seven fresh thongs that have not been dried, I'll become as weak as any other man." [8] Then the rulers of the Philistines brought her seven fresh thongs that had not been dried, and she tied him with them. [9] With men hidden in the room, she called to him, "Samson, the Philistines are upon you!" But he snapped the thongs as easily as a piece of string snaps when it comes close to a flame. So the secret of his strength was not discovered. [10] Then Delilah said to Samson, "You have made a fool of me; you lied to me. Come now, tell me how you can be tied." [11] He said, "If anyone ties me securely with new ropes that have never been used, I'll become as weak as any other man." So Delilah took new ropes and tied him with them. Then, with men hidden in the room, she called to him, "Samson, the Philistines are upon you!" But he snapped the ropes off his arms as if they were threads. Delilah then said to Samson, "Until now, you have been making a fool of me and lying to me. Tell me how you can be tied." He replied, "If you weave the seven braids of my head into the fabric on the loom and tighten it with the pin, I'll become as weak as any other man." So while he was sleeping, Delilah took the seven braids of his head, wove them into the fabric [14] and tightened it with the pin. Again she called to him, "Samson, the Philistines are upon you!" He awoke from his sleep and pulled up the pin and the loom, with the fabric. [15] Then she said to him, "How can you say, 'I love you,' when you won't confide in me? This is the third time you have made a fool of me and haven't told me the secret of your great strength." [16] With such nagging she prodded him day after day until he was tired to death. [17] So he told her everything. "No razor has ever been used on my head," he said, "because I have been a Nazirite set apart to God since birth. If my head were shaved, my strength would leave me, and I would become as weak as any other man." [18] When Delilah saw that he had told her everything, she sent word to the rulers of the Philistines, "Come back once more; he has told me everything." So the rulers of the Philistines returned with the silver in their hands.

Question 4. What did Delilah keep doing to Samson? How is that an illustration of how sin presses us?

Testimony

Sally's testimony continues ...

struggle and their support and acceptance of me helped a lot. I had periods of freedom when I was accountable to my pastor, but whenever I stopped that, I fell back in to sin.

Over the past few years, I had almost given up on freedom. I was so tired of feeling like a total hypocrite, some weeks, worshiping on Sunday and giving in to sin during the week. I was in so much pain and I asked the Lord a few times to just let me die. I couldn't go on like this anymore. I had thoughts of suicide, but thankfully I couldn't go through with it because I didn't want to cause more pain to my God, and my family. I have been mentoring my niece and led her to the Lord, and I just couldn't do it. For 3 years our church has been going through a time of revival. The emphasis on Sunday night has been to the lost, with many being saved, and to Christians to repent of sin and to ask God to change our hearts and lives. You can well imagine how difficult these sermons were for me. I was trying so hard, but I just couldn't seem to find the way to the freedom that others were experiencing.

Then in September I purchased a computer. I knew this was not wise, but I did it anyway. I thank God now he used it for good although the enemy meant it for evil. Within a few days despite all of my pastor's warnings about the pc, I was in to porn on the net off and on for 6 weeks. When I became totally disgusted with it, I vowed to stop and again repented of my sin. I was doing okay for a week and then a particular sermon that my pastor preached on October 21st, God used to jolt me in to reality. Through his message, my pastor spoke strongly on 3 areas of problems in my life, including pornography. I felt like everything in my life was unraveling and I didn't know what to do. I knew God was trying to get my attention, but I was angry. First at my pastor, but soon realized he was preaching the Word, so I had to take it to the Lord. One particular Scripture really affected me. I had to face the fact that if I continued to give in to these sins, I couldn't have God also, and I was not on my way to heaven. Also I had to face the issue of rebellion in my life. The next day was Sunday and I could not go to church. I was in total despair. I cried out to God and asked for His help. Later that night, I went on the computer looking for help. I found Setting Captives Free and went into the site. It looked great, and I was surprised and pleased to see that other women were in the group. I was a little hesitant to sign up, but I did the next day.

I know that God led me to this site. From the very first lesson, I finally understood the scripture about the woman at the well and that I had been thirsty but was drinking from dirty wells, that could never satisfy my thirst. The Lord starting working in my life from the beginning slowly and revealing truth to me through the daily lessons taken from the scriptures. I am not even sure exactly what has changed in my heart, but I know God has changed me. The support from Mike, my mentor, and others taking this course has helped so much. Finding so many other women with these issues did something life changing for me. I had always felt so alone and full of shame. And the daily accountability was invaluable to me. I believe God used all these things to help me.

I've learned about God's grace in helping me everyday to stay pure. I had a hard time during the course on the lesson on

Testimonies

repentance. I really felt I had true repentance, but had to face the truth, that I did not. Yes, I wanted to please God, but I still wanted to keep my sin also, and I still desired to go back to it. I stopped doing the course for a week, because I didn't know what to do and I was pretty upset. I then contacted Mike and Andrea, and with their help, realized that I could not change my heart. I needed to seek God and ask him to give me a truly repentant heart that hates this sin as much as he does and to take away the desire I still have some days to go back. I also realized that I was afraid to leave my so-called "friends". I had turned to them for comfort for so many years, that I didn't think I could survive without them. I need to trust God that he alone will satisfy me, and he will give me so many better things to replace what I thought I held dear, although they caused me so much pain. I have learned to go to Him instead when I am thirsty. I have started reading the Word and praying more, although I still have to focus more on doing this.

I have felt many changes in my life. As of today, I have been free for 92 days! I feel clean before the Lord, which is my greatest joy. I can now go to church and feel no shame and guilt. The worship songs have new meaning for me. I can sing about freedom and know what that feels like. A Christian friend who I have not seen for a while, said my whole countenance has changed. That made me happy and I give God the glory. I feel better around other people. I have also tried to apply all the principles I have learned to other areas of my life, including my weight issue and things are going well there too, although I still need to work on it.

I know that I still have a long way to go, but I do believe that God has set me free. I am still seeking God to take away the desires completely. This past Sunday, the Lord brought the word "wait" to me through songs at church, and through a poem that Jody sent us. One of my favorite scriptures has always been Isaiah 40:31. I will wait upon the Lord and daily walk in his grace, one day at a time. The enemy still tries to tell me some days that I am not free, (even writing this testimony), but I will not listen to him. Freedom is too precious to me now, and I will continue my accountability with my pastor who has been so supportive and patient with me for 10 long years. I thank God for his obedience to the Lord to preach His Word and address the hard issues, although I know it must be hard for him at times. He has preached the truth for so long, but I just didn't know how to let God penetrate the truth to my heart. Only God could have finally broken through!

I have lost a lot due to these sins. The hardest one is not having a husband and children. All I wanted growing up was to be married and have several children. I know that God can restore the years that the locusts have eaten, but there are still consequences that we cannot change. I know that marriage is still a possibility if the Lord desires.

I thank God for what he has done, and thank Mike and others who God has used in a powerful way. I pray for God's blessings on everyone in my life who has helped others and me on the road to freedom. I pray that I can now help to show others the way with the Lord's help.

Questions

Course Member Marc writes: "She constantly tempted Samson by saying, 'you don't really love me, you won't tell me your secret of strength, look at all I do for you, I love you, but you reject me. Oh and by the way ignore those guys who try to bind you every time you tell me something, they don't mean anything.' Sometimes you just have to wonder about God's chosen heroes. Samson certainly was proud - because no one can be that stupid."

Question 5. Share an experience you've had where temptation kept after you.

If you study the temptation of Adam and Eve in the garden of Eden (Genesis 3) you will see this same truth illustrated again: The devil kept after Adam and Eve, kept tempting them, kept arguing with them and weakening them with each word. So, guess what? We'll never win an argument with the devil. And, if we hang around long enough, we will develop enough excuses to just go ahead and sin. So, how in the world do we win against these pressing temptations?

RUN LIKE THE WIND!!

"Flee the evil desires of youth..." (2 Timothy 2:22).

"But you, man of God, flee from all this..." (1 Timothy 6:11).

Question 6. What did Joseph do when Potiphar's wife was tempting him?
- A. He changed the subject, and began talking with her about the weather.
- B. He decided to witness to her, so he sat down on the bed with her and explained the way of salvation.
- C. He left his coat and ran!

Do you long to be able to look temptation square in the face and say, "NO!?" Chances are we may never be able to do it. Temptation is more powerful than we are, it is more persistent than we are, it is more persuasive than we are. Our only hope is to RUN, RUN, RUN. Flee away from it like it is a burning house. Run from it no matter what the cost. Joseph would rather lose a good coat than a good conscience.

Question 7. What can we learn from the way Joseph handled this temptation?

Comments:

Course Member John writes: "Yesterday I was at work praising God and having a great time, and all of a sudden images of women were running through my mind. Then the excuses started. I prayed to God and it seemed to get worse. One night while gassing up the car and paying for it, it was like some kind of magnet pulling me toward the magazine rack with my heart pumping. I did not take down a porn magazine but instead God reminded me that he would always provide a way out of my temptation and at that second I grabbed a Men's Health magazine and paid for it and went to my car. As I got in the car I felt a bit relieved and let out a yell! I know about the battles in the mind and I hate them and get very upset when it happens. Thank God he helped me!"

Dear friend, the above story and much of the content of Day 24 came from a friend named John who is going through this course. Notice that he RAN from temptation. Maybe not physically, but he got himself away from it. This is no small thing. This is a huge victory! And if he continues to develop the habit of running away he is well on his way to lasting victory. Joseph was thinking of God and he ran. John was thinking of God and he ran. It's the only way to win.

Course Member Dan writes: "She kept prodding Samson for his secret. It said she 'prodded him day after day until he was tired to death'. Temptation can be like that - it keeps prodding and prodding until you almost feel compelled to give in. The pictures that get in my head from one sin prod me until they propagate another sin. It is an endless cycle that can only be broken by God."

Specifically, in regards to pornography, the hardest part is trying to clear the pictures out of my head. There have been times when I have fallen and immediately afterward vowed to never do it again. I would pray constantly for strength and I found that as I prayed there were the pictures prodding me again. I would pray to not give in to the temptation to look at pornography on the Internet and, as I did, the pictures of the last time I did it would enter my mind. It made it so I almost didn't want to pray about it anymore...

Scripture to Consider

"And it will be said: 'Build up, build up, prepare the road! Remove the obstacles out of the way of my people'" (Isaiah 57:14).

"May the God of hope fill you with all joy and peace as you trust in him, so that you may overflow with hope by the power of the Holy Spirit" (Romans 15:13).

Were you free from pornography since you did the last lesson?
    Yes   No

Were you free from masturbation since you did the last lesson?
    Yes   No

Were you free from sexual immorality since you did the last lesson?
    Yes   No

DAY 25—
FLEE, ABSTAIN, RESIST

Today, we are going to study various passages of Scripture that relate to our battle against pornography, masturbation, and all forms of sexual impurity. Our purpose is to gain understanding and practical assistance in how to win this battle, by God's grace. Please think through the following passages, specifically asking yourself how you can apply them in your own life, and then answer the questions:

> "Flee the evil desires of youth, and pursue righteousness, faith, love and peace, along with those who call on the Lord out of a pure heart" (2 Timothy 2:22).

Questions

Question 1. The verse has two commands in it, what are they?

Question 2. Please think through how to apply these two commands in your own life. The first one is to "flee the evil desires of youth." In your specific situation, how can you do this? What desires do you have and how can you flee from them?

Question 3. We are not only to flee evil desires, but we are to pursue righteousness…etc. Again, in your situation, how can you do this? Please list some specific things you can do to pursue righteousness.

Testimony

The following testimony is from Chris:

I got caught up in pornography in my early teens, getting pornography magazines with allowance money and looking at them when I was alone. This happened to be quite often, as I was very responsible and could be trusted. I also acquired a "fetish" (for lack of a better word) for pantyhose and nylons. I liked the feel of them and would wear them during my sessions of pornography and masturbation. My preference of pornography ultimately became bondage, and I would engage in acts of self-bondage after looking at various bondage scenes.

After college I became married, but the pornography and self-bondage remained a significant part of my life. I would seek out whatever time I could have to get my sessions in, separating me from my family. Although as a child I went to church with my family, once in college I became somewhat "disassociated", and with my wife not being a believer I still lacked the spiritual walk I needed. Our marriage began to dissolve, pornography being one of the reasons but there were others. I became disinterested in my wife, and she began looking outside the marriage herself. A few months before this, though, I did begin reading the Bible regularly. However, I still engaged in my porn and bondage sessions just as regularly. I can recall feeling like I was being pulled from both sides.

After five years of marriage, it all collapsed. One morning, when my wife went to work, I jumped into a session. By this time we had three children, and I would try to get in as much as I could before they woke up. I finished up, knowing they had been awake for some time, and went to check on them. What I found was marker written all over the walls. In a rage I turned to my older son and demanded to know where he got the marker. He said he did not know. I called him a liar, and before I knew it, I slapped him across the face leaving a welt. When my wife came home she wanted to know what had happened. I tried to lie my way out of it (ironic, after slapping my son for that very thing) but could not. I was asked to leave the house and could not return until I promised to take counseling, not for the porn, but for the anger. To this day my ex-wife does not know about my struggles with porn.

I took on a part-time job to help offset the costs of the counseling. It was only a couple of weeks later I was asked for a divorce. I was told it could not work anymore, and that it was better for the children. I dropped to my knees and wept before God. My life was crumbling around me. Not only was I loosing my family, but also at the time I was working with her father so I was suddenly without a job too, aside from the part-time one.

But little by little God began mending things back together. I found a place not far from
Continued on page 80

Now, you need to share these specific steps with your accountability partner, and ask him/her to hold you accountable to these things.

Here are some things that I did to "pursue righteousness" during the first six months while coming out of pornography:

1. My wife and I met with our pastor on a weekly basis for instruction in the Word and for accountability.
2. I arose early in the mornings and sought the face of God, asking Him to break the power of sin in my life.
3. My wife and I maintained daily accountability with regards to masturbation. I knew I must report to her daily in this area until the power of sin was broken.

4. I studied many of the writings of the Puritans and sought to learn from their practical and godly wisdom.
5. I attended every service that our church had, and sought the Lord during them.
6. My wife and I had daily devotionals where we sought the Lord as a couple.

Question 4. We are to pursue righteousness "along with those who call on the Lord out of a pure heart." Are you calling to the Lord?

> "I will lift up the cup of salvation and call on the name of the LORD" (Psalm 116:13).
>
> "Then will I purify the lips of the peoples, that all of them may call on the name of the LORD and serve him shoulder to shoulder. [10] From beyond the rivers of Cush my worshipers, my scattered people, will bring me offerings. [11] On that day you will not be put to shame for all the wrongs you have done to me" (Zephaniah 3:9-11).

I remember when I first came out of pornography, I was pleading with the Lord to release me from the chains of sin. I was "calling on the Lord" in sincerity. I was calling out to Him often, begging for mercy, asking for Him to set me free, and pleading with Him to make me whole. Friends, don't hesitate to beg for God's help, to plead and cry to Him, to latch onto Him as your only hope in life.

This type of crying out to God and begging Him for freedom is not a pleasant thing to watch, as people will plead with God out of desperation, and being nearly frantic for His help they cry and wail, and prostrate themselves before Him, seeking to be released from the trap they are in. Now I'm not suggesting that it is our tears, or bodily contortions that help our prayers to be heard, but I am saying that a heart that is desperate for God will call on Him in reckless abandon, until He hears and answers. "[12] For there is no difference between Jew and Gentile—the same Lord is Lord of all and richly blesses all who *call on him*, [13] for, 'Everyone who *calls on the name of the Lord* will be saved'" (Romans 10:12-13).

> "Dear friends, I urge you, as aliens and strangers in the world, to abstain from sinful desires, which war against your soul. Live such good lives among the pagans that, though they accuse you of doing wrong, they may see your good deeds and glorify God on the day he visits us" (1 Peter 2:11,12).

Question 5. Verse 11 above tells us that we are in a war. Evil desires war against our soul, and we fight internal battles every day. The goal of the enemy is to drag our soul into hell, and he uses "evil desires" to do it. According to verse 11 above, what are we to do with these evil desires?

Chris' testimony continues ...

my children so I could still be close to them. God provided me a better job than I had before, one with a good group of believers that held an in-office Bible study! And I began going to a small church, and became a part of the worship team!

It was at my part-time job that I met a woman and began seeing her. As we got to know each other, she started going to my church and accepted the Lord into her life too! If there was to be another woman for me, I promised God that everything would be different, that I wouldn't make the same mistakes again. Well, I made them again. After seeing each other for a few months, she "unexpectedly" became pregnant. Abortion was not an option; sin was not going to be covered with sin. I did the respectful thing and asked her to marry me.

The first year, especially the first several months, were absolutely rough and at times I doubted we were going to make it. Just coming off a divorce, marrying again before we got to know each other because of a conception outside of marriage, financial difficulties, and other things just barraged us constantly. But God saw us through it all. Our little daughter was born, and that perhaps was the one thing that held us together. Yet pornography still raised its ugly head, not to the same extent as in my first marriage, but it was still there and it would have its effects nonetheless. Where I was getting my fixes of pornography was at work. Needless to say I was killing my productivity and running the risk of losing my job, the very one God provided in my time of need.

I knew all of this was bad, that it was sinful. Yet I could not pull away from it. I would go a week, maybe two or three, but then I would be right in the middle of it again. I was becoming irritable and defensive at home, taking every little comment personally. The attentions I should have been giving my wife I was not because they were going to pornography instead. In a nutshell, I was walking down the same road I was before.

Praise God that this time He woke me up and set me straight before I went down in flames again! The nudging of the Holy Spirit began telling me something was not right, that things needed to be straightened out. This was confirmed by a call from my sister-in-law who wanted to let me know of the real state of affairs before it was too late. I thank God for that! We began seeing the leader of our congregation, a Messianic rabbi, and that is when I let it out that I was a porn addict. He quickly and lovingly shared the consequences of this addiction - spiritually, emotionally, physically, and mentally.

I quickly began seeking help on the Internet. The thing that once fueled my addiction God now used to begin my freedom. I found Setting Captives Free and signed up for the **Pure Freedom** course. I also found a discussion group for men addicted to pornography and became involved in that. I told a couple of deacons in our congregation about my fight with pornography, as well as a co-worker who is a believer.

From that day when my wife and I met with our rabbi I have been free of pornography and masturbation, praise the Lord! I am now done with the Setting Captives Free course. Goliath has been beheaded, and I am now looking forward to help others do the same, as God enables me so.

Questions

Abstaining is the Scriptural method for winning the battle against evil desires. We are not to give in, or to vent, or act out in other ways; we are to abstain from evil desires. In some ways, this is like the "just say no" philosophy that the world promotes, but it is different also, because the world only teaches half the truth. Yes, we are to "just say no" or rather to "abstain" but according to the next verse we are to "live such good lives among the pagans that, though they accuse us of doing wrong, they may see our good deeds…" So, we are not only to abstain, we are to live such godly lives that others see our good deeds. This is much like the first verse we studied (2 Timothy 2:22) which taught us not only to flee evil desires, but to pursue righteousness, and both of these concepts must be embraced, not just one.

> "⁸Be self-controlled and alert. Your enemy the devil prowls around like a roaring lion looking for someone to devour. ⁹Resist him, standing firm in the faith, because you know that your brothers throughout the world are undergoing the same kind of sufferings" (1 Peter 5:8-9).

Many places in Scripture picture the devil and sin as a lion seeking to devour us. This concept is important to understand because it speaks of the strength of the enemy. He is a lion. Man is no match for a lion, as many martyrs in early church history show, and the evil one and sin are as a lion. They are very strong, and their purpose is to "devour us." Note this passage in Genesis 4:7: "⁷If you do what is right, will you not be accepted? But if you do not do what is right, **sin is crouching at your door;** it desires to have you, but you must master it." Sin here is "crouching" at Cain's door, desiring to "have" and devour him, as a lion kills its prey.

We have a strong enemy, and we have weak flesh. This combination works powerfully together, and can drag us into sin and maul us, chewing us up and leaving us half dead. I remember times of praying earnestly that I would not give in to temptation to do sex-chatting on the Internet when I got to my hotel room, but as soon as I got there the desire was overpowering, and I would immediately log on and give in. I might be up the entire night indulging the lusts of my flesh, and I would get changed and come downstairs the next day absolutely exhausted—mentally, emotionally and spiritually. Sin pounced on me and beat me up and, as this experience became more and more common in my life, the enemy nearly devoured me.

Question 6. According to verse 9 above, what are we to do with this lion?

Question 7. In your own situation, how can you resist? Think through specifics of your situation, and write out how you will resist the enemy.

When I was first coming out of pornography, my plan to resist was actually a radical amputation. I gave my notebook computer away to my pastor, so I resisted by not allowing any access to the temptation. The key to knowing whether you need to resist or to amputate is if you are getting the victory or not.

According to verse 9, we are not only to resist the devil; we are to stand firm in the faith. Now here is a key to doing this. The Bible says that "faith comes by hearing, and hearing by the Word of God" (Romans 10:17). Notice it does not say, "faith comes by what you heard," but rather "faith comes by hearing." There must be an ongoing "hearing" of God's Word in order for faith to remain active. So, how can we "stand firm in the faith?" One way is we can involve ourselves in God's Word often, and as we hear anew and afresh, faith is kindled again and remains active.

Question 8. Finally, verse 9 says that our brothers throughout the world are undergoing the same trials and temptations. Have you ever thought that you were the only one who was sinning in such a horrible manner? Ever felt isolated, like nobody else would understand?

Not so! All our brothers and sisters get assaulted by the enemy, we are all under attack by evil desires. Our temptations, whatever they may be, no matter how severe or perverted they may be, are "common to man" (1 Corinthians 10:13).

So, today we learned to flee, abstain and resist. But we also learned to pursue righteousness, live good and godly, and stand firm in the faith. We have learned of the strength of our enemy, and we have thought through certain steps that we will take to ensure that we are pursuing righteousness. May our God enable us to do these things, by His grace.

Scripture to Consider

"I have been crucified with Christ and I no longer live, but Christ lives in me. The life I live in the body, I live by faith in the Son of God, who loved me and gave himself for me. I do not set aside the grace of God, for if righteousness could be gained through the law, Christ died for nothing!" (Galatians 2:20-21)

"A cry is heard on the barren heights, the weeping and pleading of the people of Israel, because they have perverted their ways and have forgotten the LORD their God. 'Return, faithless people; I will cure you of backsliding.' 'Yes, we will come to you, for you are the LORD our God. Surely the idolatrous commotion on the hills and mountains is a deception; surely in the LORD our God is the salvation of Israel. From our youth shameful gods have consumed the fruits of our fathers' labor— their flocks and herds, their sons and daughters. Let us lie down in our shame, and let our disgrace cover us. We have sinned against the LORD our God, both we and our fathers; from our youth till this day we have not obeyed the LORD our God'" Jeremiah 3: 21-25 8.

Were you free from pornography since you did the last lesson?
    Yes   No

Were you free from masturbation since you did the last lesson?
    Yes   No

Were you free from sexual immorality since you did the last lesson?
    Yes   No

Questions

Question 1. In verse 8, the young man is doing something foolish. What is it?
- A. Going out at night without a coat
- B. Going near a prostitutes home, walking in her direction

Question 2. What words are used to describe this young man?
- A. Simple, lacking judgment
- B. Blond, well-muscled
- C. Able to go near temptation and say no to it

Question 3. Notice the personal nature of the temptation. How many times does the seductress use the word "you" in verse 15?
- A. 1
- B. 2
- C. 3

Question 4. What is this "personal touch" designed to appeal to in this young man?

Personal illustration: I remember going to my hotel room after a long day, turning on cable television and barely being able to get my uniform off before a seductress came on with a very personal message: "I've been waiting for **you**, I've taken a hot shower and I smell good just for **you**. Come on, tonight I'm all **yours**!" And possibly you have seen advertisements for 900 numbers: "I want to talk to **you**, I am sitting here waiting for your call. Come on, pick up the phone, I want to talk to **you**."

Question 5. Why is this personal, intimate form of communication so hard to resist? What are your thoughts? What porn have you seen that utilizes this powerful form of seduction?

DAY 26—DON'T GO NEAR

In July of 1972 a McDonnell Douglas DC-9, loaded with 85 passengers and 5 crewmembers, was traveling from St. Louis, Missouri to Minneapolis, Minnesota. The time of departure was 2:30 p.m. and the aircraft had been airborne approximately 25 minutes. It was a typical hot and humid summer afternoon in the Midwest, with numerous thunderstorms building along the route of flight.

The Air Traffic Control monitor noticed the aircraft approaching the vicinity of several heavy thunderstorm buildups, and radioed this information: "___ ____ (airline name) flight 2164, weather radar indicates you are approaching an area of level 5 buildups with tops above Flight Level 410. Suggest an easterly deviation to heading 105 degrees within the next 10 miles."

The response from the pilots came back. "Uh, Roger, Kansas City center, we see the thunderstorms. Onboard radar indicates a possible hole to penetrate through the buildups at our 12 o'clock position and 18 miles. Do you agree?"

Air Traffic Control replied, "Negative, Flight 2164, our radar does not confirm the existence of a hole in the storm, suggest an easterly deviation to the right immediately."

This is the last transmission recorded from this aircraft on Air Traffic Control's tapes:

"Uh, Roger, Kansas City center, we will proceed straight ahead...it may be a little close, but we, uh, do see a hole to penetrate."

The aircraft penetrated the severest part of the storm, a level 5 thunderstorm, and was sent plummeting to the earth, killing all 91 people aboard. What happened?

Aircraft radar is susceptible to what is known as "attenuation" which is the blocking of any weather returns that are behind severe storms. Because there is so much moisture in severe thunderstorms, the radar is unable to penetrate

The following testimony is from Tom:

I began the practice of masturbation at age 5. Unfortunately some older cousins taught me. I remember entering grade 1 when everyone had to walk to the front of the room and give their name. I couldn't look up because I was ashamed of myself. I clearly remember on that first day of school that people would hate me if they knew what I did. By then it was already a daily habit.

Unfortunately, as a boy growing up I experimented with other boys, only reinforcing my habit.

When I was about 13 years old I discovered my first Playboy magazine. That began my introduction into pornography. Pornography and masturbation haunted me all through high school and into university. Three times a day was routine during university. Along with this came an increasing awareness that I was attracted to both men and women. Clearly a homosexual "bent" was emerging.

through the moisture to be able to accurately present any weather information immediately behind the severe storms. In the above situation the radar, because of attenuation, falsely presented the appearance of a safe route of flight. Seasoned and well-trained pilots are aware of the problem of attenuation and know to remain well clear of all thunderstorms. The key to safety is to not go anywhere near a storm.

For us, pornography is a thunderstorm. It can present the appearance of being harmless—"a little fun, something that doesn't hurt anyone, a release for pent-up sexual energy, or a stimulus for better lovemaking with a spouse." And yet pornography is a trap of the devil that has devastated the lives of countless people. How do we deal with this thunderstorm?

The answer is: **Don't go near!**

Today, we will notice Scriptural teaching on the subject: Don't go near. Please read the following passage and answer the questions at the bottom. Can you discover the approaching "thunderstorm?"

> 6 At the window of my house I looked out through the lattice. 7 I saw among the simple, I noticed among the young men, a youth who lacked judgment. 8 He was going down the street near her corner, walking along in the direction of her house 9 at twilight, as the day was fading, as the dark of night set in. 10 Then out came a woman to meet him, dressed like a prostitute and with crafty intent. 11 (She is loud and defiant, her feet never stay at home; 12 now in the street, now in the squares, at every corner she lurks.) 13 She took hold of him and kissed him and with a brazen face she said: 14 I have fellowship offerings at home; today I fulfilled my vows. 15 So I came out to meet you; I looked for you and have found you! 16 I have covered my bed with colored linens from Egypt. 17 I have perfumed my bed with myrrh, aloes and cinnamon. 18 Come, let's drink deep of love till morning; let's enjoy ourselves with love! 19 My husband is not at home; he has gone on a long journey. 20 He took his purse filled with money and will not be home till full moon. 21 With persuasive words she led him astray; she seduced him with her smooth talk. 22 All at once he followed her like an ox going to the slaughter, like a deer stepping into a noose 23 till an arrow pierces his liver, like a bird darting into a snare, little knowing it will cost him his life. 24 Now then, my sons, listen to me; pay attention to what I say. 25 Do not let your heart turn to her ways or stray into her paths. 26 Many are the victims she has brought down; her slain are a mighty throng. 27 Her house is a highway to the grave, leading down to the chambers of death (Proverbs 7:6-27).

Then in my 3rd year of university I became a believer through the Navigator ministry. This had a significant impact on my practice of P&M. It all diminished. However, I was never able to completely conquer it. I struggled as I served several years in a campus ministry. Over time I entered seminary and went into pastoral ministry. All during seminary I struggled. All through my 19 years of pastoral ministry I struggled. Five years ago I had a burnout and went for counseling. I opened up this whole area of struggle to the counselor. Although I had never acted out my homosexual desires, they existed and bothered me. Through counseling I dealt with some of the past sexual abuse and all the things I'd done as a younger boy. I had a significant release and victory. However, about that time I got connected to the Internet. In time curiosity took over and I was soon viewing pornography and masturbating. I knew it was wrong and kept trying to stop. I greatly feared being caught and devastating my family and ministry. However, nothing worked. No resolve was ever kept. I changed churches two years ago and hoped for better times. But not so.

Finally, after 47 years of fighting masturbation and after 39 years of fighting pornography

Continued on page 84

Question 6. Verse 18 says, "Come let us drink deep of love until morning..." Let's see how good your memory is. In the early days of this course we studied through John 4 about "the woman at the well." How does verse 18 above compare with the story in John 4?

Course Member Jeff writes: "We must drink deep of the living waters of Jesus Christ. He is our fountain. I notice here that part of the verse, "...until morning..." This is very obviously not a fountain with any sustenance at all. It will go dry in the morning. There is nothing satisfying here at all. It has an end. Jesus' fountain has no end. And its drink gives us life."

Note: Verse 22 says, "All at once he followed her." Here is the problem with going "near" the temptation: The choice to sin is often made all of a sudden and without rational thought. If this young man were reasonable and rational, he could have weighed out the benefits versus the disadvantages. He could have said, "I will think about it and let you know," or he could have asked a friend for advice before acting. But powerful temptation removes ones ability to be rational and decisions are often made immediately. This is "impulse buying" at it's worst. And the longer we stay involved in pornography the more things we do simply by impulse.

Ten years ago, after I had been involved in pornography for 4 or 5 years my impulses were beginning to master me. I would find myself doing inappropriate things almost by reflex, without thinking about it, and later it left me wondering why. I now know that habitual giving in to sin leads to living by impulse. It still breaks my heart to think of this, and I am so thankful to be delivered from it now.

Question 7. Have you experienced this "all of a sudden" decision with porn? What happened?

Questions

Course Member David writes: "Once I had been to the porn shop, and bought some magazines, I suddenly decided I just couldn't wait until I got home to look at one, I was so busy looking, that I ran into the car in front of me."

Question 8. Verses 22 and 23 use four analogies to describe what the end result of giving in to temptation is like. What are they? I will write the first one:

Giving in to temptation is like:

1—An Ox Going To The Slaughter

2_____

3_____

4_____

It helps to keep in mind what the final outcome of any sin will be. Sin inevitably leads to death. It may lead to physical death, as in the case of Ted Bundy and numerous others, or it may lead to the death of your marriage, or to the death of your spiritual life…etc.

Question 9. The temptress promised an enjoyment of life. But according to the last couple of verses where did her paths actually lead?

   A. To the White House
   B. To the enjoyment of life
   C. To death and the grave

Question 10. There is only one admonition in this entire passage on how to escape the "slaughter," the "noose," the "arrow," the "snare," meaning "death," and the "grave." It is found in verse 25. Please write out verse 25 here. It would be a good idea for you to memorize this verse:

Note: Don't go near! Sometimes this is extremely difficult as temptation is "now in the street, now in the squares, at every corner she lurks." Here are some of the things I do to avoid temptation. I will not get in to an elevator alone with a woman, I will not meet alone with a woman—my wife must be present. I will not counsel another woman without my wife being present. I disassemble the TV at my hotel room, or take it into a co-workers room, or drop it off at the front desk. I do not go into newsstands because of the numerous magazines of naked women. At the checkout stand in grocery stores, I make "a covenant with my eyes" to not look at the magazines.

Friends, a deadly air disaster could have been averted in 1972 had the pilots lived by the principle to not go near. In flying, when I am faced with a radarscope showing thunderstorms, my one policy is avoidance. I do not look for holes or try to find a shortcut. When dealing with pornography, like deadly thunderstorms, the only safe approach is avoidance. "In the paths of the wicked lie thorns and snares, but he who guards his soul stays far from them" (Proverbs 22:5).

Question 11. What have been your areas of temptation in the past? Please give us your avoidance plan. How will you apply this principle now to not go near?

Testimony

Tom's testimony continues …

and after many years with conflictive desires I anonymously sought out help from another pastor through the Internet. He eventually pointed me to Setting Captives Free. I began the course on Nov. 1, 2000. By then I'd already experienced 15 days of victory through self-effort. Right away I began to feel God's encouragement and help in staying pure. It as if God said, "Now you are ready". By coming out of the dark and letting others in on my struggle I was able to receive God's help and strength and grace to overcome this lifelong battle. Like everyone else who takes the course, the battle was strong. At times I felt like giving in. It is only by God's grace that I have been able to complete the course without viewing any pornography or masturbating. That is totally God's power at work. I have NEVER had any such victory since I was 5 years old. Praise God!

Recently I lost my position as senior pastor of the church I've ministered in the past two years. At first I felt it was because of the effects P&M were having on my life that kept me from being what the church needed. There is no doubt the church suffered because of my diminished spiritual vitality. However, the issues were more a spiritual gift-match issue. I've discovered that I don't have the full complement of gifts needed for a new church plant. What is amazing, through all this is that God has helped me stay pure. The discouragement of such circumstances would normally push me to seek out a little "comfort" in P&M. However, God's grace has come through strong.

Now that I'm ending the course I would like to "cut off" the giant's head by taking the mentor's course and become involved in helping others, particularly pastors who struggle in a deep, dark hole of secrecy. Church members can go to their pastor for help for P&M, but where does the pastor go when he is struggling with P&M. Perhaps God can use me in this way.

Scripture to Consider

"Do not set foot on the path of the wicked or walk in the way of evil men. Avoid it, do not travel on it; turn from it and go on your way" (Proverbs 4:14-15).

"Rather, clothe yourselves with the Lord Jesus Christ, and do not think about how to gratify the desires of the sinful nature" (Romans 13:14).

"You are to abstain from food sacrificed to idols, from blood, from the meat of strangled animals and from sexual immorality. You will do well to avoid these things" (Acts 15:29).

"Avoid every kind of evil" (1 Thessalonians 5:22).

"For everything that was written in the past was written to teach us, so that through endurance and the encouragement of the Scriptures we might have hope" (Romans 15:4).

Were you free from pornography since you did the last lesson?
    Yes   No

Were you free from masturbation since you did the last lesson?
    Yes   No

Were you free from sexual immorality since you did the last lesson?
    Yes   No

DAY 27— GROWING IN CHRIST

It is good to see from Scripture that there are different stages of growth in the Christian life. The teaching today will bring encouragement to those who stumble, strengthen the faith of those who are beginning to overcome, and confirm the faith of those walking in habitual victory.

Please read the following passage, and answer the questions :

> 12 "I write to you, dear children, because your sins have been forgiven on account of his name. 13 I write to you, fathers, because you have known him who is from the beginning. I write to you, young men, because you have overcome the evil one. I write to you, dear children, because you have known the Father. 14 I write to you, fathers, because you have known him who is from the beginning. I write to you, young men, because you are strong, and the word of God lives in you, and you have overcome the evil one" (1 John 2:12-14).

Notice the three different groups the Apostle John addresses above:
1. Children—verses 12, 13
2. Young men—verses 13, 14
3. Fathers—verses 13, 14

The Christian life is one of ongoing growth, development and maturity. We can learn much in our fight against pornography by studying what John writes to each of the above groups.

Questions

Question 1. There are two things that the Apostle John writes about "little children". What are those two things.
- A. They cried a lot and spilled their food
- B. They were forgiven, and they knew the Father
- C. They fell down and skinned their knees often

The Apostle John writes to children—"Your sins have been forgiven on account of his name." And, "you have known the Father." We come into the Christian family by being born again, and through drinking the pure milk of God's Word can soon become little children. But little children fall a lot, and so John writes to little children "your sins have been forgiven on account of his name."

Question 2. Have you come in to God's family through the forgiveness of your sins?
- A. Yes, I am part of God's family because He has forgiven me.
- B. No, I do not need to be forgiven for any sins as I'm not that bad a person.

Little children stumble as they are learning to walk, it is part of the growing process. And initially little children do more falling than walking. This is the reason that John speaks of little children as being forgiven. This should teach us caution when dealing with those who fall a lot; they may be unsaved and living in sin, or they might be saved, but are children who are just learning to walk. Be careful in judging those who fall often.

Question 3. Please provide your comments on the two following Scriptures:

> "For though a righteous man falls seven times, he rises again, but the wicked are brought down by calamity" (Proverbs 24:16).

Testimony

The following testimony is from one of our mentors, Tim:

I am an older man in my late fifties. I have been sexually addicted to one form of immorality or another for most of my life. My addictions to pornography and masturbation began at an early age when I first discovered the stash of nudist magazines, which my dad kept hidden in his closet. As a teenager and a young man growing up in the 50's and the 60's, I tried to seduce as many girls as I could find into having sex with me. I joined the Navy at age 17 and the easy availability of prostitutes back then only intensified my sexual addictions. I considered it normal to have sex with as many women as I could find who were willing to indulge me in my sexual fantasies and pleasures. I had grown up with the "Playboy Philosophy" and firmly believed that this was what all men did.

After being discharged from the Navy, I entered college and got married. I thought that being married would end my preoccupation with sex. It did not. Even though I had slept around with many women before marriage, I had no intentions of doing so after marriage. I started hanging out in strip bars and X-rated movie theaters because I did not want to be "unfaithful" to my wife. I wasted much time and money on my voyeurism during those years. My failed marriage ended three years later. I returned to my former practice of seducing women because I was now free from the constraints of marriage.

I met the woman who would later become my wife in 1969. We have now been married for 30 years. At first I hid my sexual addictions from her because I thought that she simply would not understand. (I later discovered that secrecy is one of the devil's greatest devices to keep us in bondage to our sexual sins.) Ten years after we were

Continued on page 86

Questions

"²¹ Then Peter came to Jesus and asked, 'Lord, how many times shall I forgive my brother when he sins against me? Up to seven times?' ²² Jesus answered, 'I tell you, not seven times, but seventy-seven times'" (Matthew 18:21-22).

The passage we are studying in 1 John 2 tells us how one becomes born again: through a relationship with God, "You have known the Father." Jesus said, "And this is eternal life, that they may know You, the only true God, and Jesus Christ whom You have sent" (John 17:3ᴺᴷᴶⱽ). And knowing God starts with receiving His forgiveness, "Your sins have been forgiven on account of His Name." So the little child in Christ has a relationship with God that is based on forgiveness. He may not have grown much beyond this initial relationship, and like a little child, stumbles as much as he walks. John emphasizes forgiveness for the little child. Some of us feel as if all we are doing is stumbling and falling and are in constant need of forgiveness. If this is you, keep seeking the Lord for grace, because with growth comes strength.

The Apostle John writes to young men—"You have overcome the evil one." and "You are strong, and the word of God lives in you, and you have overcome the evil one."

How do we know we are progressing in the Christian life? We begin winning battles. The Word of God becomes our sword with which we defeat the evil one. The "young man" in the Lord is described as one who walks in victory over the enemy because the Word of God lives in him. Relating this to our subject, we are no longer living in the twin sins of pornography and masturbation, but we have acquired the tools from Scripture to be strong in the Lord and overcome the evil one.

For many years of my life I was a stumbling little child spiritually. I fell so often, and then repented only to fall again, sometimes on the same day. This continued way too long, as I had nobody who could assist me into growing spiritually. I am not blaming anyone, just stating facts that there was no **Pure Freedom** course back in the days when I was doing pornography, and nobody I knew wanted to talk about it. I went to several pastors but they did not have the spiritual insight necessary to help me out, so I remained stunted in my growth, malnourished and failing to thrive.

But then, through the assistance of my pastor, I learned the principles that make up this course, and I entered a growth spurt spiritually. He helped me understand how to apply the principles of radical amputation, accountability, dragging sin into the light, feeding on the Word…etc. and now I am walking in perpetual victory over sin.

What's more is that God is even using me to help others, and this has been a great delight, too.

So, I can see that there has been "growth in grace" in my life. I have gone from an unsaved man who lived in sin continually, to a little child who stumbled often, to a young man who knows how to fight sin using the principles in God's Word, to a father who is helping others. I do praise God for growth in grace.

Question 4. According to the passage we are studying in 1 John 2, what is the evidence that one has grown from a "little child" to a "young man?" Write your thoughts here:

Question 5. Next, please provide your thoughts about the next two passages of Scripture. Include whether or not the author was a "little child" or a "young man."

"We know that the law is spiritual; but I am unspiritual, sold as a slave to sin. ¹⁵ I do not understand what I do. For what I want to do I do not do, but what I hate I do. ¹⁶ And if I do what I do not want to do, I agree that the law is good. ¹⁷ As it is, it is no longer I myself who do it, but it is sin living in me. ¹⁸ I know that nothing good lives in me, that is, in my sinful nature. For I have the desire to do what is good, but I cannot carry it out. ¹⁹ For what I do is not the good I want to do; no, the evil I do not want to do—this I keep on doing. ²⁰ Now if I do what I do not want to do, it is no longer I who do it, but it is sin living in me that does it. ²¹So I find this law at work: When I want to do good, evil is right there with me. ²²For in my inner being I delight in God's law; ²³ but I see another law at work in the members of my body, waging war against the law of my mind and making me a prisoner of the law of sin at work within my members" (Romans 7:14-23).

Testimony

Tim's testimony continues …

married, my wife and I became Christians in 1979. I was ashamed to be seen in strip bars and X-rated theaters after becoming a Christian so I concentrated my sexual addictions upon pornography alone. The 1980's brought a new form of technology to feed the sexual desires of men such as me. I soon became hooked on X-rated videos. With the advent of the "neighborhood video stores", it was no longer necessary for sex addicts such as me to go to the "seedier parts of town" to feed our lustful desires. My addiction to X-rated videos was one of the hardest things that I have ever had to face. I even contemplated suicide several times because I could not find freedom from my bondage to those sexual sins.

I cried out to God for His help and He responded to my plea. The Lord led me to confess my sins to my wife and that confession finally broke the yoke of secrecy that had pervaded my life. I also found a man to whom I confessed my sexual addictions who later became my spiritual mentor. Together, we formed a group of similarly addicted men and we met regularly to support each other and hold each other accountable. We met bi-monthly for several years before the group dissolved in 1998. Pornographic X-rated videos were no longer the problem for me that they once were and I thought that I no longer needed accountability.

Satan, however, had other plans to ensnare me into a final form of sexual addiction. The Worldwide Web became a reality in the mid 1990's and along with it came the porn

Questions

"Shouts of joy and victory resound in the tents of the righteous: 'The Lord's right hand has done mighty things! 16 The Lord's right hand is lifted high; the Lord's right hand has done mighty things!'" (Psalm 118:15-16).

The Apostle John writes to Fathers—"You have known Him Who is from the beginning." The mature father in the Lord is again characterized by relationship. He still has his dependence on the Word of God but His attention now is on the God of the Word, and he is characterized by His relationship to the Lord. He is a father, so he has children and for our purposes this mature man has not only overcome the evil one, but is also assisting others out of pornography by the grace of God.

Question 6. Can you see the growth in the Lord that is taking place here in this passage?

Question 7. Please compare the following passage of Scripture to our struggle with pornography and masturbation:

"When I was a child, I talked like a child, I thought like a child, I reasoned like a child. When I became a man, I put childish ways behind me" (1 Corinthians 13:11).

Question 8. Dear children, young men, fathers. Which are you? Explain how you know which one you are currently:

Whichever level of maturity you can just know that there is growth ahead for all of us. The **Pure Freedom** course is designed to assist in our growth, taking us from little children who fall much and are in need of forgiveness often (beginning the course), to young men who know how to fight and are characterized by winning battles (middle portions of the course), to fathers who are producing fruit of other "little children" (mentors).

Keep growing dear children, and know that victory is around the next corner. Fight hard, young men for your adversary is angry at you. Enjoy your intimacy with the Father, fathers, and encourage your little ones to grow in the Lord.

Testimony

sites that proliferate the Internet today. I soon became hooked on this newest form of technology which brings porn into the privacy of one's own home. I firmly believe that Internet porn is the scourge of many Christian men today. It is practiced in the secrecy of one's own home and most men will attempt to hide this sin from their wives, pastors and friends at church. I attempted to free myself from the Internet porn by installing several different computer filters. I even subscribed to a filtered Christian ISP service once. None of these attempts to free myself from pornography on the Internet worked because I always found ways to circumvent them.

Once again I cried out to God and He led me to the SCF website through a friend that I had met online several years earlier. I enrolled in the **Pure Freedom** course and completed it without ever falling once back into my old habits of P&M. It was relatively easy for me to abstain from P&M while taking the course because I had been on the "road to recovery" already for several years prior to my enrolment in the course. The course gave me additional tools that I found useful in keeping me pure from all of my sexual sins. After completing the basic course, I enrolled in the mentor's course and I became a mentor on January 25, 2001.

I now truly believe that I have finally been set free from all forms of sexual addictions for the first time in my life. My only regret is that it has taken me so long to achieve sexual purity. It is therefore my desire to spend the remainder of my natural life helping other men to achieve the sexual purity that God has so graciously granted to me. May the Lord Jesus Christ be eternally praised and glorified for what He has done for me.

Scripture to Consider:

"I will surely bless you and make your descendants as numerous as the stars in the sky and as the sand on the seashore. Your descendants will take possession of the cities of their enemies, and through your offspring all nations on earth will be blessed, because you have obeyed me" (Genesis 22:17-18).

"And I tell you that you are Peter, and on this rock I will build my church, and the gates of Hades will not overcome it. I will give you the keys of the kingdom of heaven; whatever you bind on earth will be bound in heaven, and whatever you loose on earth will be loosed in heaven" (Matthew 16:18-19).

Were you free from pornography since you did the last lesson?   Yes   No

Were you free from masturbation since you did the last lesson?   Yes   No

Were you free from sexual immorality since you did the last lesson?   Yes   No

DAY 28— SANCTIFICATION

Dear friend,

Have you ever wondered about God's will for your life? Well, today we are going to explore this topic. We will be considering the following questions: What is the will of God for our lives? How do we find it? How do we do it? And what does that have to do with sexual bondage?

> "Finally, brothers, we instructed you how to live in order to please God, as in fact you are living. Now we ask you and urge you in the Lord Jesus to do this more and more. ²For you know what instructions we gave you by the authority of the Lord Jesus. ³It is God's will that you should be sanctified: that you should avoid sexual immorality; ⁴ that each of you should learn to control his own body in a way that is holy and honorable, ⁵ not in passionate lust like the heathen, who do not know God; ⁶ and that in this matter no one should wrong his brother or take advantage of him. The Lord will punish men for all such sins, as we have already told you and warned you. ⁷For God did not call us to be impure, but to live a holy life. ⁸ Therefore, he who rejects this instruction does not reject man but God, who gives you his Holy Spirit" (1 Thessalonians 4:1-8).

Questions

Question 1. In this passage Paul talks about avoiding sexual immorality, controlling our bodies, and living a holy life. But before he mentions all this, in verse one he provides a motive. What is this motive?

Question 2. In your own words, please tell why you believe Paul provides this motive for holy living.

There are many good reasons why we should avoid sexual immorality and learn to control our bodies. However, if we are Christians, our primary motivation for pursuing purity should be so that we might please the Lord. Before we knew Jesus Christ we lived to please ourselves in ever increasing wickedness, but now God's grace has changed our hearts so that we now earnestly desire to please Him instead of ourselves. A sincere desire to please Him will drive us on to resist the devil, to die to our flesh daily, to forsake the pleasure of sin continually, to avoid sexual immorality and to control our bodies in a way that is holy and honorable.

Question 3. Take a second and compare your past motives with your present motives. Where were you when involved in pornography and where are you now?

When we offer ourselves to pornography or sexual impurity of any kind, we soon find that the enslavement process begins to increase. We want more pictures, we continually seek for something new and different, we go from soft core to hard core...etc. We always want "more and more."

Testimony

The following is from Ben:

I was born, the oldest of four children, in Indiana in 1944, a much more innocent age. Movies still had censors and there was not one naked woman's breast to be seen on the screen. Women models in newspapers and magazines were covered almost completely and TV had not yet invaded American homes.

I remember joining with the majority of boys my age in an almost universal boycott of girls, who we regarded as weak and soft. Certainly any male who consorted with such as these was a "sissy" and not to be trusted. In many ways, the society was sexless compared to today's superheated environs. Playing doctor was about as risqué as it got for most of us - and, even then many of us kept both feet on the floor.

I'm not exactly sure when this changed, I know there had always been a large underground audience for Henry Miller, D.H Lawrence, Fanny Hill, blue movies, and the wares of prostitutes, but it simmered beneath the surface of society in the 40s and 50s barely causing ripples in peoples' everyday life. I think I saw my first bare woman's breast in the Pawnbroker in the middle 60s. After that, the nudity (and the language) became increasingly suggestive and blatant.

So during my "growth years", I had a rather pastoral upbringing, full of baseball, butterfly collecting, bike riding and basketball. The only sex I knew about was the "forbidden fruit" of adultery and fornication, which were continuously warned about each Sunday in church. I wouldn't have recognized either one if they'd attacked me on the playground.

So, if the outer environment of my youth was conducive to a celibate (i.e. ignorant) lifestyle, my upbringing was equally uninformative. So lacking was my sex education that I received none until the day I left for college, in 1962. So, until college, I had no "formal" sex education, my knowledge was gleaned from periodic raids on my parents "hidden" sex book, my friends' meager knowledge and what little I could glean on the streets.

As a result of my timidity, my parents fear, and a decided lack of information about girls and sex, I was not a social force in grade school, high school or college. As time progressed my

Continued on page 90

Questions

Course Member Paul writes: "My lust pulled me deeper and deeper into more risqué and perverted activities. After awhile the women were not as exciting as before and I found myself drifting into homosexual erotica. This was something that would have repulsed me before I became entrapped in the cycle of more and more."

Question 4. But when we present ourselves to the Lord and become slaves of Christ we enter a path of increasing righteousness. What instruction does Paul give in verse one above to teach this truth? Write your thoughts here:

Note: The Christian life is one of ongoing improvement; growing in purity, increasing in holiness, abounding in the work of the Lord "more and more."

Question 5. Verse 3 above tells us very clearly what God's will is. Please write out all of verse 3 here:

Question 6. According to verse 4, as Christians we must "learn something." What is it?
 A. We must learn to talk the right way
 B. We must learn how to get people to make a decision for Christ
 C. We must learn how to control our bodies in an honorable way

Question 7. Verse 5 describes those who live in "passionate lust" in two different ways. What are they?
 A. Oversexed and easily stimulated
 B. Heathen who do not know God

Note: Paul is instructing Christians to not live like their Pagan neighbors who did not know God. The Pagans lived their lives in lust, giving in to the cravings of the flesh in sexual immorality, and the degrading of their bodies in sexual perversion.

History records that pornography played a major role in the culture of their day and that pornographic "art" abounded. All of this is descriptive of a culture alienated from God, a people who chose not to retain God in their knowledge, and who logically began to "worship" sex in all its perversions. Paul's description of these people as those "who do not know God" is significant here. Knowing God, that is, having an intimate relationship with Him is the key ingredient that will enable us to "escape the corruption in the world caused by evil desires" (2 Peter 1:4).

Question 8. According to verse 6, what will God do to people who live like this?
 A. In grace, He will overlook their sins
 B. He will punish
 C. He knows we are only human and He understands our weaknesses

Question 9. How does the following verse reinforce this?

> "Marriage should be honored by all, and the marriage bed kept pure, for God will judge the adulterer and all the sexually immoral" (Hebrews 13:4).

Question 10. Verse 7 states what the "calling" of the Christian is. What is it?
 A. To convert others
 B. To hold up the 10 commandments as the standard of God
 C. To live a holy life and to be pure

Question 11. How are you doing with your calling?

Friends, as we seek to live a pure life in Christ, and do so "more and more" we will also be given opportunities to encourage others toward a holy life. Some may listen and heed our warnings and instructions, embrace Christ and forsake their sin. Others will cling to sin and attempt to justify themselves. Here, at Setting Captives Free, we have heard many different excuses from people who will not forsake their sin. Sadly, many of these people will use overtly spiritual language in their rejection of the truth. Here is an example we received the other day:

> "When I was saved and regenerated by the Holy Ghost (as salvation precedes regeneration) God showed me that His grace, mercy and loving kindness are there to forgive every sin I have ever committed and the sins I will continue to commit as a born-again, adopted, grace-bought child of God. He does not expect perfection from me, nor does He demand (under this dispensation of grace) that I forsake all sin in order for Him to love me. His grace increases with my sin, and is magnified every time I fall. No, I have not forsaken masturbation and pornography, but yet remain convinced that I know God, am known by God, and loved unconditionally. I will remain His child and do not need you to tell me to forsake sin. God knows I am a human being dwelling in flesh, and is sympathetic to the frailties of my flesh."

Notice the mixture of truth and error in his message. Despite all his religious language, this gentleman is unwilling to forsake his sin and is hostile to encouragements and warnings to do so.

Questions

Question 12. According to verse 8, when people reject teaching about avoiding immorality and learning to control their bodies, and about future punishment of those who continue to live in sin, what are they really rejecting?

A. They may love God, but they are rejecting the person who brings the message.

B. While embracing God, they are rejecting the teaching of men.

C. They are rejecting God!

Question 13. What do the following verses have to do with the previous situation described?

> "But I will come to you very soon, if the Lord is willing, and then I will find out not only how these arrogant people are talking, but what power they have. [20]For the kingdom of God is not a matter of talk but of power" (1 Corinthians 4:19-20).

> "Do you not know that the wicked will not inherit the kingdom of God? Do not be deceived: Neither the sexually immoral nor idolaters nor adulterers nor male prostitutes nor homosexual offenders [10]nor thieves nor the greedy nor drunkards nor slanderers nor swindlers will inherit the kingdom of God. And that is what some of you were. But you were washed, you were sanctified, you were justified in the name of the Lord Jesus Christ and by the Spirit of our God" (1 Corinthians 6:9-11).

> "Those who belong to Christ Jesus have crucified the sinful nature with its passions and desires" (Galatians 5:24).

Testimony

Ben's testimony continued...

hunger for knowing what I didn't know began to build higher and higher. As my body matured (I was among the last to do so), my feelings began to come into sharp conflict with my childhood creed that girls were to be avoided. Some of these curled and beribboned creatures were affecting me in a way that couldn't be ignored. Were my defenses weakening?

I only dated a few times in high school and I never kissed one of the girls. Something inside made me abhor even the least chance of rejection. Even in college, I went years between dates and these never went beyond the heavy petting stage.

I had discovered masturbation (mostly by accident) when I was about 16. We had a young couple that lived next to us. The kids' room was right opposite my bedroom. One night I was adjusting the curtains (you had to stand on the bed to do this) when the young mother came in, topless. She was, in my eyes at least, quite beautiful and I marveled at her nakedness. My masturbation career began shortly thereafter. I spent many nights waiting for Fate to repeat the adventure and I was rewarded a few times but not nearly in proportion to the time I spent.

This voyeurism carried me through high school and probably retarded my dating as well (each ejaculation tends to decrease your appetite for "the real thing" and all the protocol you have to go through to get it). In college, on my own hundreds of miles away from home, I was left to what little I'd learned and retained in what already was becoming a war between P&M and the search for a real-world mate. Although I'd left my naked neighbor's bust behind, my age had entered me into the world of "adult magazines", which proved to be admirable substitutes. I worked a lot after my first year in college and confined my sex life to P&M, although my buddies would force me to date every so often. Yet, these few dates provided no release and I always came back to the magazines.

I met my first wife in my last year of college. I was married to her for seven years. I was a poor and infrequent lover because I continued to do P&M at every opportunity. We had other issues that separated us but we never had a good sex life to bind us together. And I never imagined there was a connection between the P&M and my poor performance. Duh!

Several years passed from the end of my first marriage until I married another woman. During that time, I attended law school in San Francisco. I asked no law school women out, I sought no whores, I frequented no nightclubs. I did, however, escalate P from magazines to movies... there is nothing like a moving picture. Two years later I got married to a wonderful woman. Did this new "outlet" end the P&M? Of course not! Instead, I talked her into having me order perfumes, sex toys, videos, sex games and other junk. Did this enhance our sex life? No, because the cause lay in me.

How did my epiphany occur? How long did it take for this sad song to end? Did some cosmic bolt of lightning strike me on the mountaintop? Did a soft voice whisper in my ear? Did I have a near death experience? NO! I was sitting down when my wife came in with the picture of the nude 17 year old that I'd printed out to masturbate with. Rather than lie (which at that time was an attractive alternative), I spilled out the depths of my addiction to P&M. She asked a lot of questions and I answered truthfully the best I could. And, as we talked, it began to come clear to me what I'd done to my life (and my wife's) by clinging to this evil. I used to blame a thousand other reasons for our childlessness but the "worshiping" of lewd images is a crystal clear cause. Similarly, it explains my seeming lack of sex drive for my wife - if you've "sown" most of your seed what's left is not the greatest portion. Who do I love, my wife or my solitary pleasure?

So having seen the Truth, how to repair the brokenness? What else? I sought the answers on the Internet and I found Setting Captives Free. From Day 1, I have been drinking the Living water. My cistern is repaired and filled with sweet water. Simple isn't it? Confess, Repent, Rejoice. Yes, it's easy on paper but how long it takes before one can really see! Slowly, as I read, I began taking up my Sword of Faith and hacking at the roots of my addiction. I asked, and I ask you now, Lord Jesus, to hear my cry for help. Unfailingly, he answers with his Redemption, the Salvation for which all sinners seek. I could feel his protection wrap about me as I cried out for his help. Committed to eating the word of God daily, I am his and, in his Love, he sets me free of bondage to all things carnal. His peace becomes mine.

Questions

Let us summarize the teaching of the passage of Scripture:

What is God's will for our lives? That we should be sanctified: that we should avoid sexual immorality and that we should learn how to control our bodies in a way that honors the Lord. Our motive for doing this is to live in such a way as to please the Lord. Viewing pornography and masturbating, like all sexual impurity, is a sin that if not repented of will bring punishment from the Lord. If anyone rejects this teaching they are rejecting God. If we were to continue in these sins it would be evidence that we do not know God, and no amount of "spiritual language" can fool God, who calls us to live a holy life and to be pure. God gives us His Holy Spirit to call us out of slavery to sin, to make us pure and to enable us to live holy lives.

Scripture warns us about presuming upon God's grace in this area of sexual immorality (of which pornography is a part): "We should not commit sexual immorality, as some of them did—and in one day twenty-three thousand of them died. We should not test the Lord, as some of them did—and were killed by snakes" (1 Corinthians 10:8-9).

But friend, let us also add that all of us who have come to this **Pure Freedom** course have lived in this sexual immorality, in one form or another, in the past. Personally, for years I rebelled against God while in bondage to pornography and I presumed upon the grace of God by not forsaking my sins. God was indeed patient with me, and granted me repentance in His time. There is grace for all who will turn from their sin to Christ, and grace will enable us to live a holy life now regardless of our past. Grace is an amazing thing. It does not simply forgive the penalty of our sins while leaving us under the power of sin. It forgives and enables. It pardons and empowers. And it does so "more and more" as we grow in grace.

Please heed the warnings in the following words written by L. Eiland:[20]

Too Late

Too late, twill be for you to cry, when mercy's day has passed you by! When solemn night, of dark despair, Shall come upon you halting there!

Too late, when death has barred the door, your wailings can be heard no more! Rejected, there, thy soul will be shut out, through all eternity!

Will you not heed the voice today, inviting you Christ to obey? And be prepared to enter there, a pure and spotless robe to wear?

No longer, there in sin abide! This all-important step decide! Come out, where Christ can touch thy soul, and at this moment be made whole!

Chorus: Too late, too late, poor trembling soul! O will this be your fate? Too late, too late to be made whole! Too late, too late, too late!

Testimony

Having confessed and been assured of Christ's redemption, I testify now to the freedom and love he has blessed me with. I rise every morning in prayer and, rain, wind or shades of night, I speak his name: a surge of peace and forgiveness descends upon me. Throughout the day I rejoice in my deliverance from the bonds of P&M. I walk then free of guilt, free of the need to incessantly hide and prevaricate. Great God, thank you for your forgiveness and understanding. I thrive in your limitless Joy and Righteousness.

Every day I walk a little straighter, I sing a little more, I speak as a follower seeking converts for his Master. At the end of the day, I thank God for each blessing of the day (and I see more and more as each day passes.) Father, above all, I ask you to free the young ones from the slavery of P&M. Let not another life be ruined in the name of pleasure and hedonism.

Father and Son, for setting me free, I thank you! Let me help you do the same for others wherever evil lives.

Comments:

Scripture to Consider:

"You will be secure, because there is hope; you will look about you and take your rest in safety. You will lie down, with no one to make you afraid, and many will court your favor. But the eyes of the wicked will fail, and escape will elude them; their hope will become a dying gasp" (Job 11:18-20).

Were you free from pornography since you did the last lesson?   Yes   No

Were you free from masturbation since you did the last lesson?   Yes   No

Were you free from sexual immorality since you did the last lesson? Yes   No

DAY 29—OUR IDENTITY IN CHRIST

An anonymous course graduate wrote the majority of today's course material.

Today we are going to look at several Scriptures in the book of Ephesians. You will want to have your Bible handy and maybe a pen and paper to take notes. This study may be a little bit on the long side, but I think you will appreciate its value when you are finished.

Our Glorious Inheritance as God's Children
Our Identity in Christ

One of the lies that Satan wants to get us to believe is that our faith in Christ really has no effect on our lives. We are still the same old sinners we always were. We haven't really changed a bit. But this is a lie. God says in His word the truth about who we are now as His children.

The reason we need to understand our identity in Christ is that knowing who we are will affect the way we respond to various things in our lives. When you're trying to overcome the sin of lust, for example, you need to know that you're not a lustful person in God's eyes. If you believed that you were lustful and that you couldn't help yourself when tempted, you would very easily succumb to every temptation that comes your way. Knowing who we are in Christ will help us to be victorious over pornography. We won't go near the temptation because we are not the same people.

Questions

Question 1. According to verse 1, what were we?

> Ephesians 2:1-10 (v. 1)
> As for you, you were dead in your transgressions and sins,

A. Zombies
B. Living life to the fullest
C. Dead in sins and trespasses

Note: When we were living in pornography we were in reality dead! We did not need education, or behavioral modification, or mere admonition to stop doing what we were doing. We needed life! Not that we were dead physically, (though we may have been headed there) but we were dead spiritually; dead to God, dead to His Word, dead to the church, etc...

> (v. 2) in which you used to live when you followed the ways of this world and of the ruler of the kingdom of the air, the spirit who is now at work in those who are disobedient.

Question 2. What does verse 2 tell us we were?

A. Following Christ
B. Following the way to life
C. Followers of the world and Satan

Note: We were not only dead, we were devilish as well; just following along after the "carrot" that Satan offered to lead us into his trap.

Question 3. What else does verse 2 tell us we were?

A. Satisfied by our enjoyment of pornography
B. Disobedient
C. Experiencing ever-increasing joy

Question 4. What does verse 3 tell us we were?

> (v. 3) All of us also lived among them at one time, gratifying the cravings of our sinful nature and following its desires and thoughts. Like the rest, we were by nature objects of wrath.

A. Gratifiers of our sinful lusts
B. Gentle and loving people
C. Humble servants

Question 5. What else does verse 3 tell us we were?

A. Followers of every desire and thought
B. Able to resist temptation with ease

Note: Not only were we dead, devilish, and disobedient, but we were also

Testimony

The following testimony is from Robbie:

I started my association with pornography when I was 12 years old, which is when I "found" an old pornographic magazine in the forest near our house. It satisfied my curiosity about the opposite sex and put pictures in my mind that I did not fully understand. I was never popular in junior high or high school and never had girl friends. I discovered masturbation in high school and I regularly engaged in that (often using pornography for stimulation) throughout college (until I met my wife). Twice during college I recall going to strip joints and although it was sexually stimulating, it made me feel cheap and guilty afterward.

It was my wonderful wife who taught me the true meaning of love. We did not live together prior to marriage and our first time was on our honeymoon. For several years I stayed away from pornography and gave up masturbation altogether. This lasted until I discovered the Internet and the ease of finding pornography on the Internet. I found myself slipping back into the habits that I thought were long gone. Some times I would find myself out of control seeking out pictures of nude women on the internet for no reason or just because I was bored. I realized that this was wrong and offensive to God. Often I felt guilt about these sessions and sought reconciliation, but I would still return to the web sites.

The Apostle Paul tells us in 2 Corinthians 5:17, "Therefore, if anyone is in Christ, he is a new creation; the old has gone, the new has come!" If we have accepted Jesus as our savior, then God tells us that we are in Christ. What exactly does this mean? What is Paul saying when he says we are in Christ? My Bible happens to have study notes in it. Here's what it says about being "in Christ":

"In Christ. United with Christ through faith in Him and commitment to Him."

God is telling us that we have, as believers, a spiritual union with Jesus (and hence with God Himself). The bond we have with the Lord is unseen, but it is nonetheless very real.

Jesus explains this truth in His prayer in John 14:20-21, "On that day you will realize that I am in my Father, and you are in me, and I am in you. Whoever has my commands and obeys them, he is the one who loves me. He who loves me will be loved by my Father, and I too will love him and show myself to him."

This describes our relationship with God very well. It is one of living in Him and He living in us. He gives to us His life, and we give to Him our lives. He gives to us His love; we give to Him our love.

We need to understand how God has changed our lives to enjoy our relationship with Him to the fullest. To do that we need to take time and read from Scripture what God says about us now that we are in Christ.

Let's look at some Scripture from Paul's letter to the Ephesians and contrast who we WERE with who we ARE now.

Testimony

God told me to seek out help to resolve this problem, on the way to Mass one day. I returned from Mass that day and used the Internet search engine to find www.SettingCaptivesFree.com. Thanks to your help, I have been free from pornography for two months now. I have been attending daily Mass whenever possible and have successfully gotten rid of pornography from my life. I pray each day to love God and my wife and children more each day. Thank you and God bless you!

Questions

depraved! This is the condition of all who follow their impulses and live to gratify their flesh. If we had an impulse to view porn we did it. Then if we had a desire to masturbate we did. And slowly, over time, we began to be controlled by our impulses, which were becoming stronger and stronger.

Question 6. And what does verse 3 tell us is the final description of us as we used to be?
  A. Objects of God's wrath
  B. People who knew and loved God

Note: That's right, we were the destination for God's wrath! We were the bull's-eye for the arrows of God's hatred; the object of His anger. This ought to frighten us to the core of our very being, and if we have escaped the trap of pornography we ought to be grateful for the grace of God!

Question 7. Please describe how your past life in pornography illustrates the above teaching. How were you dead, devilish, disobedient, depraved...etc. Describe how your life verified the truth of Scripture.

We readily admit that a Christian, who is indeed alive in Christ, can succumb to the temptation of pornography. The believer is alive, and though he may be disobedient at the time, he is not dead, devilish, depraved, or under the wrath of God. But the passage we have just studied is about unbelievers who live in sin. As it says in Ephesians 2 "As for you, you were dead in your transgressions and sins, in which you used to live."

Next we will notice that a great transformation has taken place. We are not who we were! Our identity is different. Read the following passage again, noticing who we are NOW.

> (v. 4) But because of his great love for us, God, who is rich in mercy,

Question 8. According to verse 4, what are we?
  A. Still hated by God
  B. Loved by God
  C. Somewhere in the middle

Note: It is God's love and grace that changes our identity.

Question 9. What else does verse 4 tell us we are?
- A. Second class Christians
- B. Recipients of God's mercy
- C. Step-children

(v. 5) made us alive with Christ even when we were dead in transgressions—it is by grace you have been saved.

Question 10. What does verse 5 tell us we are?
- A. Mummies
- B. Still dead in sin
- C. Alive with Christ

Question 11. What do verses 5 and 8 tell us we are?
- A. Trying to get saved
- B. Saved by grace
- C. Saved by our works

Note: Salvation is by grace alone. Not grace, plus what we do, it is all of grace. God chose us to be saved in eternity past (Ephesians 1; 2 Thessalonians 2:13), and then gave us grace to believe (Acts 18:27), and it is God who will keep us saved throughout eternity.

(v. 6) And God raised us up with Christ and seated us with him in the heavenly realms in Christ Jesus,

Question 12. What else are we in verse 6?
- A. Seated on David's couch
- B. Earthly people
- C. Seated with Christ in heaven

Note: This very principle, of being alive and raised up from sin, is why man's methods of helping those with addictions will not work. Man can give advice, suggestions, and counsel but man cannot impart life! Only God can raise the dead.

(v. 7) in order that in the coming ages he might show the incomparable riches of his grace, expressed in his kindness to us in Christ Jesus.

Question 13. According to verse 7 who are we?
- A. Recipients of God's grace and kindness
- B. Targets of wrath

(v. 8) For it is by grace you have been saved through faith—and this is not from yourselves, it is the gift of God—(v. 9) not by works, so that no one can boast.

Question 14. According to verses 8 and 9, what are we?
- A. Saved by faith in Christ
- B. Saved by our own efforts to overcome sin

(v. 10) For we are God's workmanship, created in Christ Jesus to do good works, which God prepared in advance for us to do.

Question 15. What does verse 10 tell us we are?
- A. Useless, broken vessels
- B. God's workmanship

Note: The Greek word for "workmanship" in verse 10 is the word poema, from which we get our word POEM. We are God's poem to the world, His art that displays His grace, His workmanship of love.

Let us summarize who we used to be, versus who we are now:

WE WERE:
1. Dead in transgressions and sins (v. 1, 5)
2. Followers of the world and Satan (v. 2)
3. Disobedient to God (v. 2)
4. Gratifiers of our sinful lusts (v. 3)
5. Followers of our every desire and thought (v. 3)
6. Objects of God's wrath (v. 3)

Next, we will examine who we are NOW. **WE ARE:**
1. Loved by God (v. 4)
2. Recipients of God's mercy (v. 4)
3. Alive with Christ (v. 5)
4. Saved by grace (v. 5, 8)
5. Raised up with Christ (v. 6)
6. Seated with Christ in heaven (v. 6)
7. Recipients of God's grace and kindness in Christ (v. 7)
8. Saved through faith in Christ (not from ourselves, it is a gift of God, and not by our works) (v. 8, 9)
9. God's workmanship (v. 10)
10. Created (this means re-created) in Christ Jesus to do good works pre-prepared for us (v. 10)

Wow! Isn't it awesome all that God has done for us? Take time right now to praise God in prayer for all the wonderful things He's done in our lives. We are not the same anymore!

My challenge to you is to take the book of Ephesians and do this same kind of study. There are even more wonderful truths you will discover about who you are now in Christ Jesus! God's Word has the power to literally transform us.

Paul said in 2 Corinthians 3:18, "And we, who with unveiled face all reflect the Lord's glory, are being transformed into his likeness with ever-increasing glory, which comes from the Lord, who is the Spirit."

Question 16. Practically speaking, what are some differences in your life, now that you have left pornography behind? Can you tell a difference, does anyone else see the change?

Scripture to Consider

"I have been crucified with Christ and I no longer live, but Christ lives in me. The life I live in the body, I live by faith in the Son of God, who loved me and gave himself for me" (Galatians 2:20).

Were you free from pornography since you did the last lesson?
    Yes   No

Were you free from masturbation since you did the last lesson?
    Yes   No

Were you free from sexual immorality since you did the last lesson?
    Yes   No

DAY 30—NEW CREATION IN CHRIST (SALVATION ILLUSTRATED)

Today we will study a passage that will encourage us toward a better understanding of how salvation works, and how it relates to our previous sexual impurity and use of pornography. It follows on the heels of yesterday's lesson that taught us we are "new CREATIONS in Christ" (2 Corinthians 5:17). I truly can't wait to share this with you! Let's get started.

> "In the beginning God created the heavens and the earth. Now the earth was formless and empty, darkness was over the surface of the deep, and the Spirit of God was hovering over the waters. And God said, 'Let there be light,' and there was light" (Genesis 1:1-2).

> "Therefore, if anyone is in Christ, he is a new creation; the old has gone, the new has come" (2 Corinthians 5:17).

Friends, we are new "creations" in Jesus. I am not a "refurbished" Mike; I am totally new. God does not shave caterpillars; He makes butterflies! And so it is profitable for us to study the biblical account of the creation of the earth, for in it we can see how God has saved us.

Notice there are three things, which are said of the earth in the beginning. It was:
1. Formless
2. Empty
3. In darkness

And if we look at Genesis 1 verse 9 we can see a fourth description of the earth:
4. Submerged underneath water.

Can you see how all of this is relating to us as new creations in Christ? Let me explain. We, too, at one time were:

Formless. This same word is translated "confusion" in Deuteronomy 32:10. Empty. Why did we turn to pornography anyway? Probably because we were trying to "fill the void." Emptiness in heart and life is the condition of all who are trapped in porn. Instead of being "filled with all the fullness of God," and having an overflowing cup as David did, we were inwardly empty, lonely, yearning people.

> *Course Member Michael writes:* "I wanted to be filled with love and companionship but by looking at porn I alienated myself from any hope of ever finding a lasting love. My heart was empty and I found the further into porno I went the further I was from satisfaction and fullness."

In Darkness. Oh friend, can you remember the darkness that pervaded your life in pornography? The absence of light, wisdom, direction, and illumination all characterized my 15-year addiction to pornography.

Submerged underneath the water. We were dead and buried under the water of our sin. Lost, sunk, submerged, and dead.

And so we have a perfect description of how we were when trapped in sin: We were "formless," confused, empty, in darkness and buried under the water of our sin.

Questions

Question 1. Please write out the description of the earth in its initial stages, using the four words in these verses:

Question 2. Does this describe your past? Can you recall any of the feelings you had when living in pornographic sin?

Question 3. Specifically focusing on "empty", can you see how using pornography may have been an attempt to be fulfilled? Satisfied? Explain.

Question 4. Referring to the word "submerged" in the lesson. Did you ever feel like you were sunk down deep in porn or sexual impurity? Ever feel submerged? How so?

> *Course Member Ben writes:* "When I was deep into it, it consumed me. A good portion of my time was spent in the pursuit of pornography."

Questions

Next, God said "let there be light". Please don't miss this: It is the Word of God that brings light. Notice this verse: "The unfolding of your words gives light; it gives understanding to the simple" (Psalm 119:130).

Dear friends, if you are saved there was a time in your life that you were in darkness. Possibly this was when you were in pornographic slavery. But then you began having an interest in Scripture. And you were drawn to Jesus Christ. He spoke light into your heart through His Word, dispelling your sin and darkness. And now you are becoming, for lack of a better word, "addicted" to God's Word. And you are receiving illumination, understanding, and wisdom (light).

The Apostle Paul, under the inspiration of the Holy Spirit, applied Genesis 1:1-3 in this fashion. Paul says in 2 Corinthians 4:6 "For God, who said, 'Let light shine out of darkness,' made His light shine in our hearts to give us the light of the knowledge of the glory of God in the face of Christ." It is the same God who spoke light into darkness in creation that illuminates our hearts with Jesus Christ in salvation. Do you see it?

Course Member Dennis writes: "When I was doing pornography, I was very confused. I struggled with the uncertainty of my personal salvation. I thought how could I enjoy this sin and still call myself a believer. I tried to rationalize my sin and that only led to more confusion. Empty: I can truly say that I felt dead inside. I felt nothing emotionally or spiritually. I was a shell of what God created anew. Darkness: I had more in common with sinful men than with believers. I was so degenerate that I was not in fellowship with God or men. My heart was only darkness continually and I hated the light although I claimed to love it. I was a hypocrite. Submerged: I was drowning in my sin. I put my hand up for help, but the people I was swimming with just waved back. They were drowning too, not waving. Thank God for rescuing me."

So, we were indeed confused, empty, in darkness, and buried in sin. But the Holy Spirit was "hovering" over us and God said, "let there be light." And the Word brought light into our hearts. Let us continue in our study:

> "And God said, 'Let the water under the sky be gathered to one place, and let dry ground appear.' And it was so" (Genesis 1:9).

Now, this is where it begins to get truly exciting. Do you see what is happening here? The earth, which was submerged beneath the water, has now come bursting up through the water, sort of like a resurrection. What was once buried is now alive, and is about to begin producing fruit!

Oh friend, this is YOU if you are in Christ. Once empty, in darkness, buried in sin; now raised from the dead, full of the glory of God, enjoying the light of Jesus Christ. And watch this...

"Then God said, 'Let the land produce vegetation: seed-bearing plants and trees on the land that bear fruit with seed in it, according to their various kinds.' And it was so" (Genesis 1:11). This gets better and better. Now the earth is alive and producing fruit. Oh how I wish you and I were sharing this Scripture together right now, feeding on the truth of it. Do you see what is happening? Now I am not going to comment on this verse, instead I'm going to ask you to answer Question 5:

Question 5. Write out how the above verse applies to you and salvation.

Testimony

The following testimony is from Tammy:

My first remembrance of lust was when I was young, in elementary school, and I found my mom's Cosmo magazines. I loved to read and too soon found the "love stories". Most were very explicit and this led to masturbation at a young age. I never knew what I was doing really, or what it was called. I just knew it felt good. Along the years, I'd find her romance novels or else more magazines. But later on when I got the Internet it all changed. I had this huge source at my fingertips, whatever I wanted to see or read it was there. After feeding my desires of the flesh, I usually felt satisfied. I never thought this was wrong, no one said it was. I always thought I was a Christian, until the summer of 1997, when I did become born again. But since no one really said what I was doing was wrong. I kept at it. In the back of my mind I suddenly had this conscience, which made me feel worse every time I did this. I finally realized I was drawing away from God when I did this. Although I tried to justify it, it wouldn't work. Did this bring me closer to God? Would I have done this with Him in the same room? No, no, no. I kept asking, pleading with God to make me stop, help me stop because I only wanted to be his. But I kept at it. Everywhere I looked I was bombarded with lust images... although I was still searching for Christian ways to help. I finally found this course and knew I was free. But after a lengthy process, and a second start at the course, it is almost a year later that I am done.

And it was just two Mondays ago, when the real change happened. God broke me and made me remorseful of what I had done. Someone who never cries was broken down crying at all the things she had done. I am finally finding peace about this and freedom through the grace of God. Thankful for He is there each day for me, because this battle, although already won by Christ, I still have to fight the devil each day, knowing that I am more than a conqueror in Christ.

Course Member Roy writes: "In hindsight, I can see that NO part of my life was unaffected by my use of pornography and my submission to my lustful thoughts. There were parts of me, intellectual, spiritual, physical that were wasted on pornography and lust. These parts of me have been released from the slavery of lust, just as my soul has been freed from the damnation of sin. These parts are now able to join the rest of me in celebrating life and the salvation Christ has freely offered to me."

Question 6. John 15:5 says, "I am the Vine, you are the branches. If a man remains in Me and I in Him, He will bear much fruit." How does that verse apply to what we are studying?

Oh, friend, it is truly quite wonderful to know God as Creator; not so much that He created the world (though that is important) but that He can create good out of bad, light out of darkness, order out of chaos in our lives.

And now you can tell your testimony to others in a very short and simple manner: "I was empty, in darkness, and buried under the waters of sin; but God spoke light into my heart, raised me from the dead, filled me with His Son, and is making me fruitful." Amen!

And one last point: Did you happen to notice that it was on the third day that the "resurrection" of the earth happened? This point is important. In creation there was initial chaos, darkness, emptiness and death. And then, on the third day, there was a resurrection unto life and fruitfulness! Do you understand? The Lord Jesus emptied Himself for us amidst the chaos of His crucifixion. Then He hung on the cross in darkness and died for our sins. But on the third day He arose from the dead; victorious over sin, death, hell and the grave. And now you and I are the fruit of His suffering. We are the living souls He died to produce, and we carry precious seed to give life to others. Please do not miss this precious picture of our Lord Jesus Christ here in the first chapter of Genesis.

Here are a number of course member comments to show that our experiences while "submerged" in the darkness of pornography are common:

Course Member Troy writes: "I hope the feelings I have do not constitute pride. But I do feel free and it seems like I have to get to know myself all over again. However, this new person is one I definitely like better than the old; new, fresh, likeable. My wife and I kept our grand kids yesterday and I actually felt like entering into their lives more than usual. Just being myself and talking to each one of them was so neat. I actually wanted to just be with them. So, I've learned that masturbation and porn certainly does dim the joy and light in one's heart and bruises one's desire for living. Thanks for your site and your loving concern."

Course Member Jonas writes: "This very much describes my past. I was submerged in the deep waters of pornography. I am now above those waters. The Lord has saved me from drowning and from a horrible death/destruction as in the case of Ted Bundy. I don't know where I would have ended up if I went further down, but I do know it would have been the path to destruction. The Lord saved me and turned me to the opposite direction of this path."

Course Member Michel writes: "I was drowning in life, without God's guidance. But now I feel like I am walking on water."

Scripture to Consider

"Therefore, there is now no condemnation for those who are in Christ Jesus, because through Christ Jesus the law of the Spirit of life set me free from the law of sin and death. For what the law was powerless to do in that it was weakened by the sinful nature, God did by sending his own Son in the likeness of sinful man to be a sin offering. And so he condemned sin in sinful man, in order that the righteous requirements of the law might be fully met in us, who do not live according to the sinful nature but according to the Spirit" (Romans 8:1-4).

Were you free from pornography since you did the last lesson?
    Yes   No

Were you free from masturbation since you did the last lesson?
    Yes   No

Were you free from sexual immorality since you did the last lesson?
    Yes   No

DAY 31—THE GREATNESS, MAJESTY, POWER AND GRACE OF GOD

This course is not just a "how to" guide for overcoming pornography and sexual impurity. The real purpose of this course is to assist us in viewing God as He really is, and loving Him supremely. For if the Holy Spirit opens our eyes to see the vastness, majesty and glory of God, and we are brought to see His power and grace, then the natural response is worship and love of God. In other words, this course is not just about ceasing sinful behavior; it is about helping us to love God. It is not just about morality, it is about holiness.

So today we will examine a passage of Scripture that shows the glory, majesty and power of God, as well as His grace and compassion. May Scripture expand our view of Who God is, and cause us to be in awe of Him, for surely we cannot be viewing the greatness and glory of God and still be involved in habitual sin. Please read the following and answer the questions:

> "See, the Sovereign LORD comes with power, and his arm rules for him. See, his reward is with him, and his recompense accompanies him" (Isaiah 40:10).

The above verse describes God as the "Sovereign Lord" who comes with power and strength. This teaches us that God is God over all, the supreme Potentate, and the ruling King. "His arm rules for Him" is a metaphor for God being strong enough to rule, doing as He pleases and being able to accomplish what He decrees.

> "He tends his flock like a shepherd: He gathers the lambs in his arms and carries them close to his heart; he gently leads those that have young" (verse 11).

Verse 10 described God as the Sovereign Lord displaying His power, but verse 11 describes Him as a loving Shepherd displaying His grace. This God is not only One Who is in control of the entire universe, but He is also the caring Shepherd who loves individual "sheep;" carrying them closely and leading them gently.

This combination of Lord and Shepherd, of Divine Power and Divine Love, of Majesty and Grace is what makes our God so amazing.

> "Who has measured the waters in the hollow of his hand, or with the breadth of his hand marked off the heavens? Who has held the dust of the earth in a basket, or weighed the mountains on the scales and the hills in a balance?" (verse 12)

Questions

Question 1. Please examine what these verses have to say about who God is, and compare the view of God that you have had up to this point. Are you growing in comprehension of the greatness of God? What are your thoughts so far?

Question 2. According to the verses, what will the proper view of man be, once we catch a glimpse of the greatness of God?

Question 3. If people think themselves to be great, what are they missing?

> "Do you not know? Have you not heard? Has it not been told you from the beginning? Have you not understood since the earth was founded? 22 He sits enthroned above the circle of the earth, and its people are like grasshoppers. He stretches out the heavens like a canopy, and spreads them out like a tent to live in. 23 He brings princes to naught and reduces the rulers of this world to nothing. 24 No sooner are they planted, no sooner are they sown, no sooner do they take root in the ground, than he blows on them and they wither, and a whirlwind sweeps them away like chaff" (verses 21-24).

The questions in verse 21 are almost a mimic of man's inability to perceive the greatness of God. What, can't you understand? Can't you perceive that God is the God of the entire universe, the great King of all creation, who uses the entire heavens for His tent, who does as He pleases with all of mankind? Isn't this obvious to you? Paul says, "19 since what may be known about God is plain to them, because God has made it plain to them. 20 For since the creation of the world God's invisible qualities—his eternal power and divine nature—have been clearly seen, being understood from what has been made, so that men are without excuse" (Romans 1:19-20).

> 25 "To whom will you compare me? Or who is my equal?" says the Holy One. 26 Lift your eyes and look to the heavens: Who created all these? He who brings out the starry host one by one, and calls them each by name. Because of his great power and mighty strength, not one of them is missing" (verses 25-26).

Though this passage compares mankind to "grasshoppers" yet God cannot be com-

Scientists tell us that the entire existing universe is so vast and expansive that it cannot be measured, and yet God marks it off with His hand. The use of the word "hand" here is not to teach us that God has body parts, for He is a Spirit, but to show the supreme greatness of God over His created universe. The vast universe, that baffles the scientific genius of man and leaves him speechless, is but a handbreadth to God. In verse 10 above we saw the power of God, in verse 11 we saw His grace, and now in verse 12 we see His glory. Who is like unto our God?

> "Who has understood the mind of the LORD, or instructed him as his counselor? 14 Whom did the LORD consult to enlighten him, and who taught him the right way? Who was it that taught him knowledge or showed him the path of understanding?" (vs. 13, 14)

These questions, and the verses that follow, are designed to show the insignificance of man in light of the greatness of God. Is there anyone on earth who might suggest to God that He measure the universe differently, or that He should use a different basket in which to carry the entire dust of the earth, or that He weigh the mountains using different scales? Some may declare, "I Am God" but when have they measured the entire universe with their hand, or carried the dust of the earth in a basket or weighed mountains? **Those who do not see the greatness of God become great in their own eyes.**

> "Surely the nations are like a drop in a bucket; they are regarded as dust on the scales; he weighs the islands as though they were fine dust. 16 Lebanon is not sufficient for altar fires, nor its animals enough for burnt offerings. 17Before him all the nations are as nothing; they are regarded by him as worthless and less than nothing" (verses 15-17).

What God can look at the teeming nations, such as China whose population is 1,238,599,424, or Russia whose population is 1,469,089,929 and call them "a drop in the bucket" and "dust on the scales?" What kind of a God can weigh an island? And in light of the greatness of God, these nations of man are considered by Him as "nothing," "worthless" and "less than nothing."

> "To whom, then, will you compare God? What image will you compare him to?" (verse 18)

God is the incomparably great God, unable to be reduced to words, inexplicable in human terminology, and unlike anything that has been or ever could be made.

pared, for He is too great. God is awesome in splendor, powerful in majesty, beautiful in grace, and He has no equal. Can the great gurus of other religions create the heavens? Can all the prophets of all the religions down through the ages bring out each star and give it a name?

> "Why do you say, O Jacob, and complain, O Israel, 'My way is hidden from the LORD; my cause is disregarded by my God'? Do you not know? Have you not heard? The LORD is the everlasting God, the Creator of the ends of the earth. He will not grow tired or weary, and his understanding no one can fathom" (verses 27-28).

Questions

Since God is so great, and since He has created all things, and is ruling over all things, can we hide from Him? When we rush to click on to the pornographic website, or we hurry to leave work so we can get to the adult bookstore, is our way hidden from God? Does God look the other way when we watch X-rated videos? "For a man's ways are in full view of the LORD, and he examines all his paths" (Proverbs 5:21). God sees everything we do, and though we think we are sinning in secret, the Light will some day expose the things done in darkness. Our way is not hidden from the Lord, and we can never sin in secret. As Moses was about to kill the Egyptian he "looked left and right" to see if anyone was looking, and having concluded that no one was watching he killed the Egyptian. Though he looked left and right, he forgot to look up.

> "He gives strength to the weary and increases the power of the weak. 30 Even youths grow tired and weary, and young men stumble and fall; 31 but those who hope in the LORD will renew their strength. They will soar on wings like eagles; they will run and not grow weary, they will walk and not be faint" (Isaiah 40:29-31).

Here is what today's teaching on the greatness and awesome power of the Lord comes down to: All God's power is employed to strengthen the weary and to increase the power of the weak.

Question 4. Verse 31 above is the "bridge" that enables us to cross over from stumbling and falling, to soaring and running. What is this bridge, and what does it mean?

Question 5. By way of review, please write down all the things that this passage teaches us about God. Please do not rush through this, but contemplate all that God is, and all that He can do.

Questions

Question 6. If God is showing you His own greatness, and your own insignificance by comparison, how do you think this will affect your life?

Dear friend, when I was involved in the habitual sins of pornography and masturbation I entertained great thoughts about myself. I thought I was more spiritual than others, that I was an authority on Scripture, and that people should look up to me. Sin hardens and deceives, and that, combined with my spiritual knowledge, led me into thinking I was somebody. All of these great thoughts about myself were because my view of God was so small.

God gave me over to sin for a time, much like He gave King Nebuchadnezzar over to an insane mind for 7 years, to live on the fields and eat grass like a cow. He showed me that my will was only free to sin, that He was in control of all things, and that He held my life (both physical and spiritual) in His hands. Through my sinning, and the subsequent loss of my marriage of 14 years, and the labels many others put on me "Adulterer, Fornicator…etc." God began bringing me low and reducing me to nothing. Finally, I had lost all self-respect, and thought God had thrown me away on the trash heap of sinful humanity. This is how I, as a young man "stumbled and fell."

But then God did an amazing thing. He began picking me back up, remaking me, giving me grace to forsake sin and embrace Christ, empowering me when I was so weak to "soar" and "run" and "walk", and now He is making me useful again. This is causing me to say, "Wow, look at Who God is, and what He can do. He not only created the heavens and the earth, but He has taken me out of the trap of the devil, is carrying me close to His heart, and giving me strength to overcome sin.

Testimony

The following is from Ronnie:

I grew up like any other kid in America. I played sports (football, wrestling, track), went to church sometimes against my will but I went. I was on the Honor Roll. I was saved and baptized in my early teens. But I had this sin I always kept hiding.

Since I could not get into R rated movies at the theater when I was in high school, I could rent them at the family rental store. So I rented what I call soft porn with only partial nudity. This grew over the years and finally I bought a Porn magazine on the way to work. When I got into my truck I started shaking violently. It really scared me. That was the only time that happened.

Every once in a while I would rent an R rated movie or buy an adult magazine. One day I decided I would go to a strip club. There was no nudity but I was hooked. A few months later I went to another one where there was full nudity and I was hooked even more and $400 poorer, $20 a dance. A few months later I walked into one and one of the dancers ran up to me and said she knew me. We went to high school together, I even took her out on a date in high school, my graduation party. After I left I have never saw her again.

I bought a computer and eventually got onto the Internet and saw the pictures at the porn sites. I was afraid I would get caught, so I made an appointment with the youth pastor at my church. He and I are close in age so I could trust him. I had him as a Sunday school teacher a few months before.

And he challenged us to confess our sins to an accountability partner. I confessed everything and held nothing back. Victory Day May 3, 2000. When I was involved in this lifestyle I felt like dirt, like I was unclean or something. I rededicated my life to God and started living for Jesus. I started the **Pure Freedom** course in Oct 2000 and between May and Oct I fell only once or twice but quickly went to my pastor and confessed.

All the time I was involved in this lifestyle I knew I was doing wrong sinning against God. Since I started the **Pure Freedom** course I try to picture myself walking with Jesus. And you know what, it has been really cool. So if you are struggling in any way I encourage you to find someone your can trust and confess your sin, believe me it is worth it. You have to want to be free. If you don't then you will just keep on living in that lifestyle and one day you will get caught.

Scripture to Consider

"But you are a chosen people, a royal priesthood, a holy nation, a people belonging to God, that you may declare the praises of him who called you out of darkness into his wonderful light. [10] Once you were not a people, but now you are the people of God; once you had not received mercy, but now you have received mercy" (1 Peter 2:9-10).

Were you free from pornography since you did the last lesson?	Yes	No
Were you free from masturbation since you did the last lesson?	Yes	No
Were you free from sexual immorality since you did the last lesson?	Yes	No

DAY 32—
BATTLE STRATEGIES

YOU ARE AT WAR, SOLDIER; TIME TO LEARN HOW TO FIGHT!

During the next several days, we will examine the tactics of the Enemy of our souls, as well as develop some battle strategies of our own to combat him. Please read the following verses, paying close attention to exactly where the Enemy wages war on us.

> "For though we live in the world, we do not wage war as the world does. The weapons we fight with are not the weapons of the world. On the contrary, they have divine power to demolish strongholds. We demolish arguments and every pretension that sets itself up against the knowledge of God, and we take captive every thought to make it obedient to Christ" (2 Corinthians 10:3-5).

Questions

Question 1. From the verses, where does the Devil attack us? In other words, where is the battle fought?
- A. In Battleground, Washington
- B. In political and cultural issues
- C. In the mind; in our thoughts

Question 2. What do the verses call evil thoughts that can get lodged in our minds?
- A. Strongholds
- B. Brain teasers
- C. Common and ordinary thoughts

Soldiers, we are in a battle! The battlefield is the mind. The Enemy desires to set up thought "strongholds" in our minds. These are thoughts that won't go away, that eventually must be acted upon. These "strongholds" are whatever is opposed to "the knowledge of God." Here is how one student put it on his enrollment form: "I want to leave behind all forms of sexual impurity that pervade my life. Firstly, the endless and repetitive pornographic thoughts I have throughout the day which leads into viewing pornography, mostly on the web, but occasionally with videos and magazines, and of course masturbation."

So, here is what happens: Everything is going just fine, and all of a sudden a pornographic picture comes into our thoughts. Possibly it is of a pornographic movie we watched years ago, or it might be a more recent image we have seen over the Internet. Soldiers, THIS is the beginning of a thought-stronghold. This image that is lodging itself in our brain is in opposition to the knowledge of God. After all, the knowledge of God is whatever is true, noble, right, pure, lovely, and admirable (Philippians 4:8) on such we are to constantly think. We can understand then that the Evil One is setting that pornographic image up in our minds to turn us away from God. This image, and the associated emotions that are conjured up in the heart, can become a stronghold of the Devil, and lead us into masturbation and/or other sins.

Or, if our particular downfall is Internet Chatting, we can be praying against going to the chat groups all day, but all of a sudden thoughts come into our heads: Everybody loves you there! Somebody is just waiting to see your name come on his or her screen. They need your gentle caring, and loving concern, as well as your quick wit and romantic style. In fact, somebody there will no doubt want to have Cyber-Sex with you and is probably waiting for you right now. Though we try to push these thoughts away, and may be successful for the first or second time, eventually the thoughts get stuck in our minds and we are off to sin.

Testimony

The following testimony is from Gregory:

My sin was in the area of lustful conversations and masturbation. Conversations didn't usually start out there, but occasionally would end up there. After stumbling across settingcaptivesfree.com from a singles web site I decided to open the site and take a peek and see what the site was all about. My first impressions were "I don't really need this site as I am not involved in porn or anything like that". So I moved on but book marked the site anyway. About a month or so later after hitting big time frustration over these kinds of conversations I decided that maybe I needed to go back to this site and see if I could find some help to staying pure in every area of my life, word and deed.

So I signed up for the 60 day **Pure Freedom** course. I liked the idea of having an accountability partner because I knew I would not want to give into sin as long as I had to be accountable to someone. I was surprised though that when I repented of my sin and made the decision to begin the course the desire to do masturbation or have anymore of these conversations totally left. I began the course with much anticipation of gaining true freedom once and for all and my relationship with the Lord really took off.

I had a hard time understanding intimacy with God because of past abuse but during the course of doing each lesson God began to restore me in all of these places and reveal what true intimacy with Jesus was...enjoying being in His presence and drinking from His Life giving waters of the Spirit of God. Where I once feared His presence because of how I thought He viewed me, I love His presence today. I know that I have been washed by the Blood of the Lamb and am made clean. I can stand in His presence assured of my salvation and free from the holds of sin that once had me bound.

His grace alone empowered me to walk away from my sin and remain free today. I am willing to be used as God leads to assist in helping others get free. Who the Son sets free is free indeed!! I live daily by the Word of God and in His presence I find my joy, which is the source of my strength. I have found the source of true life, "Living by the Spirit, Drinking from the Wells of Living Waters". Waters that will change you from the inside out, make you a new man, restore you to right relationships, give you new desires, and redeem your soul from the grips of hell and death. PRAISE GOD, Thank you Jesus for such a ministry as this!!!

Question 3. What is your particular temptation scenario?

Question 4. Now it is time for personal reflection. What experiences have you had with pornography that verify the truth that your mind is a battlefield? Have you felt at times that you were unable to control your mind? What "strongholds" have you experienced in the past?

We need to make sure we understand that our minds are a battleground. And most importantly, we need to possess "Divine weapons" and know how to fight using them. In today's study it should become obvious that the Enemy wages war on our minds. Notice the following verses:

> "The mind of sinful man is death..." (Romans 8:6).

The reason that the mind of sinful man is death is because the Devil has numerous thought-strongholds there. Sinful man is fixated on sinful thoughts, and the wages of sin is death. In our case, pornographic images can totally overwhelm and control our minds.

> "The sinful mind is hostile to God. It does not submit to God's law nor can it do so" (Romans 8:7).

The sinful mind is saturated in sinful thoughts. When God's law requires it to think of pure, lovely, truthful thoughts it is totally unable to do so. The sinful mind is filled with sinful images and is bent on fulfilling the desires of the flesh.

> "Many live as the enemies of the cross of Christ. Their destiny is destruction, their god is their stomach, and their glory is in their shame. Their mind is on earthly things" (Philippians 3:18b,19).

Friend, our minds are the battleground. If the Devil can just get our minds fixed on "earthly things," he knows that we will be "enemies of the cross," and therefore enemies of God.

> "Furthermore, since they did not think it worthwhile to retain the knowledge of God, he gave them over to a depraved mind, to do what ought not to be done. They have become filled with every kind of wickedness, evil, greed and depravity. They are full of envy, murder, strife, deceit and malice" (Romans 1:28-29).

People who do not retain the knowledge of God are given over "to a depraved mind" to do what should not be done.

> "But I see another law at work in the members of my body, waging war against the law of my mind and making me a prisoner of the law of sin at work within my members" (Romans 7:23).

In this verse we see that the war is waged against the mind, and when the enemy is successful we become prisoners of sin.

Tomorrow, we will examine the resources with which we may fight. Meanwhile, we need to know where the battlefield is—the thought life, and how the Devil gets access to our hearts—through thought strongholds. Friends, please be on guard. *"Your enemy, the devil, prowls around like a roaring lion looking for someone to devour"* (1 Peter 5:8). And one of the ways he "devours" is through these thought-strongholds.

Here are two things we can do to combat these thoughts that get lodged in our minds:

1. We can refuse to have access to any further pornography, which will cease the income of any additional pornographic images that can drag us into sin. This point is key, and without allowing ourselves zero access there really won't be any victory in this area. Please review Matthew 5:29-30, Romans 13:14 and Joshua 7:13.

2. We need to begin to immerse ourselves in Scripture, seeking God for grace to apply what we read. Taking in the Water of the Word has the effect of washing away the images that remain in the brain. Please review Joshua 1:8, Psalm 1:3.

As we continue to put these two things in place, over time we will become free from all strongholds of the enemy, by the grace of God.

Question 5. Please record the two things that are referred to above, that will rid the brain of the pornographic images:

1.

2.

Course Member Daryl writes: "In the past I sought pornography on the net and through the medium of print and video. I also frequented a strip club. This has left a thought process imprinted on my mind. When meeting women, whether at work, on the street or even in church, I find myself invariably viewing them as an object of sexual desire. I know this is wrong but it sometimes seems that I have no control over my thoughts, kind of like an old TV I had. The tuner was going bad so it kept switching channels back to channel 2. It wouldn't stay on the selected channel for more than a few minutes then it defaulted back to 2. My thought process is like that at present, though with God's help it is changing."

Questions

Course Member John writes: "I have had many a time that I would just start to think about looking at pornography, and then from the mental picture I would masturbate."

Course Member Hans writes: "The images that I have experienced pop up in my mind at the worst times for me and the best times for the adversary. He and his henchmen have studied me and know when to strike and to strike hard. I have not, by the grace of God, gone any farther than pornography and masturbation, but this alone has given Satan a stronghold on my whole being. I have become limited or damned by this. I am slowly turning to God and allowing him to fight the battle. I cannot win alone; I have tried for 15 years. The images and fantasies are the strongholds where Lucifer twists my logic and makes my addiction seem like an old comfortable friend. He is losing the fight however, day by day I feel more and more freedom."

Course Member Jim writes: "When we fight Satan, it is in our minds. We take down strongholds that he has put there. This is very true. I have experienced this for a long time now. And even more since I have started this course. Satan does not want me to be free from porn. He is far from being done with me. Day 20 seems like a big number to me. But I have fallen recently. And Day 60 is a long way away. God will get me to that point because it is His will. I am sure of this. Then, Satan will continue to attack. I would be a fool to think that after 60 days Satan will just leave me alone. But he will be a lot weaker than he is now. God has been mighty in my life recently. This is just the beginning of that. All of this has happened in my mind. It is a war. And we are in the midst of it all. I will not become a casualty of war. I will not become MIA or POW. I am going to pray that GOD will not let that happen. And, because I know that that is HIS will, HE will do it. I have taken a few bullets. But no more. Best of all, we know who wins the war. GOD DOES!"

Course member Dennis writes: "The paragraph starting with "So, here is what happens" is exactly describing the battlefield in my mind. I have pictures in my head of movies I watched as a teenager and pictures I have seen on the Internet. Up until I started this study and working on filling my mind with things of God; when one of those images flashed into my head it was all a downhill slide from there. Something would remind me of something I had seen and I would start "teasing" myself on the Internet - "Just a peek" is how I would convince myself it was okay. But, of course, that never worked. Even if I were satisfied temporarily with "just a peek" within a day or two I would give in completely. It's when Satan reminds me of the things I have done and seen that I feel the temptation the strongest to give in again (kind of twisted logic - you would think that being reminded of my sin would make me turn away from it)."

In the next lesson we will see that demolishing strongholds is only possible through Jesus Christ. Many will say we need a "higher power" to help us, but in truth there is only one source of that Higher Power.

Comments:

Scripture to Consider

"No one engaged in warfare entangles himself with the affairs of this life, that he may please him who enlisted him as a soldier." (2 Timothy 2:4 NKJV)

Were you free from pornography since you did the last lesson?
    Yes   No

Were you free from masturbation since you did the last lesson?
    Yes   No

Were you free from sexual immorality since you did the last lesson?
    Yes   No

DAY 33—DEMOLISHING STRONGHOLDS

Only Jesus Christ can give true and lasting victory.

Friends, there are many false saviors being offered today. If you were to do a search on the Internet for "help for addictions" you would discover 12-Step programs, psychological counseling programs, hypnotherapy, medication therapies, natural and alternative therapies, meditation...etc. I declare to you, on the authority of God's Word, that nothing can deliver us out of true pornographic addiction except Jesus Christ.

> "Salvation is found in no one else, for there is no other name under heaven given to men by which we must be saved" (Acts 4:12).

> "For though we live in the world, we do not wage war as the world does. The weapons we fight with are not the weapons of the world. On the contrary, they have divine power to demolish strongholds. We demolish arguments and every pretension that sets itself up against the knowledge of God, and we take captive every thought to make it obedient to Christ" (2 Corinthians 10:3-5).

Testimony

My name is Mac.

I have been involved with pornography and masturbation for the last 26 years. It started out small. I would buy a magazine, look at the pictures, and then hide it in my car trunk. But after high school, I moved into reading books about sex, which were readily available because of the job I had at the time. Within a year my addiction to porn led to premarital sex.

Then I joined the military (USMC) and ended up being stationed in 29 Palms, CA. then Camp Pendleton, CA. and Camp Hansen, Okinowa. P & M were the normal activity there. 29 Palms had easy access to Parker Dam, AZ, where all the college kids hang out. As I was an alcoholic, p & m were as far as I went; I needed my money for booze. Camp Pendleton, Oceanside, CA. was a very rough town when I was there. The movie theater in town played XXX films 24 hours a day. And at Camp Hansen, OK—if you had the money anything could be bought.

I left the Marines in 1983, worked odd jobs till 1988 when I became a garbage man and then I married. My boss required the workers to save all porn for him (what a collection!). Incidentally, the most extreme hardcore is thrown out by the upper class.

After a while I moved and became a printer's helper. In 1999, I became a partner in a bagel shop, and then my wife left me in Oct. 1999. I acquired a computer in 1998, started playing games and looking at porn when my wife was gone or sleeping. And then after she left, I spent time proving I was right and she was wrong from a biblical standpoint. As there was no one around porn became something searched for more and more. By Dec. 2000 I had sunk to new lows even for me—I was viewing bondage, animals, and worse.

I finally realized that, at some point, pictures would no longer be enough so I began seeking a companion. And while looking in a matchmaking site I saw a banner for Setting Captives Free. I looked but didn't start anything for a day or two. I started SCF 9 Dec. 2000.

Questions

Question 1. We are continuing our study today in 2 Corinthians 10:3-5. Please fill in the blanks below:

"For though we live in the world, we do not _____ _____ as the world does."

"The weapons we _____ _____ are not the weapons of the world."

"On the contrary, they have divine power to _____ _____."

Why do the programs mentioned not work? They don't work because only "divine power" and divine weapons are effective against the demonic strongholds that Satan can set up in our minds. And only Jesus Christ, as God, is "divine."

Question 2. According to the above verses, what does it take to be able to demolish thought-strongholds?
- A. A stick of dynamite
- B. Behavior Modification Therapy
- C. Divine Power

Dear friends, no 12-step plan, no un-Biblical counseling, no ___anonymous, no group therapy, no program of man (including this one) can totally deliver us from the clutches of pornography. It takes divine power and divine weapons. This teaching leaves us dependent upon God, Who alone is divine.

Demolishing thought strongholds—by God's power!

Jesus Christ Himself is God's "divine power" and His "divine weapons." Without Him we have no way to permanently win the battle against porn. So, let us examine how to demolish strongholds, and how to demolish every argument that sets itself up against the knowledge of God. Read the following verses and answer the questions.

> "We demolish arguments and every pretension that sets itself up against the knowledge of God" (2 Corinthians 10:5).

Question 3. According to the above verse, what are we to do when we are bombarded with a pornographic thought or image that can become a stronghold?
- A. We are to entertain the thought and dwell on the image
- B. We are to demolish it

Question 4. If you have ever tried to "demolish" these thought strongholds in your own power, you've learned that it is impossible to do. It takes "divine power." Have you ever tried to just not dwell on pornographic images? What happened?

"But thanks be to God Who gives us the victory through our Lord Jesus Christ" (1 Corinthians 15:57).

"No, in all these things we are more than conquerors through Him who loved us" (Romans 8:37).

We are to "demolish" thought strongholds. We are to totally annihilate, exterminate, and eradicate sinful thoughts so that our Enemy does not gain a stronghold in our lives. Friends, if we begin to dwell on porn images we are rolling out the red carpet for Satan. We are not talking "mental warfare" here, but rather spiritual warfare. The difference is that in spiritual warfare we must possess Jesus Christ, and we must beg God for divine power in order to tear down the pornographic images. In spiritual warfare, we lose the battle when a thought is able to lodge in our minds; and we win the battle when we demolish the thought. Do you see how we must become dependent on God in this battle?

"If the Son sets you free, you will be free indeed" (John 8:36).

Question 5. Please write out your thoughts on the following verses and show how they teach us dependence on God.

Having accepted Christ as a child the format appealed to me right off. Even though I no longer was indulging myself, I was still rebellious until 1 Jan. 2001. Since that day I have been attempting to live a life pleasing to God. Easy only when I let God take all my burdens. When I think I can handle a situation it gets real hard. Things that gave me a challenge: Mike stating that I would make a good mentor if I stayed pure, this was stated on 20 Dec. 2000. On 31 Dec. 2000, I made the decision to stop fighting God and let him be in control of my life.

Since that day there have been struggles but by giving them to God I am no longer responsible for them. My only job is to give God the glory. On 7 Jan 2001, after asking Mike if there was anything I could do for him, it was decided that I would be a moderator for the discussion group. I enjoy this as I can read all the posts and it keeps me from surfing questionable sites.

I am truly free and giving God the glory. I want to use what is left of my life to help others in whatever way I can. May God be glorified in all I do.

Course Member John writes: "I will no longer kneel at the altar of pornography, bound by chains of sin. He will break those chains, as only He can."

"For He has rescued us from the dominion of darkness and brought us into the kingdom of the Son He loves..." (Colossians 1:13)

Course Member Jerry writes: "God has not only saved me, He has taken me to the stronghold of the Son. Here I am safe. Here there is rest and refreshment. There is no relaxation, for I am to be about His work. But here, He keeps me. Pornography cannot venture into this place. It is thrown back by the glorious light of God Almighty Himself."

"For the grace of God that brings salvation has appeared to all men. [12] It teaches us to say No to ungodliness and worldly passions, and to live self-controlled, upright and godly lives in this present age" (Titus 2:11,12).

Course Member John writes: "The victory over pornography, like salvation, is a gift. We don't earn it, we don't work for it, and we give the battle to Christ. He is the great Warrior who destroys the strongholds in my life."

Questions

Again we see, from the verse, that we must depend upon "divine power" in order to "take every thought captive." This is not easy to do. War is difficult. And yet with Jesus Christ we can indeed win. We are to make our thoughts prisoners of war. We are to notice when a particular thought is attempting to become a stronghold and we are to take it captive to Jesus.

So, this is what it may look like practically. I'm cruising along in my day again, doing just fine, when all of a sudden BAMMO; I'm hit with an 8 X 12 glossy image of something I viewed a year ago. WOW! It's appealing, too. And I start to look at it and...." Then I stop and cry out to God: "Oh, God, please Lord Jesus, rescue me. The Devil is attempting to erect a stronghold in my mind to cause me to sin. Help! I see You, there, dying on the cross because You love me. I see You placed in the tomb so that my sins could be buried. I see You raised from the dead and know that your resurrection power is at work in me right now. Thank You, Lord Jesus, for dying for me, and for ever living to intercede for me."

Dear friend,

Tomorrow we will take a look at some stories from the Bible that illustrate the truth we've been studying. But, perhaps right now there is someone who is coming to understand why he/she is not having success over pornographic images. You might possibly be realizing for the first time that you do not have "divine power" and you simply are not able to "demolish strongholds." Maybe you realize that you need Jesus Christ. Please call to Him right now, won't you?

"I also went to a 12-step program for sexual addiction. After a year, I quit. I found it very difficult to deal with a group of individuals who would admit their problems, but who wouldn't admit that God had the power to change them. The only support was supposed to come from being able to unload within a safe group of people who had similar problems. They talked about a 'higher power', which could be anything, including a stuffed teddy bear. To this 'power' they gave the credit for their faithfulness, but then would have to admit failure again and again. It seemed to me they really had no hope and couldn't offer any. I know this system has benefits and works for some people but I was frustrated because I felt God was missing from the formula" (<u>Stone Cold in a Warm Bed</u> **Kathryn Wilson with Paul Wilson, page 35,36).**[21]

John Bunyan, in his book Pilgrim's Progress described the battle that is fought with the enemy. In scene 4, he writes: **"Apollyon, seeing an opportunity, came up close to Christian, and wrestled with him, giving him a dreadful fall; and with that Christian's sword flew out of his hand. Then Apollyon said, "I have won now," and nearly killed Christian. But, as God would have it, while Apollyon was about to strike the final blow, Christian nimbly reached out his hand for his sword, and grabbed a hold of it, saying, "Rejoice not against me, O mine enemy: when I fall, I shall arise," Micah 7:8; and with that he thrust his sword into Apollyon, which made him fall back, as one that had received a deadly wound. Christian seeing the devil retreat, rushed at him again, saying, "No, in all these things we are more than conquerors, through Him Who loved us" (Romans 8:37). And with that Apollyon spread forth his dragon wings, and hurried away, and Christian saw him no more. (James 4:7).**[22]

"The devil does not sleep, nor is the flesh yet dead; therefore, you must never cease your preparation for battle, because on the right and on the left are enemies who never rest" (Thomas a Kempis).[23]

"He gives thanks for victory. Truly we are more than conquerors through Him that loved us; for we can give thanks before the fight is done. Yes, even in the thickest of the battle we can look up to Jesus, and cry, Thanks to God. The moment a soul groaning under corruption rests the eye on Jesus, that moment his groans are changed into songs of praise. In Jesus you discover a fountain to wash away the guilt of all your sin. In Jesus you discover grace sufficient for you, grace to hold you up to the end, and a sure promise that sin shall soon be rooted out altogether" (Robert McCheyne).[24]

Course Member William writes: "I subscribe to several newsletters about the PC industry. In one of them they made mention of the fact that deleted files could be recovered, if one knew how and had the right software. I already knew how, and already had the software. I had just not even thought it. That night, in my sleep, it seems like just about every picture I used to have on a particular erased Zip disk, was played back into my brain. The temptation continued all throughout the next day. I knew I could recover those files. The following day, upon arriving home, I took that Zip disk, two others like it, and every floppy disk that I could identify as having ever contained such material, smashed each of them, and though I'm not normally one to do such as this, threw them away."

This man is taking steps to knock down the strongholds of the enemy. Are you?

Course Member Marcus writes: "The Lord has truly blessed me in pushing me to your ministry. Not only have I been able to conquer the temptations so far, but also even the strongholds are weakening. It has been 25 days (sounding more and more like an AA meeting :-) now and with the help of Jesus, I will never fall back. Of course, as you know, this is probably a time when Satan is preparing to counter-attack pretty soon, but I'm prepared for it because I've finally given my problem with porn and lust over to Christ for the first time in my Christian walk and I'm letting Him fight the war for me."

Scripture to Consider

"For the LORD your God is the one who goes with you to fight for you against your enemies to give you victory" (Deuteronomy 20:4).

"He put garrisons throughout Edom, and all the Edomites became subject to David. The LORD gave David victory wherever he went" (2 Samuel 8:14).

You give me your shield of victory; you stoop down to make me great" (2 Samuel 22:36).

"The horse is made ready for the day of battle, but victory rests with the LORD" (Proverbs 21:31).

Were you free from pornography since you did the last lesson?
    Yes   No

Were you free from masturbation since you did the last lesson?
    Yes   No

Were you free from sexual immorality since you did the last lesson?
    Yes   No

DAY 34—DEMOLISHING STRONGHOLDS II

Okay, so we have been studying about how to demolish strongholds, and taking every thought captive using God's divine power. Now, we will look at how God illustrates these truths in His Word.

In the book of Joshua, we read of the many battles the Israelites fought to conquer the land the Lord had given to them. Today, let us take note of one battle in particular in Joshua chapter 11. It is the battle of the Israelites against the northern kings. These northern kings all bonded together to fight against the Israelites and the Bible says they made "a huge army, as numerous as the sand on the seashore." They were a formidable foe to be sure; but God told Joshua, "Do not be afraid...I will hand them over to you." So Joshua and the Israelites went out in battle against the huge army of the northern kings. And Joshua 11:12 says that, "Joshua took all these royal cities (where those kings used to live) and put them to the sword. He totally destroyed them as he had been commanded." That's right; Joshua and his people totally annihilated that huge army. And the Bible says that they were victorious because the Lord fought for them!

Questions

Please answer the following questions.

Question 1. The army of the northern kings was:
  A. Very tiny
  B. As numerous as the sands on the seashore

Question 2. Joshua and the Israelites were to do what to the army of the Northern Kings?
  A. Make peace
  B. Leave them alone
  C. Destroy them

Question 3. Please write, in your own words, how this story applies to our situation with pornography. Find as many parallels as you can.

Testimony

The following testimony is from Dillon:

I was once lost in sin. I chose to pursue porn, but it eventually consumed me. Before I knew it, the images from the porn sites and movies began flooding into my mind. I defiled myself, and used others. I sank in deeper and could only see others as objects of lust. To hide my growing dependence on porn, I developed a "hidden life" surrounded by lies, secrecy, and false intimacy.

Each time I gave into my lusts and the obsessive thoughts, I was filled with guilt, shame and self-loathing. The longer the addiction went on the more withdrawn I became. I drifted in and out of jobs and relationships. I eventually fell to the bottom of the pit and that scared me. I sought counseling; but I fell again. Then I began frantically looking for more help because I was about to lose everything. I joined 12-step programs, and more counseling... but nothing helped. Then I was led to Setting Captives Free, and there I enrolled in the 60-day program called **Pure Freedom**.

At first the religious message bothered me, but the accountability and daily training really helped. Eventually the message that only Christ offers living water that refreshes sank in. I quit drinking muddy water and accepted Jesus. When I put my burdens on His shoulders, the obsessive thoughts and images vanished! It was the beginning of freedom.

The course staff and mentors suggested going to a local bible-believing church, and the next day a friend called to say he and his pastor had found one for me (without being asked!). And the next day, I got a call from the pastor of the new church with an invitation to come to service. Going to church felt good. It felt clean.

I was baptized on the same day I finished the 60-day course. I am free from obsessive destructive thoughts, toxic guilt and shame, and free to live. For the first time in many years it feels good to be me. I can't wait to start a ministry to help others find this wonderful course, and win some souls for God.

Fellow soldiers, pornographic images, as I'm sure you know by now, are a formidable foe. They can, at times, be like a huge army that is much stronger than we are. And yet Scripture tells us that we are to demolish them. Destroy them. Annihilate them. Can you see how this does indeed take divine power?

> "And we take captive every thought to make it obedient to Christ" (2 Corinthians 10:5).

Here is an illustration of taking our thoughts captive:

In the Old Testament, the nation of Israel was commanded to dislodge every nation that currently existed in the Promised Land. They had good success pulling down the strongholds of those nations, and dislodging most of them. However; a few nations were very powerful and very stubborn, and the Israelites were unable to demolish them. But notice what the Israelite nation did with those nations: "All the people left from the Amorites, Hittites, Perizzites, Hivites and Jebusites...all whom the Israelites could not exterminate—these Solomon conscripted for his slave labor force" (1 Kings 9:20-21).

Questions

Question 4. According to the verses, what did King Solomon do with the nations that the Israelites were unable to exterminate?

Friend, there might be some pornographic thoughts so powerful that we may not be able to keep them from infiltrating our minds, especially in the first couple of months after we have stopped doing porn. We may not be able to demolish them. But if that is true, then we can take those thoughts captive to Christ; we make them our "prisoners of war." Next time an image comes into your mind that threatens to make you sin, say to yourself, "That's a Hittite thought, I must take it captive." Or, "that's a Perrizite, or Jebusite thought, I must make it my prisoner." This, of course, takes Divine power to accomplish. God must "give you the victory" in this area.

Before we move on we should remind ourselves that we are in a very serious battle. We are instructed to use God's power to demolish demonic strongholds, and we are to take captive every thought to Christ. This is serious business and cannot be taken lightly. If we truly want to win the battle there must be a whole lot of crying out to God for victory, depending on God for power, and thanking God each time you win. If you have been winning battles for the past 34 days, then you can rejoice with Paul who said, *"I thank Christ Jesus our Lord, who has given me strength..." (1 Timothy 1:12)* Jesus Christ gave the strength to Paul, and Jesus must give us strength as well, in order for us to win the battle over sin. Will you pray right now that God would give you strength?

Course Member Craig writes: "Pornography is a lot bigger than I am, and alone there is no way that I could do battle against it. Without God I am a traitor. I would and have made peace with the kings. Only God's grace has brought me back to where I am ready to do battle against sin."

Course Member Dirk writes: "I have been guilty of being soft on my enemy and allowing him to gain a stronghold inside my defense perimeter. I have also sought to make peace with the enemy of my soul, rather that seek to totally destroy him. In addition when the enemy promised to also make peace I found that he really had a innumerable army arrayed against me, ready to destroy me."

Course Member Scottie writes: "The army the northern kings had was huge. God told Joshua to destroy them. In order to move into the Promised Land (A porn free life), the tenants (porn) have to move out so I can get in. They do not want to leave (strongholds). They must be defeated (torn down). They have a huge army, and they will do anything to hold on to what they have. But, God has promised that He will hand them over to me. In order to defeat them, I have to go into battle. Through God's power, I will be victorious and the current tenants will be totally annihilated! No more porn! Solomon made the remaining tenants slaves. Although we can not undo the fact that we have looked at porn, we can now use it to God's service. This story is teaching me to not be afraid of the battle, but God will hand our enemies (porn) over to us. So we can go and fight and not be afraid, because we will win, we will annihilate sin."

Next, please read the following quote by Oswald Chambers and provide your thoughts.

"Lift up your eyes on high, and behold who hath created these things" (Isaiah 40:26^{KJV}*).* **The people of God in Isaiah's day had starved their imagination by looking on the face of idols, and Isaiah made them look up at the heavens; that is, he made them begin to use their imagination aright.**

The test of spiritual concentration is bringing the imagination into captivity. Is your imagination looking on the face of an idol? Is the idol you? Your work? Your conception of what a worker should be? Your experience of salvation and sanctification? Then your imagination of God is starved, and when you are up against difficulties you have no power, you can only endure in darkness. If your imagination is starved, do not look back to your own experience; it is God Whom you need. Go right out of yourself, away from the face of your idols, away from everything that has been starving your imagination. Rouse yourself, take the gibe that Isaiah gave the people, and deliberately turn your imagination to God".[25]

Question 5. Provide your thoughts here:

Next, read the following quote from Thomas a Kempis and comment on it.

"Above all, we must be especially alert against the beginnings of temptation, for the enemy is more easily conquered if he is refused admittance to the mind and is met beyond the threshold when he knocks.

Someone has said very aptly: Resist the beginnings; remedies come too late, when by long delay the evil has gained strength. First, a mere thought comes to mind, then strong imagination, followed by pleasure, evil delight, and consent. Thus, because he is not resisted in the beginning, Satan gains full entry. And the longer a man delays in resisting, so much the weaker does he become each day, while the strength of the enemy grows against him" (Thomas a Kempis) <u>The Imitation of Christ</u>.[26]

Question 6. Provide your comments here:

Course Member John writes: "Joshua's battle was just like my own. He faced insurmountable odds. There was no physical way that Israel could defeat the northern kings' armies. There is no way that I can defeat the sin of pornography in my life. But wait. Great words, aren't they? There is One, that One who holds the universe in the palm of His hand. He fights for me. His actions are the words of His mouth. He has said in His love, mercy, and grace that He would never forsake me. He, this One, fights for me. Just as He, this One, fought for Israel."

Question 7. Write out what you have learned today. How will you apply this teaching?

Scripture to Consider

"When you go to war against your enemies, the Lord will help you defeat them so that you will take them captive" (Deuteronomy 21:10).

"Now the men of Judah approached Joshua at Gilgal, and Caleb son of Jephunneh the Kenizzite said to him, 'You know what the LORD said to Moses the man of God at Kadesh Barnea about you and me. I was forty years old when Moses the servant of the LORD sent me from Kadesh Barnea to explore the land. And I brought him back a report according to my convictions, but my brothers who went up with me made the hearts of the people melt with fear. I, however, followed the LORD my God wholeheartedly.' So on that day Moses swore to me, 'The land on which your feet have walked will be your inheritance and that of your children forever, because you have followed the LORD my God wholeheartedly.' 'Now then, just as the LORD promised, he has kept me alive for forty-five years since the time he said this to Moses, while Israel moved about in the desert. So here I am today, eighty-five years old! I am still as strong today as the day Moses sent me out; I'm just as vigorous to go out to battle now as I was then'" (Joshua 14:6-11).

"David said to the Philistine, 'You come against me with sword and spear and javelin, but I come against you in the name of the LORD Almighty, the God of the armies of Israel, whom you have defied. [46] This day the LORD will hand you over to me, and I'll strike you down and cut off your head. Today I will give the carcasses of the Philistine army to the birds of the air and the beasts of the earth, and the whole world will know that there is a God in Israel. [47] All those gathered here will know that it is not by sword or spear that the LORD saves; for the battle is the Lord's, and he will give all of you into our hands'" (1 Samuel 17:45-47).

Were you free from pornography since you did the last lesson?
    Yes   No

Were you free from masturbation since you did the last lesson?
    Yes   No

Were you free from sexual immorality since you did the last lesson?
    Yes   No

DAY 35—THE LOVE OF GOD AND TEMPTATION

"Blessed is the man who perseveres under trial, because when he has stood the test, he will receive the crown of life that God has promised to those who love him. When tempted, no one should say, 'God is tempting me.' For God cannot be tempted by evil, nor does he tempt anyone; but each one is tempted when, by his own evil desire, he is dragged away and enticed. Then, after desire has conceived, it gives birth to sin; and sin, when it is full-grown, gives birth to death. Don't be deceived, my dear brothers" (James 1:12-16).

Today we will see very clearly what it is that will get us through any temptation and trial we ever face. The teaching of God's Word in this area is powerful enough to release anyone from slavery to pornography (or any other habitual sin) who will embrace and apply the truths taught today. Jesus said, *"If you hold to my teaching, you are really my disciples. Then you will know the truth, and the truth will set you free"* (John 8:31-32). The inevitable result of embracing Truth is **pure freedom!**

In James 1:12 above we see a promise made to one who stands the test and "perseveres under trial" and we see the motive for persevering. The promise is "the crown of life" and the motive for standing and persevering is the love of God. The above verses make it clear that life will have its share of both trials and temptations, and this passage communicates God's way of victory through both. Let us see what we can learn, and may God help us to grasp His truth and enjoy the freedom that comes from it.

When I am faced with a severe trial, or an intense temptation I have a choice to either persevere in faith and stand up under the trial, or fall down in sin and deception. The passage we are studying in James promises me the "crown of life" if I stand and persevere, and shows me that death will be the end result if I follow the path of temptation, desire, and sin. So we are discussing life and death today. The critical question is this: What is the motive for choosing to stand and persevere?

Questions

Question 1. Please write out James 1:12 here:

Question 2. What motive do you see for persevering and standing under the trial?

Some may answer "the crown of life" to the question of motive, but when looking a little deeper we can see that the real motive for persevering through the trial, and standing up under temptation is the love of God. God promises the crown of life "to those who love Him."

Friends, any methodology of man for bringing freedom to those trapped in sin is doomed to fail, because it leaves out motive. For instance, worldly methodologies in the past have taught those given over to excessive drinking that they need help outside of themselves, and they are taught to ask for help from a "higher power." But this model falls short of helping people have lasting heart-change because the program fails to address that man has a need to love and is created with the desire to worship. There is no true freedom in the heart that does not love God. But once this love for God is planted in the heart it will enable us to go through any trial, and to stand up under any temptation and not fall. If we are falling to sin, we do not have proper love for God. Notice how Paul's prayer for the Thessalonians reinforces the truth that it is the love of God that enables our perseverance: *"May the Lord direct your hearts into God's love and Christ's perseverance"* (2 Thessalonians 3:5).

So this brings up the next question which is, "How, then, do I acquire love for God?" This is a difficult question and does not come with a simple answer, but here are a few thoughts, along with some practical steps I've taken in my own life to grow in love for God.

1. The first step is to ask God to give you a heart that loves Him. *"You may ask me for anything in my name, and I will do it"* (John 14:14). *"You do not have, because you do not ask God"* (James 4:2). If

Testimony

The following testimony is from Ryan:

THE HOOK OF PORNOGRAPHY

I come to you as one who was "hooked by pornography" at an early age even though I was raised in a "religious" home. My Dad did not take us to church, and didn't teach us the ways of God; he was hooked on the bottle. My Mom quit taking us to church when I was in third grade. When I was 9 or 10 I was walking in a field next to our house and found a very explicit porno magazine (the baited hook). The devil is a very slick player and knows how to bait us, and to cleverly disguise it so we will swallow it. I kept the magazine and more seemed to come my way, it was like the devil was a drug pusher and I was getting more and more hooked as time went on.

As I grew up it seemed everywhere I turned there was pornography (hooks) of some sort in the strangest places. I was into sex and masturbating like any "normal" teen so

Testimony

thought. I found out my mind was far worse twisted than my fellow high school mates could ever realize. I could not look at a female body without wanting them so bad. As I grew up I could not look at any female body without undressing them and having sex with them in my mind and masturbating. Then the day of reckoning came and the enemy basically said no more freebies if you want it, you pay baby! So being snared on Satan's hook, pay I did with hard earned money. I bought magazines and videos... the hook was getting embedded deeper. I could not have a solid relationship with a woman because of the lust in my heart and mind. Even in the sex act, I could be with a "fine" woman and my mind was racing here and there and having sex with all kinds of women in my mind.

I thrived on sexual fantasy, I could sit anywhere, watch women and basically have sex with them and no one knew it. (No one knew with the exception of God.) At that time in my life, I lived for basically 3 things and that was drugs, sex and rock-n-roll. I lived hard and fast and was sliding deeper and deeper into pornography, and the people I hung with always had porno lying around. I was so deep into my addiction (though I did not realize it) that I worshiped at the altar of the female body. In my room I had pinups of naked women with full frontals and did not care who saw them... even my Mom.

It was around this time in my life that I began to really hate "real" life; I often thought about ending it all but I (thank God) could never get the guts to do it. I was in despair because I was too much of a coward to kill myself. I married one of my druggie girlfriends and we lasted about a year before my porno addiction, and worship of "female" became more than she could stand, and we divorced.

I had a brother living in Tucson AZ who I decided to go live with and "get my life straightened out", as suggested by family members. I found a job at a factory there in Tucson. God had several Christians in place, one of them being a "female". God used this woman to invite me to church and my thought was "yeah I'll go to church with you and then we'll go do the wild thing." I went to her church, and found myself at the altar; I gave my life to the Lord, and began a life of "living" for God, yet I had not given up my porn/sexual perversion addiction, to God. I was still hooked, only the hook was deep and even when I wanted to be free I could not get free. I moved back to my hometown where there was a fellowship church.

I met a wonderful woman that was a believer and loved God with all her heart. We dated and then decided to get married. We were happily married and my addiction grew... I was raised up in the local body of believers and began to minister in different areas of the church and shamefully used the sight of all of my Christian sisters bodies to fantasize. There was not a woman in my sight that I had not had sex with in my mind. We were sent out to start a pioneer work for God in another city, and I was still "hooked". I persuaded my wife we needed these sex instruction videos to enhance our sex. I ordered the whole set and they were explicit, no holds barred they showed every detail up close, and every position imaginable. In short, I dumped my garbage of porn in my wife's lap, and she being the "good wife" (not wanting to hurt me) went along with all of it. Then God would convict me and I smashed the videos, burned the magazines, but I was horribly Hooked. Try as I might, I could not get the "hook" out of me.

To make a horribly, devastating, story short I lived with my addiction for 20 years of my "Christian?" life, a total of 34 years of my life. I would buy porn, get convicted, destroy it, and throw it away, and wriggle on the hook. I could not get free by myself, and I was too ashamed to go to the church for help. I mean, what would they think, there was no way I could ask for help. I did cry out to God for help, but I did not really mean it, I just wanted the guilt to be taken away. Then I trashed my calling, began to sit on the sidelines and basically became "religious", I was nice looking on the outside, but inside I was full of "sewer water," that just oozed from my filthy heart. Then the summer of the year 2000 I was surfing the net looking at porno, being convicted, and about to give up on ever being free, when I typed in at a search site, the words "pornography addiction". I found the site Setting Captives Free and began to check it out. I went so far as to sign up for the course, completed one day of the course and did not come back for about 2 months. The angler on the other end of the line kept jerking on the hook to embed it deeper.

Continued on page 112

Questions

this teaching is new to you, you may want to pause here and acknowledge to the Lord that your love for Him needs to be increased, and ask Him to do it. Feel free to pause in prayer, or to write out a request to God for Him to give you a heart that loves Him.

2. Dwell on the cross of Jesus Christ. *"This is how we know what love is: Jesus Christ laid down his life for us"* (1 John 3:16). There has never in all of human history been an act of love displayed to the world that demonstrates the love of God better than the cross of Christ. Meditate on this cross, asking God to give you love for the One who died in our place. Think often of His wounds in His hands and feet and side, which are really reminders of His love for us (Isaiah 49:15-16). Recall how He sweat drops of blood, how He offered His back to be smitten (Isaiah 50:6), how He was willingly beaten beyond recognition (Isaiah 52:14), all to pardon us from sin's penalty and free us from sin's power.

   "But he was pierced for our transgressions, he was crushed for our iniquities; the punishment that brought us peace was upon him, and by his wounds we are healed. We all, like sheep, have gone astray, each of us has turned to his own way; and the LORD has laid on him...the iniquity of us all" (Isaiah 53:5-6).

3. Obey God's Word. *"But if anyone obeys his word, God's love is truly made complete in him"* (1 John 2:5). Of course we know that it takes the grace of God in order for us to obey the Word of God. And it is an amazing thing to begin walking in obedience to God and to sense the love of God as we do. Do you want your heart flooded with the love of God? Walk in obedience and you will have it.

4. *"Keep yourselves in the love of God, looking for the mercy of our Lord Jesus Christ unto eternal life"* (Jude 21). Again, God alone can keep us from falling (Jude 24) but we are exhorted to keep ourselves in the love of God. This is similar to John 15 where we are told to *"abide in the Vine"* and in 1 John where we are told to *"remain in Him"* (1 John 2:27). This is a general statement that we are to do all we can to remain in God's love.

Questions

Question 3. Please write out the 4 steps to God's love, and indicate whether you are currently doing them.

Step Number 1—

Step Number 2—

Step Number 3—

Step Number 4—

Next, let us look at James 1:12-16 again:

> "Blessed is the man who perseveres under trial, because when he has stood the test, he will receive the crown of life that God has promised to those who love him. When tempted, no one should say, 'God is tempting me.' For God cannot be tempted by evil, nor does he tempt anyone; but each one is tempted when, by his own evil desire, he is dragged away and enticed. Then, after desire has conceived, it gives birth to sin; and sin, when it is full-grown, gives birth to death. Don't be deceived, my dear brothers."

Verses 13 through 16 describe the nature of temptation by using 2 analogies – fishing and delivery. Let us look at both of them:

1. Fishing. "But each one is tempted when, by his own evil desire, he is dragged away and enticed." The words "dragged away and enticed" have to do with bait. The bait is what the fisherman uses to lure the fish. When we are being tempted we only focus on the "bait" never on the hook. In the Garden of Eden, Eve saw that the fruit was "pleasing to the eye" but she did not focus on the death that would result from eating it. For years I was enamored with the "perfect" images in pornography, never looking at the death of my marriage that would follow.

Question 4. What has been the "bait" that you have been attracted to in the past?

Testimony

Ryan's testimony continues...

Then one morning early (2am), in my heart of hearts a cry came up to God, that I could not live like I was living anymore, that my life was one big lie, and had been for way too many years, I was a phony, and I wanted help. I cried before God and HE encouraged me in my spirit to start the course again. I came back to the "Setting Captives Free" website and restarted the course. I started drinking the Living Water and God began a powerful work of setting this captive free. If it were not for this course that God has so graciously used, I would be still swallowing the hook of pornography even deeper. God by His Holy Spirit uses it to remove the hook, and to "take one by the hand, and lead us from absolute total darkness into His marvelous light, and we can sing we are Free Indeed." To quote Martin Luther King we can say for the first time in our lives "Free at last, Free at last, thank God almighty we are FREE at last."

There is so very much more I could share with you of how God has healed our marriage, of how I can look at people with all kinds of problems and look at them in love rather than disdain, or how I truly have a real relationship with God that I have never known in all my "Christian?" life. I could go on and on of how God through this course has changed me and made me to be a "transparent" person, but I will close here and say in all honesty were it not for the "Setting Captives Free" course and their ministry I would of all people be most miserable and might have found the guts to get out of this trap by killing myself.

Thanks be to God that I stand before you this day free from any desire for pornography, and have victory over the images of "having sex" in my mind. I can make love to my wife as it was meant to be, and not have a desire to fantasize of other women. Don't get me wrong, the memory of the "hook" is still there, but the reality of the ONE that took the hook out is so very present in my mind at all times. I love the Lord my God with all my heart and desire to please only Him. Jesus Christ and His Word is the only way to be "set free".

Question 5. Describe how you became "hooked." (How did taking that first bite of "bait" become a life dominating sin for you?)

Question 7. What are your final thoughts on today's teaching? Did you learn anything new, or will you do anything different? How will you apply these Scriptures to the ongoing battle against pornography and all forms of impurity?

"Then, after desire has conceived, it gives birth to sin; and sin, when it is full-grown, gives birth to death" (James 1:15).

2. Delivery: When desire and lust conceive, they give birth to sin, and when sin is full grown it gives birth to death. Again, when we are being tempted all we see is the conceiving, never the birth. Temptation not only obscures the "hook" but the "birth of death" as well. In contrast, Scripture teaches us to think our actions all the way through—if we take the bait, then we might (probably will) become hooked, which if not repented of leads to death.

Question 6. You've described your "bait" and how you were "hooked," now think of ways that giving in to evil desires have given birth to death in your life. Some may describe how evil desires have taken them to such lengths that they have acquired a Sexually Transmitted Disease or even AIDS, and now they are awaiting their own physical death. For others it will be that the mating of their evil desires with lust has conceived sin, and after sin grew up their marriage died. Have you experienced a death from sin yet? If not, can you see how you were headed in that direction? What are your thoughts?

Friends, these verses end with a surprising remedy for this whole process of temptation and sin: "Don't be deceived, my dear brothers" (James 1:16). Sin is deception; by it's very nature. The fisherman is not offering the fish something good by displaying the bait, the fisherman means to kill the fish. Evil desire and lust do not ultimately relieve tension, provide excitement, and spice up our lives; they bring death. Do not be deceived. How do we overcome pornography and sexual sin? We see it for what it is. Pornography is the bait that Satan uses to "hook" us and his ultimate goal is to bring about our death.

"Then, after desire has conceived, it gives birth to sin; and sin, when it is full-grown, gives birth to death. Don't be deceived, my dear brothers."

So, to summarize today's teaching: It is the love of God that enables us to endure trials and to stand up under temptation. It is the love of God that releases us from deception and frees us from sin's power. And it is the love of God that will bring us into glory as a spotless bride. Oh for more love of God!

Scripture to Consider

"Have nothing to do with the fruitless deeds of darkness, but rather expose them. For it is shameful even to mention what the disobedient do in secret. But everything exposed by the light becomes visible, for it is light that makes everything visible. This is why it is said: 'Wake up, O sleeper, rise from the dead, and Christ will shine on you'" (Ephesians 5:11-14).

"Because of the LORD's great love we are not consumed, for his compassions never fail. [23] They are new every morning; great is your faithfulness" (Lamentations 3:22-23).

Were you free from pornography since you did the last lesson?
    Yes   No

Were you free from masturbation since you did the last lesson?
    Yes   No

Were you free from sexual immorality since you did the last lesson?
    Yes   No

Questions

Question 1. List the links in the accident chain below. I'll give you the first one:

First link: Lot and Abraham separated because of a quarrel.

Second link:

Third link:

Fourth link:

Fifth link:

Sixth link:

Any others:

Break the Chain

Friends, to stop a pornographic accident, and possibly save our souls, it is important for us to break the link in the chain. Remove one link and we don't crash. Had there been proper supervision in the loading of the cargo aircraft in Miami five people would not have lost their lives. What if Lot had broken chain link number one, or even number two? These are the links that I saw in the story of Lot:

1. Lot and Abraham quarrel and separate—chapter 13:8-11. What if Lot and Abraham had worked out their differences instead of separating? (Note: watch out for separating from fellow believers for any reason, even if the reason seems legitimate as it did in Lot's case. There may come a time when separation is necessary, but weigh it carefully against the benefits derived from fellowship).
2. Lot "looked up and saw" the valley of Sodom—chapter 13 verse 10. What if Lot had not focused on the valley but on the hill country instead? (Note: be careful what we focus on.)
3. Lot "set out toward" Sodom—chapter 13 verse 11. Would this "accident" have happened if Lot set out toward the great trees of Mamre instead of Sodom? (Note: Be careful of the general direction of your life. We are always mov-

DAY 36—BREAK THE CHAIN

Misloaded Douglas DC-8 Pitches Up Excessively On Takeoff, then Stalls and Strikes the Ground.

The cargo was not loaded aboard the airplane according to the airlines instructions. As a result, the flight crew inadvertently used a horizontal-stabilizer-trim setting that was not correct for the airplane's aft center of gravity.

FSF Editorial Staff
"On Aug. 7, 1997, (airline name) Flight 101, a Douglas DC-8-61, stalled on takeoff and struck the ground approximately 3,000 feet (915 meters) from the end of Runway 27R at Miami (Florida, U.S.) International Airport. The three flight crewmembers, a security guard aboard the airplane and one person on the ground (a motorist) were killed. The U.S. National Transportation Safety Board (NTSB), in its final report, said the accident resulted from the airplane being misloaded to produce a more aft center of gravity and a correspondingly incorrect stabilizer-trim setting that precipitated an extreme pitch-up at rotation.

NTSB said that the probable causes of the accident were: the failure of (airline name) to exercise operational control over the cargo-loading process; and, the failure of [(airline name), a freight-forwarding company] to load the airplane as specified by (airline name).

Contributing to the accident was the failure of the U.S. Federal Aviation Administration (FAA) to adequately monitor (airline name) operational-control responsibilities for cargo loading and the failure of FAA to ensure that known cargo-related deficiencies were corrected at (airline name), said NTSB.

The captain, 42, was hired by (airline name) in October 1993. He had 12,154 hours of flight time, including 2,522 hours as a (airline name) DC-8 captain. NTSB said that in 1995 the FAA suspended the captain's airman certificate and medical certificate for 30 days because he had failed to report a revocation of his motor-vehicle driver's license. FAA records indicated that the captain was convicted for misdemeanor drunk driving in California in 1986 and convicted for driving under the influence in Arizona in 1994, said NTSB.

As an airline pilot, I often read up on the how's and why's of aircraft accidents. I do this to try to learn what happened and how I can prevent something similar from happening to myself, the crew, and passengers I carry. One thing I have noticed as I read through the accident reports is that there is usually an accident "chain" with many links that make up that chain. In the above accident what "links" in the accident chain can you find? Here are some that I saw:

1. Improper loading of the aircraft by the company contracted to load.
2. The airline did not properly monitor the loading of the aircraft.
3. Failure of the FAA to properly monitor the loading operation of the airline.
4. Failure of the FAA to ensure previous known loading problems were corrected.
5. A possible 5th "link" in the accident chain could have been the Captain's known drinking problem.

All the these links in the chain caused the accident of this Cargo Flight 101, killing a total of 5 people. What if just one link in the accident chain had been broken? For instance, what if the FAA, citing known loading problems with the airline, had decided to shut it down until its problems could be corrected? That one break in the chain would have saved 5 people's lives.

You and I have had a problem with pornography. And if we examine times of failure we will always find a chain of events that led up to the "crash." Here are some of mine:
1. I did not get up early and spend quiet time with the Lord.
2. I have had a long day in the air and I am tired.
3. My wife and I are at odds over something.
4. My last flight of the day was delayed because of weather.
5. I saw a partially clothed woman at the airport and I can't get the image of her out of my head.
6. When I get to my hotel room I turn on the TV and immediately see an advertisement for a pornographic movie. Crash!

Now, I have learned to notice when links in an accident chain are developing and to break at least one link to prevent a pornographic accident. So now I rise early and spend time with the Lord, which sets me in a content and praying frame of mind throughout the day. I will communicate much with my wife and ensure we are loving each other. If my day is long I know I'm headed for trouble and I begin watching and praying. And finally, I might take the TV out of my hotel room and drop it off at my co-pilot's room (makes for an interesting discussion the next day).

Next, let us notice how these "accident links" are all there in a particular incident in Scripture.

In the life of Lot, nephew of Abraham, there was a terrible tragedy. He came to live in a city that was ultimately destroyed by God for its wickedness. Lot lost all of his possessions, his wife was killed; and he barely escaped with his own life and the lives of his two daughters. Notice the following passage of Scripture and see if you can spot the links in this developing "accident chain," then write in each "link" in the lesson:

"⁸ So Abram said to Lot, 'Let's not have any quarreling between you and me, or between your herdsmen and mine, for we are brothers. ⁹ Is not the whole land before you? Let's part company. If you go to the left, I'll go to the right; if you go to the right, I'll go to the left.' ¹⁰ Lot looked up and saw that the whole plain of the Jordan was well watered, like the garden of the LORD, like the land of Egypt, toward Zoar. (This was before the LORD destroyed Sodom and Gomorrah.) ¹¹ So Lot chose for himself the whole plain of the Jordan and set out toward the east. The two men parted company: ¹² Abram lived in the land of Canaan, while Lot lived among the cities of the plain and pitched his tents near Sodom. ¹³ Now the men of Sodom were wicked and were sinning greatly against the LORD" (Genesis 13:8-13).

"¹¹ The four kings seized all the goods of Sodom and Gomorrah and all their food; then they went away. ¹² They also carried off Abrams nephew Lot and his possessions, since he was living in Sodom" (Genesis 14:11-12).

Note: eventually the fire of God's wrath destroyed Sodom.

Did you spot the "links" that led to this disaster?

Questions

ing, either more toward righteousness or more toward sin.)

4. Lot "pitched his tent near" Sodom—chapter 13 verse 12. Lot could have broken the "accident chain" even after he separated from Abraham, after he saw and set out toward Sodom, had he simply refused to pitch his tent so close to the filth and wretchedness of Sodom. (Note: To the extent possible, pitch your tent as far away from sinful traps as you can. We still must influence the world, but we have to watch ourselves, be discretionary, use wisdom and common sense as to how close we should get.)

5. Lot "was living in" Sodom—chapter 14 verse 12. Notice the progression: Lot separated from Abraham, saw Sodom, set out toward Sodom, pitched his tent near Sodom, then was living in Sodom. And then we read of him being taken captive in battle. Friends, these can be our steps to destruction as well. We separate from fellowship, see something sinful and focus on it, set out toward it, pitch our tent near it, live in it, are taken captive by it.

Break the chain!

Now, let us focus on your accident chains. What are the links? How can you remove one link (or more) and stop the "accident"? Please describe below your accident chains and your plan to remove a link.

Question 2. What has been your accident chain in the past?

Question 3. Will you now conscientiously remove some links in the chain? What links will you remove and how will you do it?

Questions

Question 4. Will you share this plan with someone who can help you implement it and hold you accountable?

Course Member Dennis writes:
"The first link in the chain that bound me to porn was the excuse "Everyone is going to sleep and now I have time to get online and 'check my email'" I would tell my wife that I would only be a moment and after surfing the web for a couple of minutes, I knew that she would be asleep before then. The next link was to "accidentally" stumble upon some porn site and say to myself, 'Well, as long as I'm here...'

From there I would bring up the News groups, where the deviant porn is, and the sex story sites, and indulge in all manner of wicked fantasies. Then I would begin to masturbate and then there was no turning back. That was always the last link in the chain. The next day my mind would still be racing with images and I would masturbate two or three times, then I would resolve to break the chain but I was not strong enough. This was my nightly routine for seven long and frustrating years.

To break the chain, I have moved the computer to the family room and do not access it or even sit at it after a certain hour. If I have not read my mail or checked the scores or read the news by a certain time, it has to wait until tomorrow. Also now that my wife is aware of my addiction, she is watchful of what is on the screen and makes me accountable. I no longer delete the history file or the temp file. She has full access to the computer also. Additionally, when the temptation to "check my email" comes, I immediately turn off the computer and join the family. It has only been 9 days, but I have been porn free for 9 days. Already I feel the strength of the Lord enabling me. I will be victorious by His grace."

Question 5. How are you doing today?

Testimony

The following testimony is from Gill:

When I returned from a mission trip that I had taken to China, in 1997, God had taught me a lot during my year overseas. What I wasn't prepared for however is how I would be tempted and how I fell into pornography and masturbation. I had been relatively free from porn while I was in college, having struggled with it as a teenager. God had used my former girlfriend's family to bring me back to the Lord after wandering away from Him. I gave up porn at that time by God's grace. Somehow though, pride began to creep into my walk with God. Though I was very zealous for God during my college years, I did not have a very solid foundation for my faith. I was not accountable to anyone. I didn't know the principles of freedom in Christ. I was caught up in my works and what I could do for God.

In 1993-4 God began to break me of my pride. I struggled with many sins of the heart: anger, jealousy, pride, fear. God showed me how much of a sinner I was. Yet I was still proud in my faith. I would not humble myself. I thought myself better than other believers. I certainly did not have a humble thankful heart to God.

I had always struggled with masturbation since I was a teenager: Both with and without porn. It didn't matter, as long as I gratified my cravings. I lusted after my sisters in Christ in my heart. I was obsessive in my thoughts about sex. This had a stranglehold on my life.

I am convinced that many Christian men live as I once did seeing their sisters in Christ as objects of desire. Many people thought I was humble and kind, but so many times I was not.

When I got back from my trip I stumbled onto Internet porn, and the hook of Satan was set. I started viewing a little bit, but then gradually more and more. I struggled with it for about 2 1/2 years before I found out about this online course, **Pure Freedom**. God led me to join and start going through it. By the grace of God I have found freedom from both pornography and masturbation. God's grace has been working in my life greatly over the past year, especially the last few months.

The most life-changing things I have learned from this course are:

1. We must be satisfied with Jesus alone. Only He can fill us up and satisfy our hearts.
2. We must aggressively deal with sin including, confession, accountability, prayer, Bible study, cutting off the sources of sin, planning our day, avoiding temptation whenever possible.
3. We need to help others be free.

God is a good God. When I was in the sin I thought I would never get out. But by God's grace I can truly say that I am free from pornography and masturbation. Now I have the responsibility to help others be free and to be diligent to stay free myself. I must be ever watchful and in prayer and accountable. I must not relax in the battle. The war still goes on. I must do all I can to continue to grow in grace and change other areas of my life that need changing, growing in the character of Christ.

I am so thankful for this course and how it has helped me.

Scripture to Consider

"Be sober, be vigilant; because your adversary the devil walks about like a roaring lion, seeking whom he may devour. Resist him, steadfast in the faith, knowing that the same sufferings are experienced by your brotherhood in the world" (1 Peter 5: 7-9).

Were you free from pornography since you did the last lesson?	Yes	No
Were you free from masturbation since you did the last lesson?	Yes	No
Were you free from sexual immorality since you did the last lesson?	Yes	No

DAY 37—SEEK THE LORD

"But what if I've done horrible things? What if I've made a real mess of my life, I've hurt other people, I've broken promises and vows...etc. What if I've gone too far? Is it possible that what I've done is so bad that I'm unable to be forgiven?"

NO!

Read the following passage, and underline the words, "But if from there."

> "After you have had children and grandchildren and have lived in the land a long time—if you then become corrupt and make any kind of idol, doing evil in the eyes of the LORD your God and provoking him to anger, I call heaven and earth as witnesses against you this day that you will quickly perish from the land that you are crossing the Jordan to possess. You will not live there long but will certainly be destroyed. The LORD will scatter you among the peoples, and only a few of you will survive among the nations to which the LORD will drive you. There you will worship man-made gods of wood and stone, which cannot see or hear or eat or smell. But if from there you seek the LORD your God, you will find him if you look for him with all your heart and with all your soul" (Deuteronomy 4: 25-29).

Questions

Question 1. Please circle all the ways that the Israelites would do wrong, according to the above passage:
- A. They would become corrupt and make idols
- B. They would do evil and provoke God
- C. They would worship man-made gods of wood and stone
- D. All of the above

Question 2. Note the things that would happen to them for their sins:
- A. They would perish from the land
- B. They would be destroyed
- C. The Lord would scatter them among other nations

Question 3. But despite the horrendous sin that these people were involved in, was God willing to forgive them?
- A. Yes
- B. No

Question 4. How do we know that God would still forgive them? What does He say?

The following testimony is from Donald:

I first looked at pornography when I was very young. I don't remember exactly how young, but I also don't remember a time when I did not have this problem. I have brothers who are much older than me (7, 13 and more years older. I am the youngest), and they always had porn and I saw it.

Because of this, I never felt like I was included in anything. I always felt different, like if they really knew me, people would not want to associate with me. I felt the same way about Church. I went because it was expected, but I knew that what I did outside of church was not in harmony with what I learned inside. So, I tried to tune out the church part. Eventually, I stopped going.

My addiction got stronger, but thankfully not much deeper. I went from soft core, to hard-core stuff, but thankfully it never went any farther. However, the amount of time I spent on it kept going up. I always thought that once I grew up and got married that everything would be fine.

I went from magazines, to movies, to Internet. I put my pleasure in my own desires. Last year, wife and daughters took a trip back to Utah to visit family I haven't seen in 3 years (since we moved to Vermont). I didn't go, because I wanted to be able to do what I wanted.

It came to a head last November. My wife knew that there was a problem, but she just didn't know how bad things were. She checked the history on the computer one day, and found that I had surfed and found 56 sites in one day. She went ballistic. My wife told me yesterday, finally, that the only, ONLY, reason she didn't throw me out, was because, I had looked at this site, and had done day 1 that day.

Continued on page 118

Note: This passage teaches us important things about the character of God: He forgives! Any sin! Any time! The Truth taught today is "But if from there...you seek the Lord" and your "there" may be anywhere. From wherever you are if you will turn to God, seek for Him, look for Him with all your heart and soul; you will find Him. He promises!

Question 5. How were the Israelites supposed to find God and be forgiven?
- A. Seek the Lord your God
- B. Look for Him if you happen to have time
- C. Look for Him with all your heart and soul

Question 6. How does Hebrews 11:6 compare with what we are studying?

"And without faith it is impossible to please God, because anyone who comes to him must believe that he exists and that he rewards those who earnestly seek him."

Course Member Jared writes: "When we do seek Him, He rewards us. I was alienated from the blessing of God because I refused to seek Him. I grew bitter because I wanted the rewards but rejected a life of faith for a life of sin."

Question 7. What are your comments on Jeremiah 29:11-13:

"For I know the plans I have for you, declares the LORD, plans to prosper you and not to harm you, plans to give you hope and a future. 12 Then you will call upon me and come and pray to me, and I will listen to you. 13 You will seek me and find me when you seek me with all your heart."

Question 8. How does this verse compare? Psalm 10:4:

"In his pride the wicked does not seek him; in all his thoughts there is no room for God."

Question 9. What are your thoughts on 2 Samuel 14:14:

"But God does not take away life; instead, he devises ways so that a banished person may not remain estranged from him."

Question 10. Comments on Matthew 7:7

"Ask and it will be given to you; seek and you will find; knock and the door will be opened to you."

Course Member Sal writes: "I was bitter that he would not bless me, but the truth was: I would not seek him. I refused to ask. What a miserable man I have become. I have no fruit to show for my years of salvation. My ground is all thorny and over run with the weeds of lust and porn. I have become a disgrace. Only Jesus can save me from the sins that bound me. I ask, I seek and I have found Him faithful. My great prayer is to recover and help my children avoid the same sinkhole of sin."

Dear friend, there is no sin that God will not forgive , if we will seek Him wholeheartedly about it. This is serious business—no half-hearted seeking of the Lord will do. Eternity is at stake. Hell is real. Let us seek Him while He may be found and we will rejoice in His forgiveness, love and acceptance.

Question 11. Write out your comments on 1 Kings 8:46-51:

"When they sin against you—for there is no one who does not sin—and you become angry with them and give them over to the enemy, who takes them captive to his own land, far away or near; and if they have a change of heart in the land where they are held captive, and repent and plead with you in the land of their conquerors and say, We have sinned, we have done wrong, we have acted wickedly; and if they turn back to you with all their heart and soul in the land of their enemies who took them captive, and pray to you toward the land you gave their fathers, toward the city you have chosen and the temple I have built for your Name; then from heaven, your dwelling place, hear their prayer and their plea, and uphold their cause. And forgive your people, who have sinned against you; forgive all the offenses they have committed against you, and cause their conquerors to show them mercy; for they are your people and your inheritance, whom you brought out of Egypt, out of that iron-smelting furnace" (1 Kings 8:46-51).

Donald's testimony continues...

Now our marriage has changed. My daughter says I am not grumpy anymore. I am starting to feel the feelings I felt for my wife before we got married. I want to do the little things to show her I love her. In ways it feels like I am just waking up after being asleep for a long, long time.

I still have temptations especially when I get stressed. But she is helping me through that and we are deciding guidelines for how to deal with those things before they become an "I fell" instead of "I was tempted"

I may struggle with this temptation for the rest of my life. I don't know. But my plan is to immerse myself so fully in truth, that I won't pay them any attention.

When I started this website, I just wanted to get in, get "fixed" and get out. Now, I am so grateful for all the help, love support and Freedom that I am going to start helping others who want to get out.

Questions

Comments:

Today I want to again introduce you to some writings of the Puritans. The first is a letter from a Puritan pastor written to a member of his congregation. He is giving practical counsel. My prayer is that his counsel will sink right in to your heart and soul as you read. Once you get a taste of the medicinal value of these writings you will want more and more. We've got to replace the hours spent on pornography with something else; why not invaluable writings like these?

Memoirs of McCheyne: "I DO NOT and cannot forget you; and though it is very late, I have to write you a few lines to say, Follow on to know Jesus. I do not know if you can read my crooked writing, but I will make it as plain as I can. I was reading this morning, Luke 2:29, what old Simeon said when he got the child Jesus into his arms: 'Now lettest thou thy servant depart in peace, according to thy word: for mine eyes have seen thy salvation.' If you get a firm hold of the Lord Jesus, you will be able to say the same.

"If you had died in your ignorance and sin, dear soul, where would you have been this night? Ah! How shall we sufficiently praise God if He really has brought you to the blood of the Lord Jesus Christ! If you all are really brought to Christ, it will be something like the case of the wise men of the East (Matthew 2). When they were in their own country, God attracted their attention by means of a star. They followed it, and came to Jerusalem, saying, Where is he that is born King of the Jews? ...for we are come to worship him. Herod and Jerusalem were troubled at the saying. No one was seeking Christ but the wise men. The world thought they were mad; but soon they saw the star again, and it led them to the house where the infant Savior lay, His robe of state a swaddling band, His cradle the manger. Yet they kneeled down and called Him, my Lord and my God, they got their own souls saved, and gave Him gifts, the best they had, and then departed into their own country with great joy in their hearts, and heaven in their eyes.

"So it may be with you. The most around you care not for Jesus. But you are asking, Where is He? We are come to be saved by Him. None around you can tell. They think you are going out of your mind. But God is leading you to the very spot where the Redeemer is a lowly, despised, spit upon, crucified Savior. Can this be the Savior of the world? Yes, dear soul; kneel down and call Him your Redeemer. He died for such as you and me. And now you may go away into your own country again, but not as you came. You will carry with you joy unspeakable and full of glory."[27]

Matthew Henry: "Here observe, First, That whatever place we are in we may thence seek the Lord our God, though ever so remote from our own land or from his holy temple. There is no part of this earth that has a gulf fixed between it and heaven. Secondly, those, and those only, shall find God to their comfort, who seek him with all their heart, that is, who are entirely devoted to him, earnestly desirous of his favor and solicitous to obtain it. Thirdly, afflictions are sent to engage and quicken us to see God, and, by the grace of God working with them, many are thus reduced to their right mind, "When these things shall come upon thee, it is to be hoped that thou wilt turn to the Lord thy God, for thou seest what comes of turning from him; see Daniel 9:11, 12[KJV]. Fourthly, Gods faithfulness to his covenant encourages us to hope that he will not reject us, though we are driven to him by affliction. If we at length remember the covenant, we shall find that he has not forgotten it."[28]

Memoirs of McCheyne: "Some of you may have seen how short life is in those around you. Your fathers, where are they? And the prophets, do they live forever? How many friends have you lying in the grave! Some of you have more friends in the grave than in this world. They were carried away as with a flood, and we are fast hastening after them. In a little while the church where you sit will be filled with new worshipers, a new voice will lead the psalm, a new man of God fill the pulpit. It is an absolute certainty that, in a few years, all of you who read this will be lying in the grave. Oh, what need, then, to fly to Christ without delay! How great a work you have to do! How short the time you have to do it in! You have to flee from wrath, to come to Christ, to be born again, to receive the Holy Spirit, to be made meet for glory. It is high time that you seek the Lord. The longest lifetime is short enough. Seek conviction of sin and an interest in Christ. Oh, satisfy me early with thy mercy, that I may rejoice and be glad all my days."[29]

Question 12. What are your thoughts on today's lesson? How are you doing today?

Scripture to Consider

"Glory in His holy name; Let the hearts of those rejoice who seek the LORD! Seek the LORD and His strength; Seek His face evermore!" (Psalm 105:3-4)

Were you free from pornography since you did the last lesson?
    Yes   No

Were you free from masturbation since you did the last lesson?
    Yes   No

Were you free from sexual immorality since you did the last lesson?
    Yes   No

DAY 38—RESTORATION AFTER LOSS

Friend, doing pornography is tremendously exciting—for a while. It promises to give fulfillment, stimulation and satisfaction. But if you have been doing it for any length of time you know that the promises are really lies; pornography takes more than it ever gives! We will examine a story today of a young man who's heart was filled with the promise of excitement and satisfaction, and the gain of material wealth, lifelong friendships, ease and satisfaction. But he ended up losing everything. Let's read:

> "vs.11—There was a man who had two sons. vs. 12—The younger one said to his father, 'Father, give me my share of the estate.' So he divided his property between them. vs. 13—Not long after that, the younger son got together all he had, set off for a distant country and there squandered his wealth in wild living. vs. 14—After he had spent everything, there was a severe famine in that whole country, and he began to be in need. vs. 15—So he went and hired himself out to a citizen of that country, who sent him to his fields to feed pigs. vs. 16—He longed to fill his stomach with the pods that the pigs were eating, but no one gave him anything" (Luke 15:11-16).

This young man was not content with his life, so he asked his father to give him his inheritance. Then he went to a "distant country" and began living a "wild life" where he "spent everything."

Dear friend, pornography plants seeds of discontentment in a very powerful way. It can plant the seed of physical discontentment by its display of the seemingly flawless appearances of the actors and actresses. It can plant the seeds of emotional discontentment through the endless exhibitions of physical "love" repeatedly demonstrated in the scenes. And, following discontentment comes covetousness, or wanting what we do not have and in the above passage is stated in these words, "give me my share." Pornography is an extremely powerful tool in the hands of the devil to make us discontented and covetous.

But if we were to follow the lives of people who have been involved in pornography for any length of time, we would discover lives of loss. Lives of need. Lives of emptiness. Here is the way one man stated it: "I have been involved in pornographic movies, pornographic internet surfing, night clubs, strip shows, prostitution, and masturbation. I am a former pastor who could no longer remain in the ministry and keep up my involvement in this." This is a common scenario.

Questions

Please answer the following questions:

Question 1. From verse 14, there are two things that caused this young man to "be in need." What are those two things?

Note: Regarding the famine, it can often be discovered that Providence is against us when we are sinning. And yet, in some cases, God is disciplining in order to restore. This famine, in the above story, was of Divine Providence, designed to increase the "need" of the young man, and was for his restoration.

Question 2. There is a word in verse 16 that describes all who are not being satisfied in Jesus Christ. Fill in the blank.

"He _____ to fill his stomach."

So, the young man initially longed to have his inheritance and longed to live the wild life; now he was longing for food. "Longing" is the characteristic of those who are not drinking the Living Water of Jesus Christ. Remember the woman at the well and her 6 relationships?

Question 3. When we were doing pornography, we were longing for something. What were you longing for?

Question 4. Write down everything you can think of from the story that this young man lost by going to the far country:

Question 5. Have you lost anything through involvement with pornography?

Testimony

The following testimony is from Devin:

I discovered masturbation at the age of ten. It was not long after that my friends and I found and looked at some pages from a porn magazine that were just laying in someone's yard. The seed was planted then; but my addiction really began when I was in high school. The local adult bookstore did not card, and I could go in any time I wanted. I had also found an erotic novel (not romance, just pure sex) that someone had stashed in the library at school, which was fuel for the fire.

My involvement with porn went on for many years but at the age of 20 I was still a "virgin." Then I met someone; we became sexually active. Then came the break up time, after a year and a half. We broke up because her husband caught us. Yes, I knew it was wrong. I had been raised in church and had even given my life to God in High School, but my flesh longed for the "love" I felt from her.

Well, after that I fell back into porn and masturbation. There was no Internet back then, so my only source of porn was videos and magazines.

It had to have been about 9 years ago that God really grabbed hold of me. I had a really great youth pastor that really held me accountable and inspired me to get straightened out even though he did not know about my sexual impurity. By the grace of God (and some literal fights with myself, I know what Paul means when he says beating his flesh into submission), I overcame the sexual sins in my life, and was free from those sins for over 8 months. Then I met her.

Now, ultimately she became my wife, and we did not do anything until after we were engaged, but we did have sex before we were married. That was bad and sinful, but I still did not fall back into porn and masturbation. That came later.

We had been married about a year and a half, and things were not going well. Our first daughter was born seriously handicapped, and it tore us apart. I turned back to porn and masturbation, mainly because I did not want to "bother my wife so much about sex." Boy was that a mistake. With the Internet around now, I had tons of "free" porn to look at (well, it did not cost money, but what it did cost was much worse). Then, because of all the things that had happened, I turned my back on God. I basically told Him that He had hurt me, now I was going to get even.

That led to a 5-year addiction, masturbation at least once a day if not more. Finally, as my marriage dissolved around me, God got my attention and brought me back to church (that was 1/1/00). But there was still this issue with sex. It had become such a part of me that I defined myself by it. Things got so bad for me that I even went so low as to get into "petting" with a minor. I could have gone to jail. I was terrified.

That experience started a struggle within me to over come this. I told my pastor (who left the church a month later for other reasons), and he introduced me to someone else that had the same problem.

Ok, enough confession. Let's get to the deliverance part. Ultimately, we got a new pastor at church and he asked me to lead worship on Wednesday nights. I knew that I needed to tell him about this problem before he could let me do that, so I did. That has helped me so much to get through this. Then I found the Setting Captives Free site, and a month or two later started it.

God has proven Himself to me in many ways. He has shown that He knows my needs, he understands my pain, He cares about me, and He hates my sin. God's grace alone has brought me to this point. The addiction is broken, but the desire is not fully broken. There are still days, in the pit of my loneliness that my flesh craves the sin I left behind, and I am not perfect. I have overcome only by the blood of Jesus Christ working in me. I need to always be on guard for my soul, be diligent and mindful, watching for the signs of weakness so that I can run to my Savior.

God has delivered me from the pit of sin. There are still parts that need to be cleaned up in me, and the race will only be over when I reach heaven, but I know Who holds my hand all the way. Amen.

Questions

"And the God of all grace...will himself restore you and make you strong, firm and steadfast" (1 Peter 5:10).

Friend, God is a restoring God. The devil prowls around like a roaring lion seeking for someone to devour. But God is able to forgive, save, heal, deliver, and restore us when we fall. And then He is able to keep us from falling again. Notice the rest of the passage in Luke 15:

"vs. 17—When he came to his senses, he said, 'How many of my father's hired men have food to spare, and here I am starving to death! vs. 18—I will set out and go back to my father and say to him: Father, I have sinned against heaven and against you. vs. 19—I am no longer worthy to be called your son; make me like one of your hired men.' vs. 20—So he got up and went to his father. But while he was still a long way off, his father saw him and was filled with compassion for him; he ran to his son, threw his arms around him and kissed him. vs. 21—The son said to him, 'Father, I have sinned against heaven and against you. I am no longer worthy to be called your son.' vs. 22—But the father said to his servants, 'Quick! Bring the best robe and put it on him. Put a ring on his finger and sandals on his feet. vs. 23—Bring the fattened calf and kill it. Let's have a feast and celebrate. vs. 24—For this son of mine was dead and is alive again; he was lost and is found.' So they began to celebrate."

Question 6. Verse 17 says that the young man "came to his senses." So what was this man's condition while in the far country?

A. Stable, strong and healthy
B. Out of his right mind
C. Fully satisfied and happy

Note: doing pornography is insanity! It puts us out of our right mind.

Question 7. What 2 words does the father use in verse 24 above to describe his son when he was in the far country?

_____and_____

Question 8. When he "came to his senses" where did he want to go?

A. To the Far Country Bar N Grill
B. To the Super Bowl
C. Back to his father

Questions

The first indicator of true repentance is a desire for God. We know we are beginning to think correctly, after a time in the far country, when we want to go to our Heavenly Father.

Now let us review the picture we have been given of this young man. According to Jesus, this man was, for a time, not in his right mind; but did come back to his senses. According to his father, he was dead and lost. According to his own words, he had sinned and was unworthy.

Question 9. Do you see yourself and your involvement with pornography in the life of this prodigal? Write your thoughts here:

Like the prodigal, I was once discontent with what I had and pornography stirred up lust in my heart. I was longing for intimacy, and I attempted to satisfy it in the wrong way—a way that is far away from God. When involved with pornography, we are out of our minds; dead and lost spiritually, sinful and unworthy, and we may lose much while in this condition. But, when we "come to our senses," and return to our Heavenly Father, He will accept, embrace, love and restore us.

> "But while he was still a long way off, his father saw him and was filled with compassion for him; he ran to his son, threw his arms around him and kissed him" (Luke 15:20).

Are there any sweeter words in all of Scripture? This verse reveals the heart of God the Father toward those who are leaving sin and coming to Him. If you are leaving pornography and coming back to God, you will be received warmly, no matter how far away you went, how long you have been gone, or how much you lost. Our God loves those who leave their sin and come to Him.

Notice that the father was "filled with compassion." If you are returning from pornography, our God has a heart wide open for you. His heart beats with love for those who are returning, and just the sight of us when we return fills our Father's heart with compassion. "As a father has compassion on his children, so the Lord has compassion on those who fear him" (Psalm 103:13).

> "vs. 22—But the father said to his servants, 'Quick! Bring the best robe and put it on him. Put a ring on his finger and sandals on his feet. vs. 23—Bring the fattened calf and kill it. Let's have a feast and celebrate. vs. 24—For this son of mine was dead and is alive again; he was lost and is found. So they began to celebrate."

The end of this story is all about loving and joyous restoration. He who had sinned, squandered his wealth, and had been living with pigs, was now reconciled to his father, given a robe, ring and sandals, and was feasting on the fatted calf.

How instructive this is for us, who, through pornography, squandered away our spiritual inheritance, and possibly much more; but now we are reconciled to God, graced with the robe of righteousness, granted the ring of authority, and are wearing the sandals of readiness to tell the gospel. And most importantly, we are feasting on the Lord Jesus! Oh, friend, we were saved to celebrate! Reconciled to God to delight in His Son! Rescued from porn to feast on Jesus!

Today's study was all about restoration after loss. Is someone reading this who has really lost a lot through involvement with pornography? Oh my friend, if you come to God, or come back to God, you will see His heart of compassion for you. You will see your life restored, and made a blessing to others. You will look good in your new robe, and will enjoy a feast that will satisfy your longings. God will restore to you the years the locusts ate.

Question 10. What steps do you see in the young man's 180-degree turn-about?

Question 11. The young man wanted to come back and be a "servant." What did the father call him in verse 24?

Question 12. If you have "squandered," does this story give you hope of restoration? How so?

Questions

Question 13. Does this story move you to believe in the possibility of new or fresh changes in your relationship with God and/or others?

Question 14. How do the following verses reinforce the truth we have been studying today? Please write your thoughts after each one:

Joel 2:25-26 "I will repay you for the years the locusts have eaten—the great locust and the young locust, the other locusts and the locust swarm my great army that I sent among you. You will have plenty to eat, until you are full, and you will praise the name of the LORD your God, who has worked wonders for you; never again will my people be shamed."

Note: This passage from Joel seems to be a promise of God that He would restore what the disobedience of the Israelites destroyed. The "locusts" here are used to picture sin, which devours and destroys everything in its path.

Hosea 6:1-2 "Come, let us return to the LORD. He has torn us to pieces but he will heal us; he has injured us but he will bind up our wounds. After two days he will revive us; on the third day he will restore us, that we may live in his presence."

Isaiah 61:1-4 "The Spirit of the Sovereign LORD is on me, because the LORD has anointed me to preach good news to the poor. He has sent me to bind up the brokenhearted, to proclaim freedom for the captives and release from darkness for the prisoners, to proclaim the year of the Lord's favor and the day of vengeance of our God, to comfort all who mourn, and provide for those who grieve in Zion to bestow on them a crown of beauty instead of ashes, the oil of gladness instead of mourning, and a garment of praise instead of a spirit of despair. They will be called oaks of righteousness, a planting of the LORD for the display of his splendor. They will rebuild the ancient ruins and restore the places long devastated; they will renew the ruined cities that have been devastated for generations."

Scripture to Consider

"Thus says the LORD: 'Behold, I will bring back the captivity of Jacob's tents, and have mercy on his dwelling places; The city shall be built upon its own mound, And the palace shall remain according to its own plan. Then out of them shall proceed thanksgiving and the voice of those who make merry; I will multiply them, and they shall not diminish; I will also glorify them, and they shall not be small'" (Jeremiah 30: 18-19 NKJV).

Were you free from pornography since you did the last lesson?
    Yes   No

Were you free from masturbation since you did the last lesson?
    Yes   No

Were you free from sexual immorality since you did the last lesson?
    Yes   No

DAY 39—SPECIFIC STEPS TO FREEDOM FROM SIN

"Submit yourselves, then, to God. Resist the devil, and he will flee from you. Come near to God and he will come near to you. Wash your hands, you sinners, and purify your hearts, you double-minded. Grieve, mourn and wail. Change your laughter to mourning and your joy to gloom. Humble yourselves before the Lord, and he will lift you up" (James 4:7-10).

Today we will see from Scripture that we are to take specific steps to be free from sin. But first, let us notice from the above passage some characteristics of those who are in sin. Let us list them here:

1. They do not submit to God (verse 7).
2. They do not resist the devil (verse 7).
3. They remain at a distance from God (verse 8).
4. They have dirty hands and a defiled heart (verse 8).
5. They are double-minded (verse 8).
6. They are light and joking, and laugh much (verse 9).
7. They are prideful (verse 10).

I can think back into my time of habitual viewing of pornography and sexual impurity and see every one of these characteristics in my life:

1. My spirit was domineering and dictatorial, not submissive toward God or others.

2. I freely embraced pornography on many occasions, not realizing that in so doing I was worshiping at a demonic shrine (1 Corinthians 10:20-21).

Questions

Question 1. Thinking through the list of 7 characteristics, which one (or several) describe your life when you were in pornography? Please give some instances where these characteristics showed themselves most clearly.

These verses also show us the remedy for our sin-sickness, and we are about to study specific steps on how to be free from habitual sin. But let us be careful to note that doing what Scripture commands requires the grace of God. This would be a good point to stop today's lesson and beseech God for grace to actually do each of these steps. I often pray, "God help me to apply what I learn today. I need your grace to actually do what your Word says to do, so please keep me from just gaining knowledge but help me to obey You." Feel free to write out a prayer here if you would like to.

Step 1: "Submit yourselves, then, to God." (verse 7) Submission is: "A Greek military term meaning 'to arrange [troop divisions] in a military fashion under the command of a leader'. In non-military use, it was 'a voluntary attitude of giving in, cooperating, assuming responsibility, and carrying a burden'". Submission in Scripture is obeying God, whereas sinning is obeying the evil one. Job 22:21-27 contain much truth on how to be free from sin, and the first step is listed in verse 21: *"Submit to God and be at peace with him;"*

Question 2. Please write out the areas you have failed to submit to God in the past, and then explain how you will submit to Him from now on.

Testimony

The following testimony is from Stu:

I was not as much in bondage to pornography as many others have been. I had only been dabbling in it for approximately 6 months when I came in contact with Mike Cleveland through our mutual place of employment. I was a professing Christian, but was thinking that pornography was not that bad, but Mike encouraged me to examine my heart and actions in light of Scripture. I studied through the Scriptures with him, and then on my own and came to the conclusion that viewing pornography was sinful. I learned how to stop, by the grace of God, and have been completely free from all forms of pornography now for nearly one year.

I just now started going through the **Pure Freedom** course, and wow! I can see that I was saved from much heartache in my life. Praise God for freedom and purity in Jesus Christ.

3. I was far from God during this time, even though I claimed to be a servant of His. My life illustrated Proverbs 28:9 "If anyone turns a deaf ear to the law, even his prayers are detestable."

4. My hands were dirty from all my sin activity and my heart was defiled all the time. Oh what a horrible condition to be in. Now I understand why Scripture compares sin to leprosy, for leprosy is a disease that defiles one entirely, and makes them unclean. Just as lepers had to remain isolated or in colonies of other lepers, so I came to feel that I should be banished from society because my guilt and shame were so great. Oh how I thank God that He still cleanses lepers!

5. I was double minded and unstable, because while I attempted to pray and meditate on Scripture, my thoughts often slid into pornographic images. This hindered time with my family as I was always entertaining some sinful image. It made me unstable for I could not keep my thoughts together on any one subject. James says, "That man (who doubts God) should not think he will receive anything from the Lord; he is a double-minded man, unstable in all he does" (James 1:7-8, explanation added).

6. I was never very serious, but was light and airy, joking all the time and laughing quite frequently. This was a cover up for my sinful ways, as I tried to hide all my pain with laughter.

7. I was very prideful and often put others down, hoping to lift myself up.

Course Member Ike writes: I too can see each one of these characteristics in my past involvement with pornography, especially the pride part. Nobody could tell me anything; I knew it all. And when it came to spiritual things I was a self-proclaimed expert, always using Scripture to justify myself while condemning others. I can see how these verses in James point me to the way out of my bondage in pornography, Lord help me to do them!"

Questions

Step 2: "Resist the devil, and he will flee from you" (verse 7). Resist means to set yourself against someone or something, or to stand in opposition to them. For me, this meant developing a "battle plan" of how to set myself against the evil one. Among other things, this meant taking the TV out of my hotel room at night, and giving away my notebook computer.

Question 3. How will you set yourself against the devil, and stand in opposition to him? Please be specific.

Step 3: "Come near to God and He will come near to you" (verse 8). Friend, let me speak a truth to your heart right now: there will be no real freedom, nor any lasting victory in a life that is not seeking closeness and union with Christ. Sure, we may be able to "white-knuckle" it, grit our teeth and use sheer "will power" for a short time but we will not have **Pure Freedom** because that comes only through intimacy with Christ. We must not only resist the devil, but we must also draw near to God and experience His presence in order to overcome sin. For me, that meant spending much time in prayer and Bible study, attending church whenever possible, counseling with my pastor, etc...

Question 4. What will it look like for you to draw near to God? Again, please be specific.

Step 4: "Wash your hands, you sinners, and purify your hearts, you double-minded" (verse 8). There must be a cleansing of what we do (our hands) what we love (our hearts) and what we think (our minds). Scripture admonishes us to "wash" and "purify" and this requires diligence and effort, as well as proper tools for cleansing.

Question 5. Please list how you are planning to cleanse your hands, your heart and your mind.

Step 5: Become single minded (verse 8). Yes, it is entirely possible to rid our brains of those pornographic images. It requires not allowing ourselves any access to additional images, and cleansing our minds of the images that are still there from what we have viewed in the past. It also requires the ceasing of masturbation, as masturbation solidifies those images in our brains. This cleansing took me a few months to do, once I began the process of coming out of pornography, but I can tell you that I have not had a pornographic image lodge in my brain in nearly three years now.

Question 6. Are you "double minded" now? Or can you remember what it was like in the past?

Questions

Step 6: "Grieve, mourn and wail. Change your laughter to mourning and your joy to gloom" (verse 9). The basic instruction in this verse is to get serious, rid your life of flippancy, and begin to mourn over your sin. Now some will say that this is a life of morbid despair and gloom, and is contradictory to all the passages that refer to unspeakable joy (1 Peter 1:8) and being content in life (Hebrews 13:5). But this is not so. This passage in James refers to a person who is in need of repentance, whereas the other passages refer to the effects of repenting. Genuine repentance includes submitting to God, resisting the devil, gaining intimacy with Christ, purifying ourselves, changing our joy to gloom, and mourning over our sins.

Question 7. Have you sincerely mourned over your sin? Are you seeking to exchange light-hearted laughter for seriousness and sadness, at least for a time? Please explain...

Step 7: "Humble yourselves" (verse 10). During my years of pornography I thought myself to be the final say on Scripture. I considered myself to be an authority because of my much study, and I did not like to be challenged by those who I considered to be inferior to me, such as my pastor, my seminary teachers, and obviously everybody else. Oh, how deceived I was, and how ignorant of the ways of God! When I went to my pastor in January of 1999 and asked for help I determined not to argue with him, nor to teach, or "prove my point" but only to ask for help and listen to his counsel. THIS is what is required to get out of habitual sin. It requires humbling ourselves.

We can tell when God is working in the heart of a course member here because they find themselves not wanting to argue, or point out all the wrongs of the course, but simply to learn and ask for help. They recognize their need and so they humble themselves and ask God and us for help. We have noticed that the people who are serious about humbling themselves always find victory. Indeed, the last half of the verse that tells us to humble ourselves says, "and He will lift you up" (verse 10). Victory and **Pure Freedom** are the results for those who humble themselves!

Question 8. Finally, please share what you have learned today, or what you will put into practice. Have you seen yourself in this passage, and are you now aware of some things that will need to change in order to be truly free from habitual sin?

Scripture to Consider

"Flee from sexual immorality. All other sins a man commits are outside his body, but he who sins sexually sins against his own body. Do you not know that your body is a temple of the Holy Spirit, who is in you, whom you have received from God? You are not your own; you were bought at a price. Therefore honor God with your body" (1 Corinthians 6:18-20).

"But among you there must not be even a hint of sexual immorality, or of any kind of impurity, or of greed, because these are improper for God's holy people" (Ephesians 5:3).

"Submit to God and be at peace with him; in this way prosperity will come to you. Accept instruction from his mouth and lay up his words in your heart. If you return to the Almighty, you will be restored: If you remove wickedness far from your tent and assign your nuggets to the dust, your gold of Ophir to the rocks in the ravines, then the Almighty will be your gold, the choicest silver for you. Surely then you will find delight in the Almighty and will lift up your face to God. You will pray to him, and he will hear you, and you will fulfill your vows. What you decide on will be done, and light will shine on your ways" (Job 22:21-28).

"There I will give her back her vineyards, and will make the Valley of Achor (valley of Trouble) a door of hope. There she will sing as in the days of her youth, as in the day she came up out of Egypt" (Hosea 2:15).

Were you free from pornography since you did the last lesson?
    Yes   No

Were you free from masturbation since you did the last lesson?
    Yes   No

Were you free from sexual immorality since you did the last lesson?
    Yes   No

DAY 40—THE HEART, THE MIND, AND THE ACTIONS

> "Since, then, you have been raised with Christ, set your hearts on things above, where Christ is seated at the right hand of God. ²Set your minds on things above, not on earthly things. ³For you died, and your life is now hidden with Christ in God. ⁴When Christ, who is your life, appears, then you also will appear with him in glory. ⁵Put to death, therefore, whatever belongs to your earthly nature: sexual immorality, impurity, lust, evil desires and greed, which is idolatry. ⁶Because of these, the wrath of God is coming. ⁷You used to walk in these ways, in the life you once lived. ⁸But now you must rid yourselves of all such things as these: anger, rage, malice, slander, and filthy language from your lips. ⁹Do not lie to each other, since you have taken off your old self with its practices ¹⁰and have put on the new self, which is being renewed in knowledge in the image of its Creator" (Colossians 3:1-10).

When I was involved in pornography, my heart was set on impure things. I would walk around during the day with my heart racing, my hands sweating, my mind dwelling on pornographic images, just waiting to get to the hotel where I could indulge my flesh, and appease my sinful appetite. That is how many of my days went.

Today we want to study how the heart and mind affect the actions, and we want to learn how to live in ***pure freedom*** from habitual sin.

The above passage of Scripture talks about the "heart" (verse 1), the "mind" (verse 2), and the actions (verses 5-10) and shows the relationship between them all. The heart affects the mind, which in turn affects the actions. Let us look at each one of these in today's lesson.

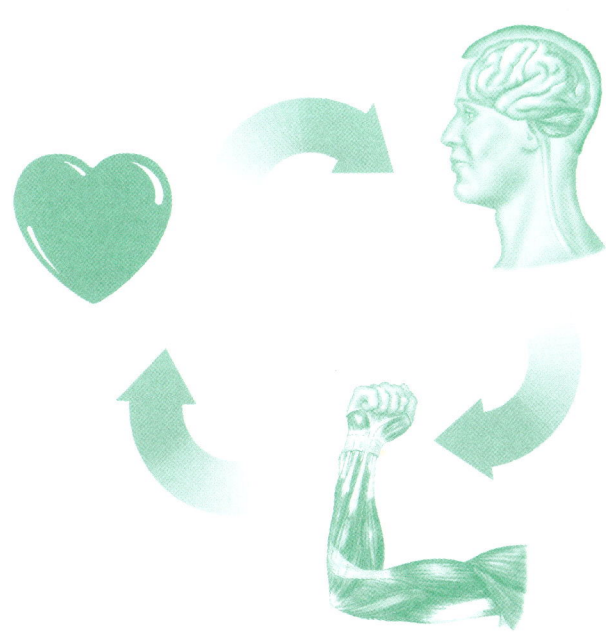

Questions

1. The Heart: The heart loves and feels excitement. The heart longs, yearns, and lusts. The heart of one in bondage loves to sin, and feels excitement when sinning. It longs, yearns, and lusts after sin, and is kept in bondage to its cravings. In contrast, the heart of one who is being set free loves God and feels excitement over growing in righteousness. That heart longs, yearns, and lusts after the holiness of God and purity.

We are instructed in the passage to "set our heart on things above, where Christ is seated at the right hand of God." In other words, we are to set our heart on loving Christ. Oh, dear friend, here is freedom from pornography! Involve your heart with Jesus Christ. Make yourself be excited about Christ. Long to be with Him, yearn for intimacy with Him, lust after a closer walk with Him. Let the cry of the beloved be yours: *"Take me away with you—let us hurry! Let the king bring me into his chambers"* (Song of Solomon 1:4).

The heart that is set on Christ is the heart that is free from sin. The heart that is apprehended by Christ refuses to let Him go, but instead embraces Him and clings to Him: *"Scarcely had I passed them when I found the one my heart loves. I held him and would not let him go till I had brought him to my mother's house, to the room of the one who conceived me"* (Song of Solomon 3:4). This is what we desire in this course of **pure freedom!** We are after the heart being affected with Christ. Colossians 3:1 tells us to "set our hearts on things above, where Christ is seated…"

Question 1. What does your heart love right now?

Question 2. List some practical ways that you will begin setting your heart on things above.

2. The Mind: The mind is obviously our thought life. The mind that is in sin is continually thinking about sinful thoughts. Pornographic images consumed my mind while awake, and my dreams while sleeping. Those thoughts and images interrupted my work, my recreation, my family time, and all other areas of life. Romans 1:28 describes my previous condition: "Furthermore, since they did not think it worthwhile to retain the knowledge of God, he gave them over to a depraved mind, to do what ought not to be done."

Colossians 3:2 tells us "set your minds on things above, not on earthly things." When I was involved in pornography I was so earthly minded that I was no heavenly good. But now we are told to set our minds on Christ, and this will inevitably bring about a real battle, because for so long we have immersed ourselves in sinful images. Now we are to think heavenly thoughts, thoughts about Christ and God, thoughts about eternity and about heaven. We are to discern whatever is true, noble, right, pure, lovely, admirable, excellent or praiseworthy (in other words, Christ!) and we are to think on these things.

The reason that we are to do these things is listed in Colossians 3:3: "For you died, and your life is now hid with Christ in God." On the cross Jesus died for us, but we also died in Him. Our old sinful nature hung on that tree with Christ. My old heart that loved sin died 2,000 years ago. My mind that was consumed with sinful images was killed at the hands of Roman soldiers, and then my old sinful self was buried in a tomb.

Question 3. Notice that verse 2 does not tell us "Stop thinking about sinful things" but rather "set your minds on things above." Why is this so?

3. The Actions: What we do is connected to what we love and what we think about. As Christians, we are not just about behavior modification without a heart change. We are about loving God passionately, about having our thoughts consumed in Christ, and then about walking in freedom from sin.

Colossians 3:5 tells us that we are to put to death whatever belongs to our flesh, and lists "sexual immorality" as the first thing to crucify. Friends, here is where the Christian life turns violent, and where murder of our pet sins is encouraged. We are to put to death sexual immorality, to crucify our lusts, and this requires spiritual acts of violence. It requires a battle plan, it uses spiritual weapons, and we won't be satisfied until there is complete annihilation of the sin. When I first started coming out of pornography I got rid of the TV in my home, and took many other "radical" steps to be free from the power of sin.

So set out to chop up your cable that has been seducing you, or burn all your magazines that have been the devil's bait, or take the TV out of your hotel room and deposit it at the front desk. Cut off your Internet access, rip up your video store card, or refuse to take any cash or credit cards with you as you drive by a favorite strip joint that has tripped you up before. And then set fences for yourself that will not allow you to go back to these sins. This may be embarrassing to you, but I have found that unless we are willing to be embarrassed we will never be free.

But not only are we to crucify sexual immorality, but also all "impurity, lust, evil desires and greed, which is idolatry." Everything has to go. Like the children of Israel when they were told to stone Achan, also stoned his family, his sheep and cattle, and destroyed everything connected with him, so we are to do violence to the entire realm of everything sinful. We are not only to destroy sexual immorality, impurity, evil desires…etc. but we are to rid our lives of anger, rage, malice, slander, and filthy language from your lips (verse 8). We will see this in upcoming lessons, as we study how to employ offensive, aggressive, violence in wiping out our sins.

Question 4. Read verse 5 above. What does it call sexual immorality, impurity, lust, evil desires, etc...?

Friend, sexual immorality, lust and all other forms of self-pleasing is idolatry. Idolatry is the worship of false gods. Did you know you were worshiping false gods when you were giving in to evil desires? When I was viewing pornography I was kneeling down to a demonic god (1 Corinthians 10:19-20), and worshiping at the shrine of the devil. When I was masturbating I was adoring myself and living to please myself, which is self-idolatry. I did not know this at the time, but the devil was deriving worship from me through pornography and masturbation. No wonder the next sentence in Colossians 3 says, "Because of these, the wrath of God is coming." God will destroy all idolaters, and as you read these words, this may be your last chance to repent of your idolatry before the wrath of God destroys you. So we must destroy sin in our lives before we are destroyed.

Question 5. How does Exodus 20:4-5 go with today's teaching?

> "You shall not make for yourself an idol in the form of anything in heaven above or on the earth beneath or in the waters below. You shall not bow down to them or worship them; for I, the LORD your God, am a jealous God…"

Questions

Today we have seen how the heart, the mind, and the actions are all connected, and we were given specific instructions about each. We are to set our hearts on things above, we are to set our minds on things above, and we are to put to death all sinful actions. This teaching really is a summary of the Christian life. We are to set our hearts toward loving God, we are to dwell on thoughts of Christ, and we are to destroy all sin in our lives.

Friends, I know people who are off-balance in these three areas. One person wants to focus only on his heart, as he believes love for God is the only thing required to walk in victory. He is very much into emotionalism, praise songs, worshiping with His eyes closed, etc... But he practically ignores the teaching about the mind being engaged to dwell on Christ, and he does not concentrate spiritual energy on putting to death the lusts of his flesh. Or there are others who are intellectuals, who have much information and learning, who know all the correct doctrine, but who have no passion for Christ, or for the destroying of sin in their lives. Still others focus all their efforts on stopping sinful behavior, of crucifying their flesh, of doing spiritual damage to their lusts, but where is their love for God?

Question 6. Think for a moment about what would happen if any one of these three things were missing in your life. Write out your thoughts as to what could happen if you did not set your heart on things above, yet you tried to do the other 2 things. Or what would happen if you did not set your mind on things above, or if you did not put to death sexual immorality, impurity, evil desires, etc...? Think through how these three spiritual truths all work together, and write out your thoughts here.

Question 7. What have you learned today, or have been reminded of, that will make a difference in your fight against sin? Please share your final thoughts here:

Scripture to Consider

"No one whose hope is in you will ever be put to shame, but they will be put to shame who are treacherous without excuse" (Psalm 25:3).

"But you, man of God, flee from all this, and pursue righteousness, godliness, faith, love, endurance and gentleness. Fight the good fight of the faith. Take hold of the eternal life to which you were called when you made your good confession in the presence of many witnesses. In the sight of God, who gives life to everything, and of Christ Jesus, who while testifying before Pontius Pilate made the good confession, I charge you to keep this command without spot or blame until the appearing of our Lord Jesus Christ, which God will bring about in his own time—God, the blessed and only Ruler, the King of kings and Lord of lords, who alone is immortal and who lives in unapproachable light, whom no one has seen or can see. To him be honor and might forever. Amen" (1 Timothy 6:11-16).

Were you free from pornography since you did the last lesson?
    Yes   No

Were you free from masturbation since you did the last lesson?
    Yes   No

Were you free from sexual immorality since you did the last lesson?
    Yes   No

Testimony

The following testimony is from Andrew:

I have been thoroughly enslaved to lust, pornography, masturbation and many other impurities ever since I can remember. My testimony is short. God saved me. He taught me how to employ biblical principles, by God's grace, to escape pornography! I have been completely free for 9 months now. I praise Him!

DAY 41—BATTLE STRATEGIES I

Dear friend,

In His Word, God tells us how to defeat the devil and overcome sin in our lives. Today's teaching will be a clear presentation of the truths of Scripture on how to eradicate bondage to pornography.

There is a primary thought expressed throughout Scripture that teaches us how to leave sin behind; it is to deal harshly with it, to be merciless in eradicating it, and to annihilate every speck of it from our lives, and to seek God for grace to accomplish this. Notice the following Scripture, and it's practical application to ridding our lives of pornography:

> "I pursued my enemies and overtook them; I did not turn back till they were destroyed. I crushed them so that they could not rise; they fell beneath my feet" (Psalm 18:37-38).

Notice how the writer of this Psalm took the offensive:
1. He pursued and overtook his enemies.
2. He was aggressive in his attack; he destroyed his enemies.
3. He was violent in the war; he crushed his enemies so they could not rise again.

Let us apply these principles to fighting against our enemies of pornography and masturbation in today's lesson.

Questions

- **We must take the offensive in our fight.** For many years, I walked around in a defensive mode, just hoping to be able to dodge the next incoming fiery dart of the devil. I lived in fear that I would succumb to the lust of my flesh, and I lived in defeat: week after week, month after month and year after year. But now I see that type of a battle plan was all wrong, and instead I pursue the enemy for the purpose of annihilation. How do I do this?

I bring home the receipts from my layovers and ask my wife to check them to verify that no pornographic movies were purchased. I put Hacker Wacker on my notebook computer which sends an email to my wife if I were to try to visit a pornographic website. We got rid of the TV in our home. I refuse to go anywhere near the magazine rack at the grocery store or in airport terminals. I try to get involved in ministry to other people who want out of pornography, wherever possible. This is our way to "get even" with the enemy for his devastation in our lives, as we use the grace of God to drag others from the jaws of the lion.

Some people say that the above is too "radical," and that it is not a "normal" life. My response is, "So?" God is enabling me to be free from the trap of the devil in pornography and masturbation and it does not bother me to be thought a little strange. Walking in purity, enjoying fellowship with Christ, and having effectiveness in ministry are more important.

Question 1. What ways are you taking the offensive in your battle against the deception of pornography? Can you do more? It gets to be fun thinking of new offensive moves after awhile. My wife and I like to be creative as we plot our next offensive move against the devil.

- **We must pursue this enemy with a healthy dose of spiritual aggression.** I drag every little temptation into the "light." Meaning, if I am tempted in some way I tell my wife right away, or I'll email a friend to "expose" it. Pornography is like a fungus; it grows best in the dark. Learn to drag it into the light to sap it of its strength. Get used to emailing a friend (or one of us in the **Pure Freedom** course) and saying "I am tempted to view pornography on the Internet just now, can you help?" One of the great joys I have been noticing lately on the discussion group is that people are writing in before they fall and asking for help and prayer. This is exposing the temptation to the light.

I often run to the Word of God for help. *"You, Oh Lord are a Strong Tower, a Sure Defense against my Foe."*

I seek to destroy the enemy when he first peeks his head around the corner. BAM! Hit him hard initially. By this, I mean, as soon as I sense an uprising of temptation, I open my Bible, or I begin singing a hymn or I call or email my wife or a friend. Be aggressive in the initial stages of temptation.

- **We must be spiritually aggressive with our "pet" sins:**

  "From the days of John the Baptist until now, the kingdom of heaven has been forcefully advancing, and forceful men lay hold of it" (Matthew 11:12).

  "If your hand causes you to sin, cut it off. It is better for you to enter life maimed than with two hands to go into

Questions

hell, where the fire never goes out. ⁴⁵ And if your foot causes you to sin, cut it off. It is better for you to enter life crippled than to have two feet and be thrown into hell. ⁴⁷ And if your eye causes you to sin, pluck it out. It is better for you to enter the kingdom of God with one eye than to have two eyes and be thrown into hell..." (Mark 9:43-47).

Treat pornography as if it were your worst enemy that is trying to drag your soul into hell, and "hack," "chop," and "pluck out" your way to freedom from it.

Remember, we don't literally pluck out our eyes. Abusing the body does nothing to lesson the power of the flesh (Colossians 2: 23).

Look for ways that you can expose the deeds done in darkness. Crush pornography, and grind it to powder, or it will rise again and you will be defeated in a weak moment.

- **Finally, we must pray for Gods grace to accomplish this aggressive battle plan against the enemy.** We make our plans but the Lord directs our steps (Proverbs 16:9), so we must seek Him for grace to carry out the plans. Notice David's understanding of grace in the rest of Psalm 18:

"You armed me with strength for battle; you made my adversaries bow at my feet. You made my enemies turn their backs in flight, and I destroyed my foes" (verses 39, 40). Jesus said, "Without Me you can do nothing" (John 15:5^{NKJV}) so we must be dependent on, and united with Him.

Testimony

This testimony is from Brent:

I grew up in a very loving Christian home. I was always shy and kept to myself most of the time. When I was fourteen I discovered masturbation while looking at Sports Illustrated swimsuit issues. This was very exciting. I was drawn to these women. This became a part of my daily routine. Over the next few years I progressed to R-rated movies and Playboys. I knew what I was doing was sin, and even though I tried to stop many times I kept going back into it.

This addiction has kept me from developing relationships with women. I was afraid to be open and vulnerable with them when the women on the pages and TV screens were always there for me. I was paralyzed with guilt. I wanted God to use my life for His glory, but because of the sin in my life I didn't have the joy in my life that He wanted to give me.

This addiction went on for 18 years through peaks and valleys, but never complete freedom. One day I discovered the Setting Captives Free website and thought that I would try going through the course. I began to see myself as God sees me and found encouragement from others who have been where I am and have found freedom. I learned that I had to get that garbage completely out of my life or I would go right back into it. I had a couple of setbacks along the way, but I did not give up. And I have found the joy that I have been seeking.

I want to use my life to glorify God. One way that I can do this is by helping others who have been where I am. I look forward to help others find freedom. God is molding me into the godly man that He wants me to be. I eagerly wait for the day that He gives me a wife with whom I can share the love that He intended.

Friends, in order to overcome pornography in our lives we must have a grace-empowered battle plan. One man I know plans his victory strategy for the entire next day before he goes to bed at night, and then prays to accomplish his plan. He knows that things don't always go according to schedule so He asks God for grace to deal with the unexpected. He is wise, and is enjoying much lasting victory.

Our desire is that this teaching would inspire you to stop treating your enemy as your friend; begin to take the offensive in the war, use healthy aggression toward eradicating the bondage to pornography, and be spiritually violent in the destruction and annihilation of it. It can be done, by the grace of God!

Please read through the following Scriptures and provide your comments on how they apply to the teaching today of using offensive, aggressive violence in this battle. We give you a "starter thought" before each passage.

Be merciless on all sin:

> "When the LORD your God brings you into the land you are entering to possess and drives out before you many nations—the Hittites, Girgashites, Amorites, Canaanites, Perizzites, Hivites and Jebusites, seven nations larger and stronger than you— and when the LORD your God has delivered them over to you and you have defeated them, then you must destroy them totally. Make no treaty with them, and show them no mercy. Do not intermarry with them. Do not give your daughters to their sons or take their daughters for your sons, for they will turn your sons away from following me to serve other gods, and the LORD's anger will burn against you and will quickly destroy you. This is what you are to do to them: Break down their altars, smash their sacred stones, cut down their Asherah poles and burn their idols in the fire. For you are a people holy to the LORD your God. The LORD your God has chosen you out of all the peoples on the face of the earth to be his people, his treasured possession" (Deuteronomy 7:1-6).

Question 2: Please record your thoughts about Deuteronomy 7:1-6 here:

No matter what it may be worth, destroy it:

> "When Moses approached the camp and saw the calf and the dancing, his anger burned and he threw the tablets out of his hands, breaking them to pieces at the foot of the mountain. And he took the calf they had made and burned it in the fire; then he ground it to powder, scattered it on the water and made the Israelites drink it" (Exodus 32:19-20).

Question 3. Record your thoughts about the above passage here:

Questions

Course Member Jeff writes: "These verses are awesome. Moses just went wild. That moment is what we are working towards here. An indignant fire against that which causes sin. By this time Moses just had had enough. Then making them drink the water, yes, it must have been bitter to the Israelites. It must have been disgusting, and there is Moses forcing it down their throats. I can imagine chards of it lodging in their mouths and throats. Crying out in pain. Then once in their stomachs, making them ill, causing them great pain. What a day that was. They swallowed their vulgarity."

Weary yet pursuing:

"Gideon and his three hundred men, exhausted yet keeping up the pursuit came to the Jordan and crossed it" (Judges 8:4).

Question 4. Record your thoughts on the above passage here:

Expose them:

"Have nothing to do with the fruitless deeds of darkness, but rather expose them. For it is shameful even to mention what the disobedient do in secret. But everything exposed by the light becomes visible, for it is light that makes everything visible. This is why it is said: 'Wake up, O sleeper, rise from the dead, and Christ will shine on you'" (Ephesians 5:11-14).

Question 5. Record your thoughts on the above passage here:

Jeff writes: "Yes. We cannot live dark lives and also live in the light. It is impossible!! It is physically impossible and it is spiritually impossible!! Part of my battle plan has been to keep the lights on. To some it sounds odd, but every time I fell to P&M, it was in the dark. I'd close all the shades, and turn off the lights. How evil. It is like preparing a temple for worship. My physical temple and my spiritual temple were dark. No light. Now that I have the lights on all the time, it is a physical reminder of the spiritual reality. The light is such a simple thing, but it does extreme violence to the darkness. There is no place for the darkness to hide."

So friends, we can see that there must be an offensive, aggressive, violent battle plan in order to eradicate our enemies of pornography and masturbation. Do you have such a battle plan? What have you learned from the Scriptures today?

Question 6. If you have not developed a battle plan in the past, will you now? Write your thoughts here:

Scripture to Consider

"He has delivered us from such a deadly peril, and he will deliver us. On him we have set our hope that he will continue to deliver us" (2 Corinthians 1:10).

Were you free from pornography since you did the last lesson?
    Yes   No

Were you free from masturbation since you did the last lesson?
    Yes   No

Were you free from sexual immorality since you did the last lesson?
    Yes   No

DAY 42—FOCUS!

"They traveled from Mount Hor along the route to the Red Sea, to go around Edom. But the people grew impatient on the way; they spoke against God and against Moses, and said, 'Why have you brought us up out of Egypt to die in the desert? There is no bread! There is no water! And we detest this miserable food!' Then the LORD sent venomous snakes among them; they bit the people and many Israelites died. The people came to Moses and said, 'We sinned when we spoke against the LORD and against you. Pray that the LORD will take the snakes away from us.' So Moses prayed for the people. The LORD said to Moses, 'Make a snake and put it up on a pole; anyone who is bitten can look at it and live.' So Moses made a bronze snake and put it up on a pole. Then when anyone was bitten by a snake and looked at the bronze snake, he lived" (Numbers 21:4-9).

Truth to memorize: *The cure for sin is to focus on Jesus Christ!*

Questions

Please review the passage above and answer the following questions:

Question 1. The people were complaining against God. What did He do to them to make them stop?
- A. Sent snakes among them
- B. Sent fire from heaven

Question 2. When the people died from snakebite, what did God tell Moses to do to fix the problem?
- A. Make a cut and suck out the venom
- B. Rush them to Sinai Medical Center
- C. Put a bronze snake up on a pole

Question 3. What were the people to do with the bronze snake upon the pole?
- A. Charm it
- B. Kill it
- C. Look at it

Please write out the "Truth to memorize" from above:

Question 4. What happened as the people looked at the snake on the pole?
- A. They died of snakebite
- B. They were cured of snakebite

Testimony

The following testimony is from Shirley:

Most people think pornography is only a man problem. It's not. Pornography is an equal opportunity destroyer, which has ruined the lives of numerous people, both men and women.

My first husband introduced me to pornography, and though I hated it at first I began wanting to see more and more of it until I was thoroughly enslaved to it. I was in bondage for 29 years, until I came to the **Pure Freedom** course, and now I have been free for 3 months.

OK, so I'm not getting it here...people get bit by snakes, Moses puts up a pole with a snake on it, people look at the snake and they're cured. So, what does that have to do with me, pornography, sin, overcoming, etc...?

Let's examine this story a little closer. Think of it like this:

The serpent of sin has bitten you and me! It's a deadly bite, the venom of sin is running through our veins, and we will die from the fatal wound. But, God erected a cross-like pole, and on that pole He hung a Savior, and if we look at the Savior we will live. We will be cured from the snakebite of sin, and we will not perish but have everlasting life!

Course member Jim writes:
"GOD sent snakes to the Israelites to make them stop complaining. Then He told Moses to put a bronze snake on a pole. All the people had to do was look on it. In much the same way, 'The cure for sin is focusing on Jesus Christ.' When the people focused on the snake, they were cured too. I often forget that pornography is a deadly condition. Just like the snakebites. Isaiah said it too; just look on Him and you will be saved. In Hebrews it again says that we are to look to Jesus. But wait a minute! Is this the correct way to interpret and understand this story? How can a snake represent Jesus Christ? Actually, it is not that the snake represents Christ, but rather that it points forward to our sin that was nailed to the cross with Christ."
"Just as Moses lifted up the snake in the desert, so the Son of Man must be lifted up, that everyone who believes in him may have eternal life" (John 3:14-15).

Observe: The people who were bitten by snakes were simply to look! That is what would cure them. Jesus Christ was lifted up on a cross, where He died for our sins. LOOK! Do you see Him there? He is being wounded in His hands for the wrong we've done with our hands. His feet are pierced because of the wrong places our feet have taken us. He is wearing a crown of thorns because of the wrong thoughts we've cherished. His heart is being gashed open because of the wrong loves we've had. LOOK! There He is! Do you see Him there on the cross? He's our cure! Look, believe and live!

There are many "cures" being offered on the market today. But if we examine most of them we will see several consistent themes: the "cure" is to examine the

Questions

snakebite. Focus on your pain, your past and your parents. Dear friends, these other "cures" are not of much value in helping us overcome bondage to pornography. The cure for the snake bitten Israelites was simple, yet profound: LOOK! The cure for habitual viewing of pornography, or impurity of any kind, is to have the focus of our lives be on Jesus Christ.

Question 5. Why do you think God chose a serpent to be uplifted on the pole? What did the serpent represent? What are your thoughts?

A snake is used in Scripture as a symbol of evil. Satan embodied a serpent when he tempted Adam and Eve.

Notice 2 Corinthians 5:21: "God made him who had no sin to be sin for us, so that in him we might become the righteousness of God."

"God made Him...to be sin for us." On the cross, Jesus Christ not only took our sins upon Himself, but was actually made to be sin itself. So the serpent really represents the sin that Christ took upon Himself. I don't fully understand all that implies, but what better picture could there be of sin than a snake? On the cross, Jesus took the lethal bite of the serpent, became sin and died for us.

And as we are looking at Him we will discover that pornography looses it's appeal, and we are cured.

Question 6. Write out how the following verses go with today's teaching:

"Look to Me, all the ends of the earth, and be saved!" (Isaiah 45:22 NKJV).

"Let us fix our eyes on Jesus, who for the joy set before Him, endured the cross" (Hebrews 12:2).

"For we have no power to face this vast army that is attacking us. We do not know what to do, but our eyes are upon you" (2 Chronicles 20:12).

Dear friends, the verses contain everything we need to know to defeat the "vast army" of pornographic images that attack us. There are three specific steps listed in that verse. Note them with me:

1. **They admitted their powerlessness.** They said, "For we have no power."
2. **They admitted their ignorance.** They said, "We do not know what to do." In order to truly defeat our enemy we must admit that we are without resources to fight it. We have neither the power to fight nor the knowledge of how to win.
3. **They focused on God.** Having admitted their own lack of power and ability, knowledge and resources, they did not stop there. They looked to God for help, and "focused" on Him as their Resource. If you read the rest of this story in 2 Chronicles 20 you will see that God totally defeats the "vast army." Here is the key, "But our eyes are upon You." Focus!

"My eyes are ever on the LORD, for only he will release my feet from the snare" (Psalm 25:15).

Note: Notice the connection between focusing on the Lord and escaping from the trap!

"When your children sinned against him, he gave them over to the penalty of their sin. But if you will look to God and plead with the Almighty,...even now he will rouse himself on your behalf and restore you to your rightful place" (Job 8:4-6).

"The gracious hand of our God is on everyone who looks to him, but his great anger is against all who forsake him" (Ezra 8:22-23).

"During the fourth watch of the night Jesus went out to them, walking on the lake. When the disciples saw him walking on the lake, they were terrified. 'It's a ghost,' they said, and cried out in fear. But Jesus immediately said to them: 'Take courage! It is I. Don't be afraid.' 'Lord, if it's you,' Peter replied, 'tell me to come to you on the water.' 'Come,' he said. Then Peter got down out of the boat, walked on the water and came toward Jesus. But when he saw the wind, he was afraid and, beginning to sink, cried out, 'Lord, save me!' Immediately Jesus reached out his hand and caught him. 'You of little faith,' he said, 'why did you doubt?' " (Matthew 14:25-31).

Questions

As long as he was looking at Jesus Peter walked on water, but when he "saw the winds and the waves" he began to sink. Please note how this passage applies to our teaching today, and draw comparisons between this story and our own victory over pornography:

Now, let us note what "looking at Jesus" means in each of these eight passages of Scripture, so we can begin to apply this teaching to our lives today:

- In Numbers 21, looking at the serpent meant they were in need of a cure for their snakebite. In just this way, we look to Jesus Christ to eradicate sin from our lives.
- In Isaiah 45:22, we are instructed to look to Jesus for salvation.
- In Hebrews 12:2, the context of the passage calls us to focus on Christ as a preventative to weariness and discouragement, and to give us strength to finish the race.
- In 2 Chronicles 20:12, we are instructed to look to Jesus to defeat the vast army of sin, and to give us victory over the world, the flesh and the devil.
- In Psalm 25:15, we are instructed to focus on Jesus in order to be released from the trap of sin.
- In Job 8:4-6 we are instructed to look to Jesus to restore us.
- In Ezra 8:22-23 we are invited to look to Jesus to receive grace.
- In Matthew 14:25-31, we are shown that looking to Jesus enables us to live supernaturally, walking on the water of our sin.

To summarize these passages, we are to look to Jesus to save us, to eradicate sin in our lives, to strengthen us for the race, to defeat all our enemies, to release us from the trap of sin, to restore us and give us grace, and to enable us to be victorious. See why focusing on Christ is so important?

Question 7. For the final question of the day, please write out what it would look like, practically, to have your life "focused" on Jesus Christ. Be specific. What will you do differently because of this teaching?

Course Member Pastor Joel writes: "Focusing on Jesus Christ means to put Him first. To look at, study, concentrate so strongly on that you see the details and characteristics of Him. NOT to focus on something else (like porn and such). More practically, we can focus on Him by praise & worship, prayer and Bible study. Focus on Jesus also by letting Him be Lord of our life (EVERY area) and following Him, by being like Him in character, morality and deed."

Oh how I wish I could sit down with you and explain to you the joy in my heart as my life is now focused on Jesus Christ. Those years involved in pornography were so detrimental to my family and me as my focus was taken off of Christ and put onto all forms of impurity. But now God has opened the eyes of this blind man, and granted me the ability to turn from my idolatry and to focus on the living God. And focusing on Him brings all other areas of my life into perspective too. I can see how to be a good husband, and father, how to bless my employer by doing a good job, how to interact with others so as to bless them, how to build up the body of Christ instead of tearing it down, and many other things. Focusing on Jesus Christ has brought amazing clarity and focus in all areas of my life. Amen to God's grace and His ability to refocus us!

Scripture to Consider

"If then you were raised with Christ, seek those things which are above, where Christ is, sitting at the right hand of God. Set your mind on things above, not on things on the earth. For you died, and your life is hidden with Christ in God" (Colossians 3: 1-3).

Were you free from pornography since you did the last lesson?
    Yes   No

Were you free from masturbation since you did the last lesson?
    Yes   No

Were you free from sexual immorality since you did the last lesson?
    Yes   No

DAY 43—DEAD TO SIN, ALIVE TO CHRIST
ROMANS 6

Today we're going to do something a little bit different. We will do a Bible study, where you will be doing the teaching simply by answering questions. This will be fun! We are about to drink from the living water!

"What shall we say, then? Shall we go on sinning so that grace may increase? By no means! We died to sin; how can we live in it any longer?" (Romans 6:1, 2)

Question 1. What is the central truth taught in the verse? Write your answer here:

Question 2. If we are indeed "dead to sin," when did we die to it? (Romans 6:6 gives the answer.) Write your thoughts here:

"Or don't you know that all of us who were baptized into Christ Jesus were baptized into his death? We were therefore buried with him through baptism into death in order that, just as Christ was raised from the dead through the glory of the father, we too may live a new life."

Question 3. There is a reason why we died to sin, why we were buried with Christ and why we have risen from the dead with him. That reason is stated at the bottom of verse 4. That we too may...

Question 4. What application does this have for us who were previously into pornography?

Question 5. This verse gives us hope! But it is a hope that is conditional (if we have…) according to this verse; upon what should we base our assurance of eternal life?

"For we know that our old self was crucified with him so that the body of sin might be done away with, that we should no longer be slaves to sin — because anyone who has died has been freed from sin" (Romans 6:6-7).

Question 6. What was crucified with Christ? And what was the purpose for our crucifixion with him?

Course Member Gene writes: "My old man, the old me, the self/flesh was crucified with Christ, that we would no longer be slaves to sin.

"Now if we died with Christ, we believe that we will also live with Him" (Romans 6:8).

Question 7. What hope is Paul expressing here?

Course Member Wally writes: "It shows that the old man (the old sinner Wally) was crucified with Jesus and therefore is a new creation, resurrected with Christ and joined with him by the indwelling of the holy spirit, I am free from the bondage of sin and its power, and can now live a life of purity and holiness in him."

"If we have been united with him like this in his death, we will certainly also be united with him in his resurrection" (Romans 6:5).

The following testimony is from Rodger:

I remember when I was about 6 years old, climbing the steps to the attic at my grandfather's home, and seeing a stash of pornography that must have been worth thousands of dollars.

Then, as a teen-ager, I watched my father plummet downward into pornography, which caused the divorce of my parents and the loss of my father's engineering job, which he had had for 30 years.

I became involved with pornography at the same time, and went spiraling downward so fast that before I knew it I was watching stuff that would have made me vomit less than a year earlier.

I stayed in this helpless and hopeless condition for 10 years, until I came to Setting Captives Free and enrolled in **Pure Freedom**. I have now been free for 3 months, which is a record for me, and I have no desire to go back!

Questions

Question 8. According to the verses, if we continue in slavery to pornography, or any other sin, should we have assurance of eternal life in Christ?

Question 9. Do you have the hope of living with Jesus Christ throughout eternity? If you do, upon what is your hope based?

"For we know that since Christ was raised from the dead, he cannot die again; death no longer has mastery over him. The death he died, he died to sin once for all; but the life he lives, he lives to God. In the same way, count yourselves dead to sin but alive to God in Christ Jesus" (Romans 6:9-11).

Question 10. Verse 9 says that death no longer has mastery over Christ. Since we are united with Christ, what does this mean for us?

Question 11. What does it mean to count ourselves dead to sin but alive to God in Christ Jesus?

Question 12. Can a dead person sin? How will this teaching help us in times of temptation?

"Therefore do not let sin reign in your mortal body so that you obey its evil desires" (Romans 6:12).

Question 13. The above verse contains imagery. We are not to let sin reign in our bodies. What is sin pictured as?
  A. A general in an army
  B. A king on the throne
  C. A teacher at school

Question 14. How does Colossians 1:13 compare with our study today? "For He has rescued us from the dominion of darkness and brought us into the kingdom of the Son He loves, in whom we have redemption, the forgiveness of sins." Please write your thoughts here:

"Do not offer the parts of your body to sin, as instruments of wickedness, but rather offer yourselves to God, as those who have been brought from death to life; and offer the parts of your body to him as instruments of righteousness" (Romans 6:13).

Question 15. The above verse states that our body's "parts" are to be offered to the Lord. Describe how you can offer each "part" to the Lord. Your head, heart, hands…etc.

"For sin shall not be your master, because you are not under law, but under grace" (Romans 6:14).

Question 16. How is being "under grace" different than being "under law?" What does it mean to be "under grace" and how are we free from sin's mastery by being under grace?

Question 17. How you are progressing in the grace of God? What is going on in your life today?

Scripture to Consider

"I put this in human terms because you are weak in your natural selves. Just as you used to offer the parts of your body in slavery to impurity and to ever-increasing wickedness, so now offer them in slavery to righteousness leading to holiness. [20] When you were slaves to sin, you were free from the control of righteousness. [21] What benefit did you reap at that time from the things you are now ashamed of? Those things result in death! [22] But now that you have been set free from sin and have become slaves to God, the benefit you reap leads to holiness, and the result is eternal life. [23] For the wages of sin is death, but the gift of God is eternal life in Christ Jesus our Lord" (Romans 6:19-23).

Were you free from pornography since you did the last lesson?
  Yes   No

Were you free from masturbation since you did the last lesson?
  Yes   No

Were you free from sexual immorality since you did the last lesson?
  Yes   No

DAY 44—DARK NIGHT OF THE SOUL ROMANS 7

> "We know that the law is spiritual; but I am unspiritual, sold as a slave to sin" (Romans 7:14).

Friends, have you ever fought pornography so hard, and lost so much that you felt that there would be no way to gain the victory? Have you felt like the apostle Paul—"sold as a slave to sin?"

Believe it or not, this is a common experience in the lives of Christians. As we will see later in this chapter, Paul struggled with sin to the point of despair (verse 24). Have you? Are you currently falling so often that you feel as if you are a slave to sin? Many people by this time in the course are walking in habitual victory over pornography, but some continue to fall. Of course, if you have followed the earlier lessons about "radical amputation" there is no opportunity for you to fall, and yet some still struggle with lust and fall often.

I went through this dark night of the soul, where sin seemed to have dominion over me, and where I felt I had been sold as a slave to sin. Does that mean I was not a Christian? It could. Or it could also have meant that I was being tried in the furnace and that I was going through a desert experience; a dark night of the soul. We must be careful in being quick to judge those who fall often, and then repent.

How did Paul describe this experience?

> "I do not understand what I do. For what I want to do I do not do, but what I hate I do" (Romans 7:15).

Questions

Question 1. Have you had this experience? Describe it here:

Course Member Rawson writes:
"My sin left me totally confused. I knew what was right, agreed that the law was good, even preached the glory of it. Yet, I did not have the power to do what I preached which left me in a state of confusion and despair."

"[16] And if I do what I do not want to do, I agree that the law is good. [17] As it is, it is no longer I myself who do it, but it is sin living in me" (Romans 7:16, 17).
"[20] Now if I do what I do not want to do, it is no longer I who do it, but it is sin living in me that does it" (Romans 7:20).

Here is one of the greatest teachings we can learn, and that is the teaching of "identity." Paul's identity, as a Christian, was in his "new man" not his old sinful self. When he sinned he said, "it is no longer I myself who do it" because he knew that his old man was crucified with Christ, as we saw in yesterday's lesson. Christians are those who are redeemed, who are new creations in Christ, whose inner man is created in true holiness and righteousness. BUT, Christians still have flesh, which is the residue of the old nature or the old man. Christians are indeed new creations, but they live in fallen flesh and so still sin.

Question 2. This is honesty time. How do you see yourself right now? Do you see your identity as a sinner, or as a saint who sins sometimes? Write your thoughts here:

Testimony

The following testimony is from Clark:

My whole life has been one dark night of the soul. I've lived in sin so much that I hardly know where to start. I guess at the beginning. I was the youngest of 6 and have been drawn to pornography ever since I can remember. I was addicted by the age of 10, and it grew worse and worse; by the time I was old enough to drive I was completely bound up in sin. In fact, the first place I drove to was a strip joint, and after that I went and found a prostitute to sleep with.

After I came to Christ I thought I would get the victory over this horrible sin, but I did not. It persisted. My first marriage broke up. My second marriage broke up. Same story, different day. Sin, sin, sin. And more sin.

Then one day as I was surfing to sin I ran across a banner add that said, "**Pure Freedom**, Want it?" and I did. Desperately. I clicked on the banner and enrolled in the **Pure Freedom** course, only to drop out a week later to return to my sin. But that site was in the back of my mind, and one day after I had completed my sinning again I went back to the site. I asked Mike if I could come back and his answer surprised me. He said, "I have been waiting for you and am running to meet you with open arms." Never had I felt such love. I took the course, employed the principles, found freedom from sin, and am a living testimony of the grace of God now. Free for 18 months and counting!

"I know that nothing good lives in me, that is, in my flesh. For I have the desire to do what is good, but I cannot carry it out" (Romans 7:18[NKJV]).

Questions

Paul, as a Christian, had the desire to do "good," but he lacked the power to carry it out. I was like Paul just a few years ago. I desired to do "good" and be free from pornography but did not have the power to accomplish it.

Question 3. Has this been your experience as well? Describe what it was like:

"For what I do is not the good I want to do; no, the evil I do not want to do—this I keep on doing" (Romans 7:19).

Paul did not want to sin. Everything within him opposed it, and yet he "kept on" sinning. Friends, this is a horribly dark night to experience. You want to do what is right, you want to cease habitual sin, but somehow you just can't. You don't have the power. Oh, the pain of this is so fresh in my memory. I think back on the years spent sinning against my family, which I did not want to do. Yet I did it anyway, and kept on doing it.

Question 4. Have you been mastered by sin as Paul describes here? Share your thoughts:

"So I find this law at work: When I want to do good, evil is right there with me" (Romans 7:21).

Are you tracking with Paul here as I am? I recall longing to be free from pornography, committing to not indulge on a particular layover, resolving all day long to stay free from it. But in all my desires to do good, evil was right there with me. Oh, what a dark night of the soul this is. If you are going through this right now, please know that the dark of night precedes the light of day. Morning is coming, and with it grace and mercy to enable you to be free from this plaguing sin.

Question 5. What are your thoughts on Romans 7:21 above?

"²² For in my inner being I delight in God's law; ²³ but I see another law at work in the members of my body, waging war against the law of my mind and making me a prisoner of the law of sin at work within my members" (Romans 7:22-23).

Oh how the long, dark night drags on sometimes. I remember praying for years, weeping out tears to God to be free from pornography. I was becoming a broken man as I felt God had left me to die in my sins. Paul describes himself above as a "slave" and a "prisoner." I felt like both of those.

Question 6. Have you felt this war going on inside you?

"What a wretched man I am! Who will rescue me from this body of death?" (Romans 7:24)

> ***Course Member Rory writes:*** "Oh how wretched I am! How wretched I have been. My pornography addiction led me to say and do things I would never have imagined. My night was so dark I could not see my hand in front of my face. I thank God for having mercy on my soul!"

The dark night can lead to overwhelming despair. It can be so dark in sin that you see no way out. All your friends tell you to read your Bible and pray, and you hear some people talk about overcoming sin as if it were a small thing for them. And you wonder if God has forsaken you for good, because their experience is not yours.

Dear friend, if this is you, take heart. God is at work even still. For God must break a man before He remakes him (Hosea 6:1-3); He must "hand all men over to sin" so that He can have mercy on them (Romans 11:32). This does not make God the author of our sin; rather it shows that He works through the sin to bring forth a good outcome.

Is your night dark? Are you frustrated, disappointed, discouraged or near suicidal? If so, you are right there with the Apostle Paul. I've been there too. I thank God that Paul did not stay in Romans 7, but moved on to Romans 8, which is what we will study tomorrow.

So please have hope, that if your darkness is thick, and you are feeling yourself to be sold as a slave to sin, and in the prison of sin and can't get out, that God's grace will make a way for you, as He has for me.

Again, it is possible that you are entirely beyond this Romans 7 experience by this time in the course. If you are walking in victory please never forget your struggle. It will help you deal in grace with your brothers and sisters who are falling.

Paul's horrible struggle with sin ended in praise of Jesus Christ. "But thanks be to God, through Jesus Christ our Lord." Here is where we need to run when the night is dark. If you are feeling the power of sin, run to Jesus. Give thanks to God for giving you His Son.

Questions

Now, please read the following quote by **Matthew Henry** and provide your comments below:

(3.) His (Paul's) great comfort lay in Jesus Christ (v. 25): *I thank God, through Jesus Christ our Lord.* **In the midst of his complaints he breaks out into praises. It is a special remedy against fears and sorrows to be much in praise: many a poor drooping soul hath found it so. And, in all our praises, this should be the burden of the son, "Blessed be God for Jesus Christ."** *Who shall deliver me?* **says he (v. 24), as one at a loss for help. At length he finds an all-sufficient friend, even Jesus Christ. When we are under the sense of the remaining power of sin and corruption, we shall see reason to bless God through Christ (for, as he is the mediator of all our prayers, so he is of all our praises)—to bless God for Christ; it is he that stands between us and the wrath due to us for this sin. If it were not for Christ, this iniquity that dwells in us would certainly be our ruin. He is our advocate with the Father, and through him God pities, and spares, and pardons, and lays not our iniquities to our charge. It is Christ that has purchased deliverance for us in due time. Through Christ death will put an end to all these complaints, and waft us to an eternity, which we shall spend without sin or sigh.** *Blessed be God that giveth us this victory through our Lord Jesus Christ!*[30]

Question 7. Please provide your comments on the above quote here:

Question 8. Where are you in your spiritual life? Is your night pitch black? Do you see some rays of dawn approaching? Or are you walking in the light of day and enjoying it? Please write your thoughts here:

Scripture to Consider

"For though a righteous man falls seven times, he rises again, but the wicked are brought down by calamity" (Proverbs 24:16).

"[21] Then Peter came to him and asked, 'Lord, how often should I forgive someone who sins against me? Seven times?' [22] 'No!' Jesus replied, 'seventy times seven!'" (Matthew 18:21-22[NLT]).

Then Christian fell down at his feet as dead, crying, Woe is me, for I am undone! At the sight of which Evangelist caught him by the right hand, saying, "All manner of sin and blasphemies shall be forgiven unto men." Matthew 12:31. "Be not faithless, but believing." John 20:27. Then did Christian again a little revive, and stood up trembling, as at first, before Evangelist. "This also shall not be, any more than that. It is the glory of God that he *multiplies to pardon*, that he spares, and forgives, to more than seventy times seven times."[31]

Were you free from pornography since you did the last lesson?
    Yes   No

Were you free from masturbation since you did the last lesson?
    Yes   No

Were you free from sexual immorality since you did the last lesson?
    Yes   No

DAY 45—NO CONDEMNATION! ROMANS 8

Oh dear friends, the dark night of the soul is temporary! The intense struggle against sin does not last forever! If we are in Christ we will be victorious! Let us see this truth from Romans 8:

> "Therefore, there is now no condemnation for those who are in Christ Jesus" (Romans 8:1).

Friends, how wonderful to know that this shining sentence declaring no condemnation follows Romans 7 where the intense war with sin is pictured. What do those who battle sin and lose often dread the most? Condemnation! And here Paul declares under the inspiration of the Holy Spirit that there is no condemnation for those who are in Christ.

Questions

Question 1. Can you sense the joy in the placement of this particular verse? Write your thoughts here, and continue on in Romans, chapter 8.

> ²because through Christ Jesus the law of the Spirit of life set me free from the law of sin and death.

Talk about **"setting captives free!"** Paul is a released captive. He has been set free from the law of sin and death. Not only is he not condemned, he is not enslaved, either. Freedom has come, through the Spirit of life. The Holy Spirit came to Paul and set him free from habitual sin, and enabled him to triumph over the law of sin and death. Friend, with God life always triumphs over death. Jesus never attended anyone's funeral that he didn't raise them back to life.

Question 2. Where are you currently? Are you under "the law of sin and death" or are you a freed captive, where life and victory are triumphing? Write your answer here:

Testimony

The following testimony is from Gary:

Like many of the others I was introduced to pornography at an early age. I didn't find a magazine out in a field somewhere; I found it in my home. I can remember sneaking into my parents bedroom and looking at the pictures. My mom caught me a couple of times and I was punished, but the lure of the images overcame the fear of being punished. I was probably 10 years old the first time I masturbated. I was an avid reader and the stories more than the pictures fueled my lust. At the time neither of my parents were walking with God. My mother's parents were Christians and my fondest memories were staying at their home for the weekend and going to church with them on Sunday morning. I went forward after a Sunday school session and asked Jesus into my heart. I knew that the porn and masturbation were wrong, but I was too embarrassed to talk about it.

As I grew up, porn and masturbation came along for the ride. I tried and failed countless times to stop on my own strength with no lasting victory. I was 20 when I met my wife. She thought I was this fine Christian man, but little did she know the hidden dragon inside. I thought, like many others, that masturbation would not be a problem anymore once I was married. At first it was no problem then when she became pregnant the frequency of intimacy diminished. I found myself filling in the gaps. After being married for 10 and one half years I finally confessed to my wife and we sought counseling with our Pastor. I can't adequately describe the lightness I felt in my spirit after I brought my sin into the light for the very first time. I walked in victory for nearly 6 months and returned to snare of P.M. I was living a lie at church and at home. Then one day I looked in my old email messages and started deleting them to make room. I found one from a friend that had a shortcut to the Setting Captives Free website. I went to the website with no real hope of this being able to make a difference in my life. After the 1st day's course I knew this was what I desperately needed. Each day in the course I could see myself in the SCF lesson. I was the prostitute ready to be stoned, the prodigal son feeding the pigs, and the King's son riding the dragon and night slowly becoming like the dragon himself.

Today marks the 59th day of **Pure Freedom.** I am not the same person who started this course. I am finally walking in a Spirit-controlled life. I no longer have the nagging doubt about how long will this last. God has given me freedom! Through this course I learned where to look for true and lasting satisfaction. I want to give all honor and glory to God and God alone. God bless anyone who reads this testimony and sees himself in it.

> ³ For what the law was powerless to do in that it was weakened by the sinful nature, God did by sending his own Son in the likeness of sinful man to be a sin offering. And so he condemned sin in sinful man.

Let's understand this well. The law was powerless. It could command me to cease viewing pornography, but not enable me to do so. It was powerless to change my heart, give me new desires, or release me from the trap of the devil in pornography and masturbation. But what the law could not do, God did! And how did He do it?

Questions

Question 3. God did what the law could not do: free us from sin's power. How did God do this?

A. He gave us the law which frees us
B. He commanded us to stop
C. He sent Jesus Christ to be a sin offering

Oh, friend, the death of Jesus Christ has everything to do with our being free from pornography! Don't miss the connection here between Jesus becoming our sin offering, and us becoming free from sin. Jesus took our sin upon Himself; therefore we are neither condemned nor enslaved! "He breaks the power of canceled sin; He sets the captives free."[32]

> [4] in order that the righteous requirements of the law might be fully met in us, who do not live according to the flesh but according to the Spirit.

Again, we see that Jesus' death has done something magnificent. It not only frees us from sin's penalty and sin's power, but it fulfills the law requiring in us. You see, the law said, "Do this or die." The law requiring death for sin was fulfilled when Jesus died. He died in order that the righteous requirements of the law might be fully met in us! And now, we who are in Christ are counted as law-keepers.

Question 4. Verse 4 describes those who are in Christ as living a certain way. What way is it?

A. We are those who do not live according to the flesh, but according to the Spirit
B. We are those who have never sinned
C. We are those who keep the law perfectly

> [5] Those who live according to the flesh have their minds set on what the flesh desires; but those who live in accordance with the Spirit have their minds set on what the Spirit desires. [6] The mind of sinful man is death, but the mind controlled by the Spirit is life and peace; [7] the sinful mind is hostile to God. It does not submit to God's law, nor can it do so. [8] Those controlled by the sinful nature cannot please God.

Question 5. Please write out everything verses 5-8 says about those who live according to the flesh. I'll write the first one:

1. **They have their minds set on what the flesh desires**

2. They_____

3. They_____

4. They_____

5. They_____

Question 6. What do verses 5-8 say about those who live according to the Spirit? Write your answer here:

> [9] You, however, are controlled not by the flesh but by the Spirit, if the Spirit of God lives in you. And if anyone does not have the Spirit of Christ, he does not belong to Christ.

The above verse makes it clear that if God's Spirit is living in us He will control us. While I was doing pornography my flesh controlled me. That is what characterized me. But God's Spirit is now living in me and controlling me.

Question 7. Overall, would you say that you are controlled by the Spirit of God or by your flesh?

> [10] But if Christ is in you, your body is dead because of sin, yet your spirit is alive because of righteousness. [11] And if the Spirit of him who raised Jesus from the dead is living in you, he who raised Christ from the dead will also give life to your mortal bodies through his Spirit, who lives in you.

According to verse 10 above, Christians are characterized by "dead flesh." Their bodies are dead because of sin. In other words, they are not characterized by giving in to the flesh and sinning, but by being controlled by the Spirit of God.

Now, see how interesting it is that Paul connects our "dead flesh" with our assurance of eternal life. Our bodies are dead because of sin, but will live forever through the Spirit of Christ who lives in us. Those who know that their flesh is crucified also know that they will live forever with Christ.

> [12] Therefore, brothers, we have an obligation—but it is not to the flesh, to live according to it. [13] For if you live according to the flesh, you will die; but if by the Spirit you put to death the misdeeds of the body, you will live, [14] because those who are led by the Spirit of God are sons of God.

This chapter started out with "no condemnation" (verse 1) and ends with "no separation" (verses 35-39), but right in the middle we are told that we have "no obligation" to live according to the flesh. Catch this truth, friend. When our flesh cries out to be satisfied, we have no obligation to gratify it.

Question 8. If we do live to gratify our flesh, according to verse 13, what will happen?

Question 9. What are we to do with the misdeeds of the body?

A. Be gracious with the sins of the body, and don't be too harsh
B. Gratify these misdeeds
C. Put them to death

Paul started off this discourse by sharing his freedom from sin with us, and here he instructs us to put to death the misdeeds of the body. Freedom from habitual sin includes the crucifying of our flesh. Paul said "I die daily" and he was referring to putting to death his flesh daily. This shows that our flesh is to be crucified, not gratified.

Questions

Question 10. Is God giving you grace to crucify your flesh? Or are you gratifying it?

Friend, let me share with you that there is much discomfort and pain involved in crucifying our flesh. For us, denying ourselves masturbation when we are burning with desire is most uncomfortable and even painful. Read how one course member describes this pain:

> **Course Member Mike writes:** "Wow, I did not know that there would be so much pain associated with denying myself. I have literally ached with pain from the denial. And yet God is granting me much grace to endure, and this is my 45thd day free from masturbation. I believe that I am now free from the law of sin, and that I am in a constant habit pattern of denying and crucifying my flesh. This also makes love making with my wife so much more enjoyable. It's good to know that I am no longer satisfying myself by sinful means, but rather I am being satisfied in Christ and in my wife. Oh, this is so much better. The pain is worth the gain!"

Please know that the pain is indeed worth the gain. Our bodies adjust, our habits change, and soon we aren't even thinking of masturbation any longer. And please don't believe the false notion that we MUST masturbate in order to relieve tension, or worse yet to prevent some physical problem from occurring. God did not make our bodies, and then require us to sin in order to stay healthy.

Question 11. Please summarize today's teaching as best as you can:

Scripture to Consider

"But now he has reconciled you by Christ's physical body through death to present you holy in his sight, without blemish and free from accusation—if you continue in your faith, established and firm, not moved from the hope held out in the gospel. This is the gospel that you heard and that has been proclaimed to every creature under heaven, and of which I, Paul, have become a servant" (Colossians 1:22-23).

"And can it be that I should gain an interest in the Savior's blood? Died He for me, who caused His pain? For me, who Him to death pursued? He left His Father's throne above, so free, so infinite His grace! Emptied Himself of all but love, and bled for Adam's helpless race. No condemnation now I dread; I am my Lord's and He is mine: Alive in Him, my living Head, and clothed in righteousness divine."

Refrain: Amazing love! How can it be that Thou, my God, shouldst die for me?"[33]

"'But I will bring the people of Israel back to their own pasture. They will eat on Mount Carmel and in Bashan. They will eat and be full on the hills of Ephraim and Gilead.' [20] The Lord says, 'At that time people will try to find Israel's guilt, but there will be no guilt. People will try to find Judah's sins, but no sins will be found, because I will leave a few people alive from Israel and Judah, and I will forgive their sins'" (Jeremiah 59:19-20[NCV]).

Were you free from pornography since you did the last lesson?
    Yes   No

Were you free from masturbation since you did the last lesson?
    Yes   No

Were you free from sexual immorality since you did the last lesson?
    Yes   No

DAY 46—PORNOGRAPHY CAN'T HOLD WATER

Today we are going to examine two things:

1. What God is like
2. What pornography is like

Please read the following scripture in preparation for today's study. You may want to memorize this verse, as there will be several questions on it today.

> "My people have committed two sins: they have forsaken me, the spring of living water, and have dug their own cisterns, broken cisterns that cannot hold water" (Jeremiah 2:13).

Questions

Question 1. In the verse, what does God describe Himself as?

   A. An angry Judge
   B. The spring of living water

Question 2. What do you believe that living water can provide?

   A. Life
   B. Refreshment
   C. Satisfaction
   D. Joy
   E. Health
   F. All of the above

Note: God describes himself as the spring of living water. He alone is the source of life, refreshment, joy, and nourishment for us. He is ever fresh and new, like a spring, and to drink of God is to receive life and be satisfied!

Please read and comment on the following Scriptures:

> "There is a river whose streams make glad the city of God, the holy place where the Most High dwells" (Psalm 46:4).

Question 3. Write your thoughts on Psalm 46:4 here:

> "Then the angel showed me the river of the water of life, as clear as crystal, flowing from the throne of God and of the Lamb down the middle of the great street of the city. On each side of the river stood the tree of life, bearing twelve crops of fruit, yielding its fruit every month. And the leaves of the tree are for the healing of the nations. No longer will there be any curse" (Revelation 22:1-3).

Question 4. Write your thoughts on Revelation 22:1-3 here:

Testimony

The following testimony is from Andy:

I was born in poverty and was determined to make something of myself. I began studying the Stock Market at a young age and became quite knowledgeable about trading and investing. In my early twenties I learned how to "Day Trade" and became hooked as I started doing very well at it.

Unfortunately, the market started to take a nosedive after I had many stocks bought on margin, and after 4 years of extremely successful trading activity I found my net worth dwindling away to nothing. Surely riches have wings, and they take off and fly away.

I continued trading, but my life became seriously stressful, and at night when I would go home I began viewing pornography as a stress releaser. Some stress releaser; I soon discovered that I could not quit, and the intensity of my passions were becoming too much for me.

My wife caught me one night, and that started a search for help. I went in to see 2 psychiatrists, and went to SA for several months. But neither of these helped, and my bondage to this sin became worse. I finally found **Pure Freedom** on the Internet, and God used it to break the power of sin. Soon after we started going through the course we were counseled to find a local church, which we did. I gave my life to Jesus Christ, and our pastor now is involved with accountability with me, and I am growing much in Christ.

By the way, stocks and trading are still eating my lunch. But pornography is nowhere in sight, and I would rather have it that way than vice versa.

Questions

"My people have committed two sins: They have forsaken me, the spring of living water, and have dug their own cisterns, broken cisterns that cannot hold water" (Jeremiah 2:13).

Question 5. Write your thoughts on Jeremiah 2:13 here:

Course Member Drew writes: "The first sin we have committed is that we have rejected God and the satisfying water that He provides. We have laid down our beautiful, holy cisterns, and picked up dirty, broken cisterns that cannot hold water, therefore, leaving us thirsty. The only way to find satisfaction again is to repent, to go back to our true cisterns and start drinking of the living water again."

Course Member Timothy writes: "This verse brings to mind Dante's Inferno. In his description of Hell, the inhabitants of one particular circle are sentenced to eternally fill and re-fill leaky jars. When I find myself constantly refilling my leaky jar of pornography it's a reminder that I'm not looking to the Lord to fulfill my needs."

Question 6. According to Jeremiah 2:13 above, when people forsake God, they turn to something else. According to the above verse, what do they turn to?
A. Something better
B. Something more enjoyable
C. Something broken, which won't hold water, and can't satisfy

Question 7. On Day 1 of this course we learned two important truths:
1. Pornography will not ultimately satisfy
2. Only Jesus can satisfy.

How does Jeremiah 2:13 teach these two truths? Please write your answer here:

Course Member Andy writes: "We are trying to find satisfaction in pornography with these broken cisterns. We try again and again, but it continues to leave us thirsty because we are using broken cisterns. We need to return to our Spring and drink of the water that Jesus provides us with. That is the only way we can truly be satisfied."

Question 8. Please read this quote from the famous preacher, **Charles Spurgeon,** and record your comments about it:

"Men are in a restless pursuit after satisfaction in earthly things. They will exhaust themselves in the deceitful delights of sin, and, finding them all to be vanity and emptiness, they will become very perplexed and disappointed. But they will still continue their fruitless search.

Though wearied, they still stagger forward under the influence of spiritual madness, and though there is no result to be reached except that of everlasting disappointment, yet they press forward. They have no forethought for their eternal state; the present hour absorbs them. They turn to another and another of earth's broken cisterns, hoping to find water where not a drop was ever discovered yet."[34]

Record your thoughts here:

Course Member Paul writes: "Madness! What a perfect description of my relentless pursuit of the next sexual image that will be the one that will satisfy. As the hours slip away and my eyes grow heavy with sleep I cannot stop. Yet, moments after I have "satisfied" myself it starts again. What madness indeed!"

Question 9. From Jeremiah 2:13, please complete these sentences:

God is like..._____

Pornography is like..._____

Questions

Question 10. How does Ephesians 4:19 apply to what we are studying? "Having lost all sensitivity, they have given themselves over to sensuality so as to indulge in every kind of impurity, with a continual lust for more." Write your answer here:

Question 11. Please comment on the following quote:

"For what is the sum and substance of these simple words? It is this: Christ is that Fountain of living water, which God has graciously provided for thirsting souls. From Him, as out of the rock smitten by Moses, there flows an abundant stream for all who travel through the wilderness of this world. In Him, as our Redeemer and Substitute, crucified for our sins and raised again for our justification, there is an endless supply of all that men can need: pardon, absolution, mercy, grace, peace, rest, relief, comfort and hope" J. C. Ryle.[35]

Write your comment here:

and fill, and at the best it will hold but a little water, and that dead and flat, and soon corrupting and becoming nauseous. No, it is a broken cistern, which cracks and cleaves in hot weather, so that the water is lost when we have most need of it. Let us therefore with purpose of heart cleave to the Lord only, for where else shall we go? He has the words of eternal life."[36]

Question 12. How are you doing today? Have you gained any insights, or been reminded of any truths by today's teaching?

Scripture to Consider

"For with You is the fountain of life..." (Psalm 36:9).

"A despairing man should have the devotion of his friends, even though he forsakes the fear of the Almighty. But my brothers are as undependable as intermittent streams, as the streams that overflow when darkened by thawing ice and swollen with melting snow, but that cease to flow in the dry season, and in the heat vanish from their channels. Caravans turn aside from their routes; they go up into the wasteland and perish. The caravans of Tema look for water, the traveling merchants of Sheba look in hope. They are distressed, because they had been confident; they arrive there, only to be disappointed. Now you too have proved to be of no help; you see something dreadful and are afraid" (Job 6:14-21).

"As a deer thirsts for streams of water, so I thirst for you, God. I thirst for the living God. When can I go to meet with him?" (Psalm 42:1-2[NCV]).

Sometimes it is difficult reading the Puritan writers because of their style. But we can hardly find writing that matches theirs for practical godliness. This is **Matthew Henry's** commentary on Jeremiah 2:13. I believe you will profit from reading this:

"There is in Him an all-sufficiency of grace and strength; all our springs are in Him and our streams from him; to forsake Him is, in effect, to deny this. He has been to us a bountiful benefactor, a fountain of living waters, overflowing, ever flowing, in the gifts of his favor; to forsake Him is to refuse to acknowledge His kindness and to withhold that tribute of love and praise which His kindness calls for.

"Those who forsake Him cheat themselves, they forsook their own mercies, but it was for lying vanities. They took a great deal of pains to hew themselves out cisterns, to dig pits or pools in the earth or rock which they would carry water to, or which should receive the rain; but they proved broken cisterns, false at the bottom, so that they could hold no water. When they came to quench their thirst there they found nothing but mud and mire, and the filthy sediments of a standing lake. Such idols were to their worshipers, and such a change did those experience who turned from God to them.

"If we make an idol of any creature-wealth, or pleasure, or honor, if we place our happiness in it, and promise ourselves the comfort and satisfaction in it which are to be had in God only, if we make it our joy and love, our hope and confidence, we shall find it a cistern, which we take a great deal of pains to hew out

Were you free from pornography since you did the last lesson?
    Yes   No

Were you free from masturbation since you did the last lesson?
    Yes   No

Were you free from sexual immorality since you did the last lesson?
    Yes   No

DAY 47—BROKENNESS: KEY TO VICTORY

Today's lesson comes out of my own experience (and the experience of others) of discovering what it takes to truly be done with habitual sin. Today we will study a truth that absolutely must be experienced in the soul if there is to be real, lasting victory over pornography. The truth is that God must break us! "Well, that is not very encouraging or hope-inspiring," you say. Actually it is. Read below what several authors have said on this subject:

"The kingdom of God is a kingdom of Paradox, where through the ugly defeat of a cross, a holy God is utterly glorified. Victory comes through defeat; healing through brokenness; finding self through losing self."
Charles Colson

"God will never plant the seed of His life upon the soil of a hard, unbroken spirit. He will only plant that seed where the conviction of His spirit has brought brokenness, where the soil has been watered with the tears of repentance as well as the tears of joy." Alan Redpath

"Deliverance can come to us only by the defeat of our old life. Safety and peace come only after we have been forced to our knees. God rescues us by breaking us, by shattering our strength and wiping out our resistance."
A. W. Tozer

"True prayer is born out of brokenness." Francis J. Roberts

So why are we devoting a whole day's study to this subject of brokenness? Because as the authors state above, brokenness brings healing, life, revival, rescue, and true prayer. So becoming broken before the Lord is indispensable.

Please read the following passage and answer the questions:

Psalm 51: Have mercy on me, O God, according to your unfailing love; according to your great compassion blot out my transgressions. Wash away all my iniquity and cleanse me from my sin. For I know my transgressions, and my sin is always before me. Against you, you only, have I sinned and done what is evil in your sight, so that you are proved right when you speak and justified when you judge. Surely I was sinful at birth, sinful from the time my mother conceived me. Surely you desire truth in the inner parts; you teach me wisdom in the inmost place. Cleanse me with hyssop, and I will be clean; wash me, and I will be whiter than snow. Let me hear joy and gladness; let the bones you have crushed rejoice. Hide your face from my sins and blot out all my iniquity. Create in me a pure heart, O God, and renew a steadfast spirit within me. Do not cast me from your presence or take your Holy Spirit from me. Restore to me the joy of your salvation and grant me a willing spirit, to sustain me. Then I will teach transgressors your ways, and sinners will turn back to you. Save me from bloodguilt, O God, the God who saves me, and my tongue will sing of your righteousness. O Lord, open my lips, and my mouth will declare your praise. You do not delight in sacrifice, or I would bring it; you do not take pleasure in burnt offerings. The sacrifices of God are a broken spirit; a broken and contrite heart, O God, you will not despise.

Note: This is a prayer for forgiveness and cleansing, made by David. The prophet Nathan had confronted him about his sin with Bathsheba and he was now brokenhearted over it.

(Quotes taken from Edith Draper, *Draper's Book of Quotations for the Christian World*—Wheaton: Tyndale House publishers, Inc. 1992)

Questions

Question 1. Please write the words David uses that ask God to do something. The first ones are "cleanse me," and "wash me." What are the others? Write them here:

Question 2. What are the sacrifices that God accepts?
A. Lambs, cattle and oxen
B. Ten percent tithe, and giving to the building fund
C. A depressed person with no hope
D. A broken spirit; a broken and contrite heart

Note: David is saying that God receives brokenness as the only acceptable sacrifice for sins committed. The previous verse states that God does not take pleasure in burnt offerings. The reason for this is obvious: someone could give burnt offerings (or tithes, or church-work, etc...) without the heart being involved.

Question 3. Hebrews 3:13 states, "But encourage one another daily, as long as it is called today, so that none of you may be hardened by sin's deceitfulness." What does sin do to our hearts?
A. Sin hardens and deceives us
B. Sin softens us, and makes us open to the needs of others

Note: Those of us who have spent many years in bondage to pornography have become hardened by sin's deceitfulness. Our hearts turned cold, brittle, unfeeling and desensitized by this sin in which we have been involved. Since God disciplines those he loves, he will break our hard hearts, cold and unyielding spirits, and harsh attitudes. God breaks us so that He can remake us (Jeremiah 18.) If you are experiencing genuine brokenness over your sin before God, know that God is working. If you are not broken before the Lord, will you pray that God would do this miraculous work in your heart lest you die in a hardhearted condition?

Question 4. Honestly assess the condition of your heart and life right now. Where are you in the process of offering the acceptable sacrifice of brokenness before the Lord? Ask the Lord to reveal your heart's condition to you right now. Write here:

Questions

Today we are going to read some very instructive writings on this important subject: one from Matthew Henry, several from Charles Spurgeon and one from John Bradford. Several course member student comments are included. Please give your thoughts on each of these writings.

Matthew Henry writes about the Passover Lamb: **"It was to be eaten with bitter herbs in remembrance of the bitterness of their bondage in Egypt. We must feed upon Christ with sorrow and brokenness of heart, in remembrance of sin; this will give an admirable relish to the lamb. Christ will be sweet to us if sin be bitter."**[37]

Question 5. Your comments about Matthew Henry's quote above:

Charles Spurgeon hits the nail on the head as usual. Read this carefully: **"True repentance has a distinct and constant reference to the Lord Jesus Christ. If you are so lamenting your sin as to forget the Savior, you have a need to begin all this work over again. Whenever we repent of sin, we must have one eye upon sin and another upon the cross; or, better still, let us have both eyes upon Christ, seeing our sin punished in him, and by no means let us look at sin except as we look at Jesus. A man may hate sin just as a murderer hates the gallows but this does not prove repentance. If I hate sin because of the punishment, I have not repented of sin; I merely regret that God is just.**

"But if I can see sin as an offense against Jesus Christ, and loathe myself because I have wounded him, then I have a true brokenness of heart. If I see the Savior and believe that those thorns upon his head were put there by my sinful words; if I believe that those wounds in his heart were made by my heart-sins; if I believe that those wounds in his feet were made by my wandering steps, and that the wounds in his hands were made by my sinful deeds, then I repent after a right fashion. Only under the cross can you repent. Repentance elsewhere is remorse, which clings to the sin and only dreads the punishment. Let us then seek, under God, to have a hatred of sin caused by a sight of Christ's love."[38]

Testimony

The following testimony is from Canon:

I was raised in a fairly moral and religious home. That is, we were average citizens. My parents did not really condone drunkenness, but didn't tell us never to do it either. The only rule was if you do drink don't drive.

You could have girls sleep over, but don't be overly obvious about it. Basically, the rules were lax and we only had to go to church on Christmas and Easter. Church was a chore and a duty.

I lived in this state for nearly 20 years. For some odd reason, while going for the God and Country merit badge in boy scouts, I learned about praying to God and decided to start doing it. I would pray every night and wanted to do what was right and good. You know, help people and be a hero. I didn't know that serving God WAS the highest good. I really didn't know anything and my life didn't change much. My knowledge of Scripture was so low, that I really didn't think it was TOO bad to go to strip clubs, watch porn movies, or put the make on girls. But inside, which I told no one about, I actually believed that sex before marriage was wrong.

I joined the Air Force, went to the Academy, and "fell" into a Bible Study that, surprisingly, actually taught the Bible. I can see God's sovereign hand in it all. As I started hearing the Word of God preached by those who actually believed it and lived it, I began to be convicted of my sinful life. I dedicated my life to the Lord and began to live purposefully for Him. That was in the spring of 1996 (sophomore year). Since that time, I stopped getting drunk, going to bars, chasing women, and even stopped swearing to a large degree (though I confess that things do slip out - to my shame.) I started to plan my life in view of what I learned in the Bible and wanted to live for God wherever His will put me.

The one sin that would not leave was lust. I had already built in my mind a sizeable library of porn and masturbated frequently. These two parts of my life I kept separate. I had a Christian girlfriend by my senior year and tried harder than ever to kick the porn habit but it got worse. By the time we broke-up in April of 1998 (thank God he protected her from me,) I had started to call phone sex lines. I got porn movies anywhere I could.

Question 6: Please comment on Spurgeon's quote:

Charles Spurgeon tells us what "normal" should be: **"When I sat on this platform on Monday night, and marked your sobs, in tears, and heard the suppressed sighs and groans of the great multitude then assembled, I could not but say, 'Behold!' And yet it ought not to be a wonder, it ought not to be a strange thing for God's people to be in earnest, or for sinners to feel brokenness of heart"**[39]

Question 7. Please write your comments on Spurgeon's quote above:

Still, I went to the Bible studies every Fri and Sat night, which kept me out of trouble. For 2 1/2 years this went on. I studied the Bible more and more (I was learning so much even on my own) and still the porn kept getting worse.

After graduation, I was sent to Delaware; but no matter where I was stationed in the Air Force, my lust followed me. I started to get into sex chat rooms where you could see the girl and call her. It was like visiting a prostitute. Soon, that would start to lose its appeal as it became old-hat. During this time I read many books and listened to tapes on how to break free, but nothing worked.

One night after a major session of porn over the Internet and in despair looking for something, ANYTHING, to help me I saw Porn Struggler's Help as I searched for "PORN" over some search engine. I found Setting Captives Free and joined the group. That was in Dec of 2000.

Since that time, I fell many times up until Jan 8. I was on about day 12 of the **Pure Freedom** course when all the teaching I had been getting finally clicked. I didn't have to anymore — I could choose purity. I had to radically amputate my access to this filth (no TV or unfiltered internet) to help me choose purity. I learned about accountability a long time ago and had a partner that I called every so often, but not one that would really ask me the hard questions. I now have that many times over.

By the grace of God, He has washed me and set me free from this sin. I am still tempted mightily and do not feel that I am ready to shepherd a wife yet. I don't even date. I also do not feel that I am ready to be a mentor. I think that it will take some time of real habitual holiness and purity to really be sure that I have the character necessary to help others. I want to be the man of high moral character and godly self-discipline that my future wife is praying for. That is not yet the case. I have lived in purity for over two months now. That is wonderful, but God is still working in my life. God's grace is real and powerful. He can pull down any stronghold, but sometimes it takes a little more time to complete the work than in others.

I look forward to completing the mentor course and learning to help others through this same journey.

Question 8. Please write your comments on the above quote here:

"Psalm 51 is the photograph of a contrite spirit. Oh, let us seek after the like brokenness of heart, for however excellent our words may be, yet if the heart is not conscious of the blackness and Hell-deservingness of sin, we cannot expect to find mercy with the Judge of all the earth. If the Lord will break your heart, consent to have it broken; asking that he may sanctify that brokenness of spirit to bring you in earnest to a savior, that you may yet be numbered with the righteous ones." Charles Spurgeon[41]

Question 9. Please provide your comments here:

Quoting **John Bradford** Spurgeon writes: **"John Bradford said, that when he was in prayer, he never liked to rise from his knees till he began to feel something of brokenness of heart: 'Get up to your chamber, then, poor sinner, if you would have a broken and contrite spirit, and come not out until you have it. Remember, you will never feel so broken in heart as when you can see Jesus bearing all your sins; faith and repentance are born together, and aid the health of each other."**

> Law and terrors do but harden,
> All the while they work alone;
> But a sense of blood-bought pardon,
> Will dissolve a heart of stone.

Spurgeon continues: **"Go as you are to Christ, and ask him to give that tenderness of heart which shall be to you the indication that pardon has come; for pardon cannot and will not come unattended by a melting of soul and a hatred of sin. Wrestle with the Lord! Say, I will not let you go except you bless me. Get a fast hold upon the savior by a vigorous faith in his great atonement. Oh! May his spirit enable you to do this! Say in your soul, here I will abide, at the horns of the altar; if I perish I will perish at the foot of the cross. From my hope in Jesus I will not depart; but I will look up and still say, savior, your heart was broken for me, break my heart! You were wounded; wound me! Your blood was freely poured forth, for me; Lord, let me pour forth my tears that I should have nailed you to the tree. Oh Lord, dissolve my soul; melt it in tenderness, and you will be forever praised for making your enemy your friend.**

"May God bless you, and make you repent, if you have not repented; and if you have, may he enable you to continue in it all your days, for Jesus Christ sake. Amen."[40]

Scripture to Consider:

"For this is what the high and lofty One says— he who lives forever, whose name is holy: 'I live in a high and holy place, but also with him who is contrite and lowly in spirit, to revive the spirit of the lowly and to revive the heart of the contrite'" (Isaiah 57:15).

Were you free from pornography since you did the last lesson?   Yes   No

Were you free from masturbation since you did the last lesson?   Yes   No

Were you free from sexual immorality since you did the last lesson? Yes   No

DAY 48—SUCH WERE SOME OF YOU

One of the greatest benefits of being a Christian is that God makes us different people than we used to be. As God rescues us from impurity and makes us slaves of righteousness, we become totally different people. This truth is so good to know, because I used to be a pornographer and an adulterer; but I am no more. Some of you may have had an extreme addiction to pornography, you may have been sleeping with prostitutes, or have become a homosexual, or a pedophile; you may have had extramarital affairs or have had sex so often that you have come down with an incurable disease. The truth of Scripture is, that no matter what you were, that is not what you are, if you are in Christ.

This truth is important because who we see ourselves to be is how we act. I am no longer a pornographer so I do not act like one. I am not addicted to anything impure, so I do not stare at women walking toward me in the airport, nor do I even glance a second time at magazines with half-naked women on them. I am not who I used to be, nor do I act as I used to act. Do you see?

Today we will see this truth in Scripture, and then we will read more testimonies of how the grace of God has changed friends of ours into totally new persons.

Please read the following passage and answer the questions:

> "⁹Do you not know that the wicked will not inherit the kingdom of God? Do not be deceived: Neither the sexually immoral nor idolaters nor adulterers nor male prostitutes nor homosexual offenders ¹⁰ nor thieves nor the greedy nor drunkards nor slanderers nor swindlers will inherit the kingdom of God. ¹¹And that is what some of you were. But you were washed, you were sanctified, you were justified in the name of the Lord Jesus Christ and by the Spirit of our God" (1 Corinthians 6:9-11).

Questions

Question 1. What kind of people made up the church at Corinth during Paul's day?
- A. Homosexuals
- B. Wicked
- C. Sexually Immoral
- D. Adulterers
- E. Male Prostitutes
- F. Thieves
- G. Drunkards
- H. All of the above

Question 2. In verses 9-10 Paul mentions the kinds of people who will not inherit the kingdom of God. Why do you think he warns against being deceived about this (verse 9)? Write your thoughts here:

Course Member Scott writes: "I think it is part of human nature to really hope that everyone can get to heaven. It's easy to fool ourselves into thinking that God will 'let you in' no matter what you say or do or believe. Paul is making it clear here that people whose lives are controlled by sin and not by God are not going to make it into God's kingdom."

Question 3. Were the people Paul was writing to still practicing these sins? Before you answer, carefully review verse 11.
- A. No, they were no longer involved in these habitual sins, but were washed, and changed
- B. Yes, they were still living in these sins.

Question 4. What verses tell us these people were no longer the same?

Testimony

This testimony is from Bobby:

I am reminded of the times I came so close to watching something impure on TV, I can honestly only claim grace and circumstance as the reasons I did not fall. I doubt those things would hold the same draw now, but a while back they did.

I'm continuing to enjoy my freedom, and God is constantly drawing people to me, not just for problems with pornography, but many believers who seem to be struggling. It's as though they can smell that I have something, and they too want it. My heart has become passionate to rescue believers who are going through this lack of life. I find myself angry that the devil has robbed and blinded so many people. Having had my eyes opened again I see the possibility for others all around me. Truly I am in a war here, but truly I am filled with such joy to be in it.

Question 5. According to the passage, what changed these people? How were they changed?

"For you died, and your life is now hidden with Christ in God. When Christ, who is your life, appears, then you also will appear with him in glory" (Colossians 3:3,4).

Write your answers here:

The New Testament church has inspired both exciting and disastrous experiments down through history. Hoping to create the perfect New Testament community, some have tried to design groups where all the gifts are expressed, worship is spontaneous and fellowship is deep. But they forget the common element of all New Testament churches — problems!

In chapters one through four of 1st Corinthians, Paul dealt with divisions in the church. Now he focuses on serious moral problems in Corinth. Incest and drunkenness (chapter 5) during communion are hardly what we hope to find in church. But we must remember that growing churches are not always filled with well-scrubbed Christians, but rather with a motley collection of sinners being saved.

Paul warns against being deceived because we're so easily deceived about this. After all, salvation is by grace, not by works, and Jesus came to save sinners. What does it matter (we think) if sinners keep on sinning? But such thinking overlooks the fact that a new life in Christ results in a new lifestyle (verse 11). Genuine salvation is to actually be saved from ongoing, habitual sin.

The sins listed referred to a continuous lifestyle or practice and not to a onetime involvement. Paul's list is similar to the works of the flesh in Galatians 5:19-21 (See also Ephesians 5:5.) In both cases a persisting in fleshly living is implied.

Likewise, Paul's mention of both male prostitutes and homosexual offenders does not mean that a person with homosexual tendencies, who is living chastely, is excluded from the kingdom. The two words Paul uses here, malakoi (men or boys who allow themselves to be misused homosexually) and arsenokoitai (a male homosexual, pederast, sodomite) both have an active meaning.

Question 6. The teaching today is that Christians are no longer who they used to be. Please state how the following passages confirm this truth:

"I have been crucified with Christ and I no longer live, but Christ lives in me. The life I live in the body, I live by faith in the Son of God, who loved me and gave himself for me" (Galatians 2:20).

Write your answer here:

Friend, let me show you how this teaching is applied practically. We do what is according to our nature. If we are sinners who are trying to be good we will inevitably fall. But if we are saints, who occasionally sin, then our nature is such that we hate sin, and our habitual pattern of life will be to walk in righteousness. See it?

Now let me share with you some writings that will confirm this truth, and have you comment on them:

"The previous character of those who seem to have been converted was various. I could name many who have been turned from the paths of open sin and profligacy, and have found pardon and purity in the blood of the Lamb, and by the Sprit of our God; so that we can say to them, as Paul said to the Corinthians, 'Such were some of you; but you were washed, but you are sanctified, but you are justified.' I often think, when conversing with some of these, that the change they have undergone might be enough to convince an atheist that there is a God, or an infidel that there is a Savior" *Memoirs of McCheyne*[42]

Question 7. Please write your comments here:

Questions

"He puts them in mind what a change the gospel and grace of God had made in them: Such were some of you (verse 11), such notorious sinners as he had been reckoning up. The Greek word is *tauta*—such things were some of you, very monsters rather than men. Note, some that are eminently good after their conversion have been as remarkably wicked before. How glorious a change does grace make! It changes the vilest of men into saints and children of God. Such were some of you, but you are not what you were. You are washed, you are sanctified; you are justified in the name of Christ and by the Spirit of our God.

"Note, the wickedness of men before conversion is no bar to their regeneration and reconciliation to God. The blood of Christ, and the washing of regeneration, can purge away all guilt and defilement. Note, none are cleansed from the guilt of sin, and reconciled to God through Christ, but those who are also sanctified by His Spirit. All who are made righteous in the sight of God are made holy by the grace of God" *Matthew Henry Commentary* [43]

Question 8. Please comment on the above quote by Matthew Henry here:

Scripture to Consider

"For you have heard of my previous way of life in Judaism, how intensely I persecuted the church of God and tried to destroy it. I was advancing in Judaism beyond many Jews of my own age and was extremely zealous for the traditions of my fathers. But when God, who set me apart from birth and called me by his grace, was pleased to reveal his Son in me so that I might preach him among the Gentiles, I did not consult any man, nor did I go up to Jerusalem to see those who were apostles before I was, but I went immediately into Arabia and later returned to Damascus. Then after three years, I went up to Jerusalem to get acquainted with Peter and stayed with him fifteen days. I saw none of the other apostles—only James, the Lord's brother. I assure you before God that what I am writing you is no lie. Later I went to Syria and Cilicia. I was personally unknown to the churches of Judea that are in Christ. They only heard the report: 'The man who formerly persecuted us is now preaching the faith he once tried to destroy.' And they praised God because of me" (Galatians 1:13-24).

Were you free from pornography since you did the last lesson?
    Yes   No

Were you free from masturbation since you did the last lesson?
    Yes   No

Were you free from sexual immorality since you did the last lesson?
    Yes   No

Course Member Brian writes: "I was reading today's lesson when I had an 'aha.' I never thought about Scripture from Paul's letter to the Corinthians quite the way you put it. I am no longer to think of myself as an ex-alcoholic, ex-smoker, or an ex-pornography addict. Those sins are behind and I need to go forth as a new man, a Christian. I believe the statement, 'You are what you think you are or if you think you can, or you think you can't, you are right' is relevant here. I can now see the freedom Jesus gave us when He paid the price for our sin. I have nothing against 12-Step programs but some seem to have the mindset that they will be addicts forever. If I am indeed free because of Jesus then I am no longer a recovering addict, I am free indeed. God bless you."

Course Member Roy writes: "I thank God for your lesson today. Satan has been planting the old thoughts back into my mind in the past few days. 'Don't you want the old stuff you use to love,' he tauntingly asks? After reading this morning's lesson, a new strength has welled up inside of me—a consolation that I'm not what I used to be! Christ has washed me clean and has sanctified me and I don't have to buckle under to the strongholds that use to bind me. It has now been 48 days of being free from pornography and masturbation. That blows me away and lifts my soul."

Friend, if we are in Christ we are not who or what we were. The story is told of Augustine who passed a familiar prostitute without turning a second glance at her. She turned and said, "Augustine, it is I." To which he replied, "Yes, but it is not I." He knew the truth that he was not who he used to be. Do you? One of our course members always signs his posts to the discussion group, "Not I, Not Ever!"

DAY 49—WALKING IN THE SPIRIT

"So I say, live by the Spirit, and you will not gratify the desires of the flesh" (Galatians 5:16).

Scripture gives us a way to live that is honoring to the Lord. That way involves a continual drinking of the Living Water, continuous and unbroken fellowship with Christ, and a refusal to gratify the desires of the flesh. This type of a life is extremely rewarding, as Scripture says, *"Happy is he who's God is the Lord"* (Psalm 144:15).

Most of us would acknowledge this truth, and yet we find that within us there are competing desires and inner conflict. *"For the flesh desires what is contrary to the Spirit, and the Spirit what is contrary to the flesh. They are in conflict with each other, so that you do not do what you want"* (Galatians 5:17).

So, are we to live the rest of our lives with this inner struggle going on all the time? Should we just give up and say that we will always have these intense temptations, these fiery darts from the enemy, and at times we will have victory over them and at other times we will give in to them? Many people do just that. They are tired of fighting, tired of resolving to stop only to fall again, tired of the vicious cycle. But friend, this does not have to continue. Scripture makes a declarative statement: *"So I say, live by the Spirit and you will not gratify the desires of the sinful nature."* We may still have the desires, but we are enabled to live above them as we live by the Spirit.

So, what does it mean to live by the Spirit? Please read this quote from **Matthew Henry** and be ready to answer the questions:

"Note, the best antidote against the poison of sin is to walk in the Spirit, to be much conversing with spiritual things, to mind the things of the soul, which is the spiritual part of man, more than those of the body, which is his carnal part, to commit ourselves to the guidance of the word, wherein the Holy Spirit makes known the will of God concerning us, and in the way of our duty to act in a dependence on his aids and influences. And, as this would be the best means of preserving them from fulfilling the lusts of the flesh, so it would be a good evidence that they were Christians indeed; for, says the apostle 'if you would be led by the Spirit, you are not under law.' As if he had said, **'You must expect a struggle between flesh and spirit as long as you are in the world, that the flesh will be lusting against the spirit as well as the spirit against the flesh; but if, in the prevailing bent and tenor of your lives, you be led by the Spirit, if you act under the guidance and government of the Holy Spirit and of that spiritual nature and disposition he has wrought in you, if you make the word of God your rule and the grace of God your principle, it will hence appear that you are not under the law, not under the condemning…'"** (Comments on Galatians 5:16-18).[44]

Questions

Question 1. Please write down everything you can find from the quote, that would define what living by the Spirit means:

Question 2. Obviously, we have come to a crucial portion of Scripture for overcoming slavery to pornography when we read, "So I say, live by the Spirit, and you will not gratify the desires of the flesh." Please explain, in your own words, what you think it means to "live by the Spirit." Write your answer here:

Please read the passage we are studying in context, and answer the questions below:

"16 So I say, live by the Spirit, and you will not gratify the desires of the flesh. 17 For the flesh desires what is contrary to the Spirit, and the Spirit what is contrary to the flesh. They are in conflict with each other, so that you do not do what you want. 18 But if you are led by the Spirit, you are not under law. 19 The acts of the flesh are obvious: sexual immorality, impurity and debauchery; 20 idolatry and witchcraft; hatred, discord, jealousy, fits of rage, selfish ambition, dissensions, factions 21and envy; drunkenness, orgies, and the like. I warn you, as I did before, that those who live like this will not inherit the kingdom of God. 22 But the fruit of the Spirit is love, joy, peace, patience, kindness, goodness, faithfulness, 23 gentleness and self-control. Against such things

Questions

there is no law. ²⁴ Those who belong to Christ Jesus have crucified the sinful nature with its passions and desires. ²⁵ Since we live by the Spirit, let us keep in step with the Spirit. ²⁶ Let us not become conceited, provoking and envying each other" (Galatians 5:16-26).

Question 3. Please list the acts of the flesh as listed in verse 19:

The first act listed here is "sexual immorality" and the second is "impurity." These two get top billing as to the acts of the flesh, and if our lives are characterized by these acts we are not living by the Spirit.

Note: There is a real possibility of being deceived when involved in acts like this. So Paul warns in verse 21 "I warn you, as I did before, that those who live like this will not inherit the kingdom of God." Oh how we need to heed the warning. Friends, please understand Paul's words, and don't try to explain them away. He is issuing a warning to those who live in the acts of the flesh, that they will not inherit the kingdom of God. In other words, hell is the destination of all who live by these acts, regardless of how much knowledge they have, how articulate the are, or what position they have in the church. This is serious. Do not be deceived.

Question 4. According to verse 24 above, what evidence must be in our lives to show that we belong to Christ?
  A. We must say that we are believers
  B. We must have bumper stickers that say "Honk if you love Jesus."
  C. We must have crucified the flesh with it's passions and desires

Question 5. What does the passage teach about our relationship to the Spirit? What are we to do in relationship to Him?

Question 6. Please list the fruit of the Spirit from verse 22:

Question 7. In the context of this passage, what does it mean to be led by the Spirit?

Question 8. What does it mean to "keep in step with the Spirit?"

Note: The Christian life can be described as a walk with God. Just as "Enoch walked with God, and was no more" so we are to be in a daily relationship with Him. And it is this daily relationship, or this walking with God, that keeps us away from sin. Compare Psalm 56:13: "because you have saved me from death. You have kept me from being defeated. So I will walk with God in light among the living." (NCV)

Testimony

The following testimony is from Carl:

Oh how desperately wicked I have been, and how deep the roots of my sin went. For 29 years I walked with sin, lived in sin, gratifying my flesh and pleasing my sinful nature. I have done all the sinful acts of the flesh listed on today's teaching; sexual immorality, impurity, greed, rage, hatred…etc. I have slept with prostitutes, other men, and even some animals.

I was like King Nebuchadnezzar who was insane until he acknowledged the sovereignty of God. I, too was out of my right mind, and it wasn't until I came to this **Pure Freedom** course that I was granted repentance and my sanity was restored. This began in June of 2000, when I enrolled in the course, but the root system of the weeds of sexual immorality were very deep, and I could not continue. I went back "out to pasture" and lived in my insanity for another 2 months, until I returned in September of 2000.

I don't know what clicked this time, but God simply granted me repentance, and I was able to radically amputate the causes of my sin, and learn how to walk with God. I have been doing this now for 6 months—free and clear!

Questions

The Christian life begins with a step of faith for salvation. Then it continues step by step toward spiritual maturity as we develop a growing closeness to God.

"It is a painful business to get through into the stride of God, it means getting your 'second wind' spiritually. In learning to walk with God there is always the difficulty of getting into His stride; but when we have got into it, the only characteristic that manifests itself is the life of God. The individual man is lost sight of in his personal union with God, and the stride and the power of God alone are manifested.

It is difficult to get into stride with God, because when we start walking with Him we find He has outstripped us before we have taken three steps. He has different ways of doing things, and we have to be trained and disciplined into His ways." (Oswald Chambers)[45]

Question 9. How does 1 John 1:7 add perspective on the above teaching? "If we walk in the light, as He is in the light, we have fellowship with one another and the blood of Jesus, His Son, purifies us from all sin." Write your answers here:

one another always and forgiving each other as we have been forgiven. The flesh resists and fights against all of this so that we cannot perfectly and, at all times, do what we want to do. Should we then despair and give up?

The passage states that there is a way to keep from fulfilling the lusts of the flesh. It is to live by the Spirit. It is to be led by the Spirit. It is to walk with the Spirit. So, our "fight" is not so much with not doing pornography, or not being greedy, selfish or divisive, it is with maintaining our walk with the Lord. For if we live by the Spirit, are led by the Spirit, and walk with the Spirit, the promise of Scripture is that we will not gratify our flesh. We will not do pornography. We will not be sexually immoral, etc... There is our answer!

Dear friend,

I have been learning, over the past 3 years what it means to walk with God. It is an experience to be sure, and it is not like anything we can learn in school. It is exercising the spiritual disciplines of being in the Word daily, of being in prayer continually, of recognizing the leading and prompting of God in our daily activities. This is all foreign to us. But I tell you that I would not trade it. I love walking in and living by the Spirit of God (though my flesh hates it) and I don't ever want to return to the acts of the flesh. My wife, also, is thankful that I am walking in the Spirit, as she and I are much closer than when I was living in sin. I hope you are finding the same thing. Or if you are single, I hope you sense anticipation of being close with your future mate.

Question 10. Paul talks about the battle between the flesh and the Spirit. The two are at war. And then he states, "so that you do not do what you want." Does this refer to believers or unbelievers?

A. Believers
B. Unbelievers

John Calvin adds some clarity here: **"So that you do not do what you want. This refers, unquestionably, to the regenerate (believers). Carnal men have no battle with depraved lusts, no proper desire to attain to the righteousness of God. Paul is speaking to believers. The things that you want must mean, not our natural inclinations, but the holy affections, which God bestows upon us by grace. Paul therefore declares, that believers, so long as they are in this life, whatever may be the earnestness of their endeavors, do not obtain such a measure of success as to serve God in a perfect manner. The highest result does not correspond to their wishes and desires"** (John Calvin, commentary on Galatians 5).[46]

Note: Because of the war in the soul of every believer (the flesh against the Spirit, the Spirit against the flesh) we are unable to perfectly do what we would like to do. We desire to seek God wholeheartedly but the flesh wars against that desire. We desire ongoing intimacy and unbroken fellowship with Jesus Christ, but the flesh vehemently resists this. We want to show others only a sweet aroma of Christ, letting our gentleness be evident to all; we want to be gracious at all times, completely humble, submitting to

Scripture to Consider

"He has shown you, O man, what is good; And what does the LORD require of you. But to do justly, To love mercy, And to walk humbly with your God?" (Micah 6:8) (NKJV)

Were you free from pornography since you did the last lesson?
  Yes   No

Were you free from masturbation since you did the last lesson?
  Yes   No

Were you free from sexual immorality since you did the last lesson?
  Yes   No

DAY 50—FREEDOM THROUGH FELLOWSHIP

The final weekend before Christmas is not the time to visit a shopping mall. If you are fortunate enough to find a parking spot, the press of people inside makes shopping almost impossible. One mother I heard was giving final instructions to her young son before plunging into the crowd: "Stay close to me and hold my hand all the time. We won't get separated if we hold on to each other."

As Jesus prepared his disciples to face life without his visible presence, he impressed on them the importance of staying close to him spiritually. He said, "Remain in Me." If you have ever longed to understand the secret of spiritual growth, you will find it in Jesus' words to us in John 15.

Here is a truth to memorize:
Truly stopping habits of pornography and masturbation requires
Ongoing intimacy with God.

Or, stated another way, enjoying true intimacy with Jesus Christ breaks the attraction of false intimacy that pornography offers. This is the reason why all psychologically based programs to "change behavior" will not produce genuine and lasting freedom. Enjoying Jesus Christ Himself must replace the love of pornography.

Please read the following Scripture:

> "⁴ Remain in me, and I will remain in you. No branch can bear fruit by itself; it must remain in the vine. Neither can you bear fruit unless you remain in me. ⁵ "I am the vine; you are the branches. If a man remains in me and I in him, he will bear much fruit; apart from me you can do nothing. ⁶ If anyone does not remain in me, he is like a branch that is thrown away and withers; such branches are picked up, thrown into the fire and burned. ⁷ If you remain in me and my words remain in you, ask whatever you wish, and it will be given you. ⁸ This is to my Father's glory, that you bear much fruit, showing yourselves to be my disciples. ⁹ "As the Father has loved me, so have I loved you. Now remain in my love. ¹⁰ If you obey my commands, you will remain in my love, just as I have obeyed my Father's commands and remain in his love. ¹¹ I have told you this so that my joy may be in you and that your joy may be complete" (John 15:4-11).

Questions

Spend a little time thinking through today's passage to the delight of your soul. When you're ready, please answer these questions:

Question 1. Jesus' instructions to his disciples in this passage revolve around 3 symbols—the vine, the gardener, and the branches. What is Jesus communicating by calling Himself the Vine?
- A. He is the Source of Life
- B. He nourishes and sustains us
- C. He lives in us
- D. All of the above

Question 2. What is the significance of calling His disciples "branches?"
- A. They were dependant on Jesus for life and fruitfulness
- B. They could do nothing on their own
- C. They were dead without Jesus
- D. All of the above

Note: See here the necessity of actually being a "branch." Nobody shares in the life of Christ unless there is an actual faith relationship with Christ.

Question 3. Please select how many times the word "remain" is used in the verses:
- A. 3
- B. 7
- C. 11

Question 4. Instead of commanding us to "bear fruit," why is Jesus' only command to "Remain in Me" (vs. 4)?

Now, let us summarize: Remain in the love of Jesus and your joy will be complete. And if your joy in Jesus is complete, you will not have to look for it anywhere else. Your slavery to sin is broken when your love and joy are complete.

Question 5. What do you think it means to remain in Christ?

Testimony

The following testimony is from Sydney:

I became addicted to Romance novels at the age of 17 when I stayed with my grandparents for the summer. They didn't much care what I was reading, and so I saturated my mind in that junk. I couldn't stop. It made me feel loved and wanted, as I became the people in those books. When I moved back home I had to hide my addiction, which only made it grow stronger (as I've learned in the **Pure Freedom** course) and I also started getting into sex chatting on the Internet. This lasted for approximately 3 years. God broke the bars of my yoke, and enabled me to walk with my head held high (Leviticus 26:13) through my pastor's teaching of God's Word. He also recommended I go through this course, and I am now on Day 59 but have been free from all forms of impurity for 9 weeks.

Questions

Question 6. The fruit produced by the remaining branch is often viewed as a reference to new converts. But branches produce grapes, not other branches. What other possible meanings are there for fruit?

Question 7. Read Galatians 5:22-23: "But the fruit of the Spirit is love, joy, peace, patience, kindness, goodness, faithfulness, gentleness and self-control." How do these verses fit into what we are studying?

Note: We can do "nothing" on our own, certainly not overcome pornography and masturbation, sexual impurity, etc... But if we remain in Jesus He will produce fruit through us, and one particular fruit of being in Him is "self-control." So, we do not focus as much on overcoming pornography as we do on abiding, or dwelling in Jesus Christ. This is the "secret" to growing in Christ, to leaving pornography behind, to experiencing genuine love and real joy!

Please read the following story:

> "Then seizing him, they led him away and took him into the house of the high priest. Peter followed at a distance. But when they had kindled a fire in the middle of the courtyard and had sat down together, Peter sat down with them. A servant girl saw him seated there in the firelight. She looked closely at him and said, 'This man was with him.' But he denied it. 'Woman, I don't know him,' he said. A little later someone else saw him and said, 'You also are one of them.' 'Man, I am not!' Peter replied. About an hour later another asserted, 'Certainly this fellow was with him, for he is a Galilean.' Peter replied, 'Man, I don't know what you're talking about!' Just as he was speaking, the rooster crowed. The Lord turned and looked straight at Peter. Then Peter remembered the word the Lord had spoken to him: 'Before the rooster crows today, you will disown me three times.' And he went outside and wept bitterly" (Luke 22:54-62).

We find in the above story that Peter denied Christ, began cursing, and stated that he did not know Jesus. And he fell 3 times in a row, one right after the other. Why? What happened?

Question 8. Please write out the second sentence of verse 54:

"And Peter followed at a distance." Friend, this is a warning for us: anytime we begin distancing ourselves from Christ we will fall. We must remain intimate with Him, enjoying fellowship with our Savior moment by moment. This is the key to ongoing victory and fruitfulness.

Next, please read the following quote from **Robert Murray McCheyne,** and write your thoughts on it below:

"Not all that seem to be branches are branches of the true Vine. Many branches fall off the trees when the high winds begin to blow—all that are rotten branches. So, in times of temptation, or trial, or persecution, many false professors drop away. Many that seemed to be believers went back, and walked no more with Jesus. They followed Jesus, they prayed with Him, they praised Him; but they went back, and walked no more with Him. So it is still. Many among us doubtless seem to be converted; they begin well and promise fair, who will fall off when winter comes. Some have fallen off, I fear, already; some more may be expected to follow. These will not be blessed in dying. Oh, of all deathbeds may I be kept from beholding the deathbed of the false professor! I have seen it before now, and I trust I may never see it again. They are not blessed after death. The rotten branches will burn more fiercely in the flames.

"Oh, think what torment it will be, to think that you spent your life in pretending to be a Christian, and lost your opportunity of becoming one indeed! Your hell will be all the deeper, blacker, hotter, that you knew so much of Christ, and were so near Him, and found Him not."[47]

Question 9. Write your thoughts on the above quote here:

Question 10. How does 1 John 2:27 compare with what we are studying today? "As for you, the anointing you received from him remains in you, and you do not need anyone to teach you. But as his anointing teaches you about all things and as that anointing is real, not counterfeit—just as it has taught you, remain in him."

Write your answer here:

Course Member Todd writes: "Just as the branches cannot bear fruit, we cannot without Christ. We cannot free ourselves from sin. We need Him in every step of this battle. Through Christ I will be freed from pornography. That is a promise in the Bible. I have asked that He would, and I am sure it is in God's will for it to be, so it is going to be done! Truly stopping a pornographic addiction requires an ongoing intimacy with God."

Question 11. Finally, provide your thoughts on this quote from Charles Spurgeon:

"We are plainly taught in the Word of God that as many as have believed are one with Christ: they are married to him, there is a conjugal union based upon mutual affection. The union is closer still, for there is a vital union between Christ and his saints. They are in him as the branches are in the vine; they are members of the body of which he is the head. They are one with Jesus in such a true and real sense that with him they died, with him they have been buried, with him they are raised; with him they are raised up together and made to sit together in heavenly places. There is an indissoluble union between Christ and all his people: I in them and they in me.

"Thus the union may be described: 'Christ is in his people the hope of glory, and they are dead and their life is hid with Christ in God.' This is a union of the most wonderful kind, which figures may faintly set forth, but which it is impossible for language completely to explain.

"Oneness to Jesus is one of the fat things full of marrow. For if it be so, indeed, that we are one with Christ, then because he lives we must live also; because he was justified by his resurrection, we also are justified in him; because he is rewarded and forever sits down at his Father's right hand, we also have obtained the inheritance in him and by faith grasp it now and enjoy its earnest."[48]

Write your comments here:

Question 12. Philippians 4:13 says, "I can do all things through Christ, who gives me strength." Can you break free from an addiction to pornography through Jesus Christ?

A. Yes
B. No
C. Through Him? You bet; I'm doing it!

Scripture to Consider

[20] "My prayer is not for them alone. I pray also for those who will believe in me through their message, [21] that all of them may be one, Father, just as you are in me and I am in you. May they also be in us so that the world may believe that you have sent me. [22] I have given them the glory that you gave me, that they may be one as we are one: [23] I in them and you in me. May they be brought to complete unity to let the world know that you sent me and have loved them even as you have loved me" (John 17:20-23).

Were you free from pornography since you did the last lesson?
    Yes   No

Were you free from masturbation since you did the last lesson?
    Yes   No

Were you free from sexual immorality since you did the last lesson?
    Yes   No

DAY 51—LIVE FOR PLEASURE!

Did you know that it is Biblical to live for pleasure? In fact, as we will see later on, it is commanded of us to live for pleasure. We are to be, as John Piper puts it, "Christian Hedonists." This was a totally new concept to me. Some people in the Christian world are not happy until they are miserable, and that is the way I was for years. But we are not doomed to this type of an existence, and today's teaching has the power to change your entire world. I know; it did mine.

Here is a challenge: Sometime when you are bored, do a search for "Sexual Addiction" on the Internet, look for some "experts" who deal with this kind of thing, and begin reading the solutions they provide. I think you will see why I truly am thankful that I did not get sucked in to the teaching that is out there today.

Most of it is a joyless "To Do" list of things to change your behavior: When hit with temptation, visualize a policeman running up to you with a big red stop sign and handcuffs. Then begin to picture an emotionally charged moment, the death of a parent or the birth of a child, so as to have an equal emotional pull as the temptation. Oh friend, how sad. How lifeless. How ineffective are the cures of the world. What about the heart? What can so motivate my heart with love and joy that I can't possibly *think* of going back to pornography? Oh friend, we have a Savior Who has come to us in *passion!* He has come not only to suffer and die to remove the penalty of our sins, but to live in our hearts and shower us with love. Oh how He does delight the soul and stir the affections. Oh how pleasurable it is to live in love with Him. A cop with a red stop sign and handcuffs, or a Savior who transforms the heart. Hmm…. let me think.

The key is that we are to be people who live for *pleasure* in God! **"It is a bad world, an incredibly bad world. But I have discovered in the midst of it a quiet and holy people who have learned a great secret. They have found a joy that is a *thousand times better* than any pleasure of our sinful life. They are despised and persecuted, but they care not. They are masters of their souls. They have overcome the world. These people are the Christians—and I am one of them."** (Saint Cyprian 200-258).[49]

Dear friend, this is what we are called to: finding a joy that is a *thousand times better* than any pleasure of our sinful life. Sometimes I cannot believe that I spent 15 long years following the "pleasures of sin" in pornography when there was Someone "a thousand times better" waiting for me. And it is the ongoing experience of Jesus Christ that keeps me from having any desire to go back. I can't get enough of Jesus—this God-Man who longs to pour His life into me, and to fill me to all the fullness of God. Today we will examine the sheer pleasure available in God. Oh friend, open your heart to this God, for you will live in pleasure for the rest of your life, and then throughout all eternity, if you do.

Questions

Question 1. According to this verse, what is at the right hand of God?
"You have made known to me the path of life; you will fill me with joy in your presence, with eternal pleasures at your right hand" (Psalm 16:11).
- A. Eternal pleasures
- B. A lot of hard to follow rules and regulations
- C. A strong bodyguard

Question 2. According to this verse, who is at the right hand of God?
"The Son is the radiance of God's glory and the exact representation of his being, sustaining all things by his powerful word. After he had provided purification for sins, he sat down at the right hand of the Majesty in heaven" (Hebrews 1:3).
- A. A strong bodyguard
- B. Jesus Christ

Note: The above verses tell us that there are eternal pleasures at the right hand of God, and that Jesus Christ is at the right hand of God. Do you see it? The message is clear: In Jesus Christ is eternal pleasure! Sin's pleasures are only "for a season" but with Jesus Christ the pleasure never ends!

"A fool finds pleasure in evil conduct, but a man of understanding delights in wisdom" (Proverbs 10:23).

Question 3. What kind of a person finds pleasure in pornography, or other evil conduct?
- A. A good-time, fun-loving person
- B. A wise and godly man
- C. A fool

"Pleasure is our greatest evil or our greatest good" (Alexander Pope 1688-1744).[50]

Question 4. According to Proverbs 10:23 above, how does a man of understanding approach wisdom?
- A. He delights in it
- B. He looks for it
- C. He gains it
- D. He endures it

"To whom can I speak and give warning? Who will listen to me? Their ears are closed so they cannot hear. The word of the LORD is offensive to them; they find no pleasure in it" (Jeremiah 6:10).

Questions

Question 5. According to Jeremiah 6:10, what is the attitude of these people toward the Word of God?
- A. They find no pleasure in it
- B. It brings them great delight
- C. They love it

Question 6. If the unrighteous are characterized as people who find no pleasure in the Word of God, how are we who love God to approach Scripture?
- A. We are to read it every Sunday at church
- B. We find pleasure in it, it is a delight to our hearts
- C. We have to read it to be saved

"Then Hannah prayed and said: 'My heart rejoices in the LORD; in the LORD my horn is lifted high. My mouth boasts over my enemies, for I delight in your deliverance'" (1 Samuel 2:1).

Question 7. This verse is the record of Hannah praying to the Lord. What is her attitude toward the Lord and His deliverance?
- A. She endures it quietly
- B. She rejoices and delights in the Lord and in His salvation

"Delight yourself in the LORD and he will give you the desires of your heart" (Psalm 37:4).

Question 8. According to Psalm 37:4 above, what are we to do with the Lord?
- A. Accept Him
- B. Delight in Him
- C. Obey Him

Question 9. According to the above verse (Psalm 37:4), what is the reward for delighting in the Lord?
- A. It's....A NEW CAR
- B. If we make the Lord our delight we receive the desires of our heart

"Praise the LORD. Blessed is the man who fears the LORD, who finds great delight in his commands" (Psalm 112:1).

Question 10. What does the man who fears the Lord delight in?
- A. Going to movies, plays, and fine art work
- B. The commands of God, the Word of God
- C. Pornography

Testimony

The following testimony is from Jimmy:

Six months ago, I was desperately seeking pleasure in everything the world has to offer. As the teacher I sought for pleasure in pleasing the flesh, in business, in social clubs, in sports, in drinking, and much more. But like the wind I could never catch it. True pleasure always eluded me. But when I was convicted of my sin, in July of 2000 and began seeking Christ, I found in Him an endless stream of delights. Oh how He encourages the heart and soul.

If you are seeking pleasure in pornography and sexual impurity you are drinking water from the wrong source. If you are seeking it in any other source than Jesus you are dooming yourself to an eternity of thirsting, and never being quenched.

Oh friend, do as I did in August of 2000, give up! Submit to God, listen to Him, remove wickedness far from your tent, and assign your golden nuggets of earthly pleasure to the dust to be trampled on, and then watch how your heart begins to delight in the Almighty God.

I'm glad I discovered that I am to delight in the Lord. And I'm glad I am finding joy in Him. I will not trade this birthright of joy in Jesus Christ for all the worldly delights there are; they are but a mess of pottage in comparison.

"Come, all you who are thirsty, come to the waters; and you who have no money, come, buy and eat! Come, buy wine and milk without money and without cost. Why spend money on what is not bread, and your labor on what does not satisfy? Listen, listen to me, and eat what is good, and your soul will delight in the richest of fare. Give ear and come to me; hear me that your soul may live. I will make an everlasting covenant with you, my faithful love promised to David" (Isaiah 55:1-3).

Question 11. These verses make it clear that there is a "delight of soul" awaiting all who will eat what is good. Are you eating what is good (God's Word)? Are you learning to delight in the Lord now? Please write your answer here:

"I delight greatly in the LORD; my soul rejoices in my God. For he has clothed me with garments of salvation and arrayed me in a robe of righteousness, as a bridegroom adorns his head like a priest, and as a bride adorns herself with her jewels" (Isaiah 61:10).

Questions

Question 12. Who or what is the author finding pleasure in?
A. The pleasures of sin
B. Being wealthy
C. The Lord

Question 13. Why is he rejoicing?
A. Because he is not naked in sin, but clothed with the garments of salvation
B. Because he won the lottery
C. Because sin is fun!

Note: Remember Adam and Eve, who after their sin were naked and ashamed. God came along and clothed them with a sacrifice. God provides all of His children with the garments of salvation; that is, with the sacrifice of Jesus Christ. This brings us pleasure and causes us to rejoice.

"To stand by the shadows of a friendly tree with the wind tugging at your coattail and the heavens hailing your heart, to gaze and glory and to give oneself again to God, what more could a man ask? Oh the fullness, pleasure, sheer excitement of knowing God on earth." (Jim Elliot in The Journals of Jim Elliot. Christianity Today, Vol. 31, no. 12.)[51]

"Nothing will supply the needs, and satisfy the desires of a soul, but water out of this rock (Jesus Christ), this fountain opened. The pleasures of sense are puddle-water; spiritual delights are rock-water, so pure, so clear, so refreshing—rivers of pleasure" (Matthew Henry).[52]

Now, please read through the following passage and give your thoughts below. This passage is a prescription for how to find delight in God:

> [21] "Submit to God and be at peace with him; in this way prosperity will come to you. [22] Accept instruction from his mouth and lay up his words in your heart. [23] If you return to the Almighty, you will be restored: If you remove wickedness far from your tent [24] and assign your nuggets to the dust, your gold of Ophir to the rocks in the ravines, [25] then the Almighty will be your gold, the choicest silver for you. [26] Surely then you will find delight in the Almighty and will lift up your face to God" (Job 22:21-26).

Question 14. There are four requirements in this passage that must be met in order to delight in God. What are they? I'll write the first one:

Number 1: Verse 21—**Submit to God**

Number 2: Verse 22—_____

Number 3: Verse 23—_____

Number 4: Verse 23,24—_____

Question 15. What does it mean when it says "Then the Almighty will be your gold, the choicest silver for you?"

Question 16. In your own words, according to the passage, what needs to be done in order to truly delight in God?

Friend, I hope you know there is exquisite joy and pleasure to be found in Jesus Christ. This has to be experienced to be understood, as words fall far short of being able to explain. Oh how sad to trade an eternity of pleasure with Christ for the temporary "pleasures of sin". With Him is fullness of joy, overflowing pleasure, ongoing delight. Won't you commit right now to seeking your pleasure in Jesus Christ? Once we taste of the joy that is found in Him we won't want to go back to the pleasures of pornography.

Scripture to Consider

"For the LORD takes pleasure in His people; He will beautify the humble with salvation. Let the saints be joyful in glory; Let them sing aloud on their beds" (Psalm 149: 4-5). NKJV

Were you free from pornography since you did the last lesson?
    Yes   No

Were you free from masturbation since you did the last lesson?
    Yes   No

Were you free from sexual immorality since you did the last lesson?
    Yes   No

DAY 52—HAPPY ARE THE HELPLESS

"Now when he saw the crowds, he went up on a mountainside and sat down. His disciples came to him, and he began to teach them, saying: 'Blessed are the poor in spirit, for theirs is the kingdom of heaven. Blessed are those who mourn, for they will be comforted'" (Matthew 5:1-4).

When Christ began this Sermon on the Mount, He began at the narrow gate of the basic need of man before God. Man needs what only God can give him—life. Without God, man is hopelessly lost and eternally condemned.

I have been amazed at the published material (sometimes Christian) caressing the pride of man today. Such things as, "Choosing Your Own Greatness", or "You're Nature's Greatest Miracle"; or "You've Got What It Takes"; or "Unlocking Your Potential." All these are misdiagnoses!

You've heard it said, "God helps those who help themselves." This is not true. According to Scripture, God helps the helpless!

We are studying today an important subject that will help us overcome pornography, masturbation, and all sexual immorality. Blessed are the poor in spirit. Or, happy are the helpless!

So, let us seek to understand what "poor in spirit" is. Here are some definitions
> Bankrupt in Self
> Self-worth is nothing without God
> All I am, have, and do is worthless without God
> I understand my **total inability** before God.

This word "poor" has to do with "one who crouches or cowers," and refers to one who is beggarly.

Questions

Question 1. Have you approached God as a beggar?

Next, let us notice the importance of coming to God spiritually bankrupt.
- This spiritual poverty is in reality the foundation of all graces. God gives grace to the humble, not to the proud. The humble, or those who recognize their own impoverished condition, are given grace.
- Emptiness Precedes Fullness. We cannot receive from God until we have empty hands. He who recognizes he has nothing to offer God will receive everything from God.
- Self must be done with for Christ to be wanted. If we are setting out in life to honor ourselves, Christ will be far from us. But he who honors God will himself be honored.
- A starving heart will give all to have the Bread of Life. It is only the hungry that sense their need of Jesus, not the full.

Question 2. Can you see the benefits of being poor in spirit? From the above thoughts, please list the blessings that come to a spiritually poor person:

Dear friend, in order to overcome life-dominating sins, such as pornography and masturbation, one must be poor in spirit. Overcoming pornography takes the presence of God and the power of God, and these are given to the destitute ones, the broken and empty ones, and the poor in spirit. God blesses those who are poor in spirit. Let us notice 4 ways in which He blesses them by examining the following verses:

1. God is near to the poor in spirit: "The LORD is close to the brokenhearted and saves those who are crushed in spirit" (Psalm 34:18).
2. God will not despise the poor in spirit: "The sacrifices of God are a broken spirit; a broken and contrite heart, O God, you will not despise" (Psalm 51:17).
3. God dwells with the poor in spir-

Testimony

The following testimony is from Lawrence:

I have been in love with myself from as early as I can remember. I have always thought I was an extremely good-looking man, and have always thought women would think that about me as well. I had myself convinced that most women I came in contact with wanted me, lusted after me, and would do anything to have me.

That was in the days of my selfish life. One of the things that God did to break me of my love affair with myself is to convince me of sin, and to show me the solid death-grip it had on my life. I could not overcome pornography and masturbation for the life of me. That is, until I came to the **Pure Freedom** course. I remember learning one truth that sank home to my heart, somewhere around Day 50, and that was that it was the poor in spirit who were blessed by God. You could have knocked me over with a feather, a

Questions

it: "For this is what the high and lofty One says— he who lives forever, whose name is holy: 'I live in a high and holy place, but also with him who is contrite and lowly in spirit, to revive the spirit of the lowly and to revive the heart of the contrite'" (Isaiah 57:15).

4. God esteems the poor in spirit: "This is the one I esteem: he who is humble and contrite in spirit, and trembles at my word" (Isaiah 66:2).

Question 3. Take a moment and write out all the blessings the poor in spirit receive, from the four items. As you are writing these, ask God to work poverty of spirit deep within you, that He might bless you in these ways.

Number 1 blessing to the poor in spirit: _____

Number 2 blessing to the poor in spirit: _____

Number 3 blessing to the poor in spirit: _____

Number 4 blessing to the poor in spirit: _____

Please read the following quote:

"A castle that has been long besieged and is ready to be taken will deliver up on any terms to save their lives. He whose heart has been a garrison for the devil and has held out long in opposition against Christ, when once God has brought him to poverty of spirit and he sees himself damned without Christ, let God propound what articles He may, he will readily subscribe to them. 'Lord, what will you have me to do?'" (Thomas Watson).[53]

Question 4. Please write your thoughts on the above quote from Thomas Watson:

Note: Watson connected the attitude "Lord, what will you have me to do?" with one who is poor in spirit. We have also noticed that those who come to the **Pure Freedom** course in humility, wanting to learn, asking questions for the purpose of implementing the answers, will always get free from pornography. Whereas those who think they have something to give and contribute, and who come into the course teaching and instructing, will usually fall often. It is the "poor in spirit" who are blessed with freedom from habitual sin.

Next, please read the following passage, paying particular attention to which of the praying men received the blessing from God:

"[9] To some who were confident of their own righteousness and looked down on everybody else, Jesus told this parable: [10] "Two men went up to the temple to pray, one a Pharisee and the other a tax collector. [11] The Pharisee stood up and prayed about himself: 'God, I thank you that I am not like other men— robbers, evildoers, adulterers—or even like this tax collector. [12] I fast twice a week and give a tenth of all I get.' [13] "But the tax collector stood at a distance. He would not even look up to heaven, but beat his breast and said, 'God, have mercy on me, a sinner.' [14] "I tell you that this man, rather than the other, went home justified before God. For everyone who exalts himself will be humbled, and he who humbles himself will be exalted" (Luke 18:9-14).

Question 5. It is obvious that the tax collector was the one who was poor in spirit. Please write out the evidences of his poverty of spirit. What things did he do and say that show us he was spiritually impoverished?

Question 6. From Luke 18:9-14 above, what blessing did the man poor in spirit receive?

God turned the search light of His Word on my heart right then and there. I began to see how grossly disgusting my love affair with myself was. I began seeing how spiritually "rich" I thought I was, and how I felt that I had so much to offer God and everyone else. This sight of myself made me sick of myself, and I repented to God for my disgusting "wealth" that I thought I had in myself. I came to God as a beggar; desperate and needy, without resources and helpless. Oh, I can't begin to describe to you the joy that has come from my own crucifixion in Christ.

Since Jesus has eradicated the sins of pornography and masturbation from my life I want to praise God all day long. I am crucified with Christ, and I no longer live. Oh how good it is to be dead to sin and alive to God! Blessed are the poor in spirit! Happy are the helpless!

Next, let us notice additional rewards and blessings of those who are poor in spirit.

1. God thinks on and delivers the poor in spirit: "Yet I am poor and needy; may the Lord think of me. You are my help and my deliverer; O my God, do not delay" (Psalm 40:17).

2. God hears and does not despise the poor in spirit: "The LORD hears the needy and does not despise his captive people" (Psalm 69:33).

3. God spares and saves the poor in

163

Questions

spirit: "He will take pity on the weak and the needy and save the needy from death" (Psalm 72:13).

4. God gives success to the poor in spirit: "But he lifted the needy out of their affliction and increased their families like flocks" (Psalm 107:41).

Question 7. Again we find that the poor in spirit are blessed. Please write down the four additional ways that God blesses them from the above four verses. Also, provide any thoughts you have while thinking through these verses:

Number 1 blessing to the poor in spirit:

_____

Number 2 blessing to the poor in spirit:

_____

Number 3 blessing to the poor in spirit:

_____

Number 4 blessing to the poor in spirit:

_____

Question 8. Psalm 107:41 from above says, "But He lifts the needy out of their affliction..." Please describe how this verse shows that the poor in spirit will be rescued from pornography, masturbation, sexual immorality, etc...

Question 9. Can you see any or all of the evidences of spiritual poverty in your life? If so, which ones?

Course Member Mel writes: "Yes, I can see this weaning from self happening now. I look at myself while I was enslaved to pornography and I see one who was thoroughly selfish, and who lived to please myself in all things. Since I have been walking in freedom from this habitual sin I am becoming less and Jesus is becoming more. I praise God for this change that He is working in my heart and in my life. My wife also said to me the other day that I am living a life that is non-selfish. Wow, never thought I would hear that from her."

Question 10. Write out any additional thoughts you have about today's lesson.

Friend, I have shared with you all throughout this course that it was not until I became poor in spirit that I received the blessing of God in being lifted out of my affliction. You know how I was teaching and preaching while involved in habitual sin on a regular basis.

But when I went to my pastor that day in January of 1999, I went as a beggar. I went as a dying man who needed life. I was willing to do anything to be free. I would listen to his advice because I trusted him, and I would do whatever he told me to do. It was embarrassing to have to take the TV out of my hotel room and deposit it at the front desk. Very embarrassing. But I was willing to do anything. And that is the key to overcoming pornography. Are you willing to do anything? Do you trust me and are you also willing to listen and obey when instructed on what to do?

Finally, please note the evidences and applications of the poor in spirit, and take the time to look up the Scripture references sometime.

Poverty of spirit brings about a:

- Weaning from self—Galatians 2:20; Philippians 1:21
- Delighting in God's glory—2 Corinthians 3:18
- Seeking God's fingerprints—Romans 8:17, 18, 28

Scripture to Consider

"Guard your steps when you go to the house of God. Go near to listen rather than to offer the sacrifice of fools, who do not know that they do wrong. ²Do not be quick with your mouth; do not be hasty in your heart to utter anything before God. God is in heaven and you are on earth, so let your words be few" (Ecclesiastes 5:1,2).

Were you free from pornography since you did the last lesson?
    Yes   No

Were you free from masturbation since you did the last lesson?
    Yes   No

Were you free from sexual immorality since you did the last lesson?
    Yes   No

DAY 53—THE POWER OF THE WORD

There is a continual need to profit from Scripture, and utilize the power of God's Word in an individual's life. The antidote to self-deception is to listen to God through His Word and to mistrust one's own capacity to reason (Proverbs 3:5-6, 13:14, 14:15, 14:27). The propensity of the human heart to rationalize and justify sin is an active force in the tangled lives of those enslaved to sin. Only by fearing the Lord (yielding oneself to the Word of God) may one find life and freedom. The following is written by one of our long-time mentors, Pastor Dave Wagner from Windsor, Ontario, Canada, and can be the basis for personal growth in Christ. Please read this excellent article and answer the questions throughout.

The Power Of The Word
Learning To Enjoy Freedom In Christ[54]

Dear friends and course members of **Pure Freedom**, this course has the ability to help shape the hearts, minds, souls and spirits of the students that come seeking freedom from addiction. On the whole, the majority of people who come to the site are Christians or have a Church background. In spite of the "availability of Scripture and truth" many come to the site hopelessly addicted to the slavery of pornography and masturbation.

Many who come have been reading the Bible for years, yet the truth has escaped them! They find no spiritual profit from their study of it. The evidence of "bad fruit" in their lives brings us rapidly to the conclusion that although their store of knowledge has increased, so also has their pride. Like a chemist engaged in making interesting experiments the intellectual searcher of the Word is quite elated when he finds or makes some discovery in it. The joy they have holds no spiritual meaning for them. Their success, and their sense of self-importance only increase and cause them to look with distain upon others they deem more ignorant than themselves.

We have found from working with course members that there is a type of person who in their answers makes frequent references to Scripture left, right and center and yet when it comes to constant scriptural accountability they end up going through cycle after cycle of checking "no's" to the accountability questions at the end of each lesson. Satan is constantly active to get this type of personality to quote much Scripture but never apply it. It is always for someone else.

Pastor Dave has written an excellent book called *Secret Sins Of The Heart, Why Christian Men Read Pornography—An Inner Look At The Addiction Process and Deliverance For Christian Men.* To order this resource:

Rev. David A. Wagner
Box # 27090
7720 Tecumseh Rd E.
Windsor, Ontario, Canada
N8T 3N5
Phone: 519-971-7664
or by email: dnh777@home.com
To order online go to www.secretsinsoftheheart.com

Questions

Note: Throughout this lesson you will apply the power of the Word of God in the following ways:

1. The Word of God will **convict you of your sin**.
2. The Word of God will make you **sorrow over sin**.
3. The Word of God leads you to **Confession of sin**.
4. The Word of God will produce in you a deeper **hatred of sin**.
5. The Word of God will produce in you a **forsaking of sin**.

Question 1. How should we read Scripture?
   A. For convincing others of our spirituality
   B. For applying it directly to life circumstances and situations
   C. For correcting others' unscriptural views

Some who come to the course are reading the Word of God for the wrong reasons, such as curiosity, or pride (in the sense that they can tell others how often they read it) and others read to accumulate knowledge as a weapon of war, but not against Satan. They use it for the purpose of being able to argue successfully with those who would differ from them or have an opposing point of view. As a result of their wrongful reading there is no thought of God, no yearning for spiritual edification, no benefit to the soul, and most important no power in their lives to overcome the addictive lifestyle they find themselves in as Christians.

Our goal is that our souls would profit from the Word of God. 2 Timothy 3:16,17 gives us clear guidance as to how the Word can influence our lives.

"All scripture is given by inspiration of God and is profitable for Doctrine, for reproof, for correction, for instruction in righteousness that the man of God may be perfect, thoroughly furnished unto all Good Works!"

Question 2. Please write down what things Scripture is profitable for:

Questions

The Word within this **Pure Freedom** course will accomplish many things!

- First the Word of God within the course will **convict of sin** and reveal our depravity, expose our vileness and make known our wickedness. One of the ways you will know that you are profiting from the Word, and not merely gaining knowledge, is when you begin to see these things occurring in your life.

Question 3. Is this happening in your life currently? If so, give an example?

- The Word of God within the course will make the addicted Christian **sorrow over sin** as many come to the course with a stony heart. As the Holy Spirit applies the Word the student is able to see and feel their inward corruption and many discover the strongholds that Satan has set up in their lives and has been working from for such a long time. This discovery by the Word produces a broken heart and leads them to humble themselves before God.

Question 4. Has God been revealing your sinfulness and causing you to sorrow over it?

You will know that you are on the right track and heading down the right road when you see this humbling of spirit start to take place. It will be shown by your humbleness of spirit, which is shown in the words you write. If God is working in your heart in this way, you will be brought to a daily repentance before Him. You will also experience liberation from guilt and shame and you will be able, with joy, to answer the daily accountability questions at the end of each lesson. This "sorrow over sin" goes

Testimony

The following testimony is from Kent:

The Word of God has changed my life dramatically. I have gone from being a homosexual and adulterer to a man who loves God, has 8 children, and enjoys my freedom in Christ. I have been free, by the power of God's Word, for 3 years now.

through a pre-defined process. God had a process for Passover Lamb-it was to be eaten with "bitter herbs" (Exodus 12:8). As the Word does the work on your heart the Holy Spirit makes it "bitter" before it becomes sweet to your taste. So we see there must be mourning before comfort. (Matthew 5:4), humbling before exalting (1 Peter 5:6).

The reading of the Word of God causes us to remember that our sinful life was a bitter experience for us. As God changes our hearts and lives, that bitterness is changed to sweetness. The cross of Jesus Christ brings us to a place of forgiveness, and the bitterness of our former sins is changed to sweetness.

- The Word of God within the course leads to **confession of sin**. The Scriptures are profitable for reproof (2 Timothy 3:16). When you come to God with an honest heart and soul, you start confessing and acknowledge your fault!

"For every one that does evil, hates the light, neither comes to the light, least his deeds should be reproved" (John 3:20 KJV).

This is a great battlefield for Christians coming to the **Pure Freedom** course with a major sin of addiction in their lives. They are like people who gather on the fringe of darkness around the campfire in a dark forest. They know that sooner or later they will have to choose, step forward and drag their sins out into the light where that sin will die or they will make the choice to stay in the comfort of the shadows slipping in and out of the light and never fully committing to the light. The sin of addiction to pornography and masturbation is often a secret or covered sin.

"He who conceals his sins does not prosper, but whoso confesses and renounces them finds mercy" (Proverbs 28:13 KJV).

There can be no spiritual prosperity or fruitfulness while we conceal within our breasts our guilty secrets. (Psalm 1:3) There is no real peace for the conscience and no rest for the heart while there is the burden of unconfessed sin.

Question 5. Is there any unconfessed or secret sin in your life? Explain.

- The Word of God if appropriated will also produce a **deeper hatred of sin**. It is when you start coming to the place where you really hate the sin and hate the addiction it brings that you will be taking the first steps towards freedom.

"Ye that love the Lord, hate evil" (Psalm 97:10 KJV)

Questions

We cannot love God without hating that which he hates. "Through thy precepts I get understanding: therefore I hate every false way (Psalm 119:104 KJV). It is not merely "I abstain from" but "I hate" not "some" or "many" but "every false way".

Question 6. Is God producing this hatred of sin in your life? If so, how is He doing it?

- The Word of God within the course will produce a **forsaking of sin.** It is very simple. Satan's job is to keep us from reading the Word. Like the parable of the sower with the seed, some will read it and it will take root. Others will read it and there will be no forsaking of sin.

"Let every one that names the name of Christ depart from iniquity" (2 Timothy 2:19).

The reading and studying of God's Word produces a purging of my ways. If it is not doing this we need to ask, "Why Not?" When the Word is personally applied to the life, the end results are dynamic. It causes mentors and students alike to "cleanse our ways". It causes us to "take heed" and it exhorts us to "flee fornication". Sin needs to be not only confessed but also forsaken. (Proverbs 28:13)

- The Word of God produces a **fortification against sin**.

"Thy Word have I hid in my heart that I might not sin against thee" (Psalm 119:11).

The more that Christ's Word dwells in us richly (Colossians 3:16) the less room there will be for the exercise of sin in the heart and life. The Word of God fortifies us. Nothing preserves from the infections of this world, delivers from the temptations of Satan and is so effective a preservative against sin as the Word of God. As long as truth is active within us, stirring the conscience and is really loved by us, we shall be kept from falling. You must be prepared and fortified ahead of time for Satan's attacks. We often call this in the course, having a "plan of action". By storing up the Word in our hearts we will be prepared for coming emergencies and the attacks of Satan.

Question 7. Please state, in your own words, what 6 things the Word of God is designed to do, and give any comments.

Scripture to Consider

"For the word of God is living and active. Sharper than any double-edged sword, it penetrates even to dividing soul and spirit, joints and marrow; it judges the thoughts and attitudes of the heart. Nothing in all creation is hidden from God's sight. Everything is uncovered and laid bare before the eyes of him to whom we must give account" (Hebrews 4:12-13).

"I write to you, fathers, because you have known him who is from the beginning. I write to you, young men, because you are strong, and the word of God lives in you, and you have overcome the evil one" (1 John 2:14).

Were you free from pornography since you did the last lesson?
    Yes   No

Were you free from masturbation since you did the last lesson?
    Yes   No

Were you free from sexual immorality since you did the last lesson?
    Yes   No

DAY 54—DO EVERYTHING TO STAND

"Therefore put on the full armor of God, so that when the day of evil comes, you may be able to stand your ground, after you have done everything to stand" (Ephesians 6:13).

By this time in the **Pure Freedom** course, most people are enjoying consistent freedom from pornography and masturbation. However, on occasion we encounter some who have come this far who are continuing to stumble. And over the course of time, we have discovered that all who continue to be defeated have at least two things in common:

1. They have not done all they can to rid their lives of the source of pornography.
2. They are not following the advice of godly mentors who can see what needs to be done to extract them from the grip of lust.

Let us examine these two things in some depth.

Today we want to talk very practically about the subject of "doing everything to stand." Let us review Ephesians 6:13 again: *"Therefore put on the full armor of God, so that when the day of evil comes, you may be able to stand your ground, after you have* done everything to stand*"*. When it comes to fighting pornography and masturbation, Ephesians 6:13 tells us we not only need to be wearing armor but we must also "do all we can to stand." Since this course began in March of 2000 we have watched many people take this verse to heart, and do all they can to stand. Here are some things that our course members have shared with us that they have done to win the war:

- Removed Cable TV from home
- Moved the computer from the "dungeon of privacy" to the open living room
- Removed TV from their home
- Refused to take cash or credit cards with them when having to drive by an old favorite strip club or movie house
- Spent all night in prayer, begging God for grace to overcome
- Locked up the VCR and gave wife the key

The following testimony is from Barrie:

I have masturbated ever since I can remember even before I knew what it was called. remember it felt good and I became addicted to that feeling. This behavior became thoroughly enslaving in my teen years when I was lusting so often after women that masturbation happened many times a day. I was controlled by my sinful nature, and had no hope of ever breaking the habit.

Then I came to Setting Captives Free and to this course **Pure Freedom**, and within 2 weeks I had ceased masturbation entirely, and have not done it now for 60 days. I'm elated. God's grace has enabled me to be severe in my dealing with lust and the power of it is completely broken in my life! Thank you Jesus!

Questions

First, if we leave ourselves access to pornography somewhere we are sure to fall. Please provide your comments on the following verses.

Question 1. What are your thoughts on Romans 13:14: "But put ye on the Lord Jesus Christ, and make not provision for the flesh, to fulfill the lusts thereof. "
Write your answers here:

Note: By leaving ourselves any access to pornography we are making provision for the flesh, and in a weak moment we will fall. We simply must remove all access.

Question 2. What are your thoughts on Matthew 5:29-30: "If your right eye causes you to sin, gouge it out and throw it away. It is better for you to lose one part of your body than for your whole body to be thrown into hell. And if your right hand causes you to sin, cut it off and throw it away. It is better for you to lose one part of your body than for your whole body to go into hell."
Write your answers here:

Question 3. What are your thoughts on Joshua 7:13: "Go, consecrate the people. Tell them, 'Consecrate yourselves in preparation for tomorrow; for this is what the LORD, the God of Israel, says: That which is devoted is among you, O Israel. *You cannot stand against your enemies until you remove it.*"

Questions

- Drove different (and longer) routes to work and back to avoid areas of temptation
- Refused to go out of town except with wife
- Cut off all Internet access
- Changed jobs
- Started going to church
- Started working with an accountability partner
- Removed TV's from hotel room
- Began counseling with pastor
- Burned all pornographic magazines
- Reformatted hard drives
- Installed Covenant Eyes, an online accountability service. Setting Captives Free is an affiliate of the company. Contact www.covenanteyes.com or call toll free: 1-877-479-1119.
- Slept with curtains open in bedroom to avoid privacy
- Stopped counseling with worldly counselors
- Refused to drive out of town where temptation has been strong
- Cut off relationships that promoted sin

Question 4. Please list here everything you have done to stand:

Friend, by now we all should recognize that being free from pornography is an act of God and by His grace: "For it is by grace you have been saved, through faith—and this not from yourselves, it is the gift of God— [9] not by works, so that no one can boast" (Ephesians 2:8-9). "For the grace of God that brings salvation has appeared to all men. [12] It teaches us to say "No" to ungodliness and worldly passions, and to live self-controlled, upright and godly lives in this present age" (Titus 2:11-12). Had it not been for God's grace we would still be serving sin, self and Satan. Sin is so powerful, and our wills so enslaved to it by nature, that we could not, on our own, extricate ourselves from its grip.

And yet there is nothing contradictory to the above truth in stating that we must "do all we can do to stand." In fact, the two work together. We do all we can do because of the grace God has given us. "I worked harder than all of them—yet not I, but the grace of God that was with me" (1 Corinthians 15:10). "For we are God's workmanship, created in Christ Jesus to do good works, which God prepared in advance for us to do" (Ephesians 2:10).

Question 5. How does Philippians 2:12,13 compare with what we are studying today?

"Therefore, my dear friends, as you have always obeyed—not only in my presence, but now much more in my absence—continue to work out your salvation with fear and trembling, for it is God who works in you to will and to act according to his good purpose." Please write your thoughts here:

Friend, we indeed must "do all we can do" to stand. We must "work harder than all the rest" by God's grace. We must work out our salvation that God is working in us, for if we don't we will continue to fall. And continuing to fall weakens us every time. Those who continue to fall may find themselves back in the death-grip of pornography and impurity again. This is serious business.

So, the passage we are studying today says that we must put on the full armor of God, and that after we "do all we can do" to stand, that we do indeed stand by grace. By grace we do not fall into sin. If we do not do all we can do to stand, we should not be surprised when we fall.

Question 6. While reading the above material, has God brought to mind anything else that you could do to stand?

Some people believe (or in some cases are taught falsely by their church) that they cannot overcome masturbation, and that masturbation is good and healthy when used in the right circumstances. Many of us who used to be captives to masturbation know that is a lie from the pit of hell. We know that as we are coming out of pornography and sexual impurity, if we masturbate we give the devil a stronghold in our minds with which he can make us his slaves again. Every time we masturbate we become weaker spiritually because we have indulged the flesh rather than deny and crucify it as we are taught in God's Word (Galatians 5:24).

Question 7. How are you doing with ceasing the masturbation habit?

Those who continue masturbating after leaving pornography behind must realize what is going on: they are yet captive to lust and a slave to carnal desires. And why? Because they are not "doing all they can do" to stand in grace. Somewhere there is a chink in their armor that is letting the evil one shoot in flaming darts to seduce and deceive them, and they are going along with his schemes to overthrow their soul. Their flesh is their master, and they gratify themselves rather than deny the pleasures of sin. And this will continue until they "do all they can do." In other words, declare war on their own lusts, make a battle plan to defeat it, and beg God for grace to carry it through to completion.

Friend, the story of Achan (which we studied on Day 19) teaches us there must be a total eradication of not only the cause of sin, but of everything associated with that sin. When we are dealing with pornography and masturbation we must declare all-out war on evil desires leading to masturbation, and do all we can do to cease this insidious habit.

Here are some things I have personally done to break the power of sin, by God's grace:
  Slept with clothes on
  Walked around the block in a blizzard
  Called a godly friend when severely tempted
  Read Scripture
  Wrote a Scripture diary
  Sang songs
  Slept outside my hotel room sitting up

Maybe these seem too radical; but not to a dying man who needs to be free from sin to live. We need to "do all we can do" until the habit of refusing masturbation is deeply ingrained into our very being. Once the habit is developed we can slowly begin to go back to a less war-oriented lifestyle, always being watchful that we are not sucked back into the trap we barely escaped from.

This day in the course was developed out of seeing heart-breaking falls from some course members as they are well along in this course. Each and every time someone falls to lust and gives in to masturbation it is evident that they have not done all they can do to rid their lives of the sin, and to stand in grace.

Oh friend, purity in Christ and freedom from sin are worth the battle. As we give up pornography and masturbation we gain far more than we lose. We gain mastery over ourselves, enjoyment of the presence of God, freedom from enslaving habits, power in witnessing, etc., etc... It is worth it. It is worth "doing all we can do" to stand by grace.

Question 8. Please make an honest assessment of where you are spiritually. Are you truly becoming free from habits that would master you? And specifically, have you done all you can do to stand?

Scripture to Consider

"Jesus looked at them and said, 'With man this is impossible, but not with God; all things are possible with God'" (Mark 10:27).

Were you free from pornography since you did the last lesson?
    Yes   No

Were you free from masturbation since you did the last lesson?
    Yes   No

Were you free from sexual immorality since you did the last lesson?
    Yes   No

DAY 55— DON'T LOOK BACK!

Dear friend,

There is much worldly teaching in the area of sexual addiction recovery that attempts to take us back to the past. If you do a search on the Internet for "sexual addiction" you will find much teaching about returning to your past, digging up repressed memories, reliving past hurts, etc... as an aid in escaping your current trap. Here is one example from a book advertisement: "Buried memories of sexual abuse can have a devastating impact on relationships, work & health. Uses case histories to stress the importance of recovering these memories as a crucial step in healing & explains various therapeutic processes used in memory retrieval."

Here is another who points to the past: "I take a history of the man's exposure to pornography and masturbation to it (or masturbation with no pornography) and sexual acting out. I do this in his wife's presence, which helps her understand more clearly that in some ways her husband was a victim usually starting at an early age. I next inquire about possible sexual abuse or early seduction of the husband as a child or as an adolescent, which have eroticized him prematurely. In taking this history, I start with his first memory of exposure to pornography—what its form was (magazine, video, phone sex, etc.) and if he masturbated to it—and continue with the history up to the day of interview."

We as Christians do not treat sexual abuse lightly. We do not pass it off as insignificant, nor tell people to "just get over it." The compassion that a Christian has in dealing with a case of real sexual abuse must exceed that of the unbelieving world, for Christ in us has compassion for the hurting. And, it is helpful for us to know a person's background in order to show that compassion as we interact with them. However, the Bible nowhere instructs us to return to our past to understand how to get out of sexual sins in the present. In fact, quite the opposite, we are instructed, "Brothers, I do not consider myself yet to have taken hold of it. But one thing I do: Forgetting what is behind and straining toward what is ahead, I press on toward the goal to win the prize for which God has called me heavenward in Christ Jesus" (Philippians 3:13-14).

The following testimony is from Jillian:

My uncle sexually abused me when I was 4 years old. Then at the age of seventeen I moved in with a family from our church so that I could attend the college near to their home. The father and son of this family molested me repeatedly. I became anorexic/bulimic while living with this family, as I attempted to vomit out all the pain and evil that was inside me. I became sexually promiscuous in the years that followed.

I went to therapists looking for an answer; some helped a little, some were not so helpful. It wasn't until I met Christ, and began applying biblical principles that I really found the freedom Jesus promises in John 8:36. I am no longer into pornography, anorexia/bulimia, or sexual impurity of any kind. I do not hide my past, nor do I dwell on it. I am not in denial about it, nor do I relive it. My God had a purpose in it, and is bringing good from it, as I assist other ladies to freedom in Jesus now.

Question 1. In Philippians 3:13-14, what did Paul say he did with his past?
  A. He forgot it
  B. He delved back into it to discover why he acted in certain ways

In the highly therapized world that we live in, this teaching may come as quite a shock to some. They have been taught that the past is key to the present, and that reliving the pain of the past will remove the pain in the present. This is not biblical truth, but rather man's theories. Personally, I was never "eroticized prematurely" but rather chose to view pornography when older. We work with many here who were never abused during childhood, but are just as thoroughly addicted as others who were abused.

Question 2. Where are you currently with understanding the past and the present? If you believe the past is key to the present, please state where you learned that. Write your thoughts here:

Christians are not focused backward and downward, but rather forward and upward. If we are in a burning building, we aren't so much interested in how the fire started; we want to get out!

Please read the following story and provide your comments.

> "So Joseph went after his brothers and found them near Dothan. ¹⁸ But they saw him in the distance, and before he reached them, they plotted to kill him. ¹⁹ 'Here comes that dreamer!' they said to each other. ²⁰ 'Come now, let's kill him and throw him into one of these cisterns and say that a ferocious animal devoured him. Then we'll see what comes of his dreams.' ²¹ When Reuben heard this, he tried to rescue him from their hands. 'Let's not take his life,' he said. ²² 'Don't shed any blood. Throw him into this cistern here in the desert, but don't lay a hand on him.' Reuben said this to rescue him from them and take him back to his father. ²³ So when Joseph came to his brothers, they

stripped him of his robe—the richly ornamented robe he was wearing—24 and they took him and threw him into the cistern. Now the cistern was empty; there was no water in it. 25 As they sat down to eat their meal, they looked up and saw a caravan of Ishmaelites coming from Gilead. Their camels were loaded with spices, balm and myrrh, and they were on their way to take them down to Egypt. 26 Judah said to his brothers, 'What will we gain if we kill our brother and cover up his blood? 27 Come, let's sell him to the Ishmaelites and not lay our hands on him; after all, he is our brother, our own flesh and blood.' His brothers agreed. So when the Midianite merchants came by, his brothers pulled Joseph up out of the cistern and sold him for twenty shekels of silver to the Ishmaelites, who took him to Egypt" (Genesis 37:17-27).

Joseph's brothers plotted his death, cruelly mistreated him by throwing him into a pit and leaving him for half-dead. Then they sold him into the hands of slave traders where he became a slave in a foreign land, and was eventually lied about and thrown in jail. These were horrible injustices done to one who was innocent of any crime. Can you imagine the temptation toward bitterness that Joseph must have had? He could have felt terribly angry in his heart towards his brothers, and even toward God.

Question 3. Please take a moment and write down any injustices that were done to you in your past. We are not asking for a book here, but rather simple statements of any mistreatment you have endured.

If we follow the story of Joseph in the remaining chapters of Genesis we read of how he became exalted to the position of Prime Minister of all Egypt, and how he was second in command of the entire nation, second only to Pharaoh himself. And because of a famine, his brothers had to travel to Egypt to buy food. Through the providence of God, they had to ask Joseph for food, and when they discovered it was he—their brother whom they had mistreated so badly—they were scared to death. Would Joseph now get even with them? Would he have them killed? Oh no, for because Joseph walked with His God, he was not bitter or angry, nor did he seek revenge. Notice his answer to his brothers as they came trembling before him:

But Joseph said to them, "'Don't be afraid. Am I in the place of God? 20 You intended to harm me, but God intended it for good to accomplish what is now being done, the saving of many lives. 21 So then, don't be afraid. I will provide for you and your children.' And he reassured them and spoke kindly to them" (Genesis 50:19-21).

How did Joseph deal with the abuse of his past? He recognized God was in control of all things, and that God had a purpose in everything that happened to him. Oh friend, if you have been abused, here is real and lasting help. Know that God was in control even during the bad times, and acknowledge that He had a purpose in it. Joseph said that "God intended it for good..." and you can say the same thing. No, this does not make God the author of sin, but it does say that God is working out His plan at all times (please see Daniel 4:35, Ephesians 1:11 and Job 42:2).

Next, notice what Joseph named one of his children, and why: "Before the years of famine came, two sons were born to Joseph by Asenath daughter of Potiphera, priest of On. Joseph named his firstborn Manasseh and said, 'It is because God has made me forget all my trouble and all my father's household'" (Genesis 41:50-51). Manasseh sounds like the Hebrew word for "forget" and Joseph named his son based on the work of God in his life. God enabled him to forget all his trouble. The psychologist and psychiatrist cannot do this; only God can enable us to know that He is in control of all things, and make us forget all our troubles. Praise Him!

Question 4. How does the name of Joseph's son correspond with the teaching we are studying today?

Again, as stated earlier, we are not teaching people to simply "forget about the past." No, we are teaching that God is in control, and that God has a purpose and a plan for all things, and that He is able to bring good out of bad. One lady I know personally, who was abused both as a little girl and as a teen-ager, is now being used greatly in ministry to others, as God is bringing good out of her past. Her constant theme is that God is sovereign, He is in charge, He is carrying out His plan in all things and at all times, and that He can and does turn bad things of the past in to good.

Nowhere is this thought of God using sin for His own purposes more clearly shown than in the cross of Jesus Christ. It was the Jews who demanded His death, though He had done nothing wrong. And it was the Romans who crucified Him, though there were no legitimate charges. And both were sinning as they did so. But ultimately it was God Who gave His Son, and He used the sin of the people involved to bring about the salvation of all who will believe. Notice how these two thoughts, of men doing the sinning, but of God being in control, are woven together in this passage: "This man was handed over to you by God's set purpose and foreknowledge; and you, with the help of wicked men, put him to death by nailing him to the cross" (Acts 2:23).

Finally, not only are we taught to "go back" if we have been abused, but if we are the abuser we will be tempted to remain in the past as well. Guilt is like the undertow that can drag us back out into the sea of sin again. Likewise, consequences of our sin can last a lifetime in some cases, and can be very discouraging at times. And finally, the devil is called "the Accuser of the brethren" and he works in that capacity very well.

But the Christian has the unique ability to run to Jesus when plagued with guilt, discouraged by consequences, or accused by the enemy. We can pour out our hearts to our Father and ask for help in time of need. Christians have the ability to turn to Scripture in these times.

If we are feeling guilty, we can read Hebrews 9:14.

If we are sad about the lasting consequences, we can read Revelation 21:3-4.

If we are being accused by the evil one, we can read Colossians 1:22-23.

Question 5. Of the 3 things listed above (guilt, consequences, the devil), which one bothers you the most at times? Write your answer here:

To friend, whether abuser or abused, we do not focus on the past to help us. We go to Christ, for He is sufficient for every problem. We have worked with those who were horribly abused in childhood and have seen them restored to wholeness, and we have worked with those who have abused and caused much pain, and have seen them restored as well. But the method is by listening to the stories of abuse, having compassion on the ones involved, and then seeking to gently point to Christ as the answer.

Scripture to Consider

"Let us look only to Jesus, the One who began our faith and who makes it perfect. He suffered death on the cross. But he accepted the shame as if it were nothing because of the joy that God put before him. And now he is sitting at the right side of God's throne. Think about Jesus' example. He held on while wicked people were doing evil things to him. So do not get tired and stop trying" (Hebrews 12:2-3[NCV]).

Were you free from pornography since you did the last lesson?
    Yes   No

Were you free from masturbation since you did the last lesson?
    Yes   No

Were you free from sexual immorality since you did the last lesson?
    Yes   No

DAY 56—NORMAL SEXUAL RELATIONS

Question 1. Please re-write the acceptable conditions for withholding intimacy in marriage. Explain them in your own words:

> "Now for the matters you wrote about: It is good for a man not to marry. ²But since there is so much immorality, each man should have his own wife, and each woman her own husband. ³ The husband should fulfill his marital duty to his wife, and likewise the wife to her husband. ⁴ The wife's body does not belong to her alone but also to her husband. In the same way, the husband's body does not belong to him alone but also to his wife. ⁵ Do not deprive each other except by mutual consent and for a time, so that you may devote yourselves to prayer. Then come together again so that Satan will not tempt you because of your lack of self-control" (1 Corinthians 7:1-5).

Today's lesson deals with some very intimate issues, and we have attempted to treat them delicately, yet forthrightly. We have saved this lesson until nearly the end of the course so as to avoid tripping people up in the beginning if at all possible. These issues need to be discussed rather than ignored, as many who come out of pornography wonder if they can have a "normal sex life". Also, today's discussion is geared toward married people, but singles should study it as well, in preparation for the future.

Please read the two following emails we have received at Setting Captives Free:

"I am so angry! I don't know what to do, and I am writing you because I really do not want to go and view pornography and masturbate like I used to, but my insides are all in turmoil. You see, my wife is having her period and during these times she wants nothing to do with intimacy yet I am "burning inside" and long to be with her. Please don't misunderstand, I am not blaming her and I do understand what her monthly cycle does to her physically, so I never pressure her, it's just that I very much want to be intimate. What do I do during these times?"

And here is the second one:
"I'm writing you in hopes that you can help me understand if there is something wrong with me and how I can change. You see, my husband has been involved with pornography for much of our 18 years of marriage, and in the

So, according to Scripture the frustrated and burning friend who wrote the email referenced earlier should have been able to turn to his wife to have his desire quenched, but he could not. We can see the fruit of her unbiblical denial of her husband was that the door was opened to the Evil One to cause strife in the marriage.

It is important to state at this point that the verses from 1 Corinthians 7 are not to be used as a weapon against our spouse to demand sex or else. 1 Peter 3 tells us that the man is to live with his wife in an understanding or considerate way. If she is feeling tired or sick or in the need of emotional support, he should be sensitive to her needs and put them ahead of his own! Yet the wife is not to deprive her husband just because she is tired or sick. These are not biblical reasons to deprive; the wife should instead seek to find other ways to quench the burning of her husband if full sexual intercourse is not possible or desirable.

On the other hand, if the man has been intoxicating himself at the devil's bar of pornography and masturbation, as in the second email, then his wife might be deprived of having her sexual needs met by her sinning husband. As men view pornography they begin to buy into the deception that only "perfect" models can satisfy them, and thus they begin to lose interest in their less-than-perfect ("real life" and not "air-brushed") wives. They often begin to withdraw from their wives as they meet their own sexual needs through masturbation. In addition, with pornography there is no need for building a relationship or being vulnerable which is what is necessary for true intimacy in marriage.

Another common hinderance we see is the belief promoted by some counselors that normal sexual relations are not possible if one spouse has been sexually abused in the past. Some have been told that their spouse's deep issues must be resolved before sexual intimacy can resume. This belief system states that the sexual abuse has produced emotional

The following testimony is from Nate:

I was born with an intense desire and drive for pleasure. And I am talking true pleasure. I can remember at a very young age wanting to have things my way, and being frustrated when the joy fizzled in my possessions. This spark was truly ignited by the lighter fluid of Pornography.

At a very young age I was introduced to it, and it became the type of thing that I sought for pleasure. I saw nothing wrong with it, even after I committed my life to God in the 7th grade. I was just being a normal kid in my eyes. Gradually, I started to notice and be frustrated by the same phenomenon, that is, the joy was fizzling out after every time I would look at porn, masturbate, and instead of feeling fulfilled, I would feel empty. So I began to look even deeper into it.

The advent of the Internet was a big step in this, and I got very deep into sexual chatting, as well as hardcore porn. I was still unhappy. This year God has started to show

last few years has begun to slowly pull away from me, and we have not made love in nearly a year. I feel like I'm going crazy, thinking I can never match those "glamour girls" and be what he needs me to be, but yet I long to be with him. Why is he not interested in me?"

The problem in each of these scenarios can be traced to the same root: lack of intimacy in marriage. Let us examine what God says on this subject, and then we will apply His truth to the above situations.

> "² But since there is so much immorality, each man should have his own wife, and each woman her own husband. ³ The husband should fulfill his marital duty to his wife, and likewise the wife to her husband."

Marriage can be a deterrent to sexual immorality. This is not to say that if a young person is in bondage to pornography that getting married will break the sinful habit. But it is to say that each of us is built with longings for intimacy, which culminate in sexual union. And while some singles have the gift of being single, the majority of us are built for relational intimacy. If this need goes unmet then temptation often comes in, and single people turn to pornography and masturbation, or sexual immorality, in attempts to satisfy the yearning within to be one with someone. This is the reason why Paul says, "Since there is so much immorality, each man should have his own wife, and each woman her own husband." The sexual intimacy that is provided in marital union satisfies the need and longing God placed within the hearts of men and women, to enjoy togetherness and closeness.

> "Do not deprive each other except by mutual consent and for a time, so that you may devote yourselves to prayer. Then come together again so that Satan will not tempt you because of your lack of self-control."

Having exhorted single people to marry, he next exhorts married people to not deprive each other of sexual intimacy, unless certain conditions are met. These conditions are:

1. Mutual consent
2. For a time
3. To seek the Lord together

trauma and scars which if not dealt with properly cause the abused victim to withdraw from marital relations and avoid dealing with the pain of the past. It is said that sexual intimacy in this situation is like re-opening a wound that was given while young. While we do not suggest that past abuse is unimportant, we also do not believe that two wrongs make a right. It is a sin to deprive our spouses of sexual relations. And to cling to a wound from the past as reason to wound our spouses now is not right. The abuse suffered in the past needs to be forgiven, by God's grace, and the one abused needs to not hold on to the abuse as a reason to deny their spouse. Scripture tells us that regularly delighting in sexual enjoyment among spouses is a deterrent to the work of the devil in our lives. And in fact, sexual relations in a loving marriage bed can even be very healing and comforting according to the biblical examples of Rebekah and Isaac (Genesis 24:66) and David and Bathsheba (2 Samuel 12:24).

Question 2. Where are you with this passage; what are your thoughts on it?

So, how are couples who have denied each other for long periods of time, and who can hardly think of being intimate with each other, to begin the process of regular intimacy?

Begin by setting goals and then start slowly toward them. Set a goal to be intimate once a week for the first month, then twice a week for the second, working toward daily intimacy. This intimacy does not necessarily have to be full sexual intercourse every day, but daily intimacy in some form should be the goal. Start with gentle touching and soft kissing and work toward the joining of the bodies in sexual unity.

But what if you agree to this, and see the truth from Scripture as well as the practical value in daily intimacy, but your spouse is unwilling to be intimate?

First, begin by asking questions. Why does your spouse not desire intimacy with you? Be sure that you are doing all you can to be in a right relationship with your spouse. If you remember that you have sinned against your spouse then go to them, confess, and ask them to forgive you.

me that if I am really serious about my relationship with Him, this stuff has got to go. I went on a Campus Crusade for Christ summer project this past summer, and I was almost completely masturbation free and completely porn free for 3 months, due to a large amount of accountability, and complete lack of access to porn. It was awesome, and I grew immensely. I thought that I had built up enough to resist it forever. But the very day that project ended, I was back into slavery. I fell harder than ever.

That's when God brought me to Setting Captives Free and to **Pure Freedom**. It is through this site that I recognized those things that helped me this past summer, the radical accountability, the radical amputation, and the radical appropriation. I realized that in order to be free forever, I just had to incorporate those things in my life. It has been immensely freeing. God has allowed me to stumble in each area, as far as amputation, accountability, and appropriation go, and it has given me a healthy respect for his word, and for his strength. I look forward to many years of basking in the light of His glory!

Questions

If the denial of intimacy is based on a lack of forgiveness for past wrongs which have been confessed and repented of, or if it is based on anything other than a biblical foundation, then see if your spouse would be willing to read through 1 Corinthians 7:1-5, and talk through it with you. Your desire is to show them the importance of not allowing the Evil One to have a foothold in your relationship. You are not threatening that you will sin if they do not meet your needs, only seeking to show the importance and evidence a desire to be united in all ways against the Evil One.

If your spouse is still depriving you for unbiblical reasons, then you may need to talk to your pastor about the matter to seek his counsel, or possibly meet with an older couple in your church with the intention of your spouse hearing the need for sexual intimacy in marriage, as according to Matthew 18:15-17. For a more detailed description of the biblical response to a sinning spouse please read Martha Peace's book *The Excellent Wife* or *The Exemplary Husband*, by Stuart Scott.

In summary, a normal couple that enjoys biblical truth will strive for intimacy often. Scripture does not say how often, but it does say that the lack of it could invite temptation from the Evil One.

Sexual intimacy in marriage should become very pleasurable when both partners are walking in habitual purity. This enjoyment of sex in marriage is a great deterrent to one or both of the spouses falling into impurity, and provides a hedge of protection around the marriage. Men and women who repent of pornography and/or sexual impurity should make it a priority to learn how to begin enjoying sexual intimacy with their spouse as soon as possible.

There should be both the giving and receiving of this exquisite pleasure in the marriage bed. Those of us who have been immersed in pornography have learned to be selfish in the areas of sexual intimacy, and we must learn how to provide pleasure to our spouses. In Stuart Scott's fantastic book, *The Exemplary Husband*, he states, **"Sex can be holy and pure. If you are married and struggle with lust you must begin to think of sex in a new way. You must plan to take a different path of thinking when you are having intimacy with your wife. It should be an opportunity to bring pleasure to your wife. Sex as God intended it is holy and pure and should be enjoyed. If you seek to give instead of to get, you will enjoy this God-given blessing in a totally new way-a pure and holy way."**[55] Dr. Scott has written an entire chapter on this subject (chapter 11) and he provides excellent, practical help. You can order his book by calling toll free 1-800-91Focus.

Finally, let us examine some select passages from the Song of Solomon that will again show what normal sexual intimacy between man and wife is:

> "Let him kiss me with the kisses of his mouth, for your love is more delightful than wine." (Song of Solomon 1:2).

Here the woman is speaking of her great desire to be intimate with her lover, and compares the delight of his love with wine. It is normal for the woman to desire her husband, even as the church desires intimacy with Christ. The woman should long to be with her husband and earnestly desire his intimacy (the kisses of his mouth).

Question 3. If you are a woman, are you showing your husband that you long to be with him?

A. Yes
B. No
C. Does not apply, I am single

> "Take me away with you—let us hurry! Let the king bring me into his chambers" (Song of Solomon 1:4).

> "Like a lily among thorns is my darling among the maidens" (Song of Solomon 2:2).

Here the man is speaking and favorably comparing his beloved. One of the greatest things a husband can do is to be in awe of his wife, and often compare her in a favorable light to other women. Statements such as "My darling, you were the most beautiful woman at the party tonight…" or "there is nobody who can hold a candle to you!" go a long way. Of course the husbands' life needs to reflect that he really feels this way, and if the husband is viewing pornography then he would be lying to say this.

Question 4. If you are a husband, are you seeing the beauty in your wife and telling her?

A. Yes
B. No
C. Does not apply, I am single

> "[3] Like an apple tree among the trees of the forest is my lover among the young men. I delight to sit in his shade, and his fruit is sweet to my taste. [4] He has taken me to the banquet hall, and his banner over me is love. [5] Strengthen me with raisins, refresh me with apples, for I am faint with love" (Song of Solomon 2:3-5).

> "Awake, north wind, and come, south wind! Blow on my garden, that its fragrance may spread abroad. Let my lover come into his garden and taste its choice fruits" (Song of Solomon 4:16).

These verses reinforce the delightful, nourishing value of sexual relations in a pure marriage.

One of the books we highly recommend is *The Excellent Wife* by Martha Peace. In her book, Mrs. Peace states, **"Pleasure resulting from physical intimacy between husband and wife is assumed by Scripture. It should be fun. There will, of course, be times when, for various reasons, the sex act may not be at the same level of intensity as other times. However, it should still be pleasurable and a sweet time between each married couple. …Generally both husband and wife should come to a climax, but if one or the other is too tired or is providentially hindered in some way (such as the wife's period or pregnancy) they can still express love to the other if not through vaginal intercourse through manual stimulation."**[56]

Friends, the devil hates intimacy between Christ and the church. He would rather we be lukewarm toward our First Love, than to be zealous and on fire for Him. He tries to ruin our devotion (2 Corinthians 11:3) and closeness with Christ. Likewise, sexual intimacy in marriage is a picture of that intimacy the church has with Christ (Ephesians 5:32). Let us not neglect either one, but enjoy them fully. What is normal sex between married people? It is the exquisite enjoyment and celebration of intimacy, as a reflection of the oneness that the church has with Jesus Christ.

Question 5. What have you learned today? Please state how you will put the truths into practice if you are married.

Scripture to Consider

> "For this is the will of God, your sanctification: that you should abstain from sexual immorality; that each of you should know how to possess own vessel in sanctification and honor, not in passion of lust, like the Gentiles who do not know God" (1 Thessalonians 4: 3-5).

Were you free from pornography since you did the last lesson? Yes No
Were you free from masturbation since you did the last lesson? Yes N
Were you free from sexual immorality since you did the last lesson? Y

DAY 57— CUT OFF HIS HEAD

There is a giant in the land, and he is wreaking havoc among God's people. He is more powerful than all of God's army, by themselves, and he is out to kill and destroy us. His hatred is against God Himself, and there is not a man (or woman) among us who can stand against him. His name is Satan! He is filthy and vile, armed with cruel hate, and he rides forth taking captive numerous slaves for his kingdom. He is never satisfied, always wanting to have more pawns to serve him, and he sets his sights specifically on the church of Jesus Christ. He despises us!

What are we to do? Is there a David among us? One who cannot stand to hear the mockings of the giant, and who knows that the battle belongs to the Lord? Who will take him on? Who has an arsenal of 5 stones of "grace" with which to knock the giant down, and can use the Sword of the Spirit, which is the Word of God, to take his head off? And who wants to take the offensive, vindicate the Name of God, and bring victory for the people of God? I hope you are saying, "ME!" because these treacherous days the church of Jesus Christ needs a David: one who takes no confidence in the armor of kings, or in his own ability, but one who relies on the sovereign grace of God and the power of the gospel to defeat sin's giant.

Are you the one who wants a piece of the giant? Are you sick and tired of seeing the devil gain more and more captives for his kingdom? Do you want to do something about it? You can!

Please read the following passage and answer the questions:

> ⁴¹ Meanwhile, the Philistine, with his shield bearer in front of him, kept coming closer to David. ⁴² He looked David over and saw that he was only a boy, ruddy and handsome, and he despised him. ⁴³ He said to David, "Am I a dog, that you come at me with sticks?" And the Philistine cursed David by his gods. ⁴⁴ "Come here," he said, "and I'll give your flesh to the birds of the air and the beasts of the field!" ⁴⁵ David said to the Philistine, "You come against me with sword and spear and javelin, but I come against you in the name of the LORD Almighty, the God of the armies of Israel, whom you have defied. ⁴⁶ This day the LORD will hand you over to me, and I'll strike you down and cut off your head. Today I will give the carcasses of the Philistine army to the birds of the air and the beasts of the earth, and the whole world will know that there is a God in Israel. ⁴⁷ All those gathered here will know that it is not by sword or spear that the LORD saves; for the battle is the Lord's, and he will give all of you into our hands." ⁴⁸ As the Philistine moved closer to attack him, David ran quickly toward the battle line to meet him. ⁴⁹ Reaching into his bag and taking out a stone, he slung it and struck the Philistine on the forehead. The stone sank into his forehead, and he fell facedown on the ground. ⁵⁰ So David triumphed over the Philistine with a sling and a stone; without a sword in his hand he struck down the Philistine and killed him. ⁵¹ David ran and stood over him. He took hold of the Philistine's sword and drew it from the scabbard. After he killed him, he cut off his head with the sword. When the Philistines saw that their hero was dead, they turned and ran. ⁵² Then the men of Israel and Judah surged forward with a shout and pursued the Philistines to the entrance of Gath and to the gates of Ekron. Their dead were strewn along the Shaaraim road to Gath and Ekron. ⁵³ When the Israelites returned from chasing the Philistines, they plundered their camp. ⁵⁴ David took the Philistine's head and brought it to Jerusalem, and he put the Philistine's weapons in his own tent" (1 Samuel 17:41-54).

Questions

Question 1. Verse 44 speaks of the intent of the Philistine toward David, and it is also the intent of the devil toward us. What is that intent?
- A. He intends to be friends with us and give us everything we want
- B. He intends to totally destroy us!

Friend, make no mistake: this is a fight to the death! Goliath wanted to kill and destroy not only David but also the entire Israelite army. This is the intention of Satan against us. Either we will triumph over this giant or we will die by his hands.

Question 2. According to verse 45, Goliath came against David with "sword, and spear and javelin." What did David come against Goliath with?
- A. An Uzzi
- B. The Lord Almighty
- C. A cannon

Question 3. Compare 2 Corinthians 10:3-4 and write your thoughts: "For though we live in the world, we do not wage war as the world does. The weapons we fight with are not the weapons of the world."

Note: If we want to do battle with the devil by rescuing others from pornography, we had better make sure that we are free ourselves, and that God is fighting for us.

Question 4. What are your thoughts on verse 48? Apply it to yourself and your life right now.

Friend, as soldiers in the Lord's army, we need to have an eagerness to kill the enemy, through the power of God. There must be a "running quickly" toward the battle line to meet him. The Bible says that the gates of hell will not prevail against us (Matthew 16:18), which implies that we take the offensive and storm the fortified

Questions

city of the devil. And we can fully expect to have success if the gates of hell will not be able to keep us out.

Let me share with you that this type of eagerness to take on the enemy comes from experiencing many previous victories over the power of the devil. In this same chapter we are studying today, David recalls previous victory and uses it as present conviction of the power of God to destroy the giant. He says, "Your servant has been keeping his father's sheep. When a lion or a bear came and carried off a sheep from the flock, I went after it, struck it and rescued the sheep from its mouth. When it turned on me, I seized it by its hair, struck it and killed it. Your servant has killed both the lion and the bear; this uncircumcised Philistine will be like one of them, because he has defied the armies of the living God" (1 Samuel 17:34-36).

If you have been experiencing several victories over sin then you may be ready to take on the giant too.

Question 5. From verse 51 in the lesson, what did David use to kill the giant?

- A. A hand grenade
- B. The giant's own sword
- C. A bow and arrow

Verse 51 tells us that David used Goliath's own weapon to kill the giant, and by so doing he freed all Israel from their fear of the giant. This is an amazing foreshadow of the work of Jesus Christ as He took death, the devil's own weapon, and used it to destroy the devil. Notice how Hebrews 2:14 compares: "…He too shared in their humanity so that by His death he might destroy him who holds the power of death—that is, the devil—and free those who all their lives were held in slavery by their fear of death." See it? Jesus took the devil's own weapon, death, and used it to destroy the devil!

Pastor Joel writes: "Just living and hoping the attacks of Satan will go away will never give us victory. I have found that I must be on the offensive in every area of spiritual life and warfare. Most of my life, I have just tried to dodge Satan's bullets. Now I seek not only to stay undefeated by his power but to defeat him in the name of the Lord Jesus and for His glory."

Question 6. According to verse 55 above, what did David do to the giant?

- A. Cut off his head
- B. Buried him
- C. Left him for dead

According to verse 55, David not only killed the giant but he also cut off his

Testimony

The following testimony is from Steven:

I had been exposed to porn in my teens. My father thought nothing about it. He said "some guys like this stuff." "Just don't let your mother catch you with it." He also told me it was OK to masturbate "just to let your frustrations out". So I did.

I bought a few magazines here & there & saw a few flicks but after a while grew tired of this. After all, it cost lots of money to really get into this stuff at the time (the 70s).

I went through one marriage not knowing the Lord & not knowing how to love a woman due to these twisted ideas. I married my present wife in 1990 & became a Christian in 1995. We had our 3 boys in 2 years time. Everything was going well. Porn seemed to be out of my mind.

Then one day my wife brought in a magazine called "Dimensions". This magazine features large women. My wife is a large woman & very attractive to me. The women in this magazine were in various states of dress & undress & attractively photographed. I still didn't get the picture. During this time I began steadily moving up the ladder in church serving on committees & teaching Sunday school. I thought I was living a righteous Christian life.

Then everything exploded.

In December 1999 we got a new computer with unlimited Internet. One of the first things I did when I set it up was to go surfing for porn sites featuring large women. My wife even encouraged me at times to spice up our love life. I suddenly found myself surfing for hours on end for this material. After all, one could look at this stuff for free. I discovered that I had unlimited unmonitored access at work as well. I was wasting many hours of the day & neglecting my work, family & Sunday school teaching. My lessons suffered. I was exhausted from the nights I spent surfing & was also afraid of being caught & confronted by any church people.

Then one day when I was on "crosswalk.com" (a Christian website) seeking relief, I found a link to "SCF". The first thing I was confronted with was the Ted Bundy Story. Seeing a picture of his body literally scared the Hell out of me. I knew that my problem was serious & would result in losing my wife, boys, job, and eventually end up in death. I would then probably hear the Lord's words "Away from me you worker of iniquity, I never knew you." That was about six months ago.

I fell twice during the early days of the course but since then, the Lord has clothed me in His armor & built defenses in my life that have set me free.

I use the sword of the Spirit each day to ward off attacks. Your site has helped me greatly. In fact, I plan to use the bulletin board & "Never Thirst" emails to keep me straight. Please feel free to use my testimony if you wish. I hope it would help someone else. In fact, I suspect that there are many men in our churches who have this problem but are too ashamed & prideful to admit it!!

Thanks for this ministry. It is truly a lifesaver.

head. Isn't this a bit much? Overkill, so to speak? Here is an important lesson for us: when dealing with our sins we need to take such drastic action against them that we prevent them from ever rearing their ugly heads in our lives again. **Do not merely kill the giant, but cut off his head!**

Question 7. What did the Israelite army do when they discovered that Goliath was dead?
 A. The retreated in fear of the rest of the Philistines
 B. They rushed forward and pursued their enemies
 C. They did nothing

Friend, your own pursuit of purity—of defeating the giant in your life—will have an effect on others to encourage them toward victory also. As the months of victory over the power of the devil roll on you soon discover that God's power is stronger and you have killed the enemy. But helping others to enjoy victory is like cutting off the enemy's head.

You are nearing the end of this 60-Day course, and if you are free from pornography that is a great victory. But now it is time for you to start thinking about, and praying about God giving you a ministry to help others out of the fire from which God rescued you. Don't merely relish your own victory over the Giant, but cut his head off and inspire numerous others to pursue victory also, as David did.

But be cautious! Please do not become involved in ministry if you are still doing pornography. The reason for this is that your soul is still in deception. You are intoxicating yourself at the devil's bar and you will not be able to truly help others to pornographic sobriety. Knowledge is not enough. Power in the life is essential. "Who can bring what is pure from the impure? No one!" (Job 14:4).

Some people have asked how long they need to be pure before they begin a ministry. We don't know. God will make it known at the time, but you simply need to know in your heart that you are completely and fully done with pornography, for good, and have an eagerness to help others out of the trap also.

There are so many ministries you could become involved in to help those enslaved to pornography and we cannot list them all here. Here are some examples. With some thought I am sure you can add to this list.

 Be a mentor and assist others to purity.

 Build your own website ministry to assist others to purity.

 Start an email list specifically for reaching people trapped in pornography.

 Share your freedom with the pastor of your church and ask for his help in starting a ministry at your church. You can use our curriculum if you would like, and we have other tools available for you to use as well.

 Begin a Bible study in your home for pornographers, sex addicts, etc... Advertise it in churches, on the Internet, in newspapers, etc... The way the cancer of pornography is spreading you may have a huge group show up.

 Open a chat room with discussions about overcoming pornography.

 Share your testimony with your church and see what God does with it.

 Write out your testimony and post it all over the Internet, while inviting people to email you.

 Begin a prison ministry to help inmates to freedom from pornography.

 Write periodicals for Christian sites such as crosswalk.com and others, about the way to be free from pornography.

 Begin a newsletter to circulate through churches and on the Internet.

Question 8. Are you ready to begin taking the offensive in the battle with the giant, to help your fellow brothers and sisters to victory?
 A. Yes, I am more than ready! I want to run into the battle!
 B. Maybe later; I want to grow stronger.
 C. No, I am still falling into the trap of the devil myself and will have to wait.

Question 9. What ministries can you think of that would fit your style, and how can you go about initiating them? Write your answer here?

Scripture to Consider

"But thanks be to God! He gives us the victory through our Lord Jesus Christ" (1 Corinthians 15:57).

Were you free from pornography since you did the last lesson?
 Yes   No

Were you free from masturbation since you did the last lesson?
 Yes   No

Were you free from sexual immorality since you did the last lesson?
 Yes   No

DAY 58—FINAL EXAM

Dear friend,

Today's material will be a review, by way of a final test of all the material covered in the 60-day course. Feel free to review the days of the course to answer the questions. Mostly we are interested in how the Scriptural truths and testimonies have affected your heart and changed your life. We are getting toward the end of the 60 Days, and the question we have is "Are you actually becoming free from pornography and masturbation?"

Please answer that question as you take this test. Here we go:

Question 1: On Days 1 and 2 of the course, we learned about quenching our thirst in the Living Water. What did Jesus say was the difference between the water the woman at the well had been drinking and the Living Water He offered her? Write your thoughts here:

Question 2: Have you learned how to drink of the Living Water?

Question 3: Day 3 is called "Into the Light" and is a reference for dragging our sins into the light to expose them and sap them of their strength. On that day, you were asked to write down ways that you could begin walking in the light. Have you begun walking in the light? Please share your thoughts:

Question 4. Day 4 is all about the cross of Jesus Christ. Why is an understanding of the cross of Jesus Christ necessary for overcoming pornography and masturbation?

Question 5. Day 5 is called "Running Light" and instructs us to throw off everything that entangles us. What does the teaching on this day compare the Christian life to?
   A. A war
   B. A foot race
   C. Climbing a mountain

Question 6. Day 6 is called "Turning" and is about the subject of repentance. From this day's teaching, how would you describe repentance?
   A. Feeling remorseful because of my sin
   B. Confessing my sin
   C. Turning from my sin to God

Question 7. Day 7 is about heading our lives in a new direction. Please write out what you remember the difference between worldly sorrow and godly sorrow is:

Question 8. On Day 8 we saw the absolute necessity of utilizing an accountability partner. From Ecclesiastes 4:9-12 please finish this sentence: "Though one can be overcome, two can _____ _____."

Question 9. "Pure Grace" was the subject of Day 9, and we used a passage of Scripture to show and define what pure grace is. What did that passage of Scripture talk about?
   A. A woman caught in adultery
   B. A tax collector who had stolen money
   C. A murderer

Question 10. On Day 10 we learned about "Surprising Grace". What illustration was used in the beginning paragraphs of that lesson?
   A. A man caught in the act of stealing
   B. A prince riding a dragon
   C. A storm that suddenly came up

Question 11. "Ongoing Freedom" was the subject of Day 11. We were instructed, in view of God's grace, to offer up our bodies and to renew our minds daily. Have you been doing these two things?

Questions

Question 12. Day 12 was called "Radical Amputation" and taught us Jesus' method for dealing with things that cause us to stumble. Have you radically amputated every place where you could access pornography?

Question 13. Day 13 was called "Setting Captives Free I" and refers to the work Jesus Christ came to do. In John 8, Jesus compared those who sin to what?
  A. Hard workers
  B. Friends of the devil
  C. Slaves

Question 14. Day 14 was called "Setting Captives Free 2" and Psalm 107 described those who are enslaved to sin as being in "iron chains." What does it mean to have an "iron chain" addiction?

Question 15. Day 15 was called "Setting Captives Free 3" and in Exodus 12, God told the Israelites to eat the Passover Lamb with their sandals on, among other things. Why did they need to eat the lamb with their sandals on?
  A. It was the fashionable thing to do.
  B. Foot odor was bad in Egypt.
  C. Because as soon as they fed on the Lamb, they would leave slavery.

Question 16. "Temptation" was the topic for Day 16, and we read about Jesus in the wilderness being tempted of the devil. What did Jesus use each time He was tempted, to get the victory over Satan?

Question 17. Day 17 was entitled "Return to the Lord" and referred to God's presence leaving the Tabernacle. The presence of God returned when what happened?
  A. The Israelites got rid of their vile images and detestable practices
  B. When God got back from vacation

Question 18. "Exclusive Drinking" was the title of Day 18, and it referred to finding all our fountains of refreshment and life in Jesus. Are you "drinking" exclusively from Christ now?

Question 19. Day 19 was all about "Purity Precedes Power." Can you summarize what this day taught?

Question 20. Day 20 was called "Idolatry" and on this day's teaching we stated that pornography and sexual impurity was:
  A. Stress-relieving
  B. Relaxing
  C. A form of worshiping idols

Question 21. Day 21 was called "Strength Through Confession." Have you confessed your sins to God and to any others that you need to?

Question 22. "Vigilance" was the title of Day 22. What two things does vigilance require?
  A. Money and hard work
  B. Watchfulness and prayer
  C. A battle plan and spiritual weapons

Question 23. Day 23 was called "Enjoying the Light." We used an illustration from Scripture in Acts 19. What did this group of people do to evidence that they were coming into the Light?
  A. They witnessed to their neighbors
  B. They removed all the curtains in their home
  C. They openly confessed their evil deeds

Question 24. Day 24 was about "Fleeing Temptation." What Old Testament story was used to teach the necessity of fleeing from temptation?
  A. Eve being tempted in the garden
  B. Joseph being tempted by Potiphar's wife

Question 25. Day 25 was called "Flee, Abstain, Resist." In this day we talked about 2 Timothy 2:22, where it tells us to "flee and pursue." What are we to flee, and what are we to pursue?

Question 26. Day 26 was called "Don't Go Near" and we used a modern day true story that illustrated this truth. What was the story?
  A. A man getting too close to a brush fire
  B. A little child getting too close to a cliff
  C. An airliner getting too close to a thunderstorm

Question 27. Day 27 was about "Growing In Christ" and discussed the different levels of growth in the Christian life. What are those different levels of maturity?
  A. Student, Co-laborer, Mentor
  B. Little children, young men, fathers

Question 28. "Sanctification" was the subject for Day 28. According to this day, what is God's will for our lives?
  A. That we be sanctified: that we avoid sexual immorality
  B. That we live healthy and wealthy
  C. That we be married

Question 29. Day 29 is about "Our Identity in Christ." Ephesians 2 is the chapter that was studied. Can you list several ways this chapter describes those who are dead in sins? How about those who are alive in Christ?

Question 30. Day 30 is called "New Creations in Christ" and used the story of creation to teach how God makes us new creations. How did God bring light out of darkness in Genesis 1?
  A. By blowing into the darkness
  B. By His Word!
  C. By putting stars in the sky

Question 31. Day 31 is about "The Greatness, Majesty, Power and Grace of God." What can you recall of Day 31's teaching?

Question 32. Day 32 is about spiritual warfare. Where does the spiritual battle take place?

Question 33. Day 33 is about demolishing thought-strongholds. What does it take to do this?
  A. An Uzzi
  B. Divine Power
  C. Persistence in refusing to think about certain thoughts

Question 34. Day 34 is also about demolishing thought-strongholds. On this day we learned that we are to do what with our thoughts?
  A. Allow them to run free
  B. Take them captive to Christ

Question 35. Day 35 was about the love of God and temptation. According to James 1:12, what is the proper motivation for enduring temptation?

Question 36. Day 36 is about breaking the accident chain. What biblical story was used to illustrate how an accident chain can form?
  A. The story of Abraham and Isaac
  B. The story of Jacob and Esau
  C. The story of Lot and Abraham

Question 37. "Seek the Lord" is the title of Day 37. Can you please write out Matthew 6:33 here?

Question 38. "Restoration After Loss" is the title for Day 38. What biblical story was used to illustrate that we have a restoring God?
  A. Cain and Abel
  B. Lot and Abraham
  C. The Prodigal son

Question 39. This day taught that there are specific steps to freedom from sin. Please write out the verse of Scripture that was used for this day's teaching.

Question 40. Day 40 talked about the heart, the mind and the actions. What does Colossians 3:3 tell us to do with our heart and affections?
  A. Set them on things above
  B. Dwell on your work and family

Questions

Question 41. Day 41 was about "Battle Strategies." Can you describe some of the battle strategies you have been using lately?

Question 42. Day 42 was about focus. It was all about fixing our eyes on Jesus in order to have victory over pornography and masturbation. What Old Testament story was used to illustrate this truth?
  A. David and Goliath
  B. The serpent uplifted on a pole
  C. The battle of Jericho

Question 43. Romans 6 was the focus of this day's teaching. Romans 6 teaches that we are dead to what?
  A. Sin
  B. Satan
  C. Sensuality

Question 44. Romans 7 describes a Christian man battling sin, and losing. Where does this battle against sin end?
  A. In the New Jerusalem
  B. In despair over this body of death, and thanking God for Christ
  C. In suicide

Question 45. Fill in the blank. Day 45 is about:

  "No _____"

Question 46. This day is about pornography's inability to satisfy us. What is pornography compared to on this day?
  A. Fresh spring water
  B. A very satisfying experience
  C. A broken cistern that cannot hold water

Question 47. This day is about brokenness being the key to victory. Do you remember learning anything from this day?

Question 48. Day 48 is called "Such Were Some of You." What was this day about?

Question 49. "Walking in the Spirit" is the subject of Day 49. Are you learning to do this?

Question 50. "Freedom Through Fellowship" is the subject of Day 50. Are you abiding in the Vine?

Question 51. Day 51 was called "Live For Pleasure." Are you finding pleasures in God?

Question 52. "Happy Are the Helpless" is the title of Day 52.

Matthew 5:3 says, "Blessed are the _____."

Question 53. "The Power of the Word" is the title of Day 53. What are some things the Word of God has power to do as taught on this day?

Question 54. Day 54 is called "Do Everything to Stand." Are you?

Question 55. Day 55 is called "Don't Look Back." Christians are to focus on:
  A. Their past
  B. Their pain
  C. Their parents
  D. Their future with Jesus

Question 56. Day 56 is called "Normal Sexual Relations." What book of Scripture speaks to this issue in detail?
  A. Romans
  B. Song of Solomon

Question 57. Day 57 was called "Cut Off His Head." What Old Testament story was used to illustrate the truth that we are not only to knock the giant down, but cut off his head as well?
  A. David and Bathsheba
  B. Jonah
  C. David and Goliath

Scripture to Consider

"For God so loved the world that He gave His only begotten Son, that whoever believes in Him should not perish but have everlasting life. For God did not send His Son into the world to condemn the world, but that the world through Him might be saved" (John 3: 15-17 NKJV).

Were you free from pornography since you did your last lesson?
    Yes   No

Were you free from masturbation since you did your last lesson?
    Yes   No

Were you free from sexual immorality since you did your last lesson?
    Yes   No

That's it!

Enjoy telling your story, and pray that God would make it useful to others who need hope that it is possible to be free from these sins, by the grace of God!

Were you free from pornography since you did your last lesson?   Yes   No

Were you free from masturbation since you did your last lesson?   Yes   No

Were you free from sexual immorality since you did your last lesson? Yes   No

DAY 59— YOUR TESTIMONY

Today, we want to give you a place to share your testimony. Feel free to share however the Lord leads you, but keep in mind that the most effective testimonies are brief (usually one page in length), and should include 3 aspects. Job 33 tells us the formula for sharing a testimony: "Then he comes to men and says, I sinned, and perverted what was right, but I did not get what I deserved. He redeemed my soul from going down to the pit, and I will live to enjoy the light" (Job 33:27-28). Notice the 3 aspects to this testimony: "I sinned…God redeemed…I will live."

A biblical testimony touches on:

- "My sin" and what areas I was involved in, and what that brought about in my life (though be cautious about sharing any details so as to not stir up sin in others).
- Redemption. This explains how I was bought out of the slave market of sin. How did God reach me, give me repentance and bring me into the Light. What means did He use?
- How I am living to enjoy the Light (Christ).

Please try to include those 3 aspects in your testimony. Take your time, and may your story of God's grace honor the Lord. (If you find that you do not yet have a testimony of true freedom from pornography, please consider working through this course again slowly.)

Please write your testimony here.

DAY 60—FEEDBACK

Dear friend,

Today is the final day of the **Pure Freedom** course, and we would like to solicit your input and receive feedback from you regarding your experience with this material.

Here are several options:
1. You will bind this form on our website, and may respond to it there. Be sure to mention that you have completed this 60-Day Course Book.
2. You may summarize the questions on this page and email a feedback report to feedback@settingcaptivesfree.com.
3. You may photocopy or send this page to: Setting Captives Free
2325 Medina Road
Medina, OH 44256

It is not necessary to identify yourself by name. If you wish, you may use simply your first name.

Question 1. Overall, what was the best part of the course?
A. The Bible Studies
B. The accountability
C. The testimonies
D. The feedback from the mentors

Question 2. On a scale of 1 to 10, how helpful was this course to you in overcoming pornography? 1 being of little help, 10 being of great help:
A. 1-2
B. 3-4
C. 5-7
D. 8-9
E. 10

Question 3. Please describe the changes have taken place in your heart and life since starting this course:

Question 4. Have you started any kind of ministry of your own to help others break free from pornography?
A. Yes, I am currently in a ministry of helping people to be free from pornography
B. No, not yet

Question 5. If you answered, "Yes" to the above question, please describe your ministry.

Question 6. Was there any specific thing that bothered you about the course as you went through it?

Question 7. How can we improve the course? What are your suggestions?

Question 8. Have you told anyone else about this course?

Question 9. Here is a place for your final comments.

Endnotes

1. Trench, Richard Chevenix, *Notes on the Parables of Our Lord*. New York, NY, D. Appleton & Co., 1895.
2. Spurgeon, Charles Haddon, *The New Park Street Pulpit, Volume 6: 1860*, London, Banner of Truth Trust, 1964.
3. Pink, Arthur W., *The Gospel of John*, Grand Rapids, MI, Zondervan, 1945.
4. Chambers, Oswald, *My Utmost for His Highest*, December 7th Devotional, Ulrichsville, OH, Barbour Publishing, 1963.
5. Henry, Matthew, *Matthew Henry's Commentary on the Whole Bible, Complete and Unabridged*, Peabody, MA, Hendrickson Publishers, 1991.
6. Ibid.
7. Ibid.
8. Ibid
9. Daniels, Robert, *The War Within: Experiencing Victory in the Battle for Sexual Purity*, Wheaton, IL, Crossway, 1997.
10. *Logos Lesson Builder*, Oak Harbor, WA, (CD-Rom) Logos Research Systems, Inc., 1997.
11. Reinicke, Melinda, "The Dragon" is one of 19 stories by Dr. Melinda Reinicke from the book *Parables for Personal Growth*, dealing with life issues for adults through parables, journaling and experiential exercises. Available for $17.95 (includes US postage and state tax) from Reinicke Counseling Associates (619) 298-8722x110 or www.christiancounseling.cc
12. Salzman, Timothy, *Sixty Days to Freedom: A Biblical Guide to Freedom from Sexual Addictions*, Colorado Springs, CO, Legacy Press, 1996.
13. Henry, Matthew, *Commentary*
14. Ibid.
15. Ibid.
16. Daniels, Robert, p.94
17. Spurgeon, Charles H. "The Chief of Sinners," a sermon on 1 Timothy 1:15, #530, *The Metropolitan Tabernacle Pulpit*, Volume 9. 1863.
18. Spurgeon, Charles H. "Christ's Plea for Ignorant Sinners," a sermon on Luke 23:34, #2263, *The Metropolitan Tabernacle Pulpit*, Volume 38, 1892.
19. Bunyan, John, *Pilgrim's Progress*, Ulrichville, OH, Barbour & Co, 1985.
20. Eiland, F.L., "Too Late", Spurgeon, Charles H., IBID.
21. Wilson, Kathryn with Paul Wilson, *Stone Cold in a Warm Bed*, pp 35.6, Christian Publications, Camp Hill, PA, 1998.
22. Bunyan, John, Ibid.
23. A. Kempis, Thomas, The *Imitation of Christ, Chicago*, Moody Press, 1984.
24. Bonar, Andrew A., *Memoir and Remains of Robert Murray McCheyne*, Grand Rapids, MI, Baker Publishers, 1978.
25. Chambers, Oswald, Ibid.
26. A Kempis, Ibid.

27. Bonar, Ibid.
28. Henry, Matthew, Ibid.
29. Bonar, Ibid.
30. Henry, Matthew, Ibid.
31. Bunyan, John, Ibid.
32. Peterson, John, Ed., *Great Hymns of the Faith*, "O For a Thousand Tongues to Sing." Wesley, Charles, Grand Rapids, MI, Zondervan Publishing House, 1968.
33. Peterson, John, Ed., Great Hymns of the Faith, "And Can It Be That I Should Gain?" Wesley, Charles, Grand Rapids, MI, Zondervan, 1968.
34. Spurgeon, Charles, H., "Christ's Plea for Ignorant Sinners." Ibid.
35. Ryle, J.C., *J.C. Ryles Tracts: "If Any Man-!"*, Scotland, Drummond's Tract Depot.
36. Henry, Matthew, Ibid.
37. Ibid.
38. Spurgeon, Charles H., "The Pierced One Pierces the Heart" A sermon on Zechariah 12:10, #575, *The Metropolitan Tabernacle Pulpit*, Volume 10, 1864.
39. Ibid.
40. Spurgeon, Charles H., quoting Bradford, "Confession of Sin Illustrated by the Cases of Dr. Pritchard and Constance Kent," a sermon on Psalm 32:5, #641, *The Metropolitan Tabernacle Pulpit*, Volume 11, 1865.
41. Spurgeon, Charles H., *Morning and Evening*, April 7th Evening Devotional, Christian Focus Publications, Portmahomack, United Kingdom, 1994.
42. Bonar, Andrew, *A Memoir and Remains of Robert Murray McCheyne*, Ibid.
43. Henry, Matthew, Ibid.
44. Ibid.
45. Calvin, John, *Calvin's New Testament Commentaries*, Volume 11 (Galatians-Colossians) Grand Rapids, MI, Erdmans Publishing Co, 1965.
46. Bonar, Andrew, Ibid.
47. Spurgeon, Charles H., "Good Cheer for Christmas" a sermon on Isaiah 25:6, #846, *The Metropolitan Tabernacle Pulpit*, Volume 14, 1868.
48. Coleman, Robery E., *Songs of Heaven*, Old Tappan, NJ, Revell, 1980.
49. Draper, Edith, *Draper's Book of Quotations for the Christian World*, Wheaton, IL, Tyndale House Publishers, Inc., 1992.
50. Elliot, Jim, Editor: Elisabeth Elliot, *The Journals of Jim Elliot*, Old Tappan, NJ, Revell, 1983.
51. Mayo, Mary Ann, *Marriage Partnership Magazine*, Volume 7, #3, 1990
52. Henry, Matthew, Ibid.
53. Watson, Thomas, *The Beatitudes: Puritan Vision of the Christian Life*, Carlisle, PA, Banner of Truth, 1971.
54. Wagner, David, *The Power of the Word: Learning to Enjoy Freedom in Christ*, Windsor, Ontario, Canada, 2000, www.settingcaptivesfree.com.
55. Scott, Stuart, *The Exemplary Husband: A Biblical Perspective*, Bemidji, MN, FocusPublishing, 2000.
56. Peace, Martha, *The Excellent Wife: A Biblical Perspective*, Bemidji, MN, Focus Publishing, 1996.

Notes

Notes

Notes

Notes